HEBREW
VOCABULARY

FOR ENGLISH SPEAKERS

ENGLISH-HEBREW

The most useful words
To expand your lexicon and sharpen
your language skills

9000 words

Hebrew vocabulary for English speakers - 9000 words

By Andrey Taranov

T&P Books vocabularies are intended for helping you learn, memorize and review foreign words. The dictionary is divided into themes, covering all major spheres of everyday activities, business, science, culture, etc.

The process of learning words using T&P Books' theme-based dictionaries gives you the following advantages:

- Correctly grouped source information predetermines success at subsequent stages of word memorization
- Availability of words derived from the same root allowing memorization of word units (rather than separate words)
- Small units of words facilitate the process of establishing associative links needed for consolidation of vocabulary
- Level of language knowledge can be estimated by the number of learned words

T&P Books Publishing
www.tpbooks.com

ISBN: 978-1-78716-409-3

This book is also available in E-book formats.
Please visit www.tpbooks.com or the major online bookstores.

HEBREW VOCABULARY
for English speakers

T&P Books vocabularies are intended to help you learn, memorize, and review foreign words. The vocabulary contains over 9000 commonly used words arranged thematically.

- Vocabulary contains the most commonly used words
- Recommended as an addition to any language course
- Meets the needs of beginners and advanced learners of foreign languages
- Convenient for daily use, revision sessions, and self-testing activities
- Allows you to assess your vocabulary

Special features of the vocabulary

- Words are organized according to their meaning, not alphabetically
- Words are presented in three columns to facilitate the reviewing and self-testing processes
- Words in groups are divided into small blocks to facilitate the learning process
- The vocabulary offers a convenient and simple transcription of each foreign word

The vocabulary has 256 topics including:

Basic Concepts, Numbers, Colors, Months, Seasons, Units of Measurement, Clothing & Accessories, Food & Nutrition, Restaurant, Family Members, Relatives, Character, Feelings, Emotions, Diseases, City, Town, Sightseeing, Shopping, Money, House, Home, Office, Working in the Office, Import & Export, Marketing, Job Search, Sports, Education, Computer, Internet, Tools, Nature, Countries, Nationalities and more ...

T&P BOOKS' THEME-BASED DICTIONARIES

The Correct System for Memorizing Foreign Words

Acquiring vocabulary is one of the most important elements of learning a foreign language, because words allow us to express our thoughts, ask questions, and provide answers. An inadequate vocabulary can impede communication with a foreigner and make it difficult to understand a book or movie well.

The pace of activity in all spheres of modern life, including the learning of modern languages, has increased. Today, we need to memorize large amounts of information (grammar rules, foreign words, etc.) within a short period. However, this does not need to be difficult. All you need to do is to choose the right training materials, learn a few special techniques, and develop your individual training system.

Having a system is critical to the process of language learning. Many people fail to succeed in this regard; they cannot master a foreign language because they fail to follow a system comprised of selecting materials, organizing lessons, arranging new words to be learned, and so on. The lack of a system causes confusion and eventually, lowers self-confidence.

T&P Books' theme-based dictionaries can be included in the list of elements needed for creating an effective system for learning foreign words. These dictionaries were specially developed for learning purposes and are meant to help students effectively memorize words and expand their vocabulary.

Generally speaking, the process of learning words consists of three main elements:

- Reception (creation or acquisition) of a training material, such as a word list
- Work aimed at memorizing new words
- Work aimed at reviewing the learned words, such as self-testing

All three elements are equally important since they determine the quality of work and the final result. All three processes require certain skills and a well-thought-out approach.

New words are often encountered quite randomly when learning a foreign language and it may be difficult to include them all in a unified list. As a result, these words remain written on scraps of paper, in book margins, textbooks, and so on. In order to systematize such words, we have to create and continually update a "book of new words." A paper notebook, a netbook, or a tablet PC can be used for these purposes.

This "book of new words" will be your personal, unique list of words. However, it will only contain the words that you came across during the learning process. For example, you might have written down the words "Sunday," "Tuesday," and "Friday." However, there are additional words for days of the week, for example, "Saturday," that are missing, and your list of words would be incomplete. Using a theme dictionary, in addition to the "book of new words," is a reasonable solution to this problem.

The theme-based dictionary may serve as the basis for expanding your vocabulary.

It will be your big "book of new words" containing the most frequently used words of a foreign language already included. There are quite a few theme-based dictionaries available, and you should ensure that you make the right choice in order to get the maximum benefit from your purchase.

Therefore, we suggest using theme-based dictionaries from T&P Books Publishing as an aid to learning foreign words. Our books are specially developed for effective use in the sphere of vocabulary systematization, expansion and review.

Theme-based dictionaries are not a magical solution to learning new words. However, they can serve as your main database to aid foreign-language acquisition. Apart from theme dictionaries, you can have copybooks for writing down new words, flash cards, glossaries for various texts, as well as other resources; however, a good theme dictionary will always remain your primary collection of words.

T&P Books' theme-based dictionaries are specialty books that contain the most frequently used words in a language.

The main characteristic of such dictionaries is the division of words into themes. For example, the *City* theme contains the words "street," "crossroads," "square," "fountain," and so on. The *Talking* theme might contain words like "to talk," "to ask," "question," and "answer".

All the words in a theme are divided into smaller units, each comprising 3–5 words. Such an arrangement improves the perception of words and makes the learning process less tiresome. Each unit contains a selection of words with similar meanings or identical roots. This allows you to learn words in small groups and establish other associative links that have a positive effect on memorization.

The words on each page are placed in three columns: a word in your native language, its translation, and its transcription. Such positioning allows for the use of techniques for effective memorization. After closing the translation column, you can flip through and review foreign words, and vice versa. "This is an easy and convenient method of review – one that we recommend you do often."

Our theme-based dictionaries contain transcriptions for all the foreign words. Unfortunately, none of the existing transcriptions are able to convey the exact nuances of foreign pronunciation. That is why we recommend using the transcriptions only as a supplementary learning aid. Correct pronunciation can only be acquired with the help of sound. Therefore our collection includes audio theme-based dictionaries.

The process of learning words using T&P Books' theme-based dictionaries gives you the following advantages:

- You have correctly grouped source information, which predetermines your success at subsequent stages of word memorization
- Availability of words derived from the same root (lazy, lazily, lazybones), allowing you to memorize word units instead of separate words
- Small units of words facilitate the process of establishing associative links needed for consolidation of vocabulary
- You can estimate the number of learned words and hence your level of language knowledge
- The dictionary allows for the creation of an effective and high-quality revision process
- You can revise certain themes several times, modifying the revision methods and techniques
- Audio versions of the dictionaries help you to work out the pronunciation of words and develop your skills of auditory word perception

The T&P Books' theme-based dictionaries are offered in several variants differing in the number of words: 1.500, 3.000, 5.000, 7.000, and 9.000 words. There are also dictionaries containing 15,000 words for some language combinations. Your choice of dictionary will depend on your knowledge level and goals.

We sincerely believe that our dictionaries will become your trusty assistant in learning foreign languages and will allow you to easily acquire the necessary vocabulary.

TABLE OF CONTENTS

T&P Books' Theme-Based Dictionaries 4
Pronunciation guide 15
Abbreviations 16

BASIC CONCEPTS 17
Basic concepts. Part 1 17

1. Pronouns 17
2. Greetings. Salutations. Farewells 17
3. How to address 18
4. Cardinal numbers. Part 1 18
5. Cardinal numbers. Part 2 20
6. Ordinal numbers 20
7. Numbers. Fractions 20
8. Numbers. Basic operations 21
9. Numbers. Miscellaneous 21
10. The most important verbs. Part 1 22
11. The most important verbs. Part 2 22
12. The most important verbs. Part 3 23
13. The most important verbs. Part 4 24
14. Colors 25
15. Questions 26
16. Prepositions 27
17. Function words. Adverbs. Part 1 27
18. Function words. Adverbs. Part 2 29

Basic concepts. Part 2 31

19. Weekdays 31
20. Hours. Day and night 31
21. Months. Seasons 32
22. Time. Miscellaneous 34
23. Opposites 35
24. Lines and shapes 37
25. Units of measurement 38
26. Containers 39
27. Materials 40
28. Metals 41

HUMAN BEING
Human being. The body

42
42

29. Humans. Basic concepts   42
30. Human anatomy   42
31. Head   43
32. Human body   44

Clothing & Accessories

45

33. Outerwear. Coats   45
34. Men's & women's clothing   45
35. Clothing. Underwear   46
36. Headwear   46
37. Footwear   46
38. Textile. Fabrics   47
39. Personal accessories   47
40. Clothing. Miscellaneous   48
41. Personal care. Cosmetics   49
42. Jewelry   50
43. Watches. Clocks   50

Food. Nutricion

52

44. Food   52
45. Drinks   54
46. Vegetables   55
47. Fruits. Nuts   55
48. Bread. Candy   56
49. Cooked dishes   57
50. Spices   58
51. Meals   58
52. Table setting   59
53. Restaurant   59

Family, relatives and friends

61

54. Personal information. Forms   61
55. Family members. Relatives   61
56. Friends. Coworkers   62
57. Man. Woman   63
58. Age   64
59. Children   64
60. Married couples. Family life   65

Character. Feelings. Emotions

67

61. Feelings. Emotions   67

62. Character. Personality 68
63. Sleep. Dreams 69
64. Humour. Laughter. Gladness 70
65. Discussion, conversation. Part 1 71
66. Discussion, conversation. Part 2 72
67. Discussion, conversation. Part 3 73
68. Agreement. Refusal 74
69. Success. Good luck. Failure 75
70. Quarrels. Negative emotions 75

Medicine 78

71. Diseases 78
72. Symptoms. Treatments. Part 1 79
73. Symptoms. Treatments. Part 2 80
74. Symptoms. Treatments. Part 3 81
75. Doctors 82
76. Medicine. Drugs. Accessories 82
77. Smoking. Tobacco products 83

HUMAN HABITAT 84
City 84

78. City. Life in the city 84
79. Urban institutions 85
80. Signs 87
81. Urban transportation 88
82. Sightseeing 89
83. Shopping 89
84. Money 90
85. Post. Postal service 91

Dwelling. House. Home 93

86. House. Dwelling 93
87. House. Entrance. Lift 94
88. House. Electricity 94
89. House. Doors. Locks 94
90. Country house 95
91. Villa. Mansion 96
92. Castle. Palace 96
93. Apartment 97
94. Apartment. Cleaning 97
95. Furniture. Interior 97
96. Bedding 98
97. Kitchen 98
98. Bathroom 100
99. Household appliances 100
100. Repairs. Renovation 101

101. Plumbing   101
102. Fire. Conflagration   102

HUMAN ACTIVITIES   104
Job. Business. Part 1   104

103. Office. Working in the office   104
104. Business processes. Part 1   105
105. Business processes. Part 2   106
106. Production. Works   107
107. Contract. Agreement   109
108. Import & Export   109
109. Finances   110
110. Marketing   111
111. Advertising   111
112. Banking   112
113. Telephone. Phone conversation   113
114. Cell phone   113
115. Stationery   114
116. Various kinds of documents   114
117. Kinds of business   116

Job. Business. Part 2   118

118. Show. Exhibition   118
119. Mass Media   119
120. Agriculture   120
121. Building. Building process   121
122. Science. Research. Scientists   122

Professions and occupations   124

123. Job search. Dismissal   124
124. Business people   124
125. Service professions   126
126. Military professions and ranks   126
127. Officials. Priests   127
128. Agricultural professions   128
129. Art professions   128
130. Various professions   129
131. Occupations. Social status   130

Sports   132

132. Kinds of sports. Sportspersons   132
133. Kinds of sports. Miscellaneous   133
134. Gym   134

135.	Hockey	134
136.	Soccer	134
137.	Alpine skiing	136
138.	Tennis. Golf	137
139.	Chess	137
140.	Boxing	138
141.	Sports. Miscellaneous	138

Education 140

142.	School	140
143.	College. University	141
144.	Sciences. Disciplines	142
145.	Writing system. Orthography	142
146.	Foreign languages	144
147.	Fairy tale characters	145
148.	Zodiac Signs	145

Arts 147

149.	Theater	147
150.	Cinema	148
151.	Painting	149
152.	Literature & Poetry	150
153.	Circus	151
154.	Music. Pop music	151

Rest. Entertainment. Travel 153

155.	Trip. Travel	153
156.	Hotel	154
157.	Books. Reading	154
158.	Hunting. Fishing	156
159.	Games. Billiards	157
160.	Games. Playing cards	157
161.	Casino. Roulette	158
162.	Rest. Games. Miscellaneous	158
163.	Photography	159
164.	Beach. Swimming	160

TECHNICAL EQUIPMENT. TRANSPORTATION 162
Technical equipment 162

165.	Computer	162
166.	Internet. E-mail	163
167.	Electricity	164
168.	Tools	165

Transportation — 168

169.	Airplane	168
170.	Train	169
171.	Ship	170
172.	Airport	172
173.	Bicycle. Motorcycle	173

Cars — 174

174.	Types of cars	174
175.	Cars. Bodywork	174
176.	Cars. Passenger compartment	176
177.	Cars. Engine	176
178.	Cars. Crash. Repair	177
179.	Cars. Road	178
180.	Traffic signs	179

PEOPLE. LIFE EVENTS — 181
Life events — 181

181.	Holidays. Event	181
182.	Funerals. Burial	182
183.	War. Soldiers	183
184.	War. Military actions. Part 1	184
185.	War. Military actions. Part 2	185
186.	Weapons	187
187.	Ancient people	188
188.	Middle Ages	189
189.	Leader. Chief. Authorities	191
190.	Road. Way. Directions	191
191.	Breaking the law. Criminals. Part 1	193
192.	Breaking the law. Criminals. Part 2	194
193.	Police. Law. Part 1	195
194.	Police. Law. Part 2	196

NATURE — 199
The Earth. Part 1 — 199

195.	Outer space	199
196.	The Earth	200
197.	Cardinal directions	201
198.	Sea. Ocean	201
199.	Seas' and Oceans' names	202
200.	Mountains	203
201.	Mountains names	204
202.	Rivers	204
203.	Rivers' names	205

| 204. | Forest | 206 |
| 205. | Natural resources | 207 |

The Earth. Part 2   209

206.	Weather	209
207.	Severe weather. Natural disasters	210
208.	Noises. Sounds	210
209.	Winter	211

Fauna   213

210.	Mammals. Predators	213
211.	Wild animals	213
212.	Domestic animals	215
213.	Dogs. Dog breeds	216
214.	Sounds made by animals	216
215.	Young animals	217
216.	Birds	217
217.	Birds. Singing and sounds	218
218.	Fish. Marine animals	219
219.	Amphibians. Reptiles	220
220.	Insects	220
221.	Animals. Body parts	221
222.	Actions of animals	222
223.	Animals. Habitats	222
224.	Animal care	223
225.	Animals. Miscellaneous	223
226.	Horses	224

Flora   226

227.	Trees	226
228.	Shrubs	227
229.	Mushrooms	227
230.	Fruits. Berries	227
231.	Flowers. Plants	228
232.	Cereals, grains	229
233.	Vegetables. Greens	230

REGIONAL GEOGRAPHY   232
Countries. Nationalities   232

234.	Western Europe	232
235.	Central and Eastern Europe	234
236.	Former USSR countries	235
237.	Asia	236

238. North America   238
239. Central and South America   239
240. Africa   240
241. Australia. Oceania   240
242. Cities   241
243. Politics. Government. Part 1   242
244. Politics. Government. Part 2   244
245. Countries. Miscellaneous   245
246. Major religious groups. Confessions   246
247. Religions. Priests   247
248. Faith. Christianity. Islam   247

MISCELLANEOUS   250

249. Various useful words   250
250. Modifiers. Adjectives. Part 1   251
251. Modifiers. Adjectives. Part 2   254

MAIN 500 VERBS   257

252. Verbs A-C   257
253. Verbs D-G   259
254. Verbs H-M   262
255. Verbs N-R   264
256. Verbs S-W   266

PRONUNCIATION GUIDE

Letter's name	Letter	Hebrew example	T&P phonetic alphabet	English example
Alef	א	אריה	[a], [ɑ:]	bath, to pass
	א	אחד	[ɛ], [ɛ:]	habit, bad
	א	מָאֶה	[]	glottal stop
Bet	ב	בית	[b]	baby, book
Gimel	ג	גמל	[g]	game, gold
Gimel+geresh	ג׳	ג׳ונגל	[dʒ]	joke, general
Dalet	ד	דג	[d]	day, doctor
Hei	ה	הר	[h]	home, have
Vav	ו	וסת	[v]	very, river
Zayin	ז	זאב	[z]	zebra, please
Zayin+geresh	ז׳	ז׳ורנָל	[ʒ]	forge, pleasure
Chet	ח	חוט	[x]	as in Scots 'loch'
Tet	ט	טוב	[t]	tourist, trip
Yud	י	יום	[j]	yes, New York
Kaph	ך כ	בריש	[k]	clock, kiss
Lamed	ל	לחם	[l]	lace, people
Mem	ם מ	מלך	[m]	magic, milk
Nun	ן נ	גר	[n]	name, normal
Samech	ס	סוס	[s]	city, boss
Ayin	ע	עין	[a], [ɑ:]	bath, to pass
	ע	חשעים	[]	voiced pharyngeal fricative
Pei	ף פ	פיל	[p]	pencil, private
Tsadi	ץ צ	צעצוע	[ts]	cats, tsetse fly
Tsadi+geresh	צ׳ץ׳	צ׳ק	[tʃ]	church, French
Qoph	ק	קוף	[k]	clock, kiss
Resh	ר	רבבת	[r]	French (guttural) R
Shin	ש	שלחן, עָשֹרֵים	[s], [ʃ]	city, machine
Tav	ת	תפוז	[t]	tourist, trip

ABBREVIATIONS
used in the vocabulary

English abbreviations

ab.	-	about
adj	-	adjective
adv	-	adverb
anim.	-	animate
as adj	-	attributive noun used as adjective
e.g.	-	for example
etc.	-	et cetera
fam.	-	familiar
fem.	-	feminine
form.	-	formal
inanim.	-	inanimate
masc.	-	masculine
math	-	mathematics
mil.	-	military
n	-	noun
pl	-	plural
pron.	-	pronoun
sb	-	somebody
sing.	-	singular
sth	-	something
v aux	-	auxiliary verb
vi	-	intransitive verb
vi, vt	-	intransitive, transitive verb
vt	-	transitive verb

Hebrew abbreviations

ז	-	masculine
ז"ר	-	masculine plural
ז , נ	-	masculine, feminine
נ	-	feminine
נ"ר	-	feminine plural

BASIC CONCEPTS

Basic concepts. Part 1

1. Pronouns

I, me	ani	אֲנִי (ז, נ)
you (masc.)	ata	אַתָּה (ז)
you (fem.)	at	אַתְּ (נ)
he	hu	הוּא (ז)
she	hi	הִיא (נ)
we	a'naxnu	אֲנַחְנוּ (ז, נ)
you (masc.)	atem	אַתֶּם (ז"ר)
you (fem.)	aten	אַתֶּן (נ"ר)
you (polite, sing.)	ata, at	אַתָּה (ז), אַתְּ (נ)
you (polite, pl)	atem, aten	אַתֶּם (ז"ר), אַתֶּן (נ"ר)
they (masc.)	hem	הֵם (ז"ר)
they (fem.)	hen	הֵן (נ"ר)

2. Greetings. Salutations. Farewells

Hello! (fam.)	ʃalom!	שָׁלוֹם!
Hello! (form.)	ʃalom!	שָׁלוֹם!
Good morning!	'boker tov!	בּוֹקֶר טוֹב!
Good afternoon!	tsaha'rayim tovim!	צָהֲרַיִים טוֹבִים!
Good evening!	'erev tov!	עֶרֶב טוֹב!
to say hello	lomar ʃalom	לוֹמַר שָׁלוֹם
Hi! (hello)	hai!	הַיי!
greeting (n)	ahlan	אַהְלָן
to greet (vt)	lomar ʃalom	לוֹמַר שָׁלוֹם
How are you? (form.)	ma ʃlomeҳ?, ma ʃlomҳa?	מָה שְׁלוֹמֵךְ? (נ), מָה שְׁלוֹמְךָ? (ז)
How are you? (fam.)	ma niʃma?	מָה נִשְׁמָע?
What's new?	ma ҳadaʃ?	מָה חָדָשׁ?
Bye-Bye! Goodbye!	lehitra'ot!	לְהִתְרָאוֹת!
Bye!	bai!	בַּיי!
See you soon!	lehitra'ot bekarov!	לְהִתְרָאוֹת בְּקָרוֹב!
Farewell!	heye ʃalom!	הֱיֵה שָׁלוֹם!
Farewell! (form.)	lehitra'ot!	לְהִתְרָאוֹת!
to say goodbye	lomar lehitra'ot	לוֹמַר לְהִתְרָאוֹת

So long!	bai!	בַּיי!
Thank you!	toda!	תּוֹדָה!
Thank you very much!	toda raba!	תּוֹדָה רַבָּה!
You're welcome	bevakaʃa	בְּבַקָשָׁה
Don't mention it!	al lo davar	עַל לֹא דָבָר
It was nothing	ein be'ad ma	אֵין בְּעַד מָה
Excuse me!	sliχa!	סְלִיחָה!
to excuse (forgive)	lis'loaχ	לִסְלוֹחַ
to apologize (vi)	lehitnatsel	לְהִתְנַצֵל
My apologies	ani mitnatsel,	אֲנִי מִתְנַצֵל (ז),
	ani mitna'tselet	אֲנִי מִתְנַצֶלֶת (נ)
I'm sorry!	ani mitsta'er,	אֲנִי מִצטַעֵר (ז),
	ani mitsta''eret	אֲנִי מִצטַעֶרֶת (נ)
to forgive (vt)	lis'loaχ	לִסְלוֹחַ
It's okay! (that's all right)	lo nora	לֹא נוֹרָא
please (adv)	bevakaʃa	בְּבַקָשָׁה
Don't forget!	al tiʃkaχ!	אַל תָּשׁכַּח! (ז)
Certainly!	'betaχ!	בֶּטַח!
Of course not!	'betaχ ʃelo!	בֶּטַח שֶלֹא!
Okay! (I agree)	okei!	אוֹקֵיי!
That's enough!	maspik!	מַספִּיק!

3. How to address

Excuse me, ...	sliχa!	סְלִיחָה!
mister, sir	adon	אָדוֹן
ma'am	gvirti	גבִרתִי
miss	'gveret	גבֶרֶת
young man	baχur tsa'ir	בָּחוּר צָעִיר
young man (little boy, kid)	'yeled	יֶלֶד
miss (little girl)	yalda	יַלדָה

4. Cardinal numbers. Part 1

0 zero	'efes	אֶפֶס (ז)
1 one	eχad	אֶחָד (ז)
1 one (fem.)	aχat	אַחַת (נ)
2 two	'ʃtayim	שׁתַיִים (נ)
3 three	ʃaloʃ	שָׁלוֹשׁ (נ)
4 four	arba	אַרבַּע (נ)
5 five	χameʃ	חָמֵשׁ (נ)
6 six	ʃeʃ	שֵׁשׁ (נ)
7 seven	'ʃeva	שֶׁבַע (נ)
8 eight	'ʃmone	שׁמוֹנֶה (נ)

9 nine	'teʃa	תֵּשַׁע (נ)
10 ten	'eser	עֶשֶׂר (נ)
11 eleven	aχat esre	אַחַת־עֶשְׂרֵה (נ)
12 twelve	ʃteim esre	שְׁתֵּים־עֶשְׂרֵה (נ)
13 thirteen	ʃloʃ esre	שְׁלוֹשׁ־עֶשְׂרֵה (נ)
14 fourteen	arba esre	אַרְבַּע־עֶשְׂרֵה (נ)
15 fifteen	χameʃ esre	חֲמֵשׁ־עֶשְׂרֵה (נ)
16 sixteen	ʃeʃ esre	שֵׁשׁ־עֶשְׂרֵה (נ)
17 seventeen	ʃva esre	שְׁבַע־עֶשְׂרֵה (נ)
18 eighteen	ʃmone esre	שְׁמוֹנֶה־עֶשְׂרֵה (נ)
19 nineteen	tʃa esre	תְּשַׁע־עֶשְׂרֵה (נ)
20 twenty	esrim	עֶשְׂרִים
21 twenty-one	esrim ve'eχad	עֶשְׂרִים וְאֶחָד
22 twenty-two	esrim u'ʃnayim	עֶשְׂרִים וּשְׁנַיִים
23 twenty-three	esrim uʃloʃa	עֶשְׂרִים וּשְׁלוֹשָׁה
30 thirty	ʃloʃim	שְׁלוֹשִׁים
31 thirty-one	ʃloʃim ve'eχad	שְׁלוֹשִׁים וְאֶחָד
32 thirty-two	ʃloʃim u'ʃnayim	שְׁלוֹשִׁים וּשְׁנַיִים
33 thirty-three	ʃloʃim uʃloʃa	שְׁלוֹשִׁים וּשְׁלוֹשָׁה
40 forty	arba'im	אַרְבָּעִים
41 forty-one	arba'im ve'eχad	אַרְבָּעִים וְאֶחָד
42 forty-two	arba'im u'ʃnayim	אַרְבָּעִים וּשְׁנַיִים
43 forty-three	arba'im uʃloʃa	אַרְבָּעִים וּשְׁלוֹשָׁה
50 fifty	χamiʃim	חֲמִשִׁים
51 fifty-one	χamiʃim ve'eχad	חֲמִשִׁים וְאֶחָד
52 fifty-two	χamiʃim u'ʃnayim	חֲמִשִׁים וּשְׁנַיִים
53 fifty-three	χamiʃim uʃloʃa	חֲמִשִׁים וּשְׁלוֹשָׁה
60 sixty	ʃiʃim	שִׁישִׁים
61 sixty-one	ʃiʃim ve'eχad	שִׁישִׁים וְאֶחָד
62 sixty-two	ʃiʃim u'ʃnayim	שִׁישִׁים וּשְׁנַיִים
63 sixty-three	ʃiʃim uʃloʃa	שִׁישִׁים וּשְׁלוֹשָׁה
70 seventy	ʃiv'im	שְׁבָעִים
71 seventy-one	ʃiv'im ve'eχad	שְׁבָעִים וְאֶחָד
72 seventy-two	ʃiv'im u'ʃnayim	שְׁבָעִים וּשְׁנַיִים
73 seventy-three	ʃiv'im uʃloʃa	שְׁבָעִים וּשְׁלוֹשָׁה
80 eighty	ʃmonim	שְׁמוֹנִים
81 eighty-one	ʃmonim ve'eχad	שְׁמוֹנִים וְאֶחָד
82 eighty-two	ʃmonim u'ʃnayim	שְׁמוֹנִים וּשְׁנַיִים
83 eighty-three	ʃmonim uʃloʃa	שְׁמוֹנִים וּשְׁלוֹשָׁה
90 ninety	tiʃim	תְּשָׁעִים
91 ninety-one	tiʃim ve'eχad	תְּשָׁעִים וְאֶחָד
92 ninety-two	tiʃim u'ʃayim	תְּשָׁעִים וּשְׁנַיִים
93 ninety-three	tiʃim uʃloʃa	תְּשָׁעִים וּשְׁלוֹשָׁה

5. Cardinal numbers. Part 2

100 one hundred	'me'a	מֵאָה (נ)
200 two hundred	ma'tayim	מָאתַיִם
300 three hundred	ʃloʃ me'ot	שְׁלוֹשׁ מֵאוֹת (נ)
400 four hundred	arba me'ot	אַרְבַּע מֵאוֹת (נ)
500 five hundred	xameʃ me'ot	חָמֵשׁ מֵאוֹת (נ)
600 six hundred	ʃeʃ me'ot	שֵׁשׁ מֵאוֹת (נ)
700 seven hundred	ʃva me'ot	שְׁבַע מֵאוֹת (נ)
800 eight hundred	ʃmone me'ot	שְׁמוֹנֶה מֵאוֹת (נ)
900 nine hundred	tʃa me'ot	תְּשַׁע מֵאוֹת (נ)
1000 one thousand	'elef	אֶלֶף (ז)
2000 two thousand	al'payim	אַלְפַּיִם (ז)
3000 three thousand	'ʃloʃet alafim	שְׁלוֹשֶׁת אֲלָפִים (ז)
10000 ten thousand	a'seret alafim	עֲשֶׂרֶת אֲלָפִים (ז)
one hundred thousand	'me'a 'elef	מֵאָה אֶלֶף (ז)
million	milyon	מִילְיוֹן (ז)
billion	milyard	מִילְיַארְד (ז)

6. Ordinal numbers

first (adj)	riʃon	רִאשׁוֹן
second (adj)	ʃeni	שֵׁנִי
third (adj)	ʃliʃi	שְׁלִישִׁי
fourth (adj)	revi'i	רְבִיעִי
fifth (adj)	xamiʃi	חֲמִישִׁי
sixth (adj)	ʃiʃi	שִׁישִׁי
seventh (adj)	ʃvi'i	שְׁבִיעִי
eighth (adj)	ʃmini	שְׁמִינִי
ninth (adj)	tʃi'i	תְּשִׁיעִי
tenth (adj)	asiri	עֲשִׂירִי

7. Numbers. Fractions

fraction	'ʃever	שֶׁבֶר (ז)
one half	'xetsi	חֲצִי (ז)
one third	ʃliʃ	שְׁלִישׁ (ז)
one quarter	'reva	רֶבַע (ז)
one eighth	ʃminit	שְׁמִינִית (נ)
one tenth	asirit	עֲשִׂירִית (נ)
two thirds	ʃnei ʃliʃim	שְׁנֵי שְׁלִישִׁים (ז)
three quarters	'ʃloʃet riv'ei	שְׁלוֹשֶׁת רְבָעֵי

8. Numbers. Basic operations

subtraction	χisur	חִיסוּר (ז)
to subtract (vi, vt)	leχaser	לְחַסֵר
division	χiluk	חִילוּק (ז)
to divide (vt)	leχalek	לְחַלֵק
addition	χibur	חִיבּוּר (ז)
to add up (vt)	leχaber	לְחַבֵּר
to add (vi, vt)	leχaber	לְחַבֵּר
multiplication	'kefel	כֶּפֶל (ז)
to multiply (vt)	lehaχpil	לְהַכְפִּיל

9. Numbers. Miscellaneous

digit, figure	sifra	סִפְרָה (נ)
number	mispar	מִסְפָּר (ז)
numeral	ʃem mispar	שֵׁם מִסְפָּר (ז)
minus sign	'minus	מִינוּס (ז)
plus sign	plus	פְּלוּס (ז)
formula	nusχa	נוּסְחָה (נ)
calculation	χiʃuv	חִישׁוּב (ז)
to count (vi, vt)	lispor	לִסְפּוֹר
to count up	leχaʃev	לְחַשֵׁב
to compare (vt)	lehaʃvot	לְהַשְׁווֹת
How much?	'kama?	כַּמָה?
How many?	'kama?	כַּמָה?
sum, total	sχum	סְכוּם (ז)
result	totsa'a	תּוֹצָאָה (נ)
remainder	ʃe'erit	שְׁאָרִית (נ)
a few (e.g., ~ years ago)	'kama	כַּמָה
little (I had ~ time)	ktsat	קְצָת
few (I have ~ friends)	me'at	מְעַט
a little (~ tired)	me'at	מְעַט
the rest	ʃe'ar	שְׁאָר (ז)
one and a half	eχad va'χetsi	אֶחָד וָחֵצִי (ז)
dozen	tresar	תְּרֵיסָר (ז)
in half (adv)	'χetsi 'χetsi	חֲצִי חֲצִי
equally (evenly)	ʃave beʃave	שָׁווֶה בְּשָׁווֶה
half	'χetsi	חֲצִי (ז)
time (three ~s)	'pa'am	פַּעַם (נ)

10. The most important verbs. Part 1

to advise (vt)	leya'ets	לְיַיעֵץ
to agree (say yes)	lehaskim	לְהַסכִּים
to answer (vi, vt)	la'anot	לַעֲנוֹת
to apologize (vi)	lehitnatsel	לְהִתנַצֵל
to arrive (vi)	leha'gi'a	לְהַגִיעַ
to ask (~ oneself)	liʃol	לִשאוֹל
to ask (~ sb to do sth)	levakeʃ	לְבַקֵש
to be (vi)	lihyot	לִהיוֹת
to be afraid	lefaxed	לְפַחֵד
to be hungry	lihyot ra'ev	לִהיוֹת רָעֵב
to be interested in ...	lehit'anyen be...	...לְהִתעַניֵין בְּ
to be needed	lehidareʃ	לְהִידָרֵש
to be surprised	lehitpale	לְהִתפַּלֵא
to be thirsty	lihyot tsame	לִהיוֹת צָמֵא
to begin (vt)	lehatxil	לְהַתחִיל
to belong to ...	lehiʃtayex	לְהִשתַייֵך
to boast (vi)	lehitravrev	לְהִתרַברֵב
to break (split into pieces)	liʃbor	לִשבּוֹר
to call (~ for help)	likro	לִקרוֹא
can (v aux)	yaxol	יָכוֹל
to catch (vt)	litfos	לִתפּוֹס
to change (vt)	leʃanot	לְשַנוֹת
to choose (select)	livxor	לִבחוֹר
to come down (the stairs)	la'redet	לָרֶדֶת
to compare (vt)	lehaʃvot	לְהַשווֹת
to complain (vi, vt)	lehitlonen	לְהִתלוֹנֵן
to confuse (mix up)	lehitbalbel	לְהִתבַּלבֵּל
to continue (vt)	lehamʃix	לְהַמשִיך
to control (vt)	liʃlot	לִשלוֹט
to cook (dinner)	levaʃel	לְבַשֵל
to cost (vt)	la'alot	לַעֲלוֹת
to count (add up)	lispor	לִספּוֹר
to count on ...	lismox al	לִסמוֹך עַל
to create (vt)	litsor	לִיצוֹר
to cry (weep)	livkot	לִבכּוֹת

11. The most important verbs. Part 2

to deceive (vi, vt)	leramot	לְרַמוֹת
to decorate (tree, street)	lekaʃet	לְקַשֵט
to defend (a country, etc.)	lehagen	לְהָגֵן

to demand (request firmly)	lidroʃ	לִדְרוֹשׁ
to dig (vt)	laχpor	לַחְפּוֹר
to discuss (vt)	ladun	לָדוּן
to do (vt)	la'asot	לַעֲשׂוֹת
to doubt (have doubts)	lefakpek	לְפַקְפֵּק
to drop (let fall)	lehapil	לְהַפִּיל
to enter	lehikanes	לְהִיכָּנֵס
(room, house, etc.)		
to excuse (forgive)	lis'loaχ	לִסְלוֹחַ
to exist (vi)	lehitkayem	לְהִתְקַיֵּים
to expect (foresee)	laχazot	לַחֲזוֹת
to explain (vt)	lehasbir	לְהַסְבִּיר
to fall (vi)	lipol	לִיפּוֹל
to find (vt)	limtso	לִמְצוֹא
to finish (vt)	lesayem	לְסַיֵּים
to fly (vi)	la'uf	לָעוּף
to follow … (come after)	la'akov aχarei	לַעֲקוֹב אַחֲרֵי
to forget (vi, vt)	liʃkoaχ	לִשְׁכּוֹחַ
to forgive (vt)	lis'loaχ	לִסְלוֹחַ
to give (vt)	latet	לָתֵת
to give a hint	lirmoz	לִרְמוֹז
to go (on foot)	la'leχet	לָלֶכֶת
to go for a swim	lehitraχets	לְהִתְרַחֵץ
to go out (for dinner, etc.)	latset	לָצֵאת
to guess (the answer)	lenaχeʃ	לְנַחֵשׁ
to have (vt)	lehaχzik	לְהַחְזִיק
to have breakfast	le'eχol aruχat 'boker	לֶאֱכוֹל אֲרוּחַת בּוֹקֶר
to have dinner	le'eχol aruχat 'erev	לֶאֱכוֹל אֲרוּחַת עֶרֶב
to have lunch	le'eχol aruχat tsaha'rayim	לֶאֱכוֹל אֲרוּחַת צָהֳרַיִים
to hear (vt)	liʃmo'a	לִשְׁמוֹעַ
to help (vt)	la'azor	לַעֲזוֹר
to hide (vt)	lehastir	לְהַסְתִּיר
to hope (vi, vt)	lekavot	לְקַווֹת
to hunt (vi, vt)	latsud	לָצוּד
to hurry (vi)	lemaher	לְמַהֵר

12. The most important verbs. Part 3

to inform (vt)	leho'dia	לְהוֹדִיעַ
to insist (vi, vt)	lehit'akeʃ	לְהִתְעַקֵּשׁ
to insult (vt)	leha'aliv	לְהַעֲלִיב
to invite (vt)	lehazmin	לְהַזְמִין
to joke (vi)	lehitba'deaχ	לְהִתְבַּדֵּחַ

to keep (vt)	liʃmor	לִשְׁמוֹר
to keep silent	liʃtok	לִשְׁתּוֹק
to kill (vt)	laharog	לַהֲרוֹג
to know (sb)	lehakir et	לְהַכִּיר אֶת
to know (sth)	la'da'at	לָדַעַת
to laugh (vi)	litsχok	לִצְחוֹק

to liberate (city, etc.)	leʃaχrer	לְשַׁחְרֵר
to like (I like …)	limtso χen be'ei'nayim	לִמְצוֹא חֵן בְּעֵינַיִים
to look for … (search)	leχapes	לְחַפֵּשׂ
to love (sb)	le'ehov	לֶאֱהוֹב
to make a mistake	lit'ot	לִטְעוֹת

to manage, to run	lenahel	לְנַהֵל
to mean (signify)	lomar	לוֹמַר
to mention (talk about)	lehazkir	לְהַזְכִּיר
to miss (school, etc.)	lehaχsir	לְהַחְסִיר
to notice (see)	lasim lev	לָשִׂים לֵב

to object (vi, vt)	lehitnaged	לְהִתְנַגֵּד
to observe (see)	litspot, lehaʃkif	לִצְפּוֹת, לְהַשְׁקִיף
to open (vt)	lif'toaχ	לִפְתּוֹחַ
to order (meal, etc.)	lehazmin	לְהַזְמִין
to order (mil.)	lifkod	לִפְקוֹד
to own (possess)	lihyot 'ba'al ʃel	לִהְיוֹת בַּעַל שֶׁל

to participate (vi)	lehiʃtatef	לְהִשְׁתַּתֵּף
to pay (vi, vt)	leʃalem	לְשַׁלֵּם
to permit (vt)	leharʃot	לְהַרְשׁוֹת
to plan (vt)	letaχnen	לְתַכְנֵן
to play (children)	lesaχek	לְשַׂחֵק

to pray (vi, vt)	lehitpalel	לְהִתְפַּלֵּל
to prefer (vt)	leha'adif	לְהַעֲדִיף
to promise (vt)	lehav'tiaχ	לְהַבְטִיחַ
to pronounce (vt)	levate	לְבַטֵּא
to propose (vt)	leha'tsi'a	לְהַצִּיעַ
to punish (vt)	leha'aniʃ	לְהַעֲנִישׁ

13. The most important verbs. Part 4

to read (vi, vt)	likro	לִקְרוֹא
to recommend (vt)	lehamlits	לְהַמְלִיץ
to refuse (vi, vt)	lesarev	לְסָרֵב
to regret (be sorry)	lehitsta'er	לְהִצְטַעֵר
to rent (sth from sb)	liskor	לִשְׂכּוֹר

to repeat (say again)	laχazor al	לַחֲזוֹר עַל
to reserve, to book	lehazmin meroʃ	לְהַזְמִין מֵרֹאשׁ
to run (vi)	laruts	לָרוּץ

to save (rescue)	lehatsil	לְהַצִּיל
to say (~ thank you)	lomar	לוֹמַר
to scold (vt)	linzof	לִנְזוֹף
to see (vt)	lir'ot	לִרְאוֹת
to sell (vt)	limkor	לִמְכּוֹר
to send (vt)	liʃloaχ	לִשְׁלוֹחַ
to shoot (vi)	lirot	לִירוֹת
to shout (vi)	lits'ok	לִצְעוֹק
to show (vt)	lehar'ot	לְהַרְאוֹת
to sign (document)	laχtom	לַחְתּוֹם
to sit down (vi)	lehityaʃev	לְהִתְיַישֵׁב
to smile (vi)	leχayeχ	לְחַיֵּיךְ
to speak (vi, vt)	ledaber	לְדַבֵּר
to steal (money, etc.)	lignov	לִגְנוֹב
to stop (for pause, etc.)	la'atsor	לַעֲצוֹר
to stop (please ~ calling me)	lehafsik	לְהַפְסִיק
to study (vt)	lilmod	לִלְמוֹד
to swim (vi)	lisχot	לִשְׂחוֹת
to take (vt)	la'kaχat	לָקַחַת
to think (vi, vt)	laχʃov	לַחְשׁוֹב
to threaten (vt)	le'ayem	לְאַיֵּים
to touch (with hands)	la'ga'at	לָגַעַת
to translate (vt)	letargem	לְתַרְגֵּם
to trust (vt)	liv'toaχ	לִבְטוֹחַ
to try (attempt)	lenasot	לְנַסּוֹת
to turn (e.g., ~ left)	lifnot	לִפְנוֹת
to underestimate (vt)	leham'it be''ereχ	לְהַמְעִיט בְּעֶרֶךְ
to understand (vt)	lehavin	לְהָבִין
to unite (vt)	le'aχed	לְאַחֵד
to wait (vt)	lehamtin	לְהַמְתִּין
to want (wish, desire)	lirtsot	לִרְצוֹת
to warn (vt)	lehazhir	לְהַזְהִיר
to work (vi)	la'avod	לַעֲבוֹד
to write (vt)	liχtov	לִכְתּוֹב
to write down	lirʃom	לִרְשׁוֹם

14. Colors

color	'tseva	צֶבַע (ז)
shade (tint)	gavan	גָּוֶון (ז)
hue	gavan	גָּוֶון (ז)
rainbow	'keʃet	קֶשֶׁת (נ)

white (adj)	lavan	לָבָן
black (adj)	ʃaχor	שָׁחוֹר
gray (adj)	afor	אָפוֹר
green (adj)	yarok	יָרוֹק
yellow (adj)	tsahov	צָהוֹב
red (adj)	adom	אָדוֹם
blue (adj)	kaχol	כָּחוֹל
light blue (adj)	taχol	תָכוֹל
pink (adj)	varod	וָרוֹד
orange (adj)	katom	כָּתוֹם
violet (adj)	segol	סָגוֹל
brown (adj)	χum	חוּם
golden (adj)	zahov	זָהוֹב
silvery (adj)	kasuf	כָּסוּף
beige (adj)	beʒ	בֵּז'
cream (adj)	be'tseva krem	בְּצֶבַע קְרֶם
turquoise (adj)	turkiz	טוּרְקִיז
cherry red (adj)	bordo	בּוֹרְדוֹ
lilac (adj)	segol	סָגוֹל
crimson (adj)	patol	פָּטוֹל
light (adj)	bahir	בָּהִיר
dark (adj)	kehe	כֵּהֶה
bright, vivid (adj)	bohek	בּוֹהֵק
colored (pencils)	tsiv'oni	צִבְעוֹנִי
color (e.g., ~ film)	tsiv'oni	צִבְעוֹנִי
black-and-white (adj)	ʃaχor lavan	שָׁחוֹר-לָבָן
plain (one-colored)	χad tsiv'i	חַד-צִבְעִי
multicolored (adj)	sasgoni	סַסְגּוֹנִי

15. Questions

Who?	mi?	מִי?
What?	ma?	מָה?
Where? (at, in)	'eifo?	אֵיפֹה?
Where (to)?	le'an?	לְאָן?
From where?	me''eifo?	מֵאֵיפֹה?
When?	matai?	מָתַי?
Why? (What for?)	'lama?	לָמָה?
Why? (~ are you crying?)	ma'du'a?	מַדּוּעַ?
What for?	biʃvil ma?	בִּשְׁבִיל מָה?
How? (in what way)	eiχ, keitsad?	כֵּיצַד? אֵיךְ?
What? (What kind of ...?)	'eize?	אֵיזֶה?
Which?	'eize?	אֵיזֶה?

To whom?	lemi?	לְמִי?
About whom?	al mi?	עַל מִי?
About what?	al ma?	עַל מָה?
With whom?	im mi?	עִם מִי?
How many? How much?	'kama?	כַּמָה?
Whose?	ʃel mi?	שֶׁל מִי?

16. Prepositions

with (accompanied by)	im	עִם
without	bli, lelo	בְּלִי, לְלֹא
to (indicating direction)	le...	...לְ
about (talking ~ ...)	al	עַל
before (in time)	lifnei	לִפְנֵי
in front of ...	lifnei	לִפְנֵי
under (beneath, below)	mi'taχat le...	...מִתַחַת לְ
above (over)	me'al	מֵעַל
on (atop)	al	עַל
from (off, out of)	mi, me	מ, מְ
of (made from)	mi, me	מ, מְ
in (e.g., ~ ten minutes)	toχ	תוֹךְ
over (across the top of)	'dereχ	דֶרֶךְ

17. Function words. Adverbs. Part 1

Where? (at, in)	'eifo?	אֵיפֹה?
here (adv)	po, kan	פֹה, כָּאן
there (adv)	ʃam	שָׁם
somewhere (to be)	'eifo ʃehu	אֵיפֹה שֶׁהוּא
nowhere (not anywhere)	beʃum makom	בְּשׁוּם מָקוֹם
by (near, beside)	leyad ...	... לְיַד
by the window	leyad haχalon	לְיַד הַחַלוֹן
Where (to)?	le'an?	לְאָן?
here (e.g., come ~!)	'hena, lekan	הֵנָה; לְכָאן
there (e.g., to go ~)	leʃam	לְשָׁם
from here (adv)	mikan	מִכָּאן
from there (adv)	miʃam	מִשָׁם
close (adv)	karov	קָרוֹב
far (adv)	raχok	רָחוֹק
near (e.g., ~ Paris)	leyad	לְיַד
nearby (adv)	karov	קָרוֹב

not far (adv)	lo raχok	לֹא רָחוֹק
left (adj)	smali	שׂמָאלִי
on the left	mismol	מִשׂמֹאל
to the left	'smola	שׂמֹאלָה
right (adj)	yemani	יְמָנִי
on the right	miyamin	מִיָמִין
to the right	ya'mina	יָמִינָה
in front (adv)	mika'dima	מִקָדִימָה
front (as adj)	kidmi	קָדמִי
ahead (the kids ran ~)	ka'dima	קָדִימָה
behind (adv)	me'aχor	מֵאָחוֹר
from behind	me'aχor	מֵאָחוֹר
back (towards the rear)	a'χora	אָחוֹרָה
middle	'emtsa	אָמצַע (ז)
in the middle	ba''emtsa	בָּאָמצַע
at the side	mehatsad	מֵהַצַד
everywhere (adv)	beχol makom	בְּכָל מָקוֹם
around (in all directions)	misaviv	מִסָבִיב
from inside	mibifnim	מִבִּפנִים
somewhere (to go)	le'an ʃehu	לְאָן שֶׁהוּא
straight (directly)	yaʃar	יָשָׁר
back (e.g., come ~)	baχazara	בַּחֲזָרָה
from anywhere	me'ei ʃam	מֵאֵי שָׁם
from somewhere	me'ei ʃam	מֵאֵי שָׁם
firstly (adv)	reʃit	רֵאשִׁית
secondly (adv)	ʃenit	שֵׁנִית
thirdly (adv)	ʃliʃit	שְׁלִישִׁית
suddenly (adv)	pit'om	פִּתאוֹם
at first (in the beginning)	behatslaχa	בַּהַתחָלָה
for the first time	lariʃona	לָרִאשׁוֹנָה
long before …	zman rav lifnei …	זמַן רַב לְפנֵי …
anew (over again)	meχadaʃ	מֵחָדָש
for good (adv)	letamid	לְתָמִיד
never (adv)	af 'pa'am, me'olam	מֵעוֹלָם, אַף פַּעַם
again (adv)	ʃuv	שׁוּב
now (adv)	axʃav, ka'et	עַכשָׁיו, כָּעֵת
often (adv)	le'itim krovot	לְעִיתִים קרוֹבוֹת
then (adv)	az	אָז
urgently (quickly)	bidχifut	בִּדחִיפוּת
usually (adv)	be'dereχ klal	בְּדֶרֶך כּלָל
by the way, …	'dereχ 'agav	דֶרֶך אַגַב
possible (that is ~)	efʃari	אֶפשָׁרִי

probably (adv)	kanir'e	כַּנִּרְאֶה
maybe (adv)	ulai	אוּלַי
besides ...	χuts mize ...	חוּץ מִזֶּה ...
that's why ...	laχen	לָכֵן
in spite of ...	lamrot ...	לַמְרוֹת ...
thanks to ...	hodot le...	הוֹדוֹת לְ...

what (pron.)	ma	מָה
that (conj.)	ʃe	שֶׁ
something	'maʃehu	מַשֶּׁהוּ
anything (something)	'maʃehu	מַשֶּׁהוּ
nothing	klum	כְּלוּם

who (pron.)	mi	מִי
someone	'miʃehu, 'miʃehi	מִישֶׁהוּ (ז), מִישֶׁהִי (נ)
somebody	'miʃehu, 'miʃehi	מִישֶׁהוּ (ז), מִישֶׁהִי (נ)

nobody	af eχad, af aχat	אַף אֶחָד (ז), אַף אַחַת (נ)
nowhere (a voyage to ~)	leʃum makom	לְשׁוּם מָקוֹם
nobody's	lo ʃayaχ le'af eχad	לֹא שַׁיָּךְ לְאַף אֶחָד
somebody's	ʃel 'miʃehu	שֶׁל מִישֶׁהוּ

so (I'm ~ glad)	kol kaχ	כָּל־כָּךְ
also (as well)	gam	גַּם
too (as well)	gam	גַּם

18. Function words. Adverbs. Part 2

Why?	ma'du'a?	מַדּוּעַ?
for some reason	miʃum ma	מִשּׁוּם־מָה
because ...	miʃum ʃe	מִשּׁוּם שֶׁ
for some purpose	lematara 'kolʃehi	לְמַטָּרָה כָּלְשֶׁהִי

and	ve ...	וְ ...
or	o	אוֹ
but	aval, ulam	אֲבָל, אוּלָם
for (e.g., ~ me)	biʃvil	בִּשְׁבִיל

too (~ many people)	yoter midai	יוֹתֵר מִדַּי
only (exclusively)	rak	רַק
exactly (adv)	bediyuk	בְּדִיּוּק
about (more or less)	be''ereχ	בְּעֵרֶךְ

approximately (adv)	be''ereχ	בְּעֵרֶךְ
approximate (adj)	meʃo'ar	מְשֹׁעָר
almost (adv)	kim'at	כִּמְעַט
the rest	ʃe'ar	שְׁאָר (ז)

| the other (second) | aχer | אַחֵר |
| other (different) | aχer | אַחֵר |

29

each (adj)	kol	כֹּל
any (no matter which)	kolʃehu	כָּלְשֶׁהוּ
many, much (a lot of)	harbe	הַרְבֵּה
many people	harbe	הַרְבֵּה
all (everyone)	kulam	כּוּלָם

in return for …	tmurat …	תְּמוּרַת ...
in exchange (adv)	bitmura	בִּתְמוּרָה
by hand (made)	bayad	בְּיָד
hardly (negative opinion)	safek im	סָפֵק אִם

probably (adv)	karov levadai	קָרוֹב לְוַודַּאי
on purpose (intentionally)	'davka	דַּווקָא
by accident (adv)	bemikre	בְּמִקְרֶה

very (adv)	me'od	מְאוֹד
for example (adv)	lemaʃal	לְמָשָׁל
between	bein	בֵּין
among	be'kerev	בְּקֶרֶב
so much (such a lot)	kol kaχ harbe	כָּל־כָּךְ הַרְבֵּה
especially (adv)	bimyuχad	בְּמְיוּחָד

Basic concepts. Part 2

19. Weekdays

Monday	yom ʃeni	יוֹם שֵׁנִי (ז)
Tuesday	yom ʃliʃi	יוֹם שְׁלִישִׁי (ז)
Wednesday	yom reviʻi	יוֹם רְבִיעִי (ז)
Thursday	yom χamiʃi	יוֹם חֲמִישִׁי (ז)
Friday	yom ʃiʃi	יוֹם שִׁישִׁי (ז)
Saturday	ʃabat	שַׁבָּת (נ)
Sunday	yom riʃon	יוֹם רִאשׁוֹן (ז)

today (adv)	hayom	הַיוֹם
tomorrow (adv)	maχar	מָחָר
the day after tomorrow	maχara'tayim	מָחֳרָתַיִם
yesterday (adv)	etmol	אֶתְמוֹל
the day before yesterday	ʃilʃom	שִׁלְשׁוֹם

day	yom	יוֹם (ז)
working day	yom avoda	יוֹם עֲבוֹדָה (ז)
public holiday	yom χag	יוֹם חַג (ז)
day off	yom menuχa	יוֹם מְנוּחָה (ז)
weekend	sof ʃa'vuʻa	סוֹף שָׁבוּעַ

all day long	kol hayom	כָּל הַיוֹם
the next day (adv)	lamaχarat	לַמָחֳרָת
two days ago	lifnei yo'mayim	לִפְנֵי יוֹמַיִים
the day before	'erev	עֶרֶב
daily (adj)	yomyomi	יוֹמְיוֹמִי
every day (adv)	midei yom	מִדֵי יוֹם

week	ʃa'vua	שָׁבוּעַ (ז)
last week (adv)	baʃa'vuʻa ʃe'avar	בַּשָׁבוּעַ שֶׁעָבַר
next week (adv)	baʃa'vuʻa haba	בַּשָׁבוּעַ הַבָּא
weekly (adj)	ʃvuʻi	שְׁבוּעִי
every week (adv)	kol ʃa'vuʻa	כָּל שָׁבוּעַ
twice a week	pa'a'mayim beʃa'vuʻa	פַּעֲמַיִים בְּשָׁבוּעַ
every Tuesday	kol yom ʃliʃi	כָּל יוֹם שְׁלִישִׁי

20. Hours. Day and night

morning	'boker	בּוֹקֶר (ז)
in the morning	ba'boker	בַּבּוֹקֶר
noon, midday	tsaha'rayim	צָהֳרַיִים (ז"ר)

in the afternoon	aχar hatsaha'rayim	אַחַר הַצָּהֳרַיִם
evening	'erev	עֶרֶב (ז)
in the evening	ba''erev	בָּעֶרֶב
night	'laila	לַיְלָה (ז)
at night	ba'laila	בַּלַּיְלָה
midnight	χatsot	חֲצוֹת (נ)
second	ʃniya	שְׁנִיָּה (נ)
minute	daka	דַּקָּה (נ)
hour	ʃa'a	שָׁעָה (נ)
half an hour	χatsi ʃa'a	חֲצִי שָׁעָה (נ)
a quarter-hour	'reva ʃa'a	רֶבַע שָׁעָה (ז)
fifteen minutes	χameʃ esre dakot	חָמֵשׁ עֶשְׂרֵה דַּקּוֹת
24 hours	yemama	יְמָמָה (נ)
sunrise	zriχa	זְרִיחָה (נ)
dawn	'ʃaχar	שַׁחַר (ז)
early morning	'ʃaχar	שַׁחַר (ז)
sunset	ʃki'a	שְׁקִיעָה (נ)
early in the morning	mukdam ba'boker	מוּקְדָּם בַּבּוֹקֶר
this morning	ha'boker	הַבּוֹקֶר
tomorrow morning	maχar ba'boker	מָחָר בַּבּוֹקֶר
this afternoon	hayom aχarei hatzaha'rayim	הַיּוֹם אַחֲרֵי הַצָּהֳרַיִם
in the afternoon	aχar hatsaha'rayim	אַחַר הַצָּהֳרַיִם
tomorrow afternoon	maχar aχarei hatsaha'rayim	מָחָר אַחֲרֵי הַצָּהֳרַיִם
tonight (this evening)	ha''erev	הָעֶרֶב
tomorrow night	maχar ba''erev	מָחָר בָּעֶרֶב
at 3 o'clock sharp	baʃa'a ʃaloʃ bediyuk	בְּשָׁעָה שָׁלוֹשׁ בְּדִיּוּק
about 4 o'clock	bisvivot arba	בִּסְבִיבוֹת אַרְבַּע
by 12 o'clock	ad ʃteim esre	עַד שְׁתֵּים־עֶשְׂרֵה
in 20 minutes	be'od esrim dakot	בְּעוֹד עֶשְׂרִים דַּקּוֹת
in an hour	be'od ʃa'a	בְּעוֹד שָׁעָה
on time (adv)	bazman	בַּזְּמַן
a quarter of …	'reva le…	רֶבַע לְ…
within an hour	toχ ʃa'a	תּוֹךְ שָׁעָה
every 15 minutes	kol 'reva ʃa'a	כָּל רֶבַע שָׁעָה
round the clock	misaviv laʃa'on	מִסָּבִיב לַשָּׁעוֹן

21. Months. Seasons

| January | 'yanu'ar | יָנוּאָר (ז) |
| February | 'febru'ar | פֶבְּרוּאָר (ז) |

March	merts	מֶרְץ (ז)
April	april	אַפְּרִיל (ז)
May	mai	מַאי (ז)
June	'yuni	יוּנִי (ז)
July	'yuli	יוּלִי (ז)
August	'ogust	אוֹגוּסְט (ז)
September	sep'tember	סֶפְּטֶמְבֶּר (ז)
October	ok'tober	אוֹקְטוֹבֶּר (ז)
November	no'vember	נוֹבֶמְבֶּר (ז)
December	de'tsember	דֶּצֶמְבֶּר (ז)
spring	aviv	אָבִיב (ז)
in spring	ba'aviv	בָּאָבִיב
spring (as adj)	avivi	אֲבִיבִי
summer	'kayits	קַיִץ (ז)
in summer	ba'kayits	בַּקַיִץ
summer (as adj)	ketsi	קֵיצִי
fall	stav	סְתָיו (ז)
in fall	bestav	בְּסְתָיו
fall (as adj)	stavi	סְתָווִי
winter	'xoref	חוֹרֶף (ז)
in winter	ba'xoref	בַּחוֹרֶף
winter (as adj)	xorpi	חוֹרְפִּי
month	'xodef	חוֹדֶשׁ (ז)
this month	ha'xodef	הַחוֹדֶשׁ
next month	ba'xodef haba	בַּחוֹדֶשׁ הַבָּא
last month	ba'xodef fe'avar	בַּחוֹדֶשׁ שֶׁעָבַר
a month ago	lifnei 'xodef	לִפְנֵי חוֹדֶשׁ
in a month (a month later)	be'od 'xodef	בְּעוֹד חוֹדֶשׁ
in 2 months (2 months later)	be'od xod'fayim	בְּעוֹד חוֹדְשַׁיִים
the whole month	kol ha'xodef	כָּל הַחוֹדֶשׁ
all month long	kol ha'xodef	כָּל הַחוֹדֶשׁ
monthly (~ magazine)	xodfi	חוֹדְשִׁי
monthly (adv)	xodfit	חוֹדְשִׁית
every month	kol 'xodef	כָּל חוֹדֶשׁ
twice a month	pa'a'mayim be'xodef	פַּעֲמַיִים בְּחוֹדֶשׁ
year	fana	שָׁנָה (נ)
this year	hafana	הַשָׁנָה
next year	bafana haba'a	בַּשָׁנָה הַבָּאָה
last year	bafana fe'avra	בַּשָׁנָה שֶׁעָבְרָה
a year ago	lifnei fana	לִפְנֵי שָׁנָה
in a year	be'od fana	בְּעוֹד שָׁנָה

in two years	be'od ʃna'tayim	בְּעוֹד שְׁנָתַיים
the whole year	kol haʃana	כָּל הַשָּׁנָה
all year long	kol haʃana	כָּל הַשָּׁנָה
every year	kol ʃana	כָּל שָׁנָה
annual (adj)	ʃnati	שְׁנָתִי
annually (adv)	midei ʃana	מִדֵי שָׁנָה
4 times a year	arba pa'amim be'xodeʃ	אַרְבַּע פְּעָמִים בְּחוֹדֶשׁ
date (e.g., today's ~)	ta'arix	תַּאֲרִיךְ (ז)
date (e.g., ~ of birth)	ta'arix	תַּאֲרִיךְ (ז)
calendar	'luax ʃana	לוּחַ שָׁנָה (ז)
half a year	xatsi ʃana	חֲצִי שָׁנָה (ז)
six months	ʃiʃa xodaʃim, xatsi ʃana	חֲצִי שָׁנָה, שִׁישָׁה חוֹדָשִׁים
season (summer, etc.)	ona	עוֹנָה (נ)
century	'me'a	מֵאָה (נ)

22. Time. Miscellaneous

time	zman	זְמַן (ז)
moment	'rega	רֶגַע (ז)
instant (n)	'rega	רֶגַע (ז)
instant (adj)	miyadi	מִיָדִי
lapse (of time)	tkufa	תְקוּפָה (נ)
life	xayim	חַיִים (ז"ר)
eternity	'netsax	נֶצַח (ז)
epoch	idan	עִידָן (ז)
era	idan	עִידָן (ז)
cycle	maxzor	מַחֲזוֹר (ז)
period	tkufa	תְקוּפָה (נ)
term (short-~)	tkufa	תְקוּפָה (נ)
the future	atid	עָתִיד (ז)
future (as adj)	haba	הַבָּא
next time	ba'pa'am haba'a	בַּפַּעַם הַבָּאָה
the past	avar	עָבָר (ז)
past (recent)	ʃe'avar	שֶׁעָבַר
last time	ba'pa'am hako'demet	בַּפַּעַם הַקוֹדֶמֶת
later (adv)	me'uxar yoter	מְאוּחָר יוֹתֵר
after (prep.)	axarei	אַחֲרֵי
nowadays (adv)	kayom	כַּיוֹם
now (adv)	axʃav, ka'et	עַכְשָׁיו, כָּעֵת
immediately (adv)	miyad	מִיָד
soon (adv)	bekarov	בְּקָרוֹב
in advance (beforehand)	meroʃ	מֵרֹאשׁ
a long time ago	mizman	מִזְמַן
recently (adv)	lo mizman	לֹא מִזְמַן

destiny	goral	גּוֹרָל (ז)
memories (childhood ~)	zixronot	זִיכרוֹנוֹת (ז"ר)
archives	arxiyon	אַרכִיוֹן (ז)
during ...	bezman ʃel ...	בְּזמַן שֶל ...
long, a long time (adv)	zman rav	זמַן רַב
not long (adv)	lo zman rav	לֹא זמַן רַב
early (in the morning)	mukdam	מוקדָם
late (not early)	me'uxar	מְאוחָר
forever (for good)	la'netsax	לָנֶצַח
to start (begin)	lehatxil	לְהַתחִיל
to postpone (vt)	lidxot	לִדחוֹת
at the same time	bo zmanit	בּוֹ זמַנִית
permanently (adv)	bikvi'ut	בִּקבִיעוּת
constant (noise, pain)	ka'vu'a	קָבוּעַ
temporary (adj)	zmani	זמַנִי
sometimes (adv)	lif'amim	לִפעָמִים
rarely (adv)	le'itim rexokot	לְעִיתִים רְחוֹקוֹת
often (adv)	le'itim krovot	לְעִיתִים קרוֹבוֹת

23. Opposites

rich (adj)	aʃir	עָשִיר
poor (adj)	ani	עָנִי
ill, sick (adj)	xole	חוֹלֶה
well (not sick)	bari	בָּרִיא
big (adj)	gadol	גָדוֹל
small (adj)	katan	קָטָן
quickly (adv)	maher	מַהֵר
slowly (adv)	le'at	לְאַט
fast (adj)	mahir	מָהִיר
slow (adj)	iti	אִיטִי
glad (adj)	sa'meax	שָׂמֵחַ
sad (adj)	atsuv	עָצוּב
together (adv)	be'yaxad	בְּיַחַד
separately (adv)	levad	לְבַד
aloud (to read)	bekol ram	בְּקוֹל רָם
silently (to oneself)	belev, be'ʃeket	בְּלֵב, בְּשֶקֶט
tall (adj)	ga'voha	גָבוֹהַ
low (adj)	namux	נָמוּך

deep (adj)	amok	עָמוֹק
shallow (adj)	radud	רָדוּד
yes	ken	כֵּן
no	lo	לֹא
distant (in space)	raχok	רָחוֹק
nearby (adj)	karov	קָרוֹב
far (adv)	raχok	רָחוֹק
nearby (adv)	samuχ	סָמוּךְ
long (adj)	aroχ	אָרוֹךְ
short (adj)	katsar	קָצָר
good (kindhearted)	tov lev	טוֹב לֵב
evil (adj)	raʃa	רָשָׁע
married (adj)	nasui	נָשׂוּי
single (adj)	ravak	רַוָּק
to forbid (vt)	le'esor al	לֶאֱסוֹר עַל
to permit (vt)	leharʃot	לְהַרְשׁוֹת
end	sof	סוֹף (ז)
beginning	hatχala	הַתחָלָה (נ)
left (adj)	smali	שׂמָאלִי
right (adj)	yemani	יְמָנִי
first (adj)	riʃon	רִאשׁוֹן
last (adj)	aχaron	אַחֲרוֹן
crime	'peʃa	פֶּשַׁע (ז)
punishment	'oneʃ	עוֹנֶשׁ (ז)
to order (vt)	letsavot	לְצַוּוֹת
to obey (vi, vt)	letsayet	לְצַיֵּת
straight (adj)	yaʃar	יָשָׁר
curved (adj)	me'ukal	מְעוּקָל
paradise	gan 'eden	גַּן עֵדֶן (ז)
hell	gehinom	גֵּיהִינוֹם (ז)
to be born	lehivaled	לְהִיוָולֵד
to die (vi)	lamut	לָמוּת
strong (adj)	χazak	חָזָק
weak (adj)	χalaʃ	חַלָּשׁ
old (adj)	zaken	זָקֵן
young (adj)	tsa'ir	צָעִיר

| old (adj) | yaʃan | יָשָׁן |
| new (adj) | χadaʃ | חָדָשׁ |

| hard (adj) | kaʃe | קָשֶׁה |
| soft (adj) | raχ | רַךְ |

| warm (tepid) | χamim | חָמִים |
| cold (adj) | kar | קַר |

| fat (adj) | ʃamen | שָׁמֵן |
| thin (adj) | raze | רָזֶה |

| narrow (adj) | tsar | צַר |
| wide (adj) | raχav | רָחָב |

| good (adj) | tov | טוֹב |
| bad (adj) | ra | רַע |

| brave (adj) | amits | אַמִיץ |
| cowardly (adj) | paχdani | פַּחְדָנִי |

24. Lines and shapes

square	ri'bu'a	רִיבּוּעַ (ז)
square (as adj)	meruba	מְרוּבָּע
circle	ma'agal, igul	מַעְגָל, עִיגוּל (ז)
round (adj)	agol	עָגוֹל
triangle	meʃulaʃ	מְשׁוּלָשׁ (ז)
triangular (adj)	meʃulaʃ	מְשׁוּלָשׁ

oval	e'lipsa	אֶלִיפְּסָה (נ)
oval (as adj)	e'lipti	אֶלִיפְּטִי
rectangle	malben	מַלְבֵּן (ז)
rectangular (adj)	malbeni	מַלְבֵּנִי

pyramid	pira'mida	פִּירָמִידָה (נ)
rhombus	me'uyan	מְעוֹיָן (ז)
trapezoid	trapez	טְרַפֶּז (ז)
cube	kubiya	קוּבִּייָה (נ)
prism	minsara	מִנְסָרָה (נ)

circumference	ma'agal	מַעְגָל (ז)
sphere	sfira	סְפִּירָה (נ)
ball (solid sphere)	kadur	כַּדוּר (ז)
diameter	'koter	קוֹטֶר (ז)
radius	'radyus	רַדְיוּס (ז)
perimeter (circle's ~)	hekef	הֶיקֵף (ז)
center	merkaz	מֶרְכָּז (ז)
horizontal (adj)	ofki	אוֹפְקִי
vertical (adj)	anaχi	אֲנָכִי

| parallel (n) | kav makbil | קַו מַקְבִּיל (ז) |
| parallel (as adj) | makbil | מַקְבִּיל |

line	kav	קַו (ז)
stroke	kav	קַו (ז)
straight line	kav yaʃar	קַו יָשָׁר (ז)
curve (curved line)	akuma	עֲקוּמָה (נ)
thin (line, etc.)	dak	דַק
contour (outline)	mit'ar	מִתְאָר (ז)

intersection	χituχ	חִיתוּךְ (ז)
right angle	zavit yaʃara	זָווִית יָשָׁרָה (נ)
segment	mikta	מִקְטָע (ז)
sector	gizra	גִזְרָה (נ)
side (of triangle)	'tsela	צֶלַע (ז)
angle	zavit	זָווִית (נ)

25. Units of measurement

weight	miʃkal	מִשְׁקָל (ז)
length	'oreχ	אוֹרֶךְ (ז)
width	'roχav	רוֹחַב (ז)
height	'gova	גוֹבַה (ז)
depth	'omek	עוֹמֶק (ז)
volume	'nefaχ	נֶפַח (ז)
area	'ʃetaχ	שֶׁטַח (ז)

gram	gram	גרַם (ז)
milligram	miligram	מִילִיגרַם (ז)
kilogram	kilogram	קִילוֹגרַם (ז)
ton	ton	טוֹן (ז)
pound	'pa'und	פָּאוּנד (ז)
ounce	'unkiya	אוּנקִיָה (נ)

meter	'meter	מֶטֶר (ז)
millimeter	mili'meter	מִילִימֶטֶר (ז)
centimeter	senti'meter	סָנטִימֶטֶר (ז)
kilometer	kilo'meter	קִילוֹמֶטֶר (ז)
mile	mail	מַייל (ז)

inch	intʃ	אִינץ' (ז)
foot	'regel	רֶגֶל (נ)
yard	yard	יַרד (ז)

| square meter | 'meter ra'vu'a | מֶטֶר רָבוּעַ (ז) |
| hectare | hektar | הֶקטָר (ז) |

liter	litr	לִיטר (ז)
degree	ma'ala	מַעֲלָה (נ)
volt	volt	ווֹלט (ז)

| ampere | amper | אַמְפֵּר (ז) |
| horsepower | 'koaχ sus | כּוֹחַ סוּס (ז) |

quantity	kamut	כַּמּוּת (נ)
a little bit of ...	ktsat ...	קְצָת ...
half	'χetsi	חֲצִי (ז)
dozen	tresar	תְּרֵיסָר (ז)
piece (item)	yeχida	יְחִידָה (נ)

| size | 'godel | גּוֹדֶל (ז) |
| scale (map ~) | kne mida | קְנֵה מִידָה (ז) |

minimal (adj)	mini'mali	מִינִימָאלִי
the smallest (adj)	hakatan beyoter	הַקָּטָן בְּיוֹתֵר
medium (adj)	memutsa	מְמוּצָע
maximal (adj)	maksi'mali	מַקְסִימָלִי
the largest (adj)	hagadol beyoter	הַגָּדוֹל בְּיוֹתֵר

26. Containers

canning jar (glass ~)	tsin'tsenet	צִנְצֶנֶת (נ)
can	paχit	פַּחִית (נ)
bucket	dli	דְּלִי (ז)
barrel	χavit	חָבִית (נ)

wash basin (e.g., plastic ~)	gigit	גִּיגִית (נ)
tank (100L water ~)	meiχal	מֵיכָל (ז)
hip flask	meimiya	מֵימִיָּה (נ)
jerrycan	'dʒerikan	גֶּ׳רִיקָן (ז)
tank (e.g., tank car)	meχalit	מֵיכָלִית (נ)

mug	'sefel	סֵפֶל (ז)
cup (of coffee, etc.)	'sefel	סֵפֶל (ז)
saucer	taχtit	תַּחְתִּית (נ)

glass (tumbler)	kos	כּוֹס (נ)
wine glass	ga'vi'a	גָּבִיעַ (ז)
stock pot (soup pot)	sir	סִיר (ז)

| bottle (~ of wine) | bakbuk | בַּקְבּוּק (ז) |
| neck (of the bottle, etc.) | tsavar habakbuk | צַוַּאר הַבַּקְבּוּק (ז) |

carafe (decanter)	kad	כַּד (ז)
pitcher	kankan	קַנְקַן (ז)
vessel (container)	kli	כְּלִי (ז)
pot (crock, stoneware ~)	sir 'χeres	סִיר חֶרֶס (ז)
vase	agartal	אֲגַרְטָל (ז)

| bottle (perfume ~) | tsloχit | צְלוֹחִית (נ) |
| vial, small bottle | bakbukon | בַּקְבּוּקוֹן (ז) |

tube (of toothpaste)	ʃfo'feret	שְׁפוֹפֶרֶת (נ)
sack (bag)	sak	שַׂק (ז)
bag (paper ~, plastic ~)	sakit	שַׂקִּית (נ)
pack (of cigarettes, etc.)	χafisa	חֲפִיסָה (נ)

box (e.g., shoebox)	kufsa	קוּפְסָה (נ)
crate	argaz	אַרְגָּז (ז)
basket	sal	סַל (ז)

27. Materials

material	'χomer	חוֹמֶר (ז)
wood (n)	ets	עֵץ (ז)
wood-, wooden (adj)	me'ets	מֵעֵץ

| glass (n) | zχuχit | זְכוּכִית (נ) |
| glass (as adj) | mizχuχit | מִזְכוּכִית |

| stone (n) | 'even | אֶבֶן (נ) |
| stone (as adj) | me''even | מֵאֶבֶן |

| plastic (n) | 'plastik | פְּלַסְטִיק (ז) |
| plastic (as adj) | mi'plastik | מִפְּלַסְטִיק |

| rubber (n) | 'gumi | גּוּמִי (ז) |
| rubber (as adj) | mi'gumi | מְגוּמִי |

| cloth, fabric (n) | bad | בַּד (ז) |
| fabric (as adj) | mibad | מְבַּד |

| paper (n) | neyar | נְיָיר (ז) |
| paper (as adj) | mineyar | מִנְּיָיר |

| cardboard (n) | karton | קַרְטוֹן (ז) |
| cardboard (as adj) | mikarton | מִקַּרְטוֹן |

| polyethylene | 'nailon | נַיְילוֹן (ז) |
| cellophane | tselofan | צֶלוֹפָן (ז) |

| linoleum | li'nole'um | לִינוֹלֵיאוּם (ז) |
| plywood | dikt | דִּיקְט (ז) |

| porcelain (n) | χar'sina | חַרְסִינָה (נ) |
| porcelain (as adj) | meχar'sina | מֵחַרְסִינָה |

| clay (n) | χarsit | חַרְסִית (נ) |
| clay (as adj) | me'χeres | מֵחֶרֶס |

| ceramic (n) | ke'ramika | קֶרָמִיקָה (נ) |
| ceramic (as adj) | ke'rami | קֶרָמִי |

28. Metals

metal (n)	ma'teχet	מַתֶּכֶת (נ)
metal (as adj)	mataχti	מַתַכְתִי
alloy (n)	sag'soget	סַגְסֹגֶת (נ)
gold (n)	zahav	זָהָב (ז)
gold, golden (adj)	mizahav, zahov	מִזָהָב, זָהֹב
silver (n)	'kesef	כֶּסֶף (ז)
silver (as adj)	kaspi	כַּסְפִּי
iron (n)	barzel	בַּרְזֶל (ז)
iron-, made of iron (adj)	mibarzel	מִבַּרְזֶל
steel (n)	plada	פְּלָדָה (נ)
steel (as adj)	miplada	מִפְּלָדָה
copper (n)	ne'χofet	נְחֹשֶׁת (נ)
copper (as adj)	mine'χofet	מִנְחֹשֶׁת
aluminum (n)	alu'minyum	אָלוּמִינְיוּם (ז)
aluminum (as adj)	me'alu'minyum	מֵאָלוּמִינְיוּם
bronze (n)	arad	אָרָד (ז)
bronze (as adj)	me'arad	מֵאָרָד
brass	pliz	פְּלִיז (ז)
nickel	'nikel	נִיקֶל (ז)
platinum	'platina	פְּלָטִינָה (נ)
mercury	kaspit	כַּסְפִּית (נ)
tin	bdil	בְּדִיל (ז)
lead	o'feret	עוֹפֶרֶת (נ)
zinc	avats	אָבָץ (ז)

HUMAN BEING

Human being. The body

29. Humans. Basic concepts

human being	ben adam	בֶּן אָדָם (ז)
man (adult male)	'gever	גֶּבֶר (ז)
woman	iʃa	אִשָּׁה (נ)
child	'yeled	יֶלֶד (ז)
girl	yalda	יַלְדָּה (נ)
boy	'yeled	יֶלֶד (ז)
teenager	'na'ar	נַעַר (ז)
old man	zaken	זָקֵן (ז)
old woman	zkena	זְקֵנָה (נ)

30. Human anatomy

organism (body)	guf ha'adam	גּוּף הָאָדָם (ז)
heart	lev	לֵב (ז)
blood	dam	דָּם (ז)
artery	'orek	עוֹרֶק (ז)
vein	vrid	וְרִיד (ז)
brain	'moaχ	מוֹחַ (ז)
nerve	atsav	עָצָב (ז)
nerves	atsabim	עֲצַבִּים (ז"ר)
vertebra	χulya	חוּלְיָה (נ)
spine (backbone)	amud haʃidra	עַמּוּד הַשִּׁדְרָה (ז)
stomach (organ)	keiva	קֵיבָה (נ)
intestines, bowels	me"ayim	מֵעַיִים (ז"ר)
intestine (e.g., large ~)	me'i	מְעִי (ז)
liver	kaved	כָּבֵד (ז)
kidney	kilya	כְּלָיָה (נ)
bone	'etsem	עֶצֶם (נ)
skeleton	'ʃeled	שֶׁלֶד (ז)
rib	'tsela	צֶלַע (ז)
skull	gul'golet	גּוּלְגּוֹלֶת (נ)
muscle	ʃrir	שְׁרִיר (ז)
biceps	ʃrir du raʃi	שְׁרִיר דּוּ־רָאשִׁי (ז)

triceps	ʃrir tlat raʃi	שְׁרִיר תְּלַת־רָאשִׁי (ז)
tendon	gid	גִּיד (ז)
joint	'perek	פֶּרֶק (ז)
lungs	re'ot	רֵיאוֹת (נ"ר)
genitals	evrei min	אֶבְרֵי מִין (ז"ר)
skin	or	עוֹר (ז)

31. Head

head	roʃ	רֹאשׁ (ז)
face	panim	פָּנִים (ז"ר)
nose	af	אַף (ז)
mouth	pe	פֶּה (ז)
eye	'ayin	עַיִן (נ)
eyes	ei'nayim	עֵינַיִים (נ"ר)
pupil	iʃon	אִישׁוֹן (ז)
eyebrow	gaba	גַּבָּה (נ)
eyelash	ris	רִיס (ז)
eyelid	af'af	עַפְעַף (ז)
tongue	laʃon	לָשׁוֹן (נ)
tooth	ʃen	שֵׁן (נ)
lips	sfa'tayim	שְׂפָתַיִים (נ"ר)
cheekbones	atsamot leχa'yayim	עַצְמוֹת לְחָיַיִם (נ"ר)
gum	χani'χayim	חֲנִיכַיִים (ז"ר)
palate	χeχ	חֵךְ (ז)
nostrils	neχi'rayim	נְחִירַיִים (ז"ר)
chin	santer	סַנְטֵר (ז)
jaw	'leset	לֶסֶת (נ)
cheek	'leχi	לְחִי (נ)
forehead	'metsaχ	מֵצַח (ז)
temple	raka	רַקָּה (נ)
ear	'ozen	אוֹזֶן (נ)
back of the head	'oref	עוֹרֶף (ז)
neck	tsavar	צַוָּואר (ז)
throat	garon	גָּרוֹן (ז)
hair	se'ar	שֵׂיעָר (ז)
hairstyle	tis'roket	תִּסְרוֹקֶת (נ)
haircut	tis'poret	תִּסְפּוֹרֶת (נ)
wig	pe'a	פֵּאָה (נ)
mustache	safam	שָׂפָם (ז)
beard	zakan	זָקָן (ז)
to have (a beard, etc.)	legadel	לְגַדֵּל
braid	tsama	צַמָּה (נ)
sideburns	pe'ot leχa'yayim	פֵּאוֹת לְחָיַיִם (נ"ר)

red-haired (adj)	'dʒindʒi	ג׳ינג׳י
gray (hair)	kasuf	כָּסוּף
bald (adj)	ke'reaχ	קֵירֵחַ
bald patch	ka'raχat	קָרַחַת (נ)
ponytail	'kuku	קוּקוּ (ז)
bangs	'poni	פּוֹנִי (ז)

32. Human body

hand	kaf yad	כַּף יָד (נ)
arm	yad	יָד (נ)
finger	'etsba	אֶצְבַּע (נ)
toe	'bohen	בּוֹהֶן (נ)
thumb	agudal	אֲגוּדָל (ז)
little finger	'zeret	זֶרֶת (נ)
nail	tsi'poren	צִיפּוֹרֶן (נ)
fist	egrof	אֶגְרוֹף (ז)
palm	kaf yad	כַּף יָד (נ)
wrist	'ʃoreʃ kaf hayad	שׁוֹרֶשׁ כַּף הַיָד (ז)
forearm	ama	אַמָה (נ)
elbow	marpek	מַרְפֵּק (ז)
shoulder	katef	כָּתֵף (נ)
leg	'regel	רֶגֶל (נ)
foot	kaf 'regel	כַּף רֶגֶל (נ)
knee	'bereχ	בֶּרֶךְ (נ)
calf (part of leg)	ʃok	שׁוֹק (נ)
hip	yareχ	יָרֵךְ (נ)
heel	akev	עָקֵב (ז)
body	guf	גוּף (ז)
stomach	'beten	בֶּטֶן (נ)
chest	χaze	חָזֶה (ז)
breast	ʃad	שַׁד (ז)
flank	tsad	צַד (ז)
back	gav	גַב (ז)
lower back	mot'nayim	מוֹתְנַיִים (ז״ר)
waist	'talya	טַלְיָה (נ)
navel (belly button)	tabur	טַבּוּר (ז)
buttocks	aχo'rayim	אֲחוֹרַיִים (ז״ר)
bottom	yaʃvan	יַשְׁבָן (ז)
beauty mark	nekudat χen	נְקוּדַת חֵן (נ)
birthmark (café au lait spot)	'ketem leida	כֶּתֶם לֵידָה (ז)
tattoo	ka'a'ku'a	קַעֲקוּעַ (ז)
scar	tsa'leket	צַלֶקֶת (נ)

Clothing & Accessories

33. Outerwear. Coats

clothes	bgadim	בְּגָדִים (ז״ר)
outerwear	levuʃ elyon	לְבוּש עֶלְיוֹן (ז)
winter clothing	bigdei 'χoref	בִּגְדֵי חוֹרֶף (ז״ר)
coat (overcoat)	me'il	מְעִיל (ז)
fur coat	me'il parva	מְעִיל פַּרְוָה (ז)
fur jacket	me'il parva katsar	מְעִיל פַּרְוָה קָצָר (ז)
down coat	me'il puχ	מְעִיל פּוּךְ (ז)
jacket (e.g., leather ~)	me'il katsar	מְעִיל קָצָר (ז)
raincoat (trenchcoat, etc.)	me'il 'geʃem	מְעִיל גֶּשֶם (ז)
waterproof (adj)	amid be'mayim	עָמִיד בְּמַיִם

34. Men's & women's clothing

shirt (button shirt)	χultsa	חוּלְצָה (נ)
pants	miχna'sayim	מִכְנָסַיִים (ז״ר)
jeans	miχnesei 'dʒins	מִכְנְסֵי ג׳ִינְס (ז״ר)
suit jacket	ʒaket	ז׳'קֶט (ז)
suit	χalifa	חֲלִיפָה (נ)
dress (frock)	simla	שִׂמְלָה (נ)
skirt	χatsa'it	חֲצָאִית (נ)
blouse	χultsa	חוּלְצָה (נ)
knitted jacket (cardigan, etc.)	ʒaket 'tsemer	ז׳'קֶט צֶמֶר (ז)
jacket (of woman's suit)	ʒaket	ז׳'קֶט (ז)
T-shirt	ti ʃert	טִי שֶרְט (ז)
shorts (short trousers)	miχna'sayim ktsarim	מִכְנָסַיִים קְצָרִים (ז״ר)
tracksuit	'trening	טְרֶנִינְג (ז)
bathrobe	χaluk raχatsa	חָלוּק רַחְצָה (ז)
pajamas	pi'dʒama	פִּיג׳'מָה (נ)
sweater	'sveder	סְוֶודֶר (ז)
pullover	afuda	אֲפוּדָה (נ)
vest	vest	וֶסְט (ז)
tailcoat	frak	פְרָאק (ז)
tuxedo	tuk'sido	טוּקְסִידוֹ (ז)

uniform	madim	מַדִים (ז"ר)
workwear	bigdei avoda	בִּגְדֵי עֲבוֹדָה (ז"ר)
overalls	sarbal	סַרְבָּל (ז)
coat (e.g., doctor's smock)	xaluk	חָלוּק (ז)

35. Clothing. Underwear

underwear	levanim	לְבָנִים (ז"ר)
boxers, briefs	taxtonim	תַחְתוֹנִים (ז"ר)
panties	taxtonim	תַחְתוֹנִים (ז"ר)
undershirt (A-shirt)	gufiya	גוּפִיָיה (נ)
socks	gar'bayim	גַרְבַּיִים (ז"ר)
nightgown	'ktonet 'laila	כּתוֹנֶת לַיְלָה (נ)
bra	xaziya	חֲזִייָה (נ)
knee highs (knee-high socks)	birkon	בִּרְכּוֹן (ז)
pantyhose	garbonim	גַרְבּוֹנִים (ז"ר)
stockings (thigh highs)	garbei 'nailon	גַרְבֵּי נַיְלוֹן (ז"ר)
bathing suit	'beged yam	בֶּגֶד יָם (ז)

36. Headwear

hat	'kova	כּוֹבַע (ז)
fedora	'kova 'leved	כּוֹבַע לֶבֶד (ז)
baseball cap	'kova 'beisbol	כּוֹבַע בֵּייסְבּוֹל (ז)
flatcap	'kova mitsxiya	כּוֹבַע מִצְחִייָה (ז)
beret	baret	בָּרֶט (ז)
hood	bardas	בַּרְדָס (ז)
panama hat	'kova 'tembel	כּוֹבַע טֶמְבֶּל (ז)
knit cap (knitted hat)	'kova 'gerev	כּוֹבַע גֶרֶב (ז)
headscarf	mit'paxat	מִטְפַּחַת (נ)
women's hat	'kova	כּוֹבַע (ז)
hard hat	kasda	קַסְדָה (נ)
garrison cap	kumta	כּוּמְתָה (נ)
helmet	kasda	קַסְדָה (נ)
derby	mig'ba'at me'u'gelet	מִגְבַּעַת מְעוּגֶלֶת (נ)
top hat	tsi'linder	צִילִינְדֶר (ז)

37. Footwear

| footwear | han'ala | הַנְעָלָה (נ) |
| shoes (men's shoes) | na'a'layim | נַעֲלַיִים (נ"ר) |

shoes (women's shoes)	na'a'layim	נַעֲלַיִם (נ״ר)
boots (e.g., cowboy ~)	maga'fayim	מַגָּפַיִם (ז״ר)
slippers	na'alei 'bayit	נַעֲלֵי בַּיִת (נ״ר)
tennis shoes (e.g., Nike ~)	na'alei sport	נַעֲלֵי סְפּוֹרְט (נ״ר)
sneakers	na'alei sport	נַעֲלֵי סְפּוֹרְט (נ״ר)
(e.g., Converse ~)		
sandals	sandalim	סַנְדָּלִים (ז״ר)
cobbler (shoe repairer)	sandlar	סַנְדְּלָר (ז)
heel	akev	עָקֵב (ז)
pair (of shoes)	zug	זוּג (ז)
shoestring	srox	שְׂרוֹך (ז)
to lace (vt)	lisrox	לִשְׂרוֹך
shoehorn	kaf na'a'layim	כַּף נַעֲלַיִם (נ)
shoe polish	miʃxat na'a'layim	מִשְׁחַת נַעֲלַיִם (נ)

38. Textile. Fabrics

cotton (n)	kutna	כּוּתְנָה (נ)
cotton (as adj)	mikutna	מְכּוּתְנָה
flax (n)	piʃtan	פִּשְׁתָּן (ז)
flax (as adj)	mipiʃtan	מִפִּשְׁתָּן
silk (n)	'meʃi	מֶשִׁי (ז)
silk (as adj)	miʃyi	מֶשְׁיִי
wool (n)	'tsemer	צֶמֶר (ז)
wool (as adj)	tsamri	צַמְרִי
velvet	ktifa	קְטִיפָה (נ)
suede	zamʃ	זָמֶשׁ (ז)
corduroy	'korderoi	קוֹרְדְּרוֹי (ז)
nylon (n)	'nailon	נַיְילוֹן (ז)
nylon (as adj)	mi'nailon	מְנַיְילוֹן
polyester (n)	poli''ester	פּוֹלִיאֶסְטֶר (ז)
polyester (as adj)	mipoli''ester	מִפּוֹלִיאֶסְטֶר
leather (n)	or	עוֹר (ז)
leather (as adj)	me'or	מֵעוֹר
fur (n)	parva	פַּרְוָה (נ)
fur (e.g., ~ coat)	miparva	מִפַּרְוָה

39. Personal accessories

gloves	kfafot	כְּפָפוֹת (נ״ר)
mittens	kfafot	כְּפָפוֹת (נ״ר)

scarf (muffler)	tsa'if	צָעִיף (ז)
glasses (eyeglasses)	miʃka'fayim	מִשְׁקָפַּיִם (ז"ר)
frame (eyeglass ~)	mis'geret	מִסְגֶּרֶת (נ)
umbrella	mitriya	מִטְרִיָּה (נ)
walking stick	makel haliχa	מַקֵּל הֲלִיכָה (ז)
hairbrush	miv'reʃet se'ar	מִבְרֶשֶׁת שֵׂיעָר (נ)
fan	menifa	מְנִיפָה (נ)
tie (necktie)	aniva	עֲנִיבָה (נ)
bow tie	anivat parpar	עֲנִיבַת פַּרְפַּר (נ)
suspenders	ktefiyot	כְּתַפִיּוֹת (נ"ר)
handkerchief	mimχata	מִמְחָטָה (נ)
comb	masrek	מַסְרֵק (ז)
barrette	sikat roʃ	סִיכַּת רֹאשׁ (נ)
hairpin	sikat se'ar	סִיכַּת שֵׂיעָר (נ)
buckle	avzam	אַבְזָם (ז)
belt	χagora	חֲגוֹרָה (נ)
shoulder strap	retsu'at katef	רְצוּעַת כָּתֵף (נ)
bag (handbag)	tik	תִּיק (ז)
purse	tik	תִּיק (ז)
backpack	tarmil	תַּרְמִיל (ז)

40. Clothing. Miscellaneous

fashion	ofna	אוֹפְנָה (נ)
in vogue (adj)	ofnati	אוֹפְנָתִי
fashion designer	me'atsev ofna	מְעַצֵּב אוֹפְנָה (ז)
collar	tsavaron	צַוָּארוֹן (ז)
pocket	kis	כִּיס (ז)
pocket (as adj)	ʃel kis	שֶׁל כִּיס
sleeve	ʃarvul	שַׁרְווּל (ז)
hanging loop	mitle	מִתְלֶה (ז)
fly (on trousers)	χanut	חֲנוּת (נ)
zipper (fastener)	roχsan	רוֹכְסָן (ז)
fastener	'keres	קֶרֶס (ז)
button	kaftor	כַּפְתּוֹר (ז)
buttonhole	lula'a	לוּלָאָה (נ)
to come off (ab. button)	lehitaleʃ	לְהִיתָּלֵשׁ
to sew (vi, vt)	litpor	לִתְפּוֹר
to embroider (vi, vt)	lirkom	לִרְקוֹם
embroidery	rikma	רִקְמָה (נ)
sewing needle	'maχat tfira	מַחַט תְּפִירָה (נ)
thread	χut	חוּט (ז)
seam	'tefer	תֶּפֶר (ז)

to get dirty (vi)	lehitlaxlex	לְהִתְלַכְלֵךְ
stain (mark, spot)	'ketem	כֶּתֶם (ז)
to crease, crumple (vi)	lehitkamet	לְהִתְקַמֵּט
to tear, to rip (vt)	lik'ro'a	לִקְרוֹעַ
clothes moth	aʃ	עָשׁ (ז)

41. Personal care. Cosmetics

toothpaste	miʃxat ʃi'nayim	מִשְׁחַת שִׁינַיִים (נ)
toothbrush	miv'reʃet ʃi'nayim	מִבְרֶשֶׁת שִׁינַיִים (נ)
to brush one's teeth	letsax'tseax ʃi'nayim	לְצַחְצֵחַ שִׁינַיִים
razor	'ta'ar	תַּעַר (ז)
shaving cream	'ketsef gi'luax	קֶצֶף גִּילוּחַ (ז)
to shave (vi)	lehitga'leax	לְהִתְגַּלֵּחַ
soap	sabon	סַבּוֹן (ז)
shampoo	ʃampu	שַׁמְפּוּ (ז)
scissors	mispa'rayim	מִסְפָּרַיִים (ז״ר)
nail file	ptsira	פְּצִירָה (נ)
nail clippers	gozez tsipor'nayim	גּוֹזֵז צִיפּוֹרְנַיִים (ז)
tweezers	pin'tseta	פִּינְצֶטָה (נ)
cosmetics	tamrukim	תַּמְרוּקִים (ז״ר)
face mask	masexa	מַסֵּכָה (נ)
manicure	manikur	מָנִיקוּר (ז)
to have a manicure	la'asot manikur	לַעֲשׂוֹת מָנִיקוּר
pedicure	pedikur	פֶּדִיקוּר (ז)
make-up bag	tik ipur	תִּיק אִיפּוּר (ז)
face powder	'pudra	פּוּדְרָה (נ)
powder compact	pudriya	פּוּדְרִייָה (נ)
blusher	'somek	סוֹמֶק (ז)
perfume (bottled)	'bosem	בּוֹשֶׂם (ז)
toilet water (lotion)	mei 'bosem	מֵי בּוֹשֶׂם (ז״ר)
lotion	mei panim	מֵי פָּנִים (ז״ר)
cologne	mei 'bosem	מֵי בּוֹשֶׂם (ז״ר)
eyeshadow	tslalit	צְלָלִית (נ)
eyeliner	ai 'lainer	אַי לַיינֶר (ז)
mascara	'maskara	מַסְקָרָה (נ)
lipstick	sfaton	שְׂפָתוֹן (ז)
nail polish, enamel	'laka letsipor'nayim	לַכָּה לְצִיפּוֹרְנַיִים (נ)
hair spray	tarsis lese'ar	תַּרְסִיס לְשֵׂיעָר (ז)
deodorant	de'odo'rant	דֵּאוֹדוֹרַנְט (ז)
cream	krem	קְרֶם (ז)
face cream	krem panim	קְרֶם פָּנִים (ז)

hand cream	krem ya'dayim	קְרֶם יָדַיים (ז)
anti-wrinkle cream	krem 'neged kmatim	קְרֶם נֶגֶד קְמָטִים (ז)
day cream	krem yom	קְרֶם יוֹם (ז)
night cream	krem 'laila	קְרֶם לַיְלָה (ז)
day (as adj)	yomi	יוֹמִי
night (as adj)	leili	לֵילִי

tampon	tampon	טַמְפּוֹן (ז)
toilet paper (toilet roll)	neyar tu'alet	נְיַיר טוֹאָלֶט (ז)
hair dryer	meyabeʃ se'ar	מְיַיבֵּשׁ שֵׂיעָר (ז)

42. Jewelry

jewelry	taxʃitim	תַּכְשִׁיטִים (ז"ר)
precious (e.g., ~ stone)	yekar 'erex	יְקַר עֵרֶךְ
hallmark stamp	tav tsorfim, bxina	תָּו צוֹרְפִים (ז), בְּחִינָה (נ)

ring	ta'ba'at	טַבַּעַת (נ)
wedding ring	ta'ba'at nisu'in	טַבַּעַת נִישׂוּאִין (נ)
bracelet	tsamid	צָמִיד (ז)

earrings	agilim	עֲגִילִים (ז"ר)
necklace (~ of pearls)	max'rozet	מַחְרוֹזֶת (נ)
crown	'keter	כֶּתֶר (ז)
bead necklace	max'rozet	מַחְרוֹזֶת (נ)

diamond	yahalom	יַהֲלוֹם (ז)
emerald	ba'reket	בָּרֶקֶת (נ)
ruby	'odem	אוֹדֶם (ז)
sapphire	sapir	סַפִּיר (ז)
pearl	pnina	פְּנִינָה (נ)
amber	inbar	עֶנְבָּר (ז)

43. Watches. Clocks

watch (wristwatch)	ʃe'on yad	שְׁעוֹן יָד (ז)
dial	'luax ʃa'on	לוּחַ שָׁעוֹן (ז)
hand (of clock, watch)	maxog	מָחוֹג (ז)
metal watch band	tsamid	צָמִיד (ז)
watch strap	retsu'a leʃa'on	רְצוּעָה לְשָׁעוֹן (נ)

battery	solela	סוֹלְלָה (נ)
to be dead (battery)	lehitroken	לְהִתְרוֹקֵן
to change a battery	lehaxlif	לְהַחְלִיף
to run fast	lemaher	לְמַהֵר
to run slow	lefager	לְפַגֵּר
wall clock	ʃe'on kir	שְׁעוֹן קִיר (ז)
hourglass	ʃe'on xol	שְׁעוֹן חוֹל (ז)

sundial	ʃeʻon ʼʃemeʃ	שְׁעוֹן שֶׁמֶשׁ (ז)
alarm clock	ʃaʻon meʻorer	שְׁעוֹן מְעוֹרֵר (ז)
watchmaker	ʃaʻan	שָׁעָן (ז)
to repair (vt)	letaken	לְתַקֵן

Food. Nutricion

44. Food

meat	basar	בָּשָׂר (ז)
chicken	of	עוֹף (ז)
Rock Cornish hen (poussin)	pargit	פַּרְגִּית (נ)
duck	barvaz	בַּרְוָז (ז)
goose	avaz	אַוָּז (ז)
game	'tsayid	צַיִד (ז)
turkey	'hodu	הוֹדוּ (ז)
pork	basar χazir	בָּשָׂר חֲזִיר (ז)
veal	basar 'egel	בָּשָׂר עֵגֶל (ז)
lamb	basar 'keves	בָּשָׂר כֶּבֶשׂ (ז)
beef	bakar	בָּקָר (ז)
rabbit	arnav	אַרְנָב (ז)
sausage (bologna, pepperoni, etc.)	naknik	נַקְנִיק (ז)
vienna sausage (frankfurter)	naknikiya	נַקְנִיקִיָּה (נ)
bacon	'kotel χazir	קוֹתֶל חֲזִיר (ז)
ham	basar χazir me'uʃan	בָּשָׂר חֲזִיר מְעוּשָׁן (ז)
gammon	'kotel χazir me'uʃan	קוֹתֶל חֲזִיר מְעוּשָׁן (ז)
pâté	pate	פָּטֶה (ז)
liver	kaved	כָּבֵד (ז)
hamburger (ground beef)	basar taχun	בָּשָׂר טָחוּן (ז)
tongue	laʃon	לָשׁוֹן (נ)
egg	beitsa	בֵּיצָה (נ)
eggs	beitsim	בֵּיצִים (נ״ר)
egg white	χelbon	חֶלְבּוֹן (ז)
egg yolk	χelmon	חֶלְמוֹן (ז)
fish	dag	דָּג (ז)
seafood	perot yam	פֵּירוֹת יָם (ז״ר)
crustaceans	sartana'im	סַרְטָנָאִים (ז״ר)
caviar	kavyar	קָוְיָאר (ז)
crab	sartan yam	סַרְטָן יָם (ז)
shrimp	ʃrimps	שְׁרִימְפְּס (ז״ר)
oyster	tsidpat ma'aχal	צִדְפַּת מַאֲכָל (נ)
spiny lobster	'lobster kotsani	לוֹבְּסְטֶר קוֹצָנִי (ז)

octopus	tamnun	תַמְנוּן (ז)
squid	kala'mari	קָלָמָארִי (ז)
sturgeon	basar haxidkan	בְּשַׂר הַחִדְקָן (ז)
salmon	'salmon	סַלְמוֹן (ז)
halibut	putit	פּוּטִית (נ)
cod	ʃibut	שִׁיבּוּט (ז)
mackerel	kolyas	קוֹלְיָס (ז)
tuna	'tuna	טוּנָה (נ)
eel	tslofax	צְלוֹפָח (ז)
trout	forel	פּוֹרֶל (ז)
sardine	sardin	סַרְדִין (ז)
pike	ze'ev 'mayim	זְאֵב מַיִם (ז)
herring	ma'liax	מָלִיחַ (ז)
bread	'lexem	לֶחֶם (ז)
cheese	gvina	גְבִינָה (נ)
sugar	sukar	סוּכָּר (ז)
salt	'melax	מֶלַח (ז)
rice	'orez	אוֹרֶז (ז)
pasta (macaroni)	'pasta	פַּסְטָה (נ)
noodles	irtiyot	אִטְרִיּוֹת (נ״ר)
butter	xem'a	חֶמְאָה (נ)
vegetable oil	'ʃemen tsimxi	שֶׁמֶן צִמְחִי (ז)
sunflower oil	'ʃemen xamaniyot	שֶׁמֶן חַמָנִיוֹת (ז)
margarine	marga'rina	מַרְגָרִינָה (נ)
olives	zeitim	זֵיתִים (ז״ר)
olive oil	'ʃemen 'zayit	שֶׁמֶן זַיִת (ז)
milk	xalav	חָלָב (ז)
condensed milk	xalav merukaz	חָלָב מְרוּכָּז (ז)
yogurt	'yogurt	יוֹגוּרט (ז)
sour cream	ʃa'menet	שַׁמֶנֶת (נ)
cream (of milk)	ʃa'menet	שַׁמֶנֶת (נ)
mayonnaise	mayonez	מָיוֹנֵז (ז)
buttercream	ka'tsefet xem'a	קַצֶפֶת חֶמְאָה (נ)
cereal grains (wheat, etc.)	grisim	גְרִיסִים (ז״ר)
flour	'kemax	קֶמַח (ז)
canned food	ʃimurim	שִׁימוּרִים (ז״ר)
cornflakes	ptitei 'tiras	פְּתִיתֵי תִירָס (ז״ר)
honey	dvaʃ	דְבַשׁ (ז)
jam	riba	רִיבָּה (נ)
chewing gum	'mastik	מַסְטִיק (ז)

45. Drinks

water	'mayim	מַיִם (ז״ר)
drinking water	mei ∫tiya	מֵי שְׁתִיָּה (ז״ר)
mineral water	'mayim mine'raliyim	מַיִם מִינֵרָלִיִּים (ז״ר)
still (adj)	lo mugaz	לֹא מוּגָז
carbonated (adj)	mugaz	מוּגָז
sparkling (adj)	mugaz	מוּגָז
ice	'kerax	קֶרַח (ז)
with ice	im 'kerax	עִם קֶרַח
non-alcoholic (adj)	natul alkohol	נָטוּל אַלכּוֹהוֹל
soft drink	ma∫ke kal	מַשׁקֶה קַל (ז)
refreshing drink	ma∫ke mera'anen	מַשׁקֶה מְרַעֲנֵן (ז)
lemonade	limo'nada	לִימוֹנָדָה (נ)
liquors	ma∫ka'ot xarifim	מַשׁקָאוֹת חָרִיפִים (ז״ר)
wine	'yayin	יַיִן (ז)
white wine	'yayin lavan	יַיִן לָבָן (ז)
red wine	'yayin adom	יַיִן אָדוֹם (ז)
liqueur	liker	לִיקֶר (ז)
champagne	∫am'panya	שַׁמפַּניָה (נ)
vermouth	'vermut	וֶרמוּט (ז)
whiskey	'viski	וִיסקִי (ז)
vodka	'vodka	וֹדקָה (נ)
gin	dʒin	גִ׳ין (ז)
cognac	'konyak	קוֹניָאק (ז)
rum	rom	רוֹם (ז)
coffee	kafe	קָפֶּה (ז)
black coffee	kafe ∫axor	קָפֶּה שָׁחוֹר (ז)
coffee with milk	kafe hafux	קָפֶּה הָפוּך (ז)
cappuccino	kapu'tʃino	קָפּוּצִ׳ינוֹ (ז)
instant coffee	kafe names	קָפֶּה נָמֵס (ז)
milk	xalav	חָלָב (ז)
cocktail	kokteil	קוֹקטֵיל (ז)
milkshake	'milk∫eik	מִילקשֵׁייק (ז)
juice	mits	מִיץ (ז)
tomato juice	mits agvaniyot	מִיץ עַגבָנִיּוֹת (ז)
orange juice	mits tapuzim	מִיץ תַּפּוּזִים (ז)
freshly squeezed juice	mits saxut	מִיץ סָחוּט (ז)
beer	'bira	בִּירָה (נ)
light beer	'bira bahira	בִּירָה בָּהִירָה (נ)
dark beer	'bira keha	בִּירָה כֵּהָה (נ)
tea	te	תֵּה (ז)

| black tea | te ʃaχor | תֵה שָׁחוֹר (ז) |
| green tea | te yarok | תֵה יָרוֹק (ז) |

46. Vegetables

| vegetables | yerakot | יְרָקוֹת (ז״ר) |
| greens | 'yerek | יָרָק (ז) |

tomato	agvaniya	עַגְבָנִיָּה (נ)
cucumber	melafefon	מְלָפְפוֹן (ז)
carrot	'gezer	גֶּזֶר (ז)
potato	ta'puaχ adama	תַּפּוּחַ אֲדָמָה (ז)
onion	batsal	בָּצָל (ז)
garlic	ʃum	שׁוּם (ז)

cabbage	kruv	כְּרוּב (ז)
cauliflower	kruvit	כְּרוּבִית (נ)
Brussels sprouts	kruv nitsanim	כְּרוּב נִצָּנִים (ז)
broccoli	'brokoli	בְּרוֹקוֹלִי (ז)

beetroot	'selek	סֶלֶק (ז)
eggplant	χatsil	חָצִיל (ז)
zucchini	kiʃu	קִשּׁוּא (ז)
pumpkin	'dla'at	דְּלַעַת (נ)
turnip	'lefet	לֶפֶת (נ)

parsley	petro'zilya	פֶּטְרוֹזִילְיָה (נ)
dill	ʃamir	שָׁמִיר (ז)
lettuce	'χasa	חַסָּה (נ)
celery	'seleri	סֶלֶרִי (ז)
asparagus	aspa'ragos	אַסְפָּרָגוֹס (ז)
spinach	'tered	תֶּרֶד (ז)

pea	afuna	אֲפוּנָה (נ)
beans	pol	פּוֹל (ז)
corn (maize)	'tiras	תִּירָס (ז)
kidney bean	ʃu'it	שְׁעוּעִית (נ)

bell pepper	'pilpel	פִּלְפֵּל (ז)
radish	tsnonit	צְנוֹנִית (נ)
artichoke	artiʃok	אַרְטִישׁוֹק (ז)

47. Fruits. Nuts

fruit	pri	פְּרִי (ז)
apple	ta'puaχ	תַּפּוּחַ (ז)
pear	agas	אַגָּס (ז)
lemon	limon	לִימוֹן (ז)

| orange | tapuz | תַּפּוּז (ז) |
| strawberry (garden ~) | tut sade | תּוּת שָׂדֶה (ז) |

mandarin	klemen'tina	קְלֶמֶנְטִינָה (נ)
plum	ʃezif	שְׁזִיף (ז)
peach	afarsek	אֲפַרְסֵק (ז)
apricot	'miʃmeʃ	מִשְׁמֵשׁ (ז)
raspberry	'petel	פֶּטֶל (ז)
pineapple	'ananas	אֲנָנָס (ז)

banana	ba'nana	בַּנָּנָה (נ)
watermelon	ava'tiax	אֲבַטִּיחַ (ז)
grape	anavim	עֲנָבִים (ז״ר)
sour cherry	duvdevan	דּוּבְדְּבָן (ז)
sweet cherry	gudgedan	גּוּדְגְּדָן (ז)
melon	melon	מֶלוֹן (ז)

grapefruit	eʃkolit	אֶשְׁכּוֹלִית (נ)
avocado	avo'kado	אֲבוֹקָדוֹ (ז)
papaya	pa'paya	פַּפָּאיָה (נ)
mango	'mango	מַנְגּוֹ (ז)
pomegranate	rimon	רִימוֹן (ז)

redcurrant	dumdemanit aduma	דּוּמְדְּמָנִית אֲדוּמָה (נ)
blackcurrant	dumdemanit ʃxora	דּוּמְדְּמָנִית שְׁחוֹרָה (נ)
gooseberry	xazarzar	חֲזַרְזַר (ז)
bilberry	uxmanit	אוּכְמָנִית (נ)
blackberry	'petel ʃaxor	פֶּטֶל שָׁחוֹר (ז)

raisin	tsimukim	צִימוּקִים (ז״ר)
fig	te'ena	תְּאֵנָה (נ)
date	tamar	תָּמָר (ז)

peanut	botnim	בּוֹטְנִים (ז״ר)
almond	ʃaked	שָׁקֵד (ז)
walnut	egoz 'melex	אֱגוֹז מֶלֶךְ (ז)
hazelnut	egoz ilsar	אֱגוֹז אִלְסָר (ז)
coconut	'kokus	קוֹקוּס (ז)
pistachios	'fistuk	פִּיסְטוּק (ז)

48. Bread. Candy

bakers' confectionery (pastry)	mutsrei kondi'torya	מוּצְרֵי קוֹנְדִיטוֹרְיָה (ז״ר)
bread	'lexem	לֶחֶם (ז)
cookies	ugiya	עוּגִיָּה (נ)

chocolate (n)	'ʃokolad	שׁוֹקוֹלָד (ז)
chocolate (as adj)	mi'ʃokolad	מְשׁוֹקוֹלָד
candy (wrapped)	sukariya	סוּכָּרִיָּה (נ)

cake (e.g., cupcake)	uga	עוּגָה (נ)
cake (e.g., birthday ~)	uga	עוּגָה (נ)
pie (e.g., apple ~)	pai	פַּאי (ז)
filling (for cake, pie)	milui	מִילּוּי (ז)
jam (whole fruit jam)	riba	רִיבָּה (נ)
marmalade	marme'lada	מַרמֶלָדָה (נ)
waffles	'vaflim	וָפלִים (ז"ר)
ice-cream	'glida	גלִידָה (נ)
pudding	'puding	פּוּדִינג (ז)

49. Cooked dishes

course, dish	mana	מָנָה (נ)
cuisine	mitbaχ	מִטבָּח (ז)
recipe	matkon	מַתכּוֹן (ז)
portion	mana	מָנָה (נ)
salad	salat	סָלָט (ז)
soup	marak	מָרָק (ז)
clear soup (broth)	marak tsaχ, tsir	מָרָק צַח, צִיר (ז)
sandwich (bread)	kariχ	כָּרִיך (ז)
fried eggs	beitsat ain	בֵּיצַת עַיִן (נ)
hamburger (beefburger)	'hamburger	הַמבּוּרגֶר (ז)
beefsteak	umtsa, steik	אוּמצָה (נ), סטֵייק (ז)
side dish	to'sefet	תּוֹסֶפֶת (נ)
spaghetti	spa'geti	ספָּגֶטִי (ז)
mashed potatoes	meχit tapuχei adama	מְחִית תַּפּוּחֵי אֲדָמָה (נ)
pizza	'pitsa	פִּיצָה (נ)
porridge (oatmeal, etc.)	daysa	דַייסָה (נ)
omelet	χavita	חֲבִיתָה (נ)
boiled (e.g., ~ beef)	mevuʃal	מְבוּשָל
smoked (adj)	me'uʃan	מְעוּשָן
fried (adj)	metugan	מְטוּגָּן
dried (adj)	meyubaʃ	מְיוּבָּש
frozen (adj)	kafu	קָפוּא
pickled (adj)	kavuʃ	כָּבוּש
sweet (sugary)	matok	מָתוֹק
salty (adj)	ma'luaχ	מָלוּחַ
cold (adj)	kar	קַר
hot (adj)	χam	חַם
bitter (adj)	marir	מָרִיר
tasty (adj)	ta'im	טָעִים
to cook in boiling water	levaʃel be'mayim rotχim	לְבַשֵל בְּמַיִם רוֹתחִים

to cook (dinner)	levaʃel	לְבַשֵּׁל
to fry (vt)	letagen	לְטַגֵּן
to heat up (food)	leχamem	לְחַמֵּם

to salt (vt)	leham'liaχ	לְהַמְלִיחַ
to pepper (vt)	lefalpel	לְפַלְפֵּל
to grate (vt)	lerasek	לְרַסֵּק
peel (n)	klipa	קְלִיפָּה (נ)
to peel (vt)	lekalef	לְקַלֵּף

50. Spices

salt	'melaχ	מֶלַח (ז)
salty (adj)	ma'luaχ	מָלוּחַ
to salt (vt)	leham'liaχ	לְהַמְלִיחַ

black pepper	'pilpel ʃaχor	פִּלְפֵּל שָׁחוֹר (ז)
red pepper (milled ~)	'pilpel adom	פִּלְפֵּל אָדוֹם (ז)
mustard	χardal	חַרְדָּל (ז)
horseradish	χa'zeret	חֲזֶרֶת (נ)

condiment	'rotev	רוֹטֶב (ז)
spice	tavlin	תַּבְלִין (ז)
sauce	'rotev	רוֹטֶב (ז)
vinegar	'χomets	חוֹמֶץ (ז)

anise	kamnon	כַּמְנוֹן (ז)
basil	reχan	רֵיחָן (ז)
cloves	tsi'poren	צִיפּוֹרֶן (ז)
ginger	'dʒindʒer	גִ'ינגֶ'ר (ז)
coriander	'kusbara	כּוּסְבָּרָה (נ)
cinnamon	kinamon	קִינָמוֹן (ז)

sesame	'ʃumʃum	שׁוּמְשׁוּם (ז)
bay leaf	ale dafna	עָלֵה דַּפְנָה (ז)
paprika	'paprika	פַּפְּרִיקָה (נ)
caraway	'kimel	קִימֶל (ז)
saffron	ze'afran	זְעַפְרָן (ז)

51. Meals

| food | 'oχel | אוֹכֶל (ז) |
| to eat (vi, vt) | le'eχol | לֶאֱכוֹל |

breakfast	aruχat 'boker	אֲרוּחַת בּוֹקֶר (נ)
to have breakfast	le'eχol aruχat 'boker	לֶאֱכוֹל אֲרוּחַת בּוֹקֶר
lunch	aruχat tsaha'rayim	אֲרוּחַת צָהֳרַיִים (נ)
to have lunch	le'eχol aruχat tsaha'rayim	לֶאֱכוֹל אֲרוּחַת צָהֳרַיִים

dinner	aruχat 'erev	אֲרוּחַת עֶרֶב (ז)
to have dinner	le'eχol aruχat 'erev	לֶאֱכֹל אֲרוּחַת עֶרֶב
appetite	te'avon	תֵּיאָבוֹן (ז)
Enjoy your meal!	betei'avon!	בְּתֵיאָבוֹן!

to open (~ a bottle)	lif'toaχ	לִפְתּוֹחַ
to spill (liquid)	liʃpoχ	לִשְׁפֹּךְ
to spill out (vi)	lehiʃapeχ	לְהִישָׁפֵךְ

to boil (vi)	lir'toaχ	לִרְתּוֹחַ
to boil (vt)	lehar'tiaχ	לְהַרְתִּיחַ
boiled (~ water)	ra'tuaχ	רָתוּחַ
to chill, cool down (vt)	lekarer	לְקָרֵר
to chill (vi)	lehitkarer	לְהִתְקָרֵר

taste, flavor	'ta'am	טַעַם (ז)
aftertaste	'ta'am levai	טַעַם לְוַואי (ז)

to slim down (lose weight)	lirzot	לִרְזוֹת
diet	di''eta	דִּיאָטָה (נ)
vitamin	vitamin	וִיטָמִין (ז)
calorie	ka'lorya	קָלוֹרִיָּה (נ)
vegetarian (n)	tsimχoni	צִמְחוֹנִי (ז)
vegetarian (adj)	tsimχoni	צִמְחוֹנִי

fats (nutrient)	ʃumanim	שׁוּמָנִים (ז״ר)
proteins	χelbonim	חֶלְבּוֹנִים (ז״ר)
carbohydrates	paχmema	פַּחְמֵימָה (נ)
slice (of lemon, ham)	prusa	פְּרוּסָה (נ)
piece (of cake, pie)	χatiχa	חֲתִיכָה (נ)
crumb (of bread, cake, etc.)	perur	פֵּירוּר (ז)

52. Table setting

spoon	kaf	כַּף (נ)
knife	sakin	סַכִּין (ז, נ)
fork	mazleg	מַזְלֵג (ז)
cup (e.g., coffee ~)	'sefel	סֵפֶל (ז)
plate (dinner ~)	tsa'laχat	צַלַּחַת (נ)
saucer	taχtit	תַּחְתִּית (נ)
napkin (on table)	mapit	מַפִּית (נ)
toothpick	keisam ʃi'nayim	קֵיסָם שִׁינַיִים (ז)

53. Restaurant

restaurant	mis'ada	מִסְעָדָה (נ)
coffee house	beit kafe	בֵּית קָפֶה (ז)

pub, bar	bar, pab	בָּר, פָּאב (ז)
tearoom	beit te	בֵּית תֶה (ז)
waiter	meltsar	מֶלְצָר (ז)
waitress	meltsarit	מֶלְצָרִית (נ)
bartender	'barmen	בַּרְמֶן (ז)
menu	tafrit	תַפְרִיט (ז)
wine list	reʃimat yeynot	רְשִׁימַת יֵינוֹת (נ)
to book a table	lehazmin ʃulxan	לְהַזְמִין שׁוּלְחָן
course, dish	mana	מָנָה (נ)
to order (meal)	lehazmin	לְהַזְמִין
to make an order	lehazmin	לְהַזְמִין
aperitif	maʃke meta'aven	מַשְׁקֶה מְתַאֲבֵן (ז)
appetizer	meta'aven	מְתַאֲבֵן (ז)
dessert	ki'nuax	קִינוּחַ (ז)
check	xeʃbon	חֶשְׁבּוֹן (ז)
to pay the check	leʃalem	לְשַׁלֵם
to give change	latet 'odef	לָתֵת עוֹדֶף
tip	tip	טִיפ (ז)

Family, relatives and friends

54. Personal information. Forms

name (first name)	ʃem	שֵׁם (ז)
surname (last name)	ʃem miʃpaχa	שֵׁם מִשְׁפָּחָה (ז)
date of birth	ta'ariχ leda	תַּאֲרִיךְ לֵידָה (ז)
place of birth	mekom leda	מְקוֹם לֵידָה (ז)
nationality	le'om	לְאוֹם (ז)
place of residence	mekom megurim	מְקוֹם מְגוּרִים (ז)
country	medina	מְדִינָה (נ)
profession (occupation)	mik'tso'a	מִקְצוֹעַ (ז)
gender, sex	min	מִין (ז)
height	'gova	גּוֹבַה (ז)
weight	miʃkal	מִשְׁקָל (ז)

55. Family members. Relatives

mother	em	אֵם (נ)
father	av	אָב (ז)
son	ben	בֵּן (ז)
daughter	bat	בַּת (נ)
younger daughter	habat haktana	הַבַּת הַקְּטַנָּה (נ)
younger son	haben hakatan	הַבֵּן הַקָּטָן (ז)
eldest daughter	habat habχora	הַבַּת הַבְּכוֹרָה (נ)
eldest son	haben habχor	הַבֵּן הַבְּכוֹר (ז)
brother	aχ	אָח (ז)
elder brother	aχ gadol	אָח גָּדוֹל (ז)
younger brother	aχ katan	אָח קָטָן (ז)
sister	aχot	אָחוֹת (נ)
elder sister	aχot gdola	אָחוֹת גְדוֹלָה (נ)
younger sister	aχot ktana	אָחוֹת קְטַנָּה (נ)
cousin (masc.)	ben dod	בֶּן דּוֹד (ז)
cousin (fem.)	bat 'doda	בַּת דּוֹדָה (נ)
mom, mommy	'ima	אִמָּא (נ)
dad, daddy	'aba	אַבָּא (ז)
parents	horim	הוֹרִים (ז"ר)
child	'yeled	יֶלֶד (ז)
children	yeladim	יְלָדִים (ז"ר)

grandmother	'savta	סַבְתָּא (נ)
grandfather	'saba	סַבָּא (ז)
grandson	'neχed	נֶכֶד (ז)
granddaughter	neχda	נֶכְדָה (נ)
grandchildren	neχadim	נְכָדִים (ז"ר)
uncle	dod	דוֹד (ז)
aunt	'doda	דוֹדָה (נ)
nephew	aχyan	אַחְיָין (ז)
niece	aχyanit	אַחְיָינִית (נ)
mother-in-law (wife's mother)	χamot	חָמוֹת (נ)
father-in-law (husband's father)	χam	חָם (ז)
son-in-law (daughter's husband)	χatan	חָתָן (ז)
stepmother	em χoreget	אֵם חוֹרֶגֶת (נ)
stepfather	av χoreg	אָב חוֹרֵג (ז)
infant	tinok	תִינוֹק (ז)
baby (infant)	tinok	תִינוֹק (ז)
little boy, kid	pa'ot	פָּעוֹט (ז)
wife	iʃa	אִשָׁה (נ)
husband	'ba'al	בַּעַל (ז)
spouse (husband)	ben zug	בֶּן זוּג (ז)
spouse (wife)	bat zug	בַּת זוּג (נ)
married (masc.)	nasui	נָשׂוּי
married (fem.)	nesu'a	נְשׂוּאָה
single (unmarried)	ravak	רַוָק
bachelor	ravak	רַוָק (ז)
divorced (masc.)	garuʃ	גָרוּש
widow	almana	אַלְמָנָה (נ)
widower	alman	אַלְמָן (ז)
relative	karov miʃpaχa	קָרוֹב מִשְׁפָּחָה (ז)
close relative	karov miʃpaχa	קָרוֹב מִשְׁפָּחָה (ז)
distant relative	karov raχok	קָרוֹב רָחוֹק (ז)
relatives	krovei miʃpaχa	קְרוֹבֵי מִשְׁפָּחָה (ז"ר)
orphan (boy)	yatom	יָתוֹם (ז)
orphan (girl)	yetoma	יְתוֹמָה (נ)
guardian (of a minor)	apo'tropos	אַפּוֹטרוֹפּוֹס (ז)
to adopt (a boy)	le'amets	לְאַמֵץ
to adopt (a girl)	le'amets	לְאַמֵץ

56. Friends. Coworkers

friend (masc.)	χaver	חָבֵר (ז)
friend (fem.)	χavera	חֲבֵרָה (נ)

friendship	yedidut	יְדִידוּת (נ)
to be friends	lihyot yadidim	לִהְיוֹת יָדִידִים
buddy (masc.)	χaver	חָבֵר (ז)
buddy (fem.)	χavera	חָבֵרָה (נ)
partner	ſutaf	שׁוּתָף (ז)
chief (boss)	menahel, roſ	מְנַהֵל (ז), רֹאש (ז)
superior (n)	memune	מְמוּנֶה (ז)
owner, proprietor	be'alim	בְּעָלִים (ז)
subordinate (n)	kafuf le	כָּפוּף לְ (ז)
colleague	amit	עָמִית (ז)
acquaintance (person)	makar	מַכָּר (ז)
fellow traveler	ben levaya	בֶּן לְוָיָה (ז)
classmate	χaver lekita	חָבֵר לְכִּיתָה (ז)
neighbor (masc.)	ſaχen	שָׁכֵן (ז)
neighbor (fem.)	ſχena	שׁכֵנָה (נ)
neighbors	ſχenim	שׁכֵנִים (ז״ר)

57. Man. Woman

woman	iſa	אִשָּׁה (נ)
girl (young woman)	baχura	בָּחוּרָה (נ)
bride	kala	כַּלָּה (נ)
beautiful (adj)	yafa	יָפָה
tall (adj)	gvoha	גבוֹהָה
slender (adj)	tmira	תְּמִירָה
short (adj)	namuχ	נָמוּך
blonde (n)	blon'dinit	בלוֹנדִינִית (נ)
brunette (n)	bru'netit	ברוּנֶטִית (נ)
ladies' (adj)	ſel naſim	שֶׁל נָשִׁים
virgin (girl)	betula	בְּתוּלָה (נ)
pregnant (adj)	hara	הָרָה
man (adult male)	'gever	גֶּבֶר (ז)
blond (n)	blon'dini	בלוֹנדִינִי (ז)
brunet (n)	ſχarχar	שׁחַרחַר
tall (adj)	ga'voha	גָּבוֹהַ
short (adj)	namuχ	נָמוּך
rude (rough)	gas	גַּס
stocky (adj)	guts	גוּץ
robust (adj)	χason	חָסוֹן
strong (adj)	χazak	חָזָק
strength	'koaχ	כּוֹחַ (ז)

stout, fat (adj)	ʃamen	שָׁמֵן
swarthy (adj)	ʃaxum	שָׁחוּם
slender (well-built)	tamir	תָּמִיר
elegant (adj)	ele'ganti	אֶלֶגַנְטִי

58. Age

age	gil	גִּיל (ז)
youth (young age)	ne'urim	נְעוּרִים (ז״ר)
young (adj)	tsa'ir	צָעִיר
younger (adj)	tsa'ir yoter	צָעִיר יוֹתֵר
older (adj)	mevugar yoter	מְבוּגָר יוֹתֵר
young man	baxur	בָּחוּר (ז)
teenager	'na'ar	נַעַר (ז)
guy, fellow	baxur	בָּחוּר (ז)
old man	zaken	זָקֵן (ז)
old woman	zkena	זְקֵנָה (נ)
adult (adj)	mevugar	מְבוּגָר (ז)
middle-aged (adj)	bagil ha'amida	בְּגִיל הָעֲמִידָה
elderly (adj)	zaken	זָקֵן
old (adj)	zaken	זָקֵן
retirement	'pensya	פֶּנְסְיָה (נ)
to retire (from job)	latset legimla'ot	לָצֵאת לְגִימְלָאוֹת
retiree	pensyoner	פֶּנְסְיוֹנֵר (ז)

59. Children

child	'yeled	יֶלֶד (ז)
children	yeladim	יְלָדִים (ז״ר)
twins	te'omim	תְּאוֹמִים (ז״ר)
cradle	arisa	עֲרִיסָה (נ)
rattle	ra'aʃan	רַעֲשָׁן (ז)
diaper	xitul	חִיתּוּל (ז)
pacifier	motsets	מוֹצֵץ (ז)
baby carriage	agala	עֲגָלָה (נ)
kindergarten	gan yeladim	גַּן יְלָדִים (ז)
babysitter	beibi'siter	בֵּיבִּיסִיטֶר (ז, נ)
childhood	yaldut	יַלְדוּת (נ)
doll	buba	בּוּבָּה (נ)
toy	tsa'a'tsu'a	צַעֲצוּעַ (ז)

construction set (toy)	misχak harkava	(ז) מִשְׂחַק הַרְכָּבָה
well-bred (adj)	meχunaχ	מְחוּנָךְ
ill-bred (adj)	lo meχunaχ	לֹא מְחוּנָךְ
spoiled (adj)	mefunak	מְפוּנָק
to be naughty	lehiſtovev	לְהִשְׁתּוֹבֵב
mischievous (adj)	ſovav	שׁוֹבָב
mischievousness	ma'ase 'kundes	(ז) מַעֲשֵׂה קוּנְדֵּס
mischievous child	'yeled ſovav	(ז) יֶלֶד שׁוֹבָב
obedient (adj)	tsaytan	צַיְּתָן
disobedient (adj)	lo memuſma	לֹא מְמוּשְׁמָע
docile (adj)	ka'nu'a	כָּנוּעַ
clever (smart)	χaχam	חָכָם
child prodigy	'yeled 'pele	(ז) יֶלֶד פֶּלֶא

60. Married couples. Family life

to kiss (vt)	lenaſek	לְנַשֵּׁק
to kiss (vi)	lehitnaſek	לְהִתְנַשֵּׁק
family (n)	miſpaχa	(נ) מִשְׁפָּחָה
family (as adj)	miſpaχti	מִשְׁפַּחְתִּי
couple	zug	(ז) זוּג
marriage (state)	nisu'im	(ז"ר) נִישּׂוּאִים
hearth (home)	aχ, ken	(ז) אָח (נ), קֵן
dynasty	ſo'ſelet	(נ) שׁוֹשֶׁלֶת
date	deit	(ז) דֵּייט
kiss	neſika	(נ) נְשִׁיקָה
love (for sb)	ahava	(נ) אַהֲבָה
to love (sb)	le'ehov	לֶאֱהֹוב
beloved	ahuv	אָהוּב
tenderness	roχ	(ז) רֹוךְ
tender (affectionate)	adin, raχ	עָדִין, רַךְ
faithfulness	ne'emanut	(נ) נֶאֱמָנוּת
faithful (adj)	masur	מָסוּר
care (attention)	de'aga	(נ) דְּאָגָה
caring (~ father)	do'eg	דּוֹאֵג
newlyweds	zug tsa'ir	(ז) זוּג צָעִיר
honeymoon	ya'reaχ dvaſ	(ז) יָרֵחַ דְּבַשׁ
to get married (ab. woman)	lehitχaten	לְהִתְחַתֵּן
to get married (ab. man)	lehitχaten	לְהִתְחַתֵּן
wedding	χatuna	(נ) חֲתוּנָה
golden wedding	χatunat hazahav	(נ) חֲתוּנַת הַזָּהָב

anniversary	yom nisu'in	יוֹם נִישׂוּאִין (ז)
lover (masc.)	me'ahev	מְאַהֵב (ז)
mistress (lover)	mea'hevet	מְאַהֶבֶת (נ)
adultery	bgida	בְּגִידָה (נ)
to cheat on … (commit adultery)	livgod be…	לִבְגוֹד בְּ...
jealous (adj)	kanai	קַנַאי
to be jealous	lekane	לְקַנֵּא
divorce	geruʃin	גֵרוּשִׁין (ז"ר)
to divorce (vi)	lehitgareʃ mi…	לְהִתְגָרֵשׁ מִ...
to quarrel (vi)	lariv	לָרִיב
to be reconciled (after an argument)	lehitpayes	לְהִתְפַּיֵיס
together (adv)	be'yaχad	בְּיַחַד
sex	min	מִין (ז)
happiness	'oʃer	אוֹשֶׁר (ז)
happy (adj)	me'uʃar	מְאוּשָׁר
misfortune (accident)	ason	אָסוֹן (ז)
unhappy (adj)	umlal	אוּמלָל

Character. Feelings. Emotions

61. Feelings. Emotions

feeling (emotion)	'regeʃ	רֶגֶשׁ (ז)
feelings	regaʃot	רְגָשׁוֹת (ז"ר)
to feel (vt)	lehargiʃ	לְהַרְגִּישׁ
hunger	'ra'av	רָעָב (ז)
to be hungry	lihyot ra'ev	לִהְיוֹת רָעֵב
thirst	tsima'on	צִמָאוֹן (ז)
to be thirsty	lihyot tsame	לִהְיוֹת צָמֵא
sleepiness	yaʃnuniyut	יַשְׁנוּנִיוּת (נ)
to feel sleepy	lirtsot liʃon	לִרְצוֹת לִישׁוֹן
tiredness	ayefut	עֲיֵפוּת (נ)
tired (adj)	ayef	עָיֵף
to get tired	lehit'ayef	לְהִתְעַיֵיף
mood (humor)	matsav 'ruax	מַצַב רוּחַ (ז)
boredom	ʃi'amum	שִׁעֲמוּם (ז)
to be bored	lehiʃta'amem	לְהִשְׁתַעֲמֵם
seclusion	hitbodedut	הִתְבּוֹדְדוּת (נ)
to seclude oneself	lehitboded	לְהִתְבּוֹדֵד
to worry (make anxious)	lehad'ig	לְהַדְאִיג
to be worried	lid'og	לִדְאוֹג
worrying (n)	de'aga	דְאָגָה (נ)
anxiety	xarada	חֲרָדָה (נ)
preoccupied (adj)	mutrad	מוּטְרָד
to be nervous	lihyot atsbani	לִהְיוֹת עַצְבָּנִי
to panic (vi)	lehibahel	לְהִיבָּהֵל
hope	tikva	תִקְוָה (נ)
to hope (vi, vt)	lekavot	לְקַוּוֹת
certainty	vada'ut	וַדָאוּת (נ)
certain, sure (adj)	vada'i	וַדָאִי
uncertainty	i vada'ut	אִי וַדָאוּת (נ)
uncertain (adj)	lo ba'tuax	לֹא בָּטוּחַ
drunk (adj)	ʃikor	שִׁיכּוֹר
sober (adj)	pi'keax	פִּיכֵּחַ
weak (adj)	xalaʃ	חַלָשׁ
happy (adj)	me'uʃar	מְאוּשָׁר
to scare (vt)	lehafxid	לְהַפְחִיד

67

fury (madness)	teruf	טֵירוּף
rage (fury)	'za'am	זַעַם (ז)
depression	dika'on	דִּיכָּאוֹן (ז)
discomfort (unease)	i noχut	אִי נוֹחוּת (נ)
comfort	noχut	נוֹחוּת (נ)
to regret (be sorry)	lehitsta'er	לְהִצְטַעֵר
regret	χarata	חֲרָטָה (נ)
bad luck	'χoser mazal	חוֹסֶר מַזָּל (ז)
sadness	'etsev	עֶצֶב (ז)
shame (remorse)	buʃa	בּוּשָׁה (נ)
gladness	simχa	שִׂמְחָה (נ)
enthusiasm, zeal	hitlahavut	הִתְלַהֲבוּת (נ)
enthusiast	mitlahev	מִתְלַהֵב
to show enthusiasm	lehitlahev	לְהִתְלַהֵב

62. Character. Personality

character	'ofi	אוֹפִי (ז)
character flaw	pgam be''ofi	פְּגָם בָּאוֹפִי (ז)
mind	'seχel	שֵׂכֶל (ז)
reason	bina	בִּינָה (נ)
conscience	matspun	מַצְפּוּן (ז)
habit (custom)	hergel	הֶרְגֵּל (ז)
ability (talent)	ye'χolet	יְכוֹלֶת (נ)
can (e.g., ~ swim)	la'da'at	לָדַעַת
patient (adj)	savlan	סַבְלָן
impatient (adj)	χasar savlanut	חֲסַר סַבְלָנוּת
curious (inquisitive)	sakran	סַקְרָן
curiosity	sakranut	סַקְרָנוּת (נ)
modesty	tsni'ut	צְנִיעוּת (נ)
modest (adj)	tsa'nu'a	צָנוּעַ
immodest (adj)	lo tsa'nu'a	לֹא צָנוּעַ
laziness	atslut	עַצְלוּת (נ)
lazy (adj)	atsel	עָצֵל
lazy person (masc.)	atslan	עַצְלָן (ז)
cunning (n)	armumiyut	עַרְמוּמִיּוּת (נ)
cunning (as adj)	armumi	עַרְמוּמִי
distrust	'χoser emun	חוֹסֶר אֵמוּן (ז)
distrustful (adj)	χadʃani	חַדְשָׁנִי
generosity	nedivut	נְדִיבוּת (נ)
generous (adj)	nadiv	נָדִיב
talented (adj)	muχʃar	מוּכְשָׁר

talent	kiʃaron	כִּישָׁרוֹן (ז)
courageous (adj)	amits	אַמִיץ
courage	'omets	אוֹמֶץ (ז)
honest (adj)	yaʃar	יָשָׁר
honesty	'yoʃer	יוֹשֶׁר (ז)
careful (cautious)	zahir	זָהִיר
brave (courageous)	amits	אַמִיץ
serious (adj)	retsini	רְצִינִי
strict (severe, stern)	χamur	חָמוּר
decisive (adj)	neχrats	נֶחְרָץ
indecisive (adj)	hasesan	הַסְּסָן
shy, timid (adj)	baiʃan	בַּיְישָׁן
shyness, timidity	baiʃanut	בַּיְישָׁנוּת (נ)
confidence (trust)	emun	אֵמוּן (ז)
to believe (trust)	leha'amin	לְהַאֲמִין
trusting (credulous)	tam	תָּם
sincerely (adv)	beχenut	בְּכֵנוּת
sincere (adj)	ken	כֵּן
sincerity	kenut	כֵּנוּת (נ)
open (person)	pa'tuaχ	פָּתוּחַ
calm (adj)	ʃalev	שָׁלֵו
frank (sincere)	glui lev	גְּלוּי לֵב
naïve (adj)	na''ivi	נָאִיבִי
absent-minded (adj)	mefuzar	מְפוּזָר
funny (odd)	matsχik	מַצְחִיק
greed	ta'avat 'betsa	תַּאֲוַות בֶּצַע (נ)
greedy (adj)	rodef 'betsa	רוֹדֵף בֶּצַע
stingy (adj)	kamtsan	קַמְצָן
evil (adj)	raʃa	רָשָׁע
stubborn (adj)	akʃan	עַקְשָׁן
unpleasant (adj)	lo na'im	לֹא נָעִים
selfish person (masc.)	ego'ist	אֶגוֹאִיסְט (ז)
selfish (adj)	anoχi	אֲנוֹכִי
coward	paχdan	פַּחְדָן (ז)
cowardly (adj)	paχdani	פַּחְדָנִי

63. Sleep. Dreams

to sleep (vi)	liʃon	לִישׁוֹן
sleep, sleeping	ʃena	שֵׁינָה (נ)
dream	χalom	חֲלוֹם (ז)
to dream (in sleep)	laχalom	לַחֲלוֹם
sleepy (adj)	radum	רָדוּם

bed	mita	מִיטָה (נ)
mattress	mizran	מִזְרָן (ז)
blanket (comforter)	smixa	שְׂמִיכָה (נ)
pillow	karit	כָּרִית (נ)
sheet	sadin	סָדִין (ז)

insomnia	nedudei ʃena	נְדוּדֵי שֵׁינָה (ז״ר)
sleepless (adj)	xasar ʃena	חֲסַר שֵׁינָה
sleeping pill	kadur ʃena	כַּדּוּר שֵׁינָה (ז)
to take a sleeping pill	la'kaxat kadur ʃena	לָקַחַת כַּדּוּר שֵׁינָה

to feel sleepy	lirtsot liʃon	לִרְצוֹת לִישׁוֹן
to yawn (vi)	lefahek	לְפַהֵק
to go to bed	la'lexet liʃon	לָלֶכֶת לִישׁוֹן
to make up the bed	leha'tsi'a mita	לְהַצִּיעַ מִיטָה
to fall asleep	leheradem	לְהֵירָדֵם

nightmare	siyut	סִיּוּט (ז)
snore, snoring	nexira	נְחִירָה (נ)
to snore (vi)	linxor	לִנְחוֹר

alarm clock	ʃa'on me'orer	שָׁעוֹן מְעוֹרֵר (ז)
to wake (vt)	leha'ir	לְהָעִיר
to wake up	lehit'orer	לְהִתְעוֹרֵר
to get up (vi)	lakum	לָקוּם
to wash up (wash face)	lehitraxets	לְהִתְרַחֵץ

64. Humour. Laughter. Gladness

humor (wit, fun)	humor	הוּמוֹר (ז)
sense of humor	xuʃ humor	חוּשׁ הוּמוֹר (ז)
to enjoy oneself	lehanot	לֵיהָנוֹת
cheerful (merry)	sa'meax	שָׂמֵחַ
merriment (gaiety)	alitsut	עֲלִיצוּת (נ)

smile	xiyux	חִיּוּךְ (ז)
to smile (vi)	lexayex	לְחַיֵּךְ
to start laughing	lifrots bitsxok	לִפְרוֹץ בִּצְחוֹק
to laugh (vi)	litsxok	לִצְחוֹק
laugh, laughter	tsxok	צְחוֹק (ז)

anecdote	anek'dota	אָנֶקְדּוֹטָה (נ)
funny (anecdote, etc.)	matsxik	מַצְחִיק
funny (odd)	meʃa'a'ʃe'a	מְשַׁעֲשֵׁעַ

to joke (vi)	lehitba'deax	לְהִתְבַּדֵּחַ
joke (verbal)	bdixa	בְּדִיחָה (נ)
joy (emotion)	simxa	שִׂמְחָה (נ)
to rejoice (vi)	lis'moax	לִשְׂמוֹחַ
joyful (adj)	sa'meax	שָׂמֵחַ

65. Discussion, conversation. Part 1

communication	'keʃer	קֶשֶׁר (ז)
to communicate	letakʃer	לְתַקְשֵׁר
conversation	siχa	שִׂיחָה (נ)
dialog	du 'siaχ	דוּ-שִׂיחַ (ז)
discussion (discourse)	diyun	דִיוּן (ז)
dispute (debate)	vi'kuaχ	וִיכּוּחַ (ז)
to dispute	lehitva'keaχ	לְהִתְוַוכֵּחַ
interlocutor	ben 'siaχ	בֶּן שִׂיחַ (ז)
topic (theme)	nose	נוֹשֵׂא (ז)
point of view	nekudat mabat	נְקוּדַת מַבָּט (נ)
opinion (point of view)	de'a	דֵעָה (נ)
speech (talk)	ne'um	נָאוּם (ז)
discussion (of report, etc.)	diyun	דִיוּן (ז)
to discuss (vt)	ladun	לָדוּן
talk (conversation)	siχa	שִׂיחָה (נ)
to talk (to chat)	leso'χeaχ	לְשׂוֹחֵחַ
meeting	pgiʃa	פְּגִישָׁה (נ)
to meet (vi, vt)	lehipageʃ	לְהִיפָּגֵש
proverb	pitgam	פִּתְגָם (ז)
saying	pitgam	פִּתְגָם (ז)
riddle (poser)	χida	חִידָה (נ)
to pose a riddle	laχud χida	לָחוּד חִידָה
password	sisma	סִיסְמָה (נ)
secret	sod	סוֹד (ז)
oath (vow)	ʃvu'a	שְׁבוּעָה (נ)
to swear (an oath)	lehiʃava	לְהִישָׁבַע
promise	havtaχa	הַבְטָחָה (נ)
to promise (vt)	lehav'tiaχ	לְהַבְטִיחַ
advice (counsel)	etsa	עֵצָה (נ)
to advise (vt)	leya'ets	לְייָעֵץ
to follow one's advice	lif'ol lefi ha'etsa	לִפְעוֹל לְפִי הָעֵצָה
to listen to … (obey)	lehiʃama	לְהִישָׁמַע
news	χadaʃot	חֲדָשׁוֹת (נ"ר)
sensation (news)	sen'satsya	סֶנְסַצְיָה (נ)
information (data)	meida	מֵידָע (ז)
conclusion (decision)	maskana	מַסְקָנָה (נ)
voice	kol	קוֹל (ז)
compliment	maχma'a	מַחְמָאָה (נ)
kind (nice)	adiv	אָדִיב
word	mila	מִילָה (נ)
phrase	miʃpat	מִשְׁפָּט (ז)

answer	tʃuva	תְּשׁוּבָה (נ)
truth	emet	אֱמֶת (נ)
lie	'ʃeker	שֶׁקֶר (ז)

thought	maxʃava	מַחְשָׁבָה (נ)
idea (inspiration)	ra'ayon	רַעְיוֹן (ז)
fantasy	fan'tazya	פַנְטַזְיָה (נ)

66. Discussion, conversation. Part 2

respected (adj)	meχubad	מְכוּבָּד
to respect (vt)	leχabed	לְכַבֵּד
respect	kavod	כָּבוֹד (ז)
Dear … (letter)	hayakar …	הַיָּקָר ...

to introduce (sb to sb)	la'asot hekerut	לַעֲשׂוֹת הֶיכֵּרוּת
to make acquaintance	lehakir	לְהַכִּיר
intention	kavana	כַּוָּנָה (נ)
to intend (have in mind)	lehitkaven	לְהִתְכַּוֵּון
wish	iχul	אִיחוּל (ז)
to wish (~ good luck)	le'aχel	לְאַחֵל

surprise (astonishment)	hafta'a	הַפְתָּעָה (נ)
to surprise (amaze)	lehaf'ti'a	לְהַפְתִּיעַ
to be surprised	lehitpale	לְהִתְפַּלֵּא

to give (vt)	latet	לָתֵת
to take (get hold of)	la'kaχat	לָקַחַת
to give back	lehaχzir	לְהַחְזִיר
to return (give back)	lehaʃiv	לְהָשִׁיב

to apologize (vi)	lehitnatsel	לְהִתְנַצֵּל
apology	hitnatslut	הִתְנַצְּלוּת (נ)
to forgive (vt)	lis'loaχ	לִסְלוֹחַ

to talk (speak)	ledaber	לְדַבֵּר
to listen (vi)	lehakʃiv	לְהַקְשִׁיב
to hear out	liʃ'mo'a	לִשְׁמוֹעַ
to understand (vt)	lehavin	לְהָבִין

to show (to display)	lehar'ot	לְהַרְאוֹת
to look at …	lehistakel	לְהִסְתַּכֵּל
to call (yell for sb)	likro le…	לִקְרוֹא לְ...
to distract (disturb)	lehaf'ri'a	לְהַפְרִיעַ
to disturb (vt)	lehaf'ri'a	לְהַפְרִיעַ
to pass (to hand sth)	limsor	לִמְסוֹר

demand (request)	bakaʃa	בַּקָּשָׁה (נ)
to request (ask)	levakeʃ	לְבַקֵּשׁ
demand (firm request)	driʃa	דְּרִישָׁה (נ)

to demand (request firmly)	lidroʃ	לִדְרוֹשׁ
to tease (call names)	lehitgarot	לְהִתְגָּרוֹת
to mock (make fun of)	lil'og	לִלְעוֹג
mockery, derision	'la'ag	לַעַג (ז)
nickname	kinui	כִּינוּי (ז)
insinuation	'remez	רֶמֶז (ז)
to insinuate (imply)	lirmoz	לִרְמוֹז
to mean (vt)	lehitkaven le...	לְהִתְכַּוֵּון לְ...
description	te'ur	תִּיאוּר (ז)
to describe (vt)	leta'er	לְתָאֵר
praise (compliments)	'ʃevax	שֶׁבַח (ז)
to praise (vt)	leʃa'beax	לְשַׁבֵּחַ
disappointment	axzava	אַכְזָבָה (נ)
to disappoint (vt)	le'axzev	לְאַכְזֵב
to be disappointed	lehit'axzev	לְהִתְאַכְזֵב
supposition	hanaxa	הֲנָחָה (נ)
to suppose (assume)	leʃa'er	לְשַׁעֵר
warning (caution)	azhara	אַזְהָרָה (נ)
to warn (vt)	lehazhir	לְהַזְהִיר

67. Discussion, conversation. Part 3

to talk into (convince)	leʃaxˈneˈa	לְשַׁכְנֵעַ
to calm down (vt)	lehar'giˈa	לְהַרְגִּיעַ
silence (~ is golden)	ʃtika	שְׁתִיקָה (נ)
to be silent (not speaking)	liʃtok	לִשְׁתּוֹק
to whisper (vi, vt)	lilxoʃ	לִלְחוֹשׁ
whisper	lexiʃa	לְחִישָׁה (נ)
frankly, sincerely (adv)	bexenut	בְּכֵנוּת
in my opinion ...	leda'ati ...	לְדַעְתִּי ...
detail (of the story)	prat	פְּרָט (ז)
detailed (adj)	meforat	מְפוֹרָט
in detail (adv)	bimfurat	בִּמְפוֹרָט
hint, clue	'remez	רֶמֶז (ז)
to give a hint	lirmoz	לִרְמוֹז
look (glance)	mabat	מַבָּט (ז)
to have a look	lehabit	לְהַבִּיט
fixed (look)	kafu	קָפוּא
to blink (vi)	lematsmets	לְמַצְמֵץ
to wink (vi)	likrots	לִקְרוֹץ
to nod (in assent)	lehanhen	לְהַנְהֵן

sigh	anaxa	אֲנָחָה (נ)
to sigh (vi)	lehe'anax	לְהֵיאָנַח
to shudder (vi)	lir'od	לִרְעוֹד
gesture	mexva	מֶחֱוָה (נ)
to touch (one's arm, etc.)	la'ga'at be...	לָגַעַת בְּ...
to seize (e.g., ~ by the arm)	litfos	לִתְפּוֹס
to tap (on the shoulder)	lit'poax	לִטְפּוֹחַ

Look out!	zehirut!	זְהִירוּת!
Really?	be'emet?	בֶּאֱמֶת?
Are you sure?	ata ba'tuax?	אַתָּה בָּטוּחַ?
Good luck!	behatslaxa!	בְּהַצְלָחָה!
I see!	muvan!	מוּבָן!
What a pity!	xaval!	חֲבָל!

68. Agreement. Refusal

consent	haskama	הַסכָּמָה (נ)
to consent (vi)	lehaskim	לְהַסכִּים
approval	iʃur	אִישׁוּר (ז)
to approve (vt)	le'aʃer	לְאַשֵׁר
refusal	siruv	סֵירוּב (ז)
to refuse (vi, vt)	lesarev	לְסָרֵב

Great!	metsuyan!	מְצוּיָן!
All right!	tov!	טוֹב!
Okay! (I agree)	be'seder!	בְּסֵדֶר!

forbidden (adj)	asur	אָסוּר
it's forbidden	asur	אָסוּר
it's impossible	'bilti efʃari	בִּלתִּי אֶפשָׁרִי
incorrect (adj)	ʃagui	שָׁגוּי

to reject (~ a demand)	lidxot	לִדחוֹת
to support (cause, idea)	litmox be...	לִתמוֹך בְּ...
to accept (~ an apology)	lekabel	לְקַבֵּל

to confirm (vt)	le'aʃer	לְאַשֵׁר
confirmation	iʃur	אִישׁוּר (ז)
permission	reʃut	רְשׁוּת (נ)
to permit (vt)	leharʃot	לְהַרשׁוֹת
decision	haxlata	הַחלָטָה (נ)
to say nothing (hold one's tongue)	liʃtok	לִשׁתוֹק

condition (term)	tnai	תְּנַאי (ז)
excuse (pretext)	teruts	תֵּירוּץ (ז)
praise (compliments)	'ʃevax	שֶׁבַח (ז)
to praise (vt)	leʃa'beax	לְשַׁבֵּחַ

69. Success. Good luck. Failure

success	hatsala	הַצְלָחָה (נ)
successfully (adv)	behatslaχa	בְּהַצְלָחָה
successful (adj)	mutslaχ	מוּצְלָח
luck (good luck)	mazal	מַזָל (ז)
Good luck!	behatslaχa!	בְּהַצְלָחָה!
lucky (e.g., ~ day)	mutslaχ	מוּצְלָח
lucky (fortunate)	bar mazal	בַּר מַזָל
failure	kiʃalon	כִּישָׁלוֹן (ז)
misfortune	'χoser mazal	חוֹסֶר מַזָל (ז)
bad luck	'χoser mazal	חוֹסֶר מַזָל (ז)
unsuccessful (adj)	lo mutslaχ	לֹא מוּצְלָח
catastrophe	ason	אָסוֹן (ז)
pride	ga'ava	גַאֲוָה (נ)
proud (adj)	ge'e	גֵאֶה
to be proud	lehitga'ot	לְהִתְגָאוֹת
winner	zoχe	זוֹכֶה (ז)
to win (vi)	lena'tseaχ	לְנַצֵחַ
to lose (not win)	lehafsid	לְהַפְסִיד
try	nisayon	נִיסָיוֹן (ז)
to try (vi)	lenasot	לְנַסוֹת
chance (opportunity)	hizdamnut	הִזְדַמְנוּת (נ)

70. Quarrels. Negative emotions

shout (scream)	tse'aka	צְעָקָה (נ)
to shout (vi)	lits'ok	לִצְעוֹק
to start to cry out	lehatχil lits'ok	לְהַתְחִיל לִצְעוֹק
quarrel	riv	רִיב (ז)
to quarrel (vi)	lariv	לָרִיב
fight (squabble)	riv	רִיב (ז)
to make a scene	lariv	לָרִיב
conflict	siχsuχ	סִכְסוּךְ (ז)
misunderstanding	i havana	אִי הֲבָנָה (נ)
insult	elbon	עֶלְבּוֹן (ז)
to insult (vt)	leha'aliv	לְהַעֲלִיב
insulted (adj)	ne'elav	נֶעֱלָב
resentment	tina	טִינָה (נ)
to offend (vt)	lif'go'a	לִפְגוֹעַ
to take offense	lehipaga	לְהִיפָּגַע
indignation	hitmarmerut	הִתְמַרְמְרוּת (נ)
to be indignant	lehitra'em	לְהִתְרַעֵם

| complaint | tluna | תְּלוּנָה (נ) |
| to complain (vi, vt) | lehitlonen | לְהִתְלוֹנֵן |

apology	hitnatslut	הִתְנַצְּלוּת (נ)
to apologize (vi)	lehitnatsel	לְהִתְנַצֵּל
to beg pardon	levakeʃ sliχa	לְבַקֵּשׁ סְלִיחָה

criticism	bi'koret	בִּיקּוֹרֶת (נ)
to criticize (vt)	levaker	לְבַקֵּר
accusation	ha'aʃama	הַאֲשָׁמָה (נ)
to accuse (vt)	leha'aʃim	לְהַאֲשִׁים

revenge	nekama	נְקָמָה (נ)
to avenge (get revenge)	linkom	לִנְקוֹם
to pay back	lehaχzir	לְהַחְזִיר

disdain	zilzul	זִלְזוּל (ז)
to despise (vt)	lezalzel be…	לְזַלְזֵל בְּ…
hatred, hate	sin'a	שִׂנְאָה (נ)
to hate (vt)	lisno	לִשְׂנוֹא

nervous (adj)	atsbani	עַצְבָּנִי
to be nervous	lihyot atsbani	לִהְיוֹת עַצְבָּנִי
angry (mad)	ka'us	כָּעוּס
to make angry	lehargiz	לְהַרְגִּיז

humiliation	haʃpala	הַשְׁפָּלָה (נ)
to humiliate (vt)	lehaʃpil	לְהַשְׁפִּיל
to humiliate oneself	lehaʃpil et atsmo	לְהַשְׁפִּיל אֶת עַצְמוֹ

| shock | 'helem | הֶלֶם (ז) |
| to shock (vt) | leza'a'ze'a | לְזַעְזֵעַ |

| trouble (e.g., serious ~) | tsara | צָרָה (נ) |
| unpleasant (adj) | lo na'im | לֹא נָעִים |

fear (dread)	'paχad	פַּחַד (ז)
terrible (storm, heat)	nora	נוֹרָא
scary (e.g., ~ story)	mafχid	מַפְחִיד
horror	zva'a	זְוָועָה (נ)
awful (crime, news)	ayom	אָיוֹם

to begin to tremble	lehera'ed	לְהֵירָעֵד
to cry (weep)	livkot	לִבְכּוֹת
to start crying	lehatχil livkot	לְהַתְחִיל לִבְכּוֹת
tear	dim'a	דִּמְעָה (נ)

fault	aʃma	אַשְׁמָה (נ)
guilt (feeling)	rigʃei aʃam	רְגָשֵׁי אָשָׁם (ז"ר)
dishonor (disgrace)	χerpa	חֶרְפָּה (נ)
protest	meχa'a	מְחָאָה (נ)
stress	'laχats	לַחַץ (ז)

to disturb (vt)	lehaf'ri'a	לְהַפְרִיעַ
to be furious	lix'os	לִכעוֹס
mad, angry (adj)	zo'em	זוֹעֵם
to end (~ a relationship)	lesayem	לְסַייֵם
to swear (at sb)	lekalel	לְקַלֵל
to scare (become afraid)	lehibahel	לְהִיבָּהֵל
to hit (strike with hand)	lehakot	לְהַכּוֹת
to fight (street fight, etc.)	lehitkotet	לְהִתקוֹטֵט
to settle (a conflict)	lehasdir	לְהַסדִיר
discontented (adj)	lo merutse	לֹא מְרוּצֶה
furious (adj)	metoraf	מְטוֹרָף
It's not good!	ze lo tov!	זֶה לֹא טוֹב!
It's bad!	ze ra!	זֶה רַע!

Medicine

71. Diseases

sickness	maχala	מַחֲלָה (נ)
to be sick	lihyot χole	לִהְיוֹת חוֹלֶה
health	bri'ut	בְּרִיאוּת (נ)

runny nose (coryza)	na'zelet	נַזֶּלֶת (נ)
tonsillitis	da'leket ʃkedim	דַּלֶּקֶת שְׁקֵדִים (נ)
cold (illness)	hitstanenut	הִצְטַנְּנוּת (נ)
to catch a cold	lehitstanen	לְהִצְטַנֵּן

bronchitis	bron'χitis	בְּרוֹנְכִיטִיס (ז)
pneumonia	da'leket re'ot	דַּלֶּקֶת רֵיאוֹת (נ)
flu, influenza	ʃa'pa'at	שַׁפַּעַת (נ)

nearsighted (adj)	ktsar re'iya	קְצַר רְאִיָּה
farsighted (adj)	reχok re'iya	רְחוֹק רְאִיָּה
strabismus (crossed eyes)	pzila	פְּזִילָה (נ)
cross-eyed (adj)	pozel	פּוֹזֵל
cataract	katarakt	קָטָרַקְט (ז)
glaucoma	gla'u'koma	גְּלָאוֹקוֹמָה (נ)

stroke	ʃavats moχi	שָׁבָץ מוֹחִי (ז)
heart attack	hetkef lev	הֶתְקֵף לֵב (ז)
myocardial infarction	'otem ʃrir halev	אוֹטֶם שְׁרִיר הַלֵּב (ז)
paralysis	ʃituk	שִׁתּוּק (ז)
to paralyze (vt)	leʃatek	לְשַׁתֵּק

allergy	a'lergya	אָלֶרְגְיָה (נ)
asthma	'astma, ka'tseret	אַסְתְמָה, קַצֶּרֶת (נ)
diabetes	su'keret	סוּכֶּרֶת (נ)

| toothache | ke'ev ʃi'nayim | כְּאֵב שִׁנַּיִים (ז) |
| caries | a'ʃeʃet | עַשֶּׁשֶׁת (נ) |

diarrhea	ʃilʃul	שִׁלְשׁוּל (ז)
constipation	atsirut	עֲצִירוּת (נ)
stomach upset	kilkul keiva	קִלְקוּל קֵיבָה (ז)
food poisoning	har'alat mazon	הַרְעָלַת מָזוֹן (נ)
to get food poisoning	laχatof har'alat mazon	לַחֲטוֹף הַרְעָלַת מָזוֹן

arthritis	da'leket mifrakim	דַּלֶּקֶת מִפְרָקִים (נ)
rickets	ra'keχet	רַכֶּבֶת (נ)
rheumatism	ʃigaron	שִׁיגָּרוֹן (ז)

atherosclerosis	ar'teryo skle'rosis	אַרְטֶרְיוֹ־סְקְלֶרוֹסִיס (ז)
gastritis	da'leket keiva	דַּלֶּקֶת קֵיבָה (נ)
appendicitis	da'leket toseftan	דַּלֶּקֶת תּוֹסֶפְתָּן (נ)
cholecystitis	da'leket kis hamara	דַּלֶּקֶת כִּיס הַמָּרָה (נ)
ulcer	'ulkus, kiv	אוּלְקוּס, כִּיב (ז)

measles	xa'tsevet	חַצֶּבֶת (נ)
rubella (German measles)	a'demet	אַדֶּמֶת (נ)
jaundice	tsa'hevet	צַהֶבֶת (נ)
hepatitis	da'leket kaved	דַּלֶּקֶת כָּבֵד (נ)

schizophrenia	sxizo'frenya	סְכִיזוֹפְרֶנְיָה (נ)
rabies (hydrophobia)	ka'levet	כַּלֶּבֶת (נ)
neurosis	noi'roza	נוֹירוֹזָה (נ)
concussion	za'a'zu'a 'moax	זַעֲזוּעַ מוֹחַ (ז)

cancer	sartan	סַרְטָן (ז)
sclerosis	ta'refet	טָרֶשֶׁת (נ)
multiple sclerosis	ta'refet nefotsa	טָרֶשֶׁת נְפוֹצָה (נ)

alcoholism	alkoholizm	אַלְכּוֹהוֹלִיזם (ז)
alcoholic (n)	alkoholist	אַלְכּוֹהוֹלִיסט (ז)
syphilis	a'gevet	עַגֶּבֶת (נ)
AIDS	eids	אֵיידְס (ז)

tumor	gidul	גִּידוּל (ז)
malignant (adj)	mam'ir	מַמְאִיר
benign (adj)	ʃapir	שַׁפִיר

fever	ka'daxat	קַדַּחַת (נ)
malaria	ma'larya	מָלַרְיָה (נ)
gangrene	gan'grena	גַּנְגְּרֶנָה (נ)
seasickness	maxalat yam	מַחֲלַת יָם (נ)
epilepsy	maxalat hanefila	מַחֲלַת הַנְּפִילָה (נ)

epidemic	magefa	מַגֵּיפָה (נ)
typhus	'tifus	טִיפוּס (ז)
tuberculosis	ʃa'xefet	שַׁחֶפֶת (נ)
cholera	ko'lera	כּוֹלֵרָה (נ)
plague (bubonic ~)	davar	דֶּבֶר (ז)

72. Symptoms. Treatments. Part 1

symptom	simptom	סִימְפְּטוֹם (ז)
temperature	xom	חוֹם (ז)
high temperature (fever)	xom ga'voha	חוֹם גָּבוֹהַּ (ז)
pulse	'dofek	דּוֹפֶק (ז)

| dizziness (vertigo) | sxar'xoret | סְחַרְחוֹרֶת (נ) |
| hot (adj) | xam | חַם |

| shivering | tsmar'moret | צְמַרְמוֹרֶת (נ) |
| pale (e.g., ~ face) | χiver | חִיוֵּר |

cough	ʃi'ul	שִׁיעוּל (ז)
to cough (vi)	lehiʃta'el	לְהִשְׁתַּעֵל
to sneeze (vi)	lehit'ateʃ	לְהִתְעַטֵּשׁ
faint	ilafon	עִילָפוֹן (ז)
to faint (vi)	lehit'alef	לְהִתְעַלֵּף

bruise (hématome)	χabura	חַבּוּרָה (נ)
bump (lump)	blita	בְּלִיטָה (נ)
to bang (bump)	lekabel maka	לְקַבֵּל מַכָּה
contusion (bruise)	maka	מַכָּה (נ)
to get a bruise	lekabel maka	לְקַבֵּל מַכָּה

to limp (vi)	lits'lo'a	לִצְלוֹעַ
dislocation	'neka	נֶקַע (ז)
to dislocate (vt)	lin'ko'a	לִנְקוֹעַ
fracture	'ʃever	שֶׁבֶר (ז)
to have a fracture	liʃbor	לִשְׁבּוֹר

cut (e.g., paper ~)	χataχ	חָתָךְ (ז)
to cut oneself	lehiχateχ	לְהֵיחָתֵךְ
bleeding	dimum	דִּימוּם (ז)

| burn (injury) | kviya | כְּוִויָה (נ) |
| to get burned | laχatof kviya | לַחֲטוֹף כְּוִויָה |

to prick (vt)	lidkor	לִדְקוֹר
to prick oneself	lehidaker	לְהִידָקֵר
to injure (vt)	lif'tso'a	לִפְצוֹעַ
injury	ptsi'a	פְּצִיעָה (נ)
wound	'petsa	פֶּצַע (ז)
trauma	'tra'uma	טְרָאוּמָה (נ)

to be delirious	lahazot	לַהֲזוֹת
to stutter (vi)	legamgem	לְגַמְגֵּם
sunstroke	makat 'ʃemeʃ	מַכַּת שֶׁמֶשׁ (נ)

73. Symptoms. Treatments. Part 2

| pain, ache | ke'ev | כְּאֵב (ז) |
| splinter (in foot, etc.) | kots | קוֹץ (ז) |

sweat (perspiration)	ze'a	זֵיעָה (נ)
to sweat (perspire)	leha'zi'a	לְהַזִיעַ
vomiting	haka'a	הֲקָאָה (נ)
convulsions	pirkusim	פִּירְכּוּסִים (ז״ר)
pregnant (adj)	hara	הָרָה
to be born	lehivaled	לְהִיוָּלֵד

delivery, labor	leda	לֵידָה (נ)
to deliver (~ a baby)	la'ledet	לָלֶדֶת
abortion	hapala	הַפָּלָה (נ)

breathing, respiration	neʃima	נְשִׁימָה (נ)
in-breath (inhalation)	ʃe'ifa	שְׁאִיפָה (נ)
out-breath (exhalation)	neʃifa	נְשִׁיפָה (נ)
to exhale (breathe out)	linʃof	לִנְשׁוֹף
to inhale (vi)	liʃ'of	לִשְׁאוֹף

disabled person	naxe	נָכֶה (ז)
cripple	naxe	נָכֶה (ז)
drug addict	narkoman	נַרקוֹמָן (ז)

deaf (adj)	xereʃ	חֵירֵשׁ
mute (adj)	ilem	אִילֵם
deaf mute (adj)	xereʃ-ilem	חֵירֵשׁ־אִילֵם

mad, insane (adj)	meʃuga	מְשׁוּגָע
madman	meʃuga	מְשׁוּגָע (ז)
(demented person)		
madwoman	meʃu'ga'at	מְשׁוּגַעַת (נ)
to go insane	lehiʃta'ge'a	לְהִשְׁתַּגֵּעַ

gene	gen	גֵן (ז)
immunity	xasinut	חֲסִינוּת (נ)
hereditary (adj)	toraʃti	תּוֹרַשְׁתִּי
congenital (adj)	mulad	מוּלָד

virus	'virus	וִירוּס (ז)
microbe	xaidak	חַיידַק (ז)
bacterium	bak'terya	בַּקְטֶריָה (נ)
infection	zihum	זִיהוּם (ז)

74. Symptoms. Treatments. Part 3

| hospital | beit xolim | בֵּית חוֹלִים (ז) |
| patient | metupal | מְטוּפָּל (ז) |

diagnosis	avxana	אַבחָנָה (נ)
cure	ripui	רִיפּוּי (ז)
medical treatment	tipul refu'i	טִיפּוּל רְפוּאִי (ז)
to get treatment	lekabel tipul	לְקַבֵּל טִיפּוּל
to treat (~ a patient)	letapel be...	לְטַפֵּל בְּ...
to nurse (look after)	letapel be...	לְטַפֵּל בְּ...
care (nursing ~)	tipul	טִיפּוּל (ז)

operation, surgery	ni'tuax	נִיתוּחַ (ז)
to bandage (head, limb)	laxboʃ	לַחבּוֹשׁ
bandaging	xaviʃa	חֲבִישָׁה (נ)

vaccination	χisun	חִיסוּן (ז)
to vaccinate (vt)	leχasen	לְחַסֵן
injection, shot	zrika	זְרִיקָה (נ)
to give an injection	lehazrik	לְהַזְרִיק

attack	hetkef	הֶתְקֵף (ז)
amputation	kti'a	קְטִיעָה (נ)
to amputate (vt)	lik'to'a	לִקְטוֹעַ
coma	tar'demet	תַרְדֶמֶת (נ)
to be in a coma	lihyot betar'demet	לִהְיוֹת בְּתַרְדֶמֶת
intensive care	tipul nimrats	טִיפּוּל נִמְרָץ (ז)

to recover (~ from flu)	lehaχlim	לְהַחְלִים
condition (patient's ~)	matsav	מַצָב (ז)
consciousness	hakara	הַכָּרָה (נ)
memory (faculty)	zikaron	זִיכָּרוֹן (ז)

to pull out (tooth)	la'akor	לַעֲקוֹר
filling	stima	סְתִימָה (נ)
to fill (a tooth)	la'asot stima	לַעֲשוֹת סְתִימָה

| hypnosis | hip'noza | הִיפְּנוֹזָה (נ) |
| to hypnotize (vt) | lehapnet | לְהַפְנֵט |

75. Doctors

doctor	rofe	רוֹפֵא (ז)
nurse	aχot	אָחוֹת (נ)
personal doctor	rofe iſi	רוֹפֵא אִישִי (ז)

dentist	rofe ſi'nayim	רוֹפֵא שִינַיִים (ז)
eye doctor	rofe ei'nayim	רוֹפֵא עֵינַיִים (ז)
internist	rofe pnimi	רוֹפֵא פְּנִימִי (ז)
surgeon	kirurg	כִּירוּרג (ז)

psychiatrist	psiχi''ater	פְּסִיכְיָאטֶר (ז)
pediatrician	rofe yeladim	רוֹפֵא יְלָדִים (ז)
psychologist	psiχolog	פְּסִיכוֹלוֹג (ז)
gynecologist	rofe naſim	רוֹפֵא נָשִים (ז)
cardiologist	kardyolog	קַרְדִיוֹלוֹג (ז)

76. Medicine. Drugs. Accessories

medicine, drug	trufa	תְרוּפָה (נ)
remedy	trufa	תְרוּפָה (נ)
to prescribe (vt)	lirſom	לִרְשוֹם
prescription	mirſam	מִרְשָם (ז)
tablet, pill	kadur	כַּדוּר (ז)

ointment	miʃχa	מִשְׁחָה (נ)
ampule	'ampula	אַמְפּוּלָה (נ)
mixture	ta'a'rovet	תַּעֲרוֹבֶת (נ)
syrup	sirop	סִירוֹפ (ז)
pill	gluya	גְּלוּיָה (נ)
powder	avka	אַבְקָה (נ)

gauze bandage	taχ'boʃet 'gaza	תַּחְבּוֹשֶׁת גָּאזָה (נ)
cotton wool	'tsemer 'gefen	צֶמֶר גֶּפֶן (ז)
iodine	yod	יוֹד (ז)

Band-Aid	'plaster	פְּלַסְטֶר (ז)
eyedropper	taf'tefet	טַפְטֶפֶת (נ)
thermometer	madχom	מַדְחוֹם (ז)
syringe	mazrek	מַזְרֵק (ז)

| wheelchair | kise galgalim | כִּיסֵא גַלְגַּלִים (ז) |
| crutches | ka'bayim | קַבַּיִים (ז"ר) |

painkiller	meʃakeχ ke'evim	מְשַׁכֵּךְ כְּאֵבִים (ז)
laxative	trufa meʃal'ʃelet	תְרוּפָה מְשַׁלְשֶׁלֶת (נ)
spirits (ethanol)	'kohal	כּוֹהַל (ז)
medicinal herbs	isvei marpe	עִשְׂבֵי מַרְפֵּא (ז"ר)
herbal (~ tea)	ʃel asavim	שֶׁל עֲשָׂבִים

77. Smoking. Tobacco products

tobacco	'tabak	טַבָּק (ז)
cigarette	si'garya	סִיגַרְיָה (נ)
cigar	sigar	סִיגָר (ז)
pipe	mik'teret	מִקְטֶרֶת (נ)
pack (of cigarettes)	χafisa	חֲפִיסָה (נ)

matches	gafrurim	גַּפְרוּרִים (ז"ר)
matchbox	kufsat gafrurim	קוּפְסַת גַּפְרוּרִים (נ)
lighter	matsit	מַצִּית (ז)
ashtray	ma'afera	מַאֲפֵרָה (נ)
cigarette case	nartik lesi'garyot	נַרְתִּיק לְסִיגַרְיוֹת (ז)

| cigarette holder | piya | פִּייָה (נ) |
| filter (cigarette tip) | 'filter | פִילְטֶר (ז) |

to smoke (vi, vt)	le'aʃen	לְעַשֵּׁן
to light a cigarette	lehadlik si'garya	לְהַדְלִיק סִיגַרְיָה
smoking	iʃun	עִישּׁוּן (ז)
smoker	me'aʃen	מְעַשֵּׁן (ז)

stub, butt (of cigarette)	bdal si'garya	בְּדַל סִיגַרְיָה (ז)
smoke, fumes	aʃan	עָשָׁן (ז)
ash	'efer	אֵפֶר (ז)

HUMAN HABITAT

City

78. City. Life in the city

city, town	ir	עִיר (נ)
capital city	ir bira	עִיר בִּירָה (נ)
village	kfar	כְּפָר (ז)
city map	mapat ha'ir	מַפַּת הָעִיר (נ)
downtown	merkaz ha'ir	מֶרְכַּז הָעִיר (ז)
suburb	parvar	פַּרְוָר (ז)
suburban (adj)	parvari	פַּרְוָרִי
outskirts	parvar	פַּרְוָר (ז)
environs (suburbs)	svivot	סְבִיבוֹת (נ״ר)
city block	ʃxuna	שְׁכוּנָה (נ)
residential block (area)	ʃxunat megurim	שְׁכוּנַת מְגוּרִים (נ)
traffic	tnu'a	תְּנוּעָה (נ)
traffic lights	ramzor	רַמְזוֹר (ז)
public transportation	taxbura tsiburit	תַּחְבּוּרָה צִיבּוּרִית (נ)
intersection	'tsomet	צוֹמֶת (ז)
crosswalk	ma'avar xatsaya	מַעֲבַר חֲצָיָה (ז)
pedestrian underpass	ma'avar tat karka'i	מַעֲבָר תַּת־קַרְקָעִי (ז)
to cross (~ the street)	laxatsot	לַחֲצוֹת
pedestrian	holex 'regel	הוֹלֵךְ רֶגֶל (ז)
sidewalk	midraxa	מִדְרָכָה (נ)
bridge	'geʃer	גֶּשֶׁר (ז)
embankment (river walk)	ta'yelet	טַיֶּלֶת (נ)
fountain	mizraka	מִזְרָקָה (נ)
allée (garden walkway)	sdera	שְׂדֵרָה (נ)
park	park	פַּארְק (ז)
boulevard	sdera	שְׂדֵרָה (נ)
square	kikar	כִּיכָּר (נ)
avenue (wide street)	rexov raʃi	רְחוֹב רָאשִׁי (ז)
street	rexov	רְחוֹב (ז)
side street	simta	סִמְטָה (נ)
dead end	mavoi satum	מָבוֹי סָתוּם (ז)
house	'bayit	בַּיִת (ז)
building	binyan	בְּנְיָן (ז)

skyscraper	gored ʃҳakim	גּוֹרֵד שְׁחָקִים (ז)
facade	ҳazit	חָזִית (נ)
roof	gag	גַּג (ז)
window	ҳalon	חַלּוֹן (ז)
arch	'keʃet	קֶשֶׁת (נ)
column	amud	עַמּוּד (ז)
corner	pina	פִּינָה (נ)

store window	ҳalon ra'ava	חַלּוֹן רַאֲוָה (ז)
signboard (store sign, etc.)	'ʃelet	שֶׁלֶט (ז)
poster	kraza	כְּרָזָה (נ)
advertising poster	'poster	פּוֹסְטֶר (ז)
billboard	'luaҳ pirsum	לוּחַ פִּרְסוּם (ז)

garbage, trash	'zevel	זֶבֶל (ז)
trashcan (public ~)	paҳ aʃpa	פַּח אַשְׁפָּה (ז)
to litter (vi)	lelaҳleҳ	לְלַכְלֵךְ
garbage dump	mizbala	מִזְבָּלָה (נ)

phone booth	ta 'telefon	תָּא טֶלֶפוֹן (ז)
lamppost	amud panas	עַמּוּד פָּנָס (ז)
bench (park ~)	safsal	סַפְסָל (ז)

police officer	ʃoter	שׁוֹטֵר (ז)
police	miʃtara	מִשְׁטָרָה (נ)
beggar	kabtsan	קַבְּצָן (ז)
homeless (n)	ҳasar 'bayit	חֲסַר בַּיִת (ז)

79. Urban institutions

store	ҳanut	חֲנוּת (נ)
drugstore, pharmacy	beit mir'kaҳat	בֵּית מִרְקַחַת (ז)
eyeglass store	ҳanut miʃka'fayim	חֲנוּת מִשְׁקָפַיִם (נ)
shopping mall	kanyon	קַנְיוֹן (ז)
supermarket	super'market	סוּפֶּרְמַרְקֶט (ז)

bakery	ma'afiya	מַאֲפִיָּה (נ)
baker	ofe	אוֹפֶה (ז)
pastry shop	ҳanut mamtakim	חֲנוּת מַמְתַּקִים (נ)
grocery store	ma'kolet	מַכֹּלֶת (נ)
butcher shop	itliz	אִטְלִיז (ז)

| produce store | ҳanut perot viyerakot | חֲנוּת פֵּירוֹת וִירָקוֹת (נ) |
| market | ʃuk | שׁוּק (ז) |

coffee house	beit kafe	בֵּית קָפֶּה (ז)
restaurant	mis'ada	מִסְעָדָה (נ)
pub, bar	pab	פָּאבּ (ז)
pizzeria	pi'tseriya	פִּיצֶּרְיָּה (נ)
hair salon	mispara	מִסְפָּרָה (נ)

post office	'do'ar	דּוֹאַר (ז)
dry cleaners	nikui yaveʃ	נִיקּוּי יָבֵשׁ (ז)
photo studio	'studyo letsilum	סְטוּדְיוֹ לְצִילוּם (ז)
shoe store	χanut na'a'layim	חֲנוּת נַעֲלַיִים (נ)
bookstore	χanut sfarim	חֲנוּת סְפָרִים (נ)
sporting goods store	χanut sport	חֲנוּת סְפּוֹרְט (נ)
clothes repair shop	χanut tikun bgadim	חֲנוּת תִּיקּוּן בְּגָדִים (נ)
formal wear rental	χanut haskarat bgadim	חֲנוּת הַשְׂכָּרַת בְּגָדִים (נ)
video rental store	χanut haʃalat sratim	חֲנוּת הַשְׁאָלַת סְרָטִים (נ)
circus	kirkas	קִרְקָס (ז)
zoo	gan hayot	גַּן חַיּוֹת (ז)
movie theater	kol'no'a	קוֹלְנוֹעַ (ז)
museum	muze'on	מוּזֵיאוֹן (ז)
library	sifriya	סִפְרִייָה (נ)
theater	te'atron	תֵּיאַטְרוֹן (ז)
opera (opera house)	beit 'opera	בֵּית אוֹפֶּרָה (ז)
nightclub	mo'adon 'laila	מוֹעֲדוֹן לַיְלָה (ז)
casino	ka'zino	קָזִינוֹ (ז)
mosque	misgad	מִסְגָּד (ז)
synagogue	beit 'kneset	בֵּית כְּנֶסֶת (ז)
cathedral	kated'rala	קָתֶדְרָלָה (נ)
temple	mikdaʃ	מִקְדָּשׁ (ז)
church	knesiya	כְּנֵסִייָה (נ)
college	miχlala	מִכְלָלָה (נ)
university	uni'versita	אוּנִיבֶרְסִיטָה (נ)
school	beit 'sefer	בֵּית סֵפֶר (ז)
prefecture	maχoz	מָחוֹז (ז)
city hall	iriya	עִירִייָה (נ)
hotel	beit malon	בֵּית מָלוֹן (ז)
bank	bank	בַּנְק (ז)
embassy	ʃagrirut	שַׁגְרִירוּת (נ)
travel agency	soχnut nesi'ot	סוֹכְנוּת נְסִיעוֹת (נ)
information office	modi'in	מוֹדִיעִין (ז)
currency exchange	misrad hamarat mat'be'a	מִשְׂרַד הַמָרַת מַטְבֵּעַ (ז)
subway	ra'kevet taχtit	רַכֶּבֶת תַּחְתִּית (נ)
hospital	beit χolim	בֵּית חוֹלִים (ז)
gas station	taχanat 'delek	תַּחֲנַת דֶּלֶק (נ)
parking lot	migraʃ χanaya	מִגְרַשׁ חֲנָיָה (ז)

80. Signs

signboard (store sign, etc.)	'ʃelet	שֶׁלֶט (ז)
notice (door sign, etc.)	moda'a	מוֹדָעָה (נ)
poster	'poster	פּוֹסטֶר (ז)
direction sign	tamrur	תַּמרוּר (ז)
arrow (sign)	χeʦ	חֵץ (ז)
caution	azhara	אַזהָרָה (נ)
warning sign	'ʃelet azhara	שֶׁלֶט אַזהָרָה (ז)
to warn (vt)	lehazhir	לְהַזהִיר
rest day (weekly ~)	yom 'χofeʃ	יוֹם חוֹפֶשׁ (ז)
timetable (schedule)	'luaχ zmanim	לוּחַ זמַנִים (ז)
opening hours	ʃa'ot avoda	שְׁעוֹת עֲבוֹדָה (נ״ר)
WELCOME!	bruχim haba'im!	בּרוּכִים הַבָּאִים!
ENTRANCE	knisa	כּנִיסָה
EXIT	yeʦi'a	יְצִיאָה
PUSH	dχof	דחוֹף
PULL	mʃoχ	משׁוֹךְ
OPEN	pa'tuaχ	פָּתוּחַ
CLOSED	sagur	סָגוּר
WOMEN	lenaʃim	לְנָשִׁים
MEN	legvarim	לְגבָרִים
DISCOUNTS	hanaχot	הֲנָחוֹת
SALE	mivʦa	מִבצָע
NEW!	χadaʃ!	חָדָשׁ!
FREE	χinam	חִינָם
ATTENTION!	sim lev!	שִׁים לֵב!
NO VACANCIES	ein makom panui	אֵין מָקוֹם פָּנוּי
RESERVED	ʃamur	שָׁמוּר
ADMINISTRATION	hanhala	הַנהָלָה
STAFF ONLY	le'ovdim bilvad	לְעוֹבדִים בִּלבַד
BEWARE OF THE DOG!	zehirut 'kelev noʃeχ!	זְהִירוּת, כֶּלֶב נוֹשֵׁךְ!
NO SMOKING	asur le'aʃen!	אָסוּר לְעַשֵּׁן!
DO NOT TOUCH!	lo lagaat!	לֹא לָגַעַת!
DANGEROUS	mesukan	מְסוּכָּן
DANGER	sakana	סַכָּנָה
HIGH VOLTAGE	'metaχ ga'voha	מֶתַח גָבוֹהַ
NO SWIMMING!	haraχaʦa asura!	הָרַחֲצָה אֲסוּרָה!
OUT OF ORDER	lo oved	לֹא עוֹבֵד
FLAMMABLE	dalik	דָלִיק
FORBIDDEN	asur	אָסוּר

NO TRESPASSING!	asur la'avor	אָסוּר לַעֲבוֹר
WET PAINT	'tseva laχ	צֶבַע לַח

81. Urban transportation

bus	'otobus	אוֹטוֹבּוּס (ז)
streetcar	ra'kevet kala	רַכֶּבֶת קַלָּה (נ)
trolley bus	tro'leibus	טרוֹלֵייבּוּס (ז)
route (of bus, etc.)	maslul	מַסלוּל (ז)
number (e.g., bus ~)	mispar	מְסְפָּר (ז)
to go by ...	lin'so'a be...	לִנסוֹעַ בְּ...
to get on (~ the bus)	la'alot	לַעֲלוֹת
to get off ...	la'redet mi...	לָרֶדֶת מ...
stop (e.g., bus ~)	taχana	תַּחֲנָה (נ)
next stop	hataχana haba'a	הַתַּחֲנָה הַבָּאָה (נ)
terminus	hataχana ha'aχrona	הַתַּחֲנָה הָאַחרוֹנָה (נ)
schedule	'luaχ zmanim	לוּחַ זמַנִּים (ז)
to wait (vt)	lehamtin	לְהַמתִּין
ticket	kartis	כַּרטִיס (ז)
fare	meχir hanesiya	מְחִיר הַנְּסִיעָה (ז)
cashier (ticket seller)	kupai	קוּפַּאי (ז)
ticket inspection	bi'koret kartisim	בִּיקוֹרֶת כַּרטִיסִים (נ)
ticket inspector	mevaker	מְבַקֵּר (ז)
to be late (for ...)	le'aχer	לְאַחֵר
to miss (~ the train, etc.)	lefasfes	לְפַסּפֵס
to be in a hurry	lemaher	לְמַהֵר
taxi, cab	monit	מוֹנִית (נ)
taxi driver	nahag monit	נָהַג מוֹנִית (ז)
by taxi	bemonit	בְּמוֹנִית
taxi stand	taχanat moniyot	תַּחֲנַת מוֹנִיּוֹת (נ)
to call a taxi	lehazmin monit	לְהַזמִין מוֹנִית
to take a taxi	la'kaχat monit	לָקַחַת מוֹנִית
traffic	tnu'a	תנוּעָה (נ)
traffic jam	pkak	פּקָק (ז)
rush hour	ʃa'ot 'omes	שָׁעוֹת עוֹמֶס (נ״ר)
to park (vi)	laχanot	לַחֲנוֹת
to park (vt)	lehaχnot	לְהַחנוֹת
parking lot	χanaya	חֲנָיָה (נ)
subway	ra'kevet taχtit	רַכֶּבֶת תַּחתִּית (נ)
station	taχana	תַּחֲנָה (נ)
to take the subway	lin'so'a betaχtit	לִנסוֹעַ בְּתַחתִּית
train	ra'kevet	רַכֶּבֶת (נ)
train station	taχanat ra'kevet	תַּחֲנַת רַכֶּבֶת (נ)

15

82. Sightseeing

monument	an'darta	אַנְדַּרְטָה (נ)
fortress	mivtsar	מִבְצָר (ז)
palace	armon	אַרְמוֹן (ז)
castle	tira	טִירָה (נ)
tower	migdal	מִגְדָּל (ז)
mausoleum	ma'uzo'le'um	מָאוּזוֹלֵיאוֹם (ז)

architecture	adrixalut	אַדְרִיכָלוּת (נ)
medieval (adj)	benaimi	בֵּינַיְימִי
ancient (adj)	atik	עַתִּיק
national (adj)	le'umi	לְאוּמִי
famous (monument, etc.)	mefursam	מְפוּרְסָם

tourist	tayar	תַּיָּיר (ז)
guide (person)	madrix tiyulim	מַדְרִיךְ טִיוּלִים (ז)
excursion, sightseeing tour	tiyul	טִיּוּל (ז)
to show (vt)	lehar'ot	לְהַרְאוֹת
to tell (vt)	lesaper	לְסַפֵּר

to find (vt)	limtso	לִמְצוֹא
to get lost (lose one's way)	la'lexet le'ibud	לָלֶכֶת לְאִיבּוּד
map (e.g., subway ~)	mapa	מַפָּה (נ)
map (e.g., city ~)	tarfim	תַּרְשִׁים (ז)

souvenir, gift	maz'keret	מַזְכֶּרֶת (נ)
gift shop	xanut matanot	חֲנוּת מַתָּנוֹת (נ)
to take pictures	letsalem	לְצַלֵּם
to have one's picture taken	lehitstalem	לְהִצְטַלֵּם

83. Shopping

to buy (purchase)	liknot	לִקְנוֹת
purchase	kniya	קְנִיָּה (נ)
to go shopping	la'lexet lekniyot	לָלֶכֶת לִקְנִיּוֹת
shopping	arixat kniyot	עֲרִיכַת קְנִיּוֹת (נ)

| to be open (ab. store) | pa'tuax | פָּתוּחַ |
| to be closed | sagur | סָגוּר |

footwear, shoes	na'a'layim	נַעֲלַיִים (נ"ר)
clothes, clothing	bgadim	בְּגָדִים (ז"ר)
cosmetics	tamrukim	תַּמְרוּקִים (ז"ר)
food products	mutsrei mazon	מוּצְרֵי מָזוֹן (ז"ר)
gift, present	matana	מַתָּנָה (נ)

| salesman | moxer | מוֹכֵר (ז) |
| saleswoman | mo'xeret | מוֹכֶרֶת (נ) |

check out, cash desk	kupa	קוּפָּה (נ)
mirror	mar'a	מַרְאָה (נ)
counter (store ~)	duχan	דוּכָן (ז)
fitting room	'χeder halbaʃa	חֶדֶר הַלְבָּשָׁה (ז)
to try on	limdod	לִמְדוֹד
to fit (ab. dress, etc.)	lehat'im	לְהַתְאִים
to like (I like …)	limtso χen be'ei'nayim	לִמְצוֹא חֵן בְּעֵינַיִים
price	meχir	מְחִיר (ז)
price tag	tag meχir	תָּג מְחִיר (ז)
to cost (vt)	la'alot	לַעֲלוֹת
How much?	'kama?	כַּמָה?
discount	hanaχa	הֲנָחָה (נ)
inexpensive (adj)	lo yakar	לֹא יָקָר
cheap (adj)	zol	זוֹל
expensive (adj)	yakar	יָקָר
It's expensive	ze yakar	זֶה יָקָר
rental (n)	haskara	הַשְׂכָּרָה (נ)
to rent (~ a tuxedo)	liskor	לִשְׂכּוֹר
credit (trade credit)	aʃrai	אַשְׁרַאי (ז)
on credit (adv)	be'aʃrai	בְּאַשְׁרַאי

84. Money

money	'kesef	כֶּסֶף (ז)
currency exchange	hamara	הֲמָרָה (נ)
exchange rate	'ʃa'ar χalifin	שַׁעַר חֲלִיפִין (ז)
ATM	kaspomat	כַּספּוֹמָט (ז)
coin	mat'be'a	מַטְבֵּעַ (ז)
dollar	'dolar	דוֹלָר (ז)
euro	'eiro	אֵירוֹ (ז)
lira	'lira	לִירָה (נ)
Deutschmark	mark germani	מַרק גֶרְמָנִי (ז)
franc	frank	פְרַנק (ז)
pound sterling	'lira 'sterling	לִירָה שְׁטֶרְלִינג (נ)
yen	yen	יֶן (ז)
debt	χov	חוֹב (ז)
debtor	'ba'al χov	בַּעַל חוֹב (ז)
to lend (money)	lehalvot	לְהַלְווֹת
to borrow (vi, vt)	lilvot	לִלְווֹת
bank	bank	בַּנק (ז)
account	χeʃbon	חֶשְׁבּוֹן (ז)
to deposit (vt)	lehafkid	לְהַפְקִיד

to deposit into the account	lehafkid lexeʃbon	לְהַפְקִיד לְחֶשְבּוֹן
to withdraw (vt)	limʃox mexeʃbon	לִמשוֹך מֵחֶשבּוֹן
credit card	kartis aʃrai	כַּרְטִיס אַשרַאי (ז)
cash	mezuman	מְזוּמָן
check	tʃek	צֶ'ק (ז)
to write a check	lixtov tʃek	לִכתוֹב צֶ'ק
checkbook	pinkas 'tʃekim	פִּנקָס צֶ'קִים (ז)
wallet	arnak	אַרְנָק (ז)
change purse	arnak lematbe''ot	אַרְנָק לְמַטבְּעוֹת (ז)
safe	ka'sefet	כַּסֶפֶת (נ)
heir	yoreʃ	יוֹרֵש (ז)
inheritance	yeruʃa	יְרוּשָה (נ)
fortune (wealth)	'oʃer	עוֹשֶר (ז)
lease	xoze sxirut	חוֹזֶה שׂכִירוּת (ז)
rent (money)	sxar dira	שׂכַר דִירָה (ז)
to rent (sth from sb)	liskor	לִשׂכּוֹר
price	mexir	מְחִיר (ז)
cost	alut	עֲלוּת (נ)
sum	sxum	סְכוּם (ז)
to spend (vt)	lehotsi	לְהוֹצִיא
expenses	hotsa'ot	הוֹצָאוֹת (נ"ר)
to economize (vi, vt)	laxasox	לַחֲסוֹך
economical	xesxoni	חֶסְכוֹנִי
to pay (vi, vt)	leʃalem	לְשַלֵם
payment	taʃlum	תַשלוּם (ז)
change (give the ~)	'odef	עוֹדֶף (ז)
tax	mas	מַס (ז)
fine	knas	קנָס (ז)
to fine (vt)	liknos	לִקנוֹס

85. Post. Postal service

post office	'do'ar	דוֹאַר (ז)
mail (letters, etc.)	'do'ar	דוֹאַר (ז)
mailman	davar	דַוָר (ז)
opening hours	ʃa'ot avoda	שְעוֹת עֲבוֹדָה (נ"ר)
letter	mixtav	מִכתָב (ז)
registered letter	mixtav raʃum	מִכתָב רָשוּם (ז)
postcard	gluya	גלוּיָה (נ)
telegram	mivrak	מִברָק (ז)
package (parcel)	xavila	חֲבִילָה (נ)

money transfer	ha'avarat ksafim	הַעֲבָרַת כְּסָפִים (נ)
to receive (vt)	lekabel	לְקַבֵּל
to send (vt)	liʃ'loax	לִשְׁלוֹחַ
sending	ʃlixa	שְׁלִיחָה (נ)

address	'ktovet	כְּתוֹבֶת (נ)
ZIP code	mikud	מִיקוּד (ז)
sender	ʃo'leax	שׁוֹלֵחַ (ז)
receiver	nim'an	נִמְעָן (ז)

| name (first name) | ʃem prati | שֵׁם פְּרָטִי (ז) |
| surname (last name) | ʃem miʃpaxa | שֵׁם מִשְׁפָּחָה (ז) |

postage rate	ta'arif	תַּעֲרִיף (ז)
standard (adj)	ragil	רָגִיל
economical (adj)	xesxoni	חֶסְכוֹנִי

weight	miʃkal	מִשְׁקָל (ז)
to weigh (~ letters)	liʃkol	לִשְׁקוֹל
envelope	ma'atafa	מַעֲטָפָה (נ)
postage stamp	bul 'do'ar	בּוּל דּוֹאַר (ז)
to stamp an envelope	lehadbik bul	לְהַדְבִּיק בּוּל

Dwelling. House. Home

86. House. Dwelling

house	'bayit	בַּיִת (ז)
at home (adv)	ba'bayit	בַּבַּיִת
yard	χatser	חָצֵר (נ)
fence (iron ~)	gader	גָּדֵר (נ)

brick (n)	levena	לְבֵנָה (נ)
brick (as adj)	milevenim	מִלְבֵנִים
stone (n)	'even	אֶבֶן (נ)
stone (as adj)	me''even	מֵאֶבֶן
concrete (n)	beton	בֶּטוֹן (ז)
concrete (as adj)	mibeton	מִבֶּטוֹן

new (new-built)	χadaʃ	חָדָשׁ
old (adj)	yaʃan	יָשָׁן
decrepit (house)	balui	בָּלוּי
modern (adj)	mo'derni	מוֹדֶרְנִי
multistory (adj)	rav komot	רַב־קוֹמוֹת
tall (~ building)	ga'voha	גָּבוֹהַ

floor, story	'koma	קוֹמָה (נ)
single-story (adj)	χad komati	חַד־קוֹמָתִי
1st floor	komat 'karka	קוֹמַת קַרְקַע (נ)
top floor	hakoma ha'elyona	הַקּוֹמָה הָעֶלְיוֹנָה (נ)
roof	gag	גַּג (ז)
chimney	aruba	אֲרוּבָּה (נ)
roof tiles	'ra'af	רַעַף (ז)
tiled (adj)	mere'afim	מְרֻעָפִים
attic (storage place)	aliyat gag	עֲלִיַּת גַּג (נ)

window	χalon	חַלּוֹן (ז)
glass	zχuχit	זְכוּכִית (נ)
window ledge	'eden χalon	אֶדֶן חַלּוֹן (ז)
shutters	trisim	תְּרִיסִים (ז"ר)

wall	kir	קִיר (ז)
balcony	mir'peset	מִרְפֶּסֶת (נ)
downspout	marzev	מַרְזֵב (ז)

upstairs (to be ~)	le'mala	לְמַעְלָה
to go upstairs	la'alot bemadregot	לַעֲלוֹת בְּמַדְרֵגוֹת
to come down (the stairs)	la'redet bemadregot	לָרֶדֶת בְּמַדְרֵגוֹת
to move (to new premises)	la'avor	לַעֲבוֹר

87. House. Entrance. Lift

entrance	knisa	כְּנִיסָה (נ)
stairs (stairway)	madregot	מַדְרֵגוֹת (נ״ר)
steps	madregot	מַדְרֵגוֹת (נ״ר)
banister	ma'ake	מַעֲקֶה (ז)
lobby (hotel ~)	'lobi	לוֹבִּי (ז)
mailbox	teivat 'do'ar	תֵּיבַת דוֹאַר (נ)
garbage can	paχ 'zevel	פַּח זֶבֶל (ז)
trash chute	merik aʃpa	מֵרִיק אַשְׁפָּה (ז)
elevator	ma'alit	מַעֲלִית (נ)
freight elevator	ma'alit masa	מַעֲלִית מַשָׂא (נ)
elevator cage	ta ma'alit	תָּא מַעֲלִית (ז)
to take the elevator	lin'so'a bema'alit	לִנְסוֹעַ בְּמַעֲלִית
apartment	dira	דִּירָה (נ)
residents (~ of a building)	dayarim	דַּיָּירִים (ז״ר)
neighbor (masc.)	ʃaχen	שָׁכֵן (ז)
neighbor (fem.)	ʃχena	שְׁכֵנָה (נ)
neighbors	ʃχenim	שְׁכֵנִים (ז״ר)

88. House. Electricity

electricity	χaʃmal	חַשְׁמַל (ז)
light bulb	nura	נוּרָה (נ)
switch	'meteg	מֶתֶג (ז)
fuse (plug fuse)	natiχ	נָתִיךְ (ז)
cable, wire (electric ~)	χut	חוּט (ז)
wiring	χivut	חִיווּט (ז)
electricity meter	mone χaʃmal	מוֹנֶה חַשְׁמַל (ז)
readings	kri'a	קְרִיאָה (נ)

89. House. Doors. Locks

door	'delet	דֶּלֶת (נ)
gate (vehicle ~)	'ʃa'ar	שַׁעַר (ז)
handle, doorknob	yadit	יָדִית (נ)
to unlock (unbolt)	lif'toaχ	לִפְתּוֹחַ
to open (vt)	lif'toaχ	לִפְתּוֹחַ
to close (vt)	lisgor	לִסְגּוֹר
key	maf'teaχ	מַפְתֵּחַ (ז)
bunch (of keys)	tsror mafteχot	צְרוֹר מַפְתְּחוֹת (ז)
to creak (door, etc.)	laχarok	לַחֲרוֹק

creak	χarika	חֲרִיקָה (נ)
hinge (door ~)	tsir	צִיר (ז)
doormat	ʃtiχon	שְׁטִיחוֹן (ז)

door lock	man'ul	מַנְעוּל (ז)
keyhole	χor haman'ul	חוֹר הַמַנְעוּל (ז)
crossbar (sliding bar)	'briaχ	בְּרִיחַ (ז)
door latch	'briaχ	בְּרִיחַ (ז)
padlock	man'ul	מַנְעוּל (ז)

to ring (~ the door bell)	letsaltsel	לְצַלְצֵל
ringing (sound)	tsiltsul	צִלְצוּל (ז)
doorbell	pa'amon	פַּעֲמוֹן (ז)
doorbell button	kaftor	כַּפְתּוֹר (ז)
knock (at the door)	hakaʃa	הַקָשָׁה (נ)
to knock (vi)	lehakiʃ	לְהַקִישׁ

code	kod	קוֹד (ז)
combination lock	man'ul kod	מַנְעוּל קוֹד (ז)
intercom	'interkom	אִינְטֶרְקוֹם (ז)
number (on the door)	mispar	מִסְפָּר (ז)
doorplate	luχit	לוּחִית (נ)
peephole	einit	עֵינִית (נ)

90. Country house

village	kfar	כְּפָר (ז)
vegetable garden	gan yarak	גַּן יָרָק (ז)
fence	gader	גָּדֵר (נ)

picket fence	gader yetedot	גָּדֵר יְתֵדוֹת (נ)
wicket gate	piʃpaʃ	פִּשְׁפָּשׁ (ז)

granary	asam	אָסָם (ז)
root cellar	martef	מַרְתֵּף (ז)

shed (garden ~)	maχsan	מַחְסָן (ז)
well (water)	be'er	בְּאֵר (נ)

stove (wood-fired ~)	aχ	אָח (נ)
to stoke the stove	lehasik et ha'aχ	לְהַסִיק אֶת הָאָח

firewood	atsei hasaka	עֲצֵי הַסָקָה (ז"ר)
log (firewood)	bul ets	בּוּל עֵץ (ז)

veranda	mir'peset mekora	מִרְפֶּסֶת מְקוֹרָה (נ)
deck (terrace)	mir'peset	מִרְפֶּסֶת (נ)

stoop (front steps)	madregot ba'petaχ 'bayit	מַדְרֵגוֹת בַּפֶּתַח בַּיִת (נ"ר)
swing (hanging seat)	nadneda	נַדְנֵדָה (נ)

91. Villa. Mansion

country house	'bayit bakfar	בָּיִת בַּכְּפָר (ז)
villa (seaside ~)	'vila	וִילָה (נ)
wing (~ of a building)	agaf	אֲגַף (ז)

garden	gan	גַּן (ז)
park	park	פָּארק (ז)
tropical greenhouse	xamama	חֲמָמָה (נ)
to look after (garden, etc.)	legadel	לְגַדֵּל

swimming pool	brexat sxiya	בְּרֵיכַת שְׂחִיָּה (נ)
gym (home gym)	'xeder 'kofer	חֶדֶר כּוֹשֶׁר (ז)
tennis court	migraf 'tenis	מִגְרַשׁ טֶנִיס (ז)
home theater (room)	'xeder hakrana beiti	חֶדֶר הַקְרָנָה בֵּיתִי (ז)
garage	musax	מוּסָךְ (ז)

private property	rexuf prati	רְכוּשׁ פְּרָטִי (ז)
private land	'fetax prati	שֶׁטַח פְּרָטִי (ז)

warning (caution)	azhara	אַזְהָרָה (נ)
warning sign	'felet azhara	שֶׁלֶט אַזְהָרָה (ז)

security	avtaxa	אַבְטָחָה (נ)
security guard	fomer	שׁוֹמֵר (ז)
burglar alarm	ma'a'rexet az'aka	מַעֲרֶכֶת אַזְעָקָה (נ)

92. Castle. Palace

castle	tira	טִירָה (נ)
palace	armon	אַרְמוֹן (ז)
fortress	mivtsar	מִבְצָר (ז)

wall (round castle)	xoma	חוֹמָה (נ)
tower	migdal	מִגְדָּל (ז)
keep, donjon	migdal merkazi	מִגְדָּל מֶרְכַּזִי (ז)

portcullis	'fa'ar anaxi	שַׁעַר אֲנָכִי (ז)
underground passage	ma'avar tat karka'i	מַעֲבָר תַּת־קַרְקָעִי (ז)
moat	xafir	חָפִיר (ז)

chain	fal'felet	שַׁלְשֶׁלֶת (נ)
arrow loop	efnav 'yeri	אֶשְׁנַב יֶרִי (ז)

magnificent (adj)	mefo'ar	מְפוֹאָר
majestic (adj)	malxuti	מַלְכוּתִי

impregnable (adj)	'bilti xadir	בִּלְתִּי חָדִיר
medieval (adj)	benaimi	בֵּינַיְמִי

93. Apartment

apartment	dira	דִּירָה (נ)
room	'xeder	חֶדֶר (ז)
bedroom	xadar ʃena	חֲדַר שֵׁינָה (ז)
dining room	pinat 'oxel	פִּינַת אוֹכֶל (נ)
living room	salon	סָלוֹן (ז)
study (home office)	xadar avoda	חֲדַר עֲבוֹדָה (ז)
entry room	prozdor	פְּרוֹזְדוֹר (ז)
bathroom (room with a bath or shower)	xadar am'batya	חֲדַר אַמְבַּטְיָה (ז)
half bath	ʃerutim	שֵׁירוּתִים (ז"ר)
ceiling	tikra	תִּקְרָה (נ)
floor	ritspa	רִצְפָּה (נ)
corner	pina	פִּינָה (נ)

94. Apartment. Cleaning

to clean (vi, vt)	lenakot	לְנַקּוֹת
to put away (to stow)	lefanot	לְפַנּוֹת
dust	avak	אָבָק (ז)
dusty (adj)	me'ubak	מְאוּבָּק
to dust (vt)	lenakot avak	לְנַקּוֹת אָבָק
vacuum cleaner	ʃo'ev avak	שׁוֹאֵב אָבָק (ז)
to vacuum (vt)	liʃov avak	לִשְׁאוֹב אָבָק
to sweep (vi, vt)	letate	לְטַאטֵא
sweepings	'psolet ti'tu	פְּסוֹלֶת טִאטוּא (נ)
order	'seder	סֵדֶר (ז)
disorder, mess	i 'seder	אִי סֵדֶר (ז)
mop	magev im smartut	מַגֵּב עִם סְמַרְטוּט (ז)
dust cloth	smartut avak	סְמַרְטוּט אָבָק (ז)
short broom	mat'ate katan	מַטְאֲטֵא קָטָן (ז)
dustpan	ya'e	יָעֶה (ז)

95. Furniture. Interior

furniture	rehitim	רָהִיטִים (ז"ר)
table	ʃulxan	שׁוּלְחָן (ז)
chair	kise	כִּסֵּא (ז)
bed	mita	מִיטָה (נ)
couch, sofa	sapa	סַפָּה (נ)
armchair	kursa	כּוּרְסָה (נ)
bookcase	aron sfarim	אֲרוֹן סְפָרִים (ז)

shelf	madaf	מַדָף (ז)
wardrobe	aron bgadim	אָרוֹן בּגָדִים (ז)
coat rack (wall-mounted ~)	mitle	מִתלֶה (ז)
coat stand	mitle	מִתלֶה (ז)
bureau, dresser	ʃida	שִׁידָה (נ)
coffee table	ʃulχan itonim	שׁוּלחַן עִיתוֹנִים (ז)
mirror	mar'a	מַרְאָה (נ)
carpet	ʃa'tiaχ	שָׁטִיחַ (ז)
rug, small carpet	ʃa'tiaχ	שָׁטִיחַ (ז)
fireplace	aχ	אָח (נ)
candle	ner	נֵר (ז)
candlestick	pamot	פָמוֹט (ז)
drapes	vilonot	וִילוֹנוֹת (ז״ר)
wallpaper	tapet	טַפֵּט (ז)
blinds (jalousie)	trisim	תרִיסִים (ז״ר)
table lamp	menorat ʃulχan	מְנוֹרַת שׁוּלחָן (נ)
wall lamp (sconce)	menorat kir	מְנוֹרַת קִיר (נ)
floor lamp	menora o'medet	מְנוֹרָה עוֹמֶדֶת (נ)
chandelier	niv'reʃet	נִברֶשֶׁת (נ)
leg (of chair, table)	'regel	רֶגֶל (נ)
armrest	miʃ'enet yad	מִשׁעֶנֶת יָד (נ)
back (backrest)	miʃ'enet	מִשׁעֶנֶת (נ)
drawer	megera	מְגֵירָה (נ)

96. Bedding

bedclothes	matsa'im	מַצָעִים (ז״ר)
pillow	karit	כָּרִית (נ)
pillowcase	tsipit	צִיפִּית (נ)
duvet, comforter	smiχa	שׂמִיכָה (נ)
sheet	sadin	סָדִין (ז)
bedspread	kisui mita	כִּיסוּי מִיטָה (ז)

97. Kitchen

kitchen	mitbaχ	מִטבָּח (ז)
gas	gaz	גָז (ז)
gas stove (range)	tanur gaz	תַנוּר גָז (ז)
electric stove	tanur χaʃmali	תַנוּר חַשׁמַלִי (ז)
oven	tanur afiya	תַנוּר אֲפִיָה (ז)
microwave oven	mikrogal	מִיקרוֹגַל (ז)
refrigerator	mekarer	מְקָרֵר (ז)

freezer	makpi	מַקְפִּיא (ז)
dishwasher	me'diax kelim	מֵדִיחַ כֵּלִים (ז)
meat grinder	matxenat basar	מַטְחֵנַת בָּשָׂר (נ)
juicer	masxeta	מַסְחֵטָה (נ)
toaster	'toster	טוֹסְטֶר (ז)
mixer	'mikser	מִיקְסֵר (ז)
coffee machine	mexonat kafe	מְכוֹנַת קָפֶה (נ)
coffee pot	findʒan	פִינְגִ'אן (ז)
coffee grinder	matxenat kafe	מַטְחֵנַת קָפֶה (נ)
kettle	kumkum	קוּמְקוּם (ז)
teapot	kumkum	קוּמְקוּם (ז)
lid	mixse	מִכְסֶה (ז)
tea strainer	mis'nenet te	מְסַנֶּנֶת תֵּה (נ)
spoon	kaf	כַּף (נ)
teaspoon	kapit	כַּפִּית (נ)
soup spoon	kaf	כַּף (נ)
fork	mazleg	מַזְלֵג (ז)
knife	sakin	סַכִּין (ז, נ)
tableware (dishes)	kelim	כֵּלִים (ז"ר)
plate (dinner ~)	tsa'laxat	צַלַּחַת (נ)
saucer	taxtit	תַּחְתִּית (נ)
shot glass	kosit	כּוֹסִית (נ)
glass (tumbler)	kos	כּוֹס (נ)
cup	'sefel	סֵפֶל (ז)
sugar bowl	mis'keret	מִסְכֶּרֶת (נ)
salt shaker	milxiya	מִלְחִיָּה (נ)
pepper shaker	pilpeliya	פִּלְפְּלִיָּה (נ)
butter dish	maxame'a	מַחֲמָאָה (ז)
stock pot (soup pot)	sir	סִיר (ז)
frying pan (skillet)	maxvat	מַחֲבַת (נ)
ladle	tarvad	תַּרְוָד (ז)
colander	mis'nenet	מְסַנֶּנֶת (נ)
tray (serving ~)	magaʃ	מַגָּשׁ (ז)
bottle	bakbuk	בַּקְבּוּק (ז)
jar (glass)	tsin'tsenet	צִנְצֶנֶת (נ)
can	paxit	פַּחִית (נ)
bottle opener	potxan bakbukim	פּוֹתְחָן בַּקְבּוּקִים (ז)
can opener	potxan kufsa'ot	פּוֹתְחָן קוּפְסָאוֹת (ז)
corkscrew	maxlets	מַחְלֵץ (ז)
filter	'filter	פִילְטֶר (ז)
to filter (vt)	lesanen	לְסַנֵּן
trash, garbage (food waste, etc.)	'zevel	זֶבֶל (ז)
trash can (kitchen ~)	pax 'zevel	פַּח זֶבֶל (ז)

98. Bathroom

bathroom	χadar am'batya	חֲדַר אַמְבַּטְיָה (ז)
water	'mayim	מַיִם (ז"ר)
faucet	'berez	בֶּרֶז (ז)
hot water	'mayim χamim	מַיִם חַמִּים (ז"ר)
cold water	'mayim karim	מַיִם קָרִים (ז"ר)
toothpaste	mifχat ʃi'nayim	מִשְׁחַת שִׁינַיִים (נ)
to brush one's teeth	letsaχ'tseaχ ʃi'nayim	לְצַחְצֵחַ שִׁינַיִים
toothbrush	miv'reʃet ʃi'nayim	מִבְרֶשֶׁת שִׁינַיִים (נ)
to shave (vi)	lehitga'leaχ	לְהִתְגַּלֵּחַ
shaving foam	'ketsef gi'luaχ	קֶצֶף גִּילּוּחַ (ז)
razor	'ta'ar	תַּעַר (ז)
to wash (one's hands, etc.)	liʃtof	לִשְׁטוֹף
to take a bath	lehitraχets	לְהִתְרַחֵץ
shower	mik'laχat	מִקְלַחַת (נ)
to take a shower	lehitka'leaχ	לְהִתְקַלֵּחַ
bathtub	am'batya	אַמְבַּטְיָה (נ)
toilet (toilet bowl)	asla	אַסְלָה (נ)
sink (washbasin)	kiyor	כִּיּוֹר (ז)
soap	sabon	סַבּוֹן (ז)
soap dish	saboniya	סַבּוֹנִייָה (נ)
sponge	sfog 'lifa	סְפוֹג לִיפָה (ז)
shampoo	ʃampu	שַׁמְפּוּ (ז)
towel	ma'gevet	מַגֶּבֶת (נ)
bathrobe	χaluk raχatsa	חָלוּק רַחְצָה (ז)
laundry (process)	kvisa	כְּבִיסָה (נ)
washing machine	meχonat kvisa	מְכוֹנַת כְּבִיסָה (נ)
to do the laundry	leχabes	לְכַבֵּס
laundry detergent	avkat kvisa	אַבְקַת כְּבִיסָה (נ)

99. Household appliances

TV set	tele'vizya	טֶלֶוִוִיזְיָה (נ)
tape recorder	teip	טֵייפּ (ז)
VCR (video recorder)	maχʃir 'vide'o	מַכְשִׁיר וִידֵאוֹ (ז)
radio	'radyo	רַדְיוֹ (ז)
player (CD, MP3, etc.)	nagan	נַגָּן (ז)
video projector	makren	מַקְרֵן (ז)
home movie theater	kol'no'a beiti	קוֹלְנוֹעַ בֵּיתִי (ז)
DVD player	nagan dividi	נַגָּן DVD (ז)

| amplifier | magber | מַגְבֵּר (ז) |
| video game console | maxʃir plei'steiʃen | מַכְשִׁיר פְּלֵייסְטֵיישֶׁן (ז) |

video camera	matslemat 'vide'o	מַצְלֵמַת וִידֵאוֹ (נ)
camera (photo)	matslema	מַצְלֵמָה (נ)
digital camera	matslema digi'talit	מַצְלֵמָה דִיגִיטָלִית (נ)

vacuum cleaner	ʃo'ev avak	שׁוֹאֵב אָבָק (ז)
iron (e.g., steam ~)	maghets	מַגְהֵץ (ז)
ironing board	'kereʃ gihuts	קֶרֶשׁ גִיהוּץ (ז)

telephone	'telefon	טֶלֶפוֹן (ז)
cell phone	'telefon nayad	טֶלֶפוֹן נַייָד (ז)
typewriter	meχonat ktiva	מְכוֹנַת כְּתִיבָה (נ)
sewing machine	meχonat tfira	מְכוֹנַת תְּפִירָה (נ)

microphone	mikrofon	מִיקְרוֹפוֹן (ז)
headphones	ozniyot	אוֹזְנִיוֹת (נ״ר)
remote control (TV)	'ʃelet	שֶׁלֶט (ז)

CD, compact disc	taklitor	תַקְלִיטוֹר (ז)
cassette, tape	ka'letet	קַלֶטֶת (נ)
vinyl record	taklit	תַקְלִיט (ז)

100. Repairs. Renovation

renovations	ʃiputs	שִׁיפּוּץ (ז)
to renovate (vt)	leʃapets	לְשַׁפֵּץ
to repair, to fix (vt)	letaken	לְתַקֵן
to put in order	lesader	לְסַדֵר
to redo (do again)	la'asot meχadaʃ	לַעֲשׂוֹת מֵחָדָשׁ

paint	'tseva	צֶבַע (ז)
to paint (~ a wall)	lits'bo'a	לִצְבּוֹעַ
house painter	tsaba'i	צַבָּעִי (ז)
paintbrush	mikχol	מִכְחוֹל (ז)
whitewash	sid	סִיד (ז)
to whitewash (vt)	lesayed	לְסַייֵד

wallpaper	tapet	טַפֵּט (ז)
to wallpaper (vt)	lehadbik ta'petim	לְהַדְבִּיק טַפֵּטִים
varnish	'laka	לַכָּה (נ)
to varnish (vt)	lim'roaχ 'laka	לִמְרוֹחַ לַכָּה

101. Plumbing

| water | 'mayim | מַיִם (ז״ר) |
| hot water | 'mayim χamim | מַיִם חַמִים (ז״ר) |

cold water	'mayim karim	מַיִם קָרִים (ז״ר)
faucet	'berez	בֶּרֶז (ז)
drop (of water)	tipa	טִיפָּה (נ)
to drip (vi)	letaftef	לְטַפְטֵף
to leak (ab. pipe)	lidlof	לִדלוֹף
leak (pipe ~)	dlifa	דלִיפָה (נ)
puddle	ʃlulit	שלוּלִית (נ)
pipe	tsinor	צִינוֹר (ז)
valve (e.g., ball ~)	'berez	בֶּרֶז (ז)
to be clogged up	lehisatem	לְהִיסָתֵם
tools	klei avoda	כּלֵי עֲבוֹדָה (ז״ר)
adjustable wrench	maf'teaχ mitkavnen	מַפּתֵחַ מִתכַּוונֵן (ז)
to unscrew (lid, filter, etc.)	lif'toaχ	לִפתוֹחַ
to screw (tighten)	lehavrig	לְהַברִיג
to unclog (vt)	lif'toaχ et hastima	לִפתוֹחַ אֶת הַסתִימָה
plumber	ʃravrav	שרַברָב (ז)
basement	martef	מַרתֵף (ז)
sewerage (system)	biyuv	בִּיוּב (ז)

102. Fire. Conflagration

fire (accident)	srefa	שׂרֵיפָה (נ)
flame	lehava	לֶהָבָה (נ)
spark	nitsots	נִיצוֹץ (ז)
smoke (from fire)	aʃan	עָשָן (ז)
torch (flaming stick)	lapid	לַפִּיד (ז)
campfire	medura	מְדוּרָה (נ)
gas, gasoline	'delek	דֶלֶק (ז)
kerosene (type of fuel)	kerosin	קֶרוֹסִין (ז)
flammable (adj)	dalik	דָלִיק
explosive (adj)	nafits	נָפִיץ
NO SMOKING	asur le'aʃen!	אָסוּר לְעַשֵן!
safety	betiχut	בְּטִיחוּת (נ)
danger	sakana	סַכָּנָה (נ)
dangerous (adj)	mesukan	מְסוּכָּן
to catch fire	lehidalek	לְהִידָלֵק
explosion	pitsuts	פִּיצוּץ (ז)
to set fire	lehatsit	לְהַצִית
arsonist	matsit	מַצִית (ז)
arson	hatsata	הַצָתָה (נ)
to blaze (vi)	liv'or	לִבעוֹר
to burn (be on fire)	la'alot be'eʃ	לַעֲלוֹת בָּאֵש

to burn down	lehisaref	לְהִישָׂרֵף
to call the fire department	lehazmin meχabei eʃ	לְהַזְמִין מְכַבֵּי אֵש
firefighter, fireman	kabai	כַּבַּאי (ז)
fire truck	'reχev kibui	רֶכֶב כִּיבּוּי (ז)
fire department	meχabei eʃ	מְכַבֵּי אֵש (ז״ר)
fire truck ladder	sulam kaba'im	סוּלַם כַּבָּאים (ז)
fire hose	zarnuk	זַרְנוּק (ז)
fire extinguisher	mataf	מַטָף (ז)
helmet	kasda	קַסְדָה (נ)
siren	tsofar	צוֹפָר (ז)
to cry (for help)	lits'ok	לִצְעוֹק
to call for help	likro le'ezra	לִקְרוֹא לְעֶזְרָה
rescuer	matsil	מַצִיל (ז)
to rescue (vt)	lehatsil	לְהַצִיל
to arrive (vi)	leha'gi'a	לְהַגִיעַ
to extinguish (vt)	leχabot	לְכַבּוֹת
water	'mayim	מַיִם (ז״ר)
sand	χol	חוֹל (ז)
ruins (destruction)	χoravot	חוֹרְבוֹת (נ״ר)
to collapse (building, etc.)	likros	לִקְרוֹס
to fall down (vi)	likros	לִקְרוֹס
to cave in (ceiling, floor)	lehitmotet	לְהִתְמוֹטֵט
piece of debris	pisat χoravot	פִּיסַת חוֹרְבוֹת (נ)
ash	'efer	אֵפֶר (ז)
to suffocate (die)	lehiχanek	לְהֵיחָנֵק
to be killed (perish)	lehihareg	לְהֵיהָרֵג

HUMAN ACTIVITIES

Job. Business. Part 1

103. Office. Working in the office

office (company ~)	misrad	מִשְׂרָד (ז)
office (of director, etc.)	misrad	מִשְׂרָד (ז)
reception desk	kabala	קַבָּלָה (נ)
secretary	mazkir	מַזְכִּיר (ז)
secretary (fem.)	mazkira	מַזְכִּירָה (נ)
director	menahel	מְנַהֵל (ז)
manager	menahel	מְנַהֵל (ז)
accountant	menahel xeʃbonot	מְנַהֵל חֶשְׁבּוֹנוֹת (ז)
employee	oved	עוֹבֵד (ז)
furniture	rehitim	רָהִיטִים (ז״ר)
desk	ʃulxan	שׁוּלְחָן (ז)
desk chair	kursa	כּוּרְסָה (נ)
drawer unit	ʃidat megerot	שִׁידַת מְגֵירוֹת (נ)
coat stand	mitle	מִתְלֶה (ז)
computer	maxʃev	מַחְשֵׁב (ז)
printer	mad'peset	מַדְפֶּסֶת (נ)
fax machine	faks	פַקְס (ז)
photocopier	mexonat tsilum	מְכוֹנַת צִילוּם (נ)
paper	neyar	נְיָיר (ז)
office supplies	tsiyud misradi	צִיוּד מִשְׂרָדִי (ז)
mouse pad	ʃa'tiax le'axbar	שְׁטִיחַ לְעַכְבָּר (ז)
sheet (of paper)	daf	דַף (ז)
binder	klaser	קְלָסֵר (ז)
catalog	katalog	קָטָלוֹג (ז)
phone directory	madrix 'telefon	מַדְרִיךְ טֶלֶפוֹן (ז)
documentation	ti'ud	תִיעוּד (ז)
brochure (e.g., 12 pages ~)	xo'veret	חוֹבֶרֶת (נ)
leaflet (promotional ~)	alon	עָלוֹן (ז)
sample	dugma	דוּגְמָה (נ)
training meeting	yeʃivat hadraxa	יְשִׁיבַת הַדְרָכָה (נ)
meeting (of managers)	yeʃiva	יְשִׁיבָה (נ)
lunch time	hafsakat tsaha'rayim	הַפְסָקַת צָהֳרַיִים (נ)

to make a copy	letsalem mismax	לְצַלֵם מִסמָך
to make multiple copies	lehaxin mispar otakim	לְהָכִין מִספָּר עוֹתָקִים
to receive a fax	lekabel faks	לְקַבֵּל פָקס
to send a fax	lifloax faks	לְשלוֹחַ פָקס
to call (by phone)	lehitkafer	לְהִתקַשֵר
to answer (vt)	la'anot	לַעֲנוֹת
to put through	lekafer	לְקַשֵר
to arrange, to set up	lik'bo'a pgifa	לִקבּוֹעַ פּגִישָה
to demonstrate (vt)	lehadgim	לְהַדגִים
to be absent	lehe'ader	לְהֵיעָדֵר
absence	he'adrut	הֵיעָדרוּת (נ)

104. Business processes. Part 1

business	'esek	עֵסֶק (ז)
occupation	isuk	עִיסוּק (ז)
firm	xevra	חֶברָה (נ)
company	xevra	חֶברָה (נ)
corporation	ta'agid	תַאֲגִיד (ז)
enterprise	'esek	עֵסֶק (ז)
agency	soxnut	סוֹכנוּת (נ)
agreement (contract)	heskem	הֶסכֵּם (ז)
contract	xoze	חוֹזֶה (ז)
deal	iska	עסקָה (נ)
order (to place an ~)	hazmana	הַזמָנָה (נ)
terms (of the contract)	tnai	תנַאי (ז)
wholesale (adv)	besitonut	בְּסִיטוֹנוּת
wholesale (adj)	sitona'i	סִיטוֹנָאִי
wholesale (n)	sitonut	סִיטוֹנוּת (נ)
retail (adj)	kim'oni	קמעוֹנִי
retail (n)	kim'onut	קמעוֹנוּת (נ)
competitor	mitxare	מִתחָרֶה (ז)
competition	taxarut	תַחֲרוּת (נ)
to compete (vi)	lehitxarot	לְהִתחָרוֹת
partner (associate)	futaf	שוּתָף (ז)
partnership	futafa	שוּתָפוּת (נ)
crisis	mafber	מַשבֵּר (ז)
bankruptcy	pfitat 'regel	פּשִיטַת רֶגֶל (נ)
to go bankrupt	liffot 'regel	לִפשוֹט רֶגֶל
difficulty	'kofi	קוֹשִי (ז)
problem	be'aya	בְּעָיָה (נ)
catastrophe	ason	אָסוֹן (ז)
economy	kalkala	כַּלכָּלָה (נ)

| economic (~ growth) | kalkali | כַּלְכָּלִי |
| economic recession | mitun kalkali | מִיתוּן כַּלְכָּלִי (ז) |

| goal (aim) | matara | מַטָרָה (נ) |
| task | mesima | מְשִׂימָה (נ) |

to trade (vi)	lisxor	לִסְחוֹר
network (distribution ~)	'reʃet	רֶשֶת (נ)
inventory (stock)	maxsan	מַחְסָן (ז)
range (assortment)	mivxar	מִבְחָר (ז)

leader (leading company)	manhig	מַנְהִיג (ז)
large (~ company)	gadol	גָדוֹל
monopoly	'monopol	מוֹנוֹפּוֹל (ז)

theory	te''orya	תֵיאוֹרְיָה (נ)
practice	'praktika	פְּרַקְטִיקָה (נ)
experience (in my ~)	nisayon	נִיסָיוֹן (ז)
trend (tendency)	megama	מְגַמָה (נ)
development	pi'tuax	פִּיתוּחַ (ז)

105. Business processes. Part 2

| profit (foregone ~) | 'revax | רֶוַוח (ז) |
| profitable (~ deal) | rivxi | רְוַוחִי |

delegation (group)	miʃ'laxat	מִשְלַחַת (נ)
salary	mas'koret	מַשְׂכּוֹרֶת (נ)
to correct (an error)	letaken	לְתַקֵן
business trip	nesi'a batafkid	נְסִיעָה בַּתַפְקִיד (נ)
commission	amla	עָמְלָה (נ)

to control (vt)	liʃlot	לִשְלוֹט
conference	kinus	כִּינוּס (ז)
license	riʃayon	רִישָיוֹן (ז)
reliable (~ partner)	amin	אָמִין

initiative (undertaking)	yozma	יוֹזְמָה (נ)
norm (standard)	'norma	נוֹרְמָה (נ)
circumstance	nesibot	נְסִיבּוֹת (נ"ר)
duty (of employee)	xova	חוֹבָה (נ)

organization (company)	irgun	אִרְגוּן (ז)
organization (process)	hit'argenut	הִתְאַרְגְנוּת (נ)
organized (adj)	me'urgan	מְאוּרְגָן
cancellation	bitul	בִּיטוּל (ז)
to cancel (call off)	levatel	לְבַטֵל
report (official ~)	dox	דוֹחַ (ז)
patent	patent	פָּטֶנְט (ז)
to patent (obtain patent)	lirʃom patent	לִרְשוֹם פָּטֶנְט

to plan (vt)	letaxnen	לְתַכְנֵן
bonus (money)	'bonus	בּוֹנוּס (ז)
professional (adj)	miktso'i	מִקְצוֹעִי
procedure	'nohal	נוֹהַל (ז)

to examine (contract, etc.)	livxon	לִבְחוֹן
calculation	xiʃuv	חִישׁוּב (ז)
reputation	monitin	מוֹנִיטִין (ז"ר)
risk	sikun	סִיכּוּן (ז)

to manage, to run	lenahel	לְנַהֵל
information	meida	מֵידָע (ז)
property	ba'alut	בַּעֲלוּת (נ)
union	igud	אִיגוּד (ז)

life insurance	bi'tuax xayim	בִּיטוּחַ חַיִים (ז)
to insure (vt)	leva'teax	לְבַטֵחַ
insurance	bi'tuax	בִּיטוּחַ (ז)

auction (~ sale)	mexira 'pombit	מְכִירָה פּוֹמְבִּית (נ)
to notify (inform)	leho'dia	לְהוֹדִיעַ
management (process)	nihul	נִיהוּל (ז)
service (~ industry)	ʃirut	שֵׁירוּת (ז)

forum	'forum	פוֹרוּם (ז)
to function (vi)	letafked	לְתַפְקֵד
stage (phase)	ʃalav	שָׁלָב (ז)
legal (~ services)	miʃpati	מִשְׁפָּטִי
lawyer (legal advisor)	orex din	עוֹרֵךְ דִין (ז)

106. Production. Works

plant	mif'al	מִפְעָל (ז)
factory	beit xa'roʃet	בֵּית חֲרוֹשֶׁת (ז)
workshop	agaf	אֲגַף (ז)
works, production site	mif'al	מִפְעָל (ז)

industry (manufacturing)	ta'asiya	תַעֲשִׂיָה (נ)
industrial (adj)	ta'asiyati	תַעֲשִׂיָיתִי
heavy industry	ta'asiya kveda	תַעֲשִׂיָה כְּבֵדָה (נ)
light industry	ta'asiya kala	תַעֲשִׂיָה קַלָה (נ)

products	to'tseret	תוֹצֶרֶת (נ)
to produce (vt)	leyatser	לְייַצֵר
raw materials	'xomer 'gelem	חוֹמֶר גֶלֶם (ז)

foreman (construction ~)	menahel avoda	מְנַהֵל עֲבוֹדָה (ז)
workers team (crew)	'tsevet ovdim	צֶוֶות עוֹבְדִים (ז)
worker	po'el	פּוֹעֵל (ז)
working day	yom avoda	יוֹם עֲבוֹדָה (ז)

pause (rest break)	hafsaka	הַפְסָקָה (נ)
meeting	yeʃiva	יְשִׁיבָה (נ)
to discuss (vt)	ladun	לָדוּן
plan	toxnit	תוֹכְנִית (נ)
to fulfill the plan	leva'tse'a et hatoxnit	לְבַצֵעַ אֶת הַתוֹכְנִית
rate of output	'ketsev tfuka	קֶצֶב תפוּקָה (ז)
quality	eixut	אֵיכוּת (נ)
control (checking)	bakara	בַּקָרָה (נ)
quality control	bakarat eixut	בַּקָרַת אֵיכוּת (נ)
workplace safety	betixut beavoda	בְּטִיחוּת בָּעֲבוֹדָה (נ)
discipline	miʃma'at	מִשְׁמַעַת (נ)
violation (of safety rules, etc.)	hafara	הֲפָרָה (נ)
to violate (rules)	lehafer	לְהָפֵר
strike	ʃvita	שְׁבִיתָה (נ)
striker	ʃovet	שׁוֹבֵת (ז)
to be on strike	liʃbot	לִשְׁבּוֹת
labor union	igud ovdim	אִיגוּד עוֹבְדִים (ז)
to invent (machine, etc.)	lehamtsi	לְהַמְצִיא
invention	hamtsa'a	הַמְצָאָה (נ)
research	mexkar	מֶחְקָר (ז)
to improve (make better)	leʃaper	לְשַׁפֵּר
technology	texno'logya	טֶכְנוֹלוֹגְיָה (נ)
technical drawing	sirtut	שְׂרְטוּט (ז)
load, cargo	mit'an	מִטְעָן (ז)
loader (person)	sabal	סַבָּל (ז)
to load (vehicle, etc.)	leha'amis	לְהַעֲמִיס
loading (process)	ha'amasa	הַעֲמָסָה (נ)
to unload (vi, vt)	lifrok mit'an	לפְרוֹק מִטְעָן
unloading	prika	פְּרִיקָה (נ)
transportation	hovala	הוֹבָלָה (נ)
transportation company	xevrat hovala	חָבְרַת הוֹבָלָה (נ)
to transport (vt)	lehovil	לְהוֹבִיל
freight car	karon	קָרוֹן (ז)
tank (e.g., oil ~)	mexalit	מֵיכָלִית (נ)
truck	masa'it	מַשָׂאִית (נ)
machine tool	mexonat ibud	מְכוֹנַת עִיבּוּד (נ)
mechanism	manganon	מַנְגָנוֹן (ז)
industrial waste	'psolet ta'asiyatit	פְּסוֹלֶת תַעֲשִׂיָיתִית (נ)
packing (process)	ariza	אֲרִיזָה (נ)
to pack (vt)	le'eroz	לֶאֱרוֹז

107. Contract. Agreement

contract	χoze	חוֹזֶה (ז)
agreement	heskem	הֶסְכֵּם (ז)
addendum	'sefaχ	סְפַח (ז)
to sign a contract	la'aroχ heskem	לַעֲרוֹךְ הֶסְכֵּם
signature	χatima	חֲתִימָה (נ)
to sign (vt)	laχtom	לַחְתּוֹם
seal (stamp)	χo'temet	חוֹתֶמֶת (נ)
subject of contract	nose haχoze	נוֹשֵׂא הַחוֹזֶה (ז)
clause	se'if	סָעִיף (ז)
parties (in contract)	tsdadim	צְדָדִים (ז״ר)
legal address	'ktovet mifpatit	כְּתוֹבֶת מִשְׁפָּטִית (נ)
to violate the contract	lehafer χoze	לְהָפֵר חוֹזֶה
commitment (obligation)	hitχaivut	הִתְחַיְּיבוּת (נ)
responsibility	aχrayut	אַחֲרָיוּת (נ)
force majeure	'koaχ elyon	כּוֹחַ עֶלְיוֹן (ז)
dispute	vi'kuaχ	וִיכּוּחַ (ז)
penalties	itsumim	עִיצוּמִים (ז״ר)

108. Import & Export

import	ye'vu'a	יְבוּא (ז)
importer	yevu'an	יְבוּאָן (ז)
to import (vt)	leyabe	לְיַבֵּא
import (as adj.)	meyuba	מְיוּבָּא
export (exportation)	yitsu	יִיצוּא (ז)
exporter	yetsu'an	יְצוּאָן (ז)
to export (vi, vt)	leyatse	לְיַצֵּא
export (as adj.)	fel yitsu	שֶׁל יִיצוּא
goods (merchandise)	sχora	סְחוֹרָה (נ)
consignment, lot	mif'loaχ	מִשְׁלוֹחַ (ז)
weight	mifkal	מִשְׁקָל (ז)
volume	'nefaχ	נֶפַח (ז)
cubic meter	'meter me'ukav	מֶטֶר מְעוּקָב (ז)
manufacturer	yatsran	יַצְרָן (ז)
transportation company	χevrat hovala	חֶבְרַת הוֹבָלָה (נ)
container	meχula	מְכוּלָה (נ)
border	gvul	גְבוּל (ז)
customs	'meχes	מֶכֶס (ז)
customs duty	mas 'meχes	מַס מֶכֶס (ז)

customs officer	pakid 'meχes	פָּקִיד מֶכֶס (ז)
smuggling	havraχa	הַבְרָחָה (נ)
contraband (smuggled goods)	sχora muv'reχet	סחוֹרָה מוּבְרַחַת (נ)

109. Finances

stock (share)	menaya	מְנָיָה (נ)
bond (certificate)	i'geret χov	אִיגֶּרֶת חוֹב (נ)
promissory note	ʃtar χalifin	שְׁטַר חֲלִיפִין (ז)

| stock exchange | 'bursa | בּוּרְסָה (נ) |
| stock price | meχir hamenaya | מְחִיר הַמְּנָיָה (ז) |

| to go down (become cheaper) | la'redet bemeχir | לָרֶדֶת בְּמְחִיר |
| to go up (become more expensive) | lehityaker | לְהִתְיַיקֵר |

| share | menaya | מְנָיָה (נ) |
| controlling interest | ʃlita | שְׁלִיטָה (נ) |

investment	haʃka'ot	הַשְׁקָעוֹת (נ״ר)
to invest (vt)	lehaʃ'ki'a	לְהַשְׁקִיעַ
percent	aχuz	אָחוּז (ז)
interest (on investment)	ribit	רִיבִּית (נ)

profit	'revaχ	רֶווַח (ז)
profitable (adj)	rivχi	רִווְחִי
tax	mas	מַס (ז)

currency (foreign ~)	mat'be'a	מַטְבֵּעַ (ז)
national (adj)	le'umi	לְאוּמִי
exchange (currency ~)	hamara	הָמָרָה (נ)

| accountant | ro'e χeʃbon | רוֹאֵה חֶשְׁבּוֹן (ז) |
| accounting | hanhalat χeʃbonot | הַנְהָלַת חֶשְׁבּוֹנוֹת (נ) |

bankruptcy	pʃitat 'regel	פְּשִׁיטַת רֶגֶל (נ)
collapse, crash	krisa	קְרִיסָה (נ)
ruin	pʃitat 'regel	פְּשִׁיטַת רֶגֶל (נ)
to be ruined (financially)	lifʃot 'regel	לִפְשׁוֹט רֶגֶל
inflation	inf'latsya	אִינְפְלַצְיָה (נ)
devaluation	piχut	פִּיחוּת (ז)

capital	hon	הוֹן (ז)
income	haχnasa	הַכְנָסָה (נ)
turnover	maχzor	מַחְזוֹר (ז)
resources	maʃabim	מַשְׁאַבִּים (ז״ר)
monetary resources	emtsa'im kaspiyim	אֶמְצָעִים כַּסְפִּיִים (ז״ר)

| overhead | hotsa'ot | הוֹצָאוֹת (נ"ר) |
| to reduce (expenses) | letsamtsem | לְצַמְצֵם |

110. Marketing

marketing	ʃivuk	שִׁיווּק (ז)
market	ʃuk	שׁוּק (ז)
market segment	'pelaχ ʃuk	פֶּלַח שׁוּק (ז)
product	mutsar	מוּצָר (ז)
goods (merchandise)	sχora	סְחוֹרָה (נ)

brand	mutag	מוּתָג (ז)
trademark	'semel misχari	סֶמֶל מִסְחָרִי (ז)
logotype	'semel haχevra	סֶמֶל הַחֶבְרָה (ז)
logo	'logo	לוֹגוֹ (ז)

demand	bikuʃ	בִּיקוּשׁ (ז)
supply	he'tse'a	הֵיצֵעַ (ז)
need	'tsoreχ	צוֹרֶךְ (ז)
consumer	tsarχan	צַרְכָן (ז)

analysis	ni'tuaχ	נִיתוּחַ (ז)
to analyze (vt)	lena'teaχ	לְנַתֵחַ
positioning	mitsuv	מִיצוּב (ז)
to position (vt)	lematsev	לְמַצֵב

price	meχir	מְחִיר (ז)
pricing policy	mediniyut timχur	מְדִינִיוּת תִמְחוּר (נ)
price formation	hamχara	הַמְחָרָה (נ)

111. Advertising

advertising	pirsum	פִּרְסוּם (ז)
to advertise (vt)	lefarsem	לְפַרְסֵם
budget	taktsiv	תַקְצִיב (ז)

ad, advertisement	pir'somet	פִּרְסוֹמֶת (נ)
TV advertising	pir'somet tele'vizya	פִּרְסוֹמֶת טֶלֶווִיזְיָה (נ)
radio advertising	pir'somet 'radyo	פִּרְסוֹמֶת רַדְיוֹ (נ)
outdoor advertising	pirsum χutsot	פִּרְסוּם חוּצוֹת (ז)

mass media	emtsa'ei tik'ʃoret hamonim	אֶמְצָעֵי תִקְשוֹרֶת הָמוֹנִים (ז"ר)
periodical (n)	ktav et	כְּתַב עֵת (ז)
image (public appearance)	tadmit	תַדְמִית (נ)

slogan	sisma	סִיסְמָה (נ)
motto (maxim)	'moto	מוֹטוֹ (ז)
campaign	masa	מַסָע (ז)

advertising campaign	masa pirsum	מַסָע פִּרסוּם (ז)
target group	oxlusiyat 'ya'ad	אוֹכלוּסִיַית יַעַד (נ)
business card	kartis bikur	כַּרטִיס בִּיקוּר (ז)
leaflet (promotional ~)	alon	עָלוֹן (ז)
brochure (e.g., 12 pages ~)	xo'veret	חוֹבֶרֶת (נ)
pamphlet	alon	עָלוֹן (ז)
newsletter	alon meida	עָלוֹן מֵידָע (ז)
signboard (store sign, etc.)	'ʃelet	שֶׁלֶט (ז)
poster	'poster	פּוֹסטֶר (ז)
billboard	'luax pirsum	לוּחַ פִּרסוּם (ז)

112. Banking

bank	bank	בַּנק (ז)
branch (of bank, etc.)	snif	סנִיף (ז)
bank clerk, consultant	yo'ets	יוֹעֵץ (ז)
manager (director)	menahel	מְנַהֵל (ז)
bank account	xeʃbon	חֶשׁבּוֹן (ז)
account number	mispar xeʃbon	מִספָּר חֶשׁבּוֹן (ז)
checking account	xeʃbon over vaʃav	חֶשׁבּוֹן עוֹבֵר וַשָׁב (ז)
savings account	xeʃbon xisaxon	חֶשׁבּוֹן חִסָכוֹן (ז)
to open an account	lif'toax xeʃbon	לִפתוֹחַ חֶשׁבּוֹן
to close the account	lisgor xeʃbon	לִסגוֹר חֶשׁבּוֹן
to deposit into the account	lehafkid lexeʃbon	לְהַפקִיד לְחֶשׁבּוֹן
to withdraw (vt)	limʃox mexeʃbon	לִמשׁוֹך מֵחֶשׁבּוֹן
deposit	pikadon	פִּיקָדוֹן (ז)
to make a deposit	lehafkid	לְהַפקִיד
wire transfer	ha'avara banka'it	הַעֲבָרָה בַּנקָאִית (נ)
to wire, to transfer	leha'avir 'kesef	לְהַעֲבִיר כֶּסֶף
sum	sxum	סכוּם (ז)
How much?	'kama?	כַּמָה?
signature	xatima	חֲתִימָה (נ)
to sign (vt)	laxtom	לַחתוֹם
credit card	kartis aʃrai	כַּרטִיס אַשׁרַאי (ז)
code (PIN code)	kod	קוֹד (ז)
credit card number	mispar kartis aʃrai	מִספָּר כַּרטִיס אַשׁרַאי (ז)
ATM	kaspomat	כַּספּוֹמָט (ז)
check	tʃek	צֶ'ק (ז)
to write a check	lixtov tʃek	לִכתוֹב צֶ'ק

checkbook	pinkas 'tʃekim	פִּנְקַס צֶ׳קִים (ז)
loan (bank ~)	halva'a	הַלְוָאָה (נ)
to apply for a loan	levakeʃ halva'a	לְבַקֵּשׁ הַלְוָאָה
to get a loan	lekabel halva'a	לְקַבֵּל הַלְוָאָה
to give a loan	lehalvot	לְהַלְוֹות
guarantee	arvut	עַרְבוּת (נ)

113. Telephone. Phone conversation

telephone	'telefon	טֶלֶפוֹן (ז)
cell phone	'telefon nayad	טֶלֶפוֹן נַיָּיד (ז)
answering machine	meʃivon	מְשִׁיבוֹן (ז)
to call (by phone)	letsaltsel	לְצַלְצֵל
phone call	siχat 'telefon	שִׂיחַת טֶלֶפוֹן (נ)
to dial a number	leχayeg mispar	לְחַיֵּיג מִסְפָּר
Hello!	'halo!	הָלוֹ!
to ask (vt)	liʃol	לִשְׁאוֹל
to answer (vi, vt)	la'anot	לַעֲנוֹת
to hear (vt)	liʃmo'a	לִשְׁמוֹעַ
well (adv)	tov	טוֹב
not well (adv)	lo tov	לֹא טוֹב
noises (interference)	hafra'ot	הַפְרָעוֹת (נ״ר)
receiver	ʃfo'feret	שְׁפוֹפֶרֶת (נ)
to pick up (~ the phone)	leharim ʃfo'feret	לְהָרִים שְׁפוֹפֶרֶת
to hang up (~ the phone)	leha'niaχ ʃfo'feret	לְהָנִיחַ שְׁפוֹפֶרֶת
busy (engaged)	tafus	תָּפוּס
to ring (ab. phone)	letsaltsel	לְצַלְצֵל
telephone book	'sefer tele'fonim	סֵפֶר טֶלֶפוֹנִים (ז)
local (adj)	mekomi	מְקוֹמִי
local call	siχa mekomit	שִׂיחָה מְקוֹמִית (נ)
long distance (~ call)	bein ironi	בֵּין עִירוֹנִי
long-distance call	siχa bein ironit	שִׂיחָה בֵּין עִירוֹנִית (נ)
international (adj)	benle'umi	בֵּינְלְאוּמִי
international call	siχa benle'umit	שִׂיחָה בֵּינְלְאוּמִית (נ)

114. Cell phone

cell phone	'telefon nayad	טֶלֶפוֹן נַיָּיד (ז)
display	masaχ	מָסָךְ (ז)
button	kaftor	כַּפְתּוֹר (ז)
SIM card	kartis sim	כַּרְטִיס סִים (ז)
battery	solela	סוֹלְלָה (נ)

| to be dead (battery) | lehitroken | לְהִתְרוֹקֵן |
| charger | mit'an | מַטְעָן (ז) |

menu	tafrit	תַּפְרִיט (ז)
settings	hagdarot	הַגְדָרוֹת (נ״ר)
tune (melody)	mangina	מַנְגִינָה (נ)
to select (vt)	livχor	לִבְחוֹר

calculator	maχʃevon	מַחְשְׁבוֹן (ז)
voice mail	ta koli	תָּא קוֹלִי (ז)
alarm clock	ʃa'on me'orer	שָׁעוֹן מְעוֹרֵר (ז)
contacts	anʃei 'keʃer	אַנְשֵׁי קֶשֶׁר (ז״ר)

| SMS (text message) | misron | מִסְרוֹן (ז) |
| subscriber | manui | מָנוּי (ז) |

115. Stationery

| ballpoint pen | et kaduri | עֵט כַּדוּרִי (ז) |
| fountain pen | et no've'a | עֵט נוֹבֵעַ (ז) |

pencil	iparon	עִיפָּרוֹן (ז)
highlighter	'marker	מַרְקֵר (ז)
felt-tip pen	tuʃ	טוּשׁ (ז)

| notepad | pinkas | פִּנְקָס (ז) |
| agenda (diary) | yoman | יוֹמָן (ז) |

ruler	sargel	סַרְגֵּל (ז)
calculator	maχʃevon	מַחְשְׁבוֹן (ז)
eraser	'maχak	מַחַק (ז)
thumbtack	'na'ats	נַעַץ (ז)
paper clip	mehadek	מְהַדֵק (ז)

glue	'devek	דֶבֶק (ז)
stapler	ʃadχan	שַׁדְכָן (ז)
hole punch	menakev	מְנַקֵב (ז)
pencil sharpener	maχded	מַחְדֵד (ז)

116. Various kinds of documents

account (report)	doχ	דוֹ״ח (ז)
agreement	heskem	הֶסְכֵּם (ז)
application form	'tofes bakaʃa	טוֹפֶס בַּקָשָׁה (ז)
authentic (adj)	mekori	מְקוֹרִי
badge (identity tag)	tag	תָּג (ז)
business card	kartis bikur	כַּרְטִיס בִּיקוּר (ז)
certificate (~ of quality)	te'uda	תְּעוּדָה (נ)

check (e.g., draw a ~)	tʃek	צֶ'ק (ז)
check (in restaurant)	xeʃbon	חֶשְׁבּוֹן (ז)
constitution	xuka	חוּקָה (נ)
contract (agreement)	xoze	חוֹזֶה (ז)
copy	'otek	עוֹתֶק (ז)
copy (of contract, etc.)	'otek	עוֹתֶק (ז)
customs declaration	hatʃharat mexes	הַצְהָרַת מֶכֶס (נ)
document	mismax	מִסְמָךְ (ז)
driver's license	riʃyon nehiga	רִשְׁיוֹן נְהִיגָה (ז)
addendum	to'sefet	תּוֹסֶפֶת (נ)
form	'tofes	טוֹפֶס (ז)
ID card (e.g., FBI ~)	te'uda mezaha	תְּעוּדָה מְזַהָה (נ)
inquiry (request)	xakira	חֲקִירָה (נ)
invitation card	kartis hazmana	כַּרְטִיס הַזְמָנָה (ז)
invoice	xeʃbonit	חֶשְׁבּוֹנִית (נ)
law	xok	חוֹק (ז)
letter (mail)	mixtav	מִכְתָּב (ז)
letterhead	neyar 'logo	נְיָיר לוֹגוֹ (ז)
list (of names, etc.)	reʃima	רְשִׁימָה (נ)
manuscript	ktav yad	כְּתַב יָד (ז)
newsletter	alon meida	עָלוֹן מֵידָע (ז)
note (short letter)	'petek	פֶּתֶק (ז)
pass (for worker, visitor)	iʃur knisa	אִישׁוּר כְּנִיסָה (ז)
passport	darkon	דַּרְכּוֹן (ז)
permit	riʃayon	רִישָׁיוֹן (ז)
résumé	korot xayim	קוֹרוֹת חַיִּים (נ״ר)
debt note, IOU	ʃtar xov	שְׁטָר חוֹב (ז)
receipt (for purchase)	kabala	קַבָּלָה (נ)
sales slip, receipt	tʃek	צֶ'ק (ז)
report (mil.)	dox	דּוֹ״ח (ז)
to show (ID, etc.)	lehatsig	לְהַצִּיג
to sign (vt)	laxtom	לַחְתּוֹם
signature	xatima	חֲתִימָה (נ)
seal (stamp)	xo'temet	חוֹתֶמֶת (נ)
text	tekst	טֶקְסְט (ז)
ticket (for entry)	kartis	כַּרְטִיס (ז)
to cross out	limxok	לִמְחוֹק
to fill out (~ a form)	lemale	לְמַלֵּא
waybill (shipping invoice)	ʃtar mit'an	שְׁטָר מִטְעָן (ז)
will (testament)	tsava'a	צַוָּאָה (נ)

117. Kinds of business

accounting services	ferutei hanhalat xefbonot	שֵׁירוּתֵי הַנהָלַת חֶשבּוֹנוֹת (ז״ר)
advertising	pirsum	פִּרסוּם (ז)
advertising agency	soxnut pirsum	סוֹכנוּת פִּרסוּם (נ)
air-conditioners	mazganim	מַזגָנִים (ז״ר)
airline	xevrat te'ufa	חֶברַת תעוּפָה (נ)
alcoholic beverages	mafka'ot xarifim	מַשקָאוֹת חָרִיפִים (נ״ר)
antiques (antique dealers)	atikot	עַתִיקוֹת (נ״ר)
art gallery (contemporary ~)	ga'lerya le'amanut	גָלֶריָה לְאָמָנוּת (נ)
audit services	ferutei bi'koret xefbonot	שֵׁירוּתֵי בִּיקוֹרֶת חֶשבּוֹנוֹת (ז״ר)
banking industry	banka'ut	בַּנקָאוּת (נ)
bar	bar	בָּר (ז)
beauty parlor	mexon 'yofi	מְכוֹן יוֹפִי (ז)
bookstore	xanut sfarim	חֲנוּת סְפָרִים (נ)
brewery	miv'felet 'bira	מִבשֶׁלֶת בִּירָה (נ)
business center	merkaz asakim	מֶרכַּז עֲסָקִים (ז)
business school	beit 'sefer le'asakim	בֵּית סֵפֶר לַעֲסָקִים (ז)
casino	ka'zino	קָזִינוֹ (ז)
construction	bniya	בּנִיָה (נ)
consulting	yi'uts	יִיעוּץ (ז)
dental clinic	mirpa'at fi'nayim	מִרפָּאַת שִׁינַיִים (נ)
design	itsuv	עִיצוּב (ז)
drugstore, pharmacy	beit mir'kaxat	בֵּית מִרקַחַת (ז)
dry cleaners	nikui yavef	נִיקוּי יָבֵש (ז)
employment agency	soxnut 'koax adam	סוֹכנוּת כּוֹחַ אָדָם (נ)
financial services	ferutim fi'nansim	שֵׁירוּתִים פִינַנסִיִים (ז״ר)
food products	mutsrei mazon	מוּצרֵי מָזוֹן (ז״ר)
funeral home	beit levayot	בֵּית לְוָויוֹת (ז)
furniture (e.g., house ~)	rehitim	רָהִיטִים (ז״ר)
clothing, garment	bgadim	בּגָדִים (ז״ר)
hotel	beit malon	בֵּית מָלוֹן (ז)
ice-cream	'glida	גלִידָה (נ)
industry (manufacturing)	ta'asiya	תַעֲשִׂיָה (נ)
insurance	bi'tuax	בִּיטוּחַ (ז)
Internet	'internet	אִינטֶרנֶט (ז)
investments (finance)	hafka'ot	הַשקָעוֹת (נ״ר)
jeweler	tsoref	צוֹרֵף (ז)
jewelry	taxfitim	תַכשִׁיטִים (ז״ר)
laundry (shop)	mixbasa	מִכבָּסָה (נ)
legal advisor	yo'ets miffati	יוֹעֵץ מִשפָּטִי (ז)
light industry	ta'asiya kala	תַעֲשִׂיָה קַלָה (נ)
magazine	ʒurnal	ז׳וּרנָל (ז)

mail-order selling	meχira be'do'ar	מְכִירָה בְּדוֹאַר (נ)
medicine	refu'a	רְפוּאָה (נ)
movie theater	kol'no'a	קוֹלְנוֹעַ (ז)
museum	muze'on	מוּזֵיאוֹן (ז)
news agency	soχnut yedi'ot	סוֹכְנוּת יְדִיעוֹת (נ)
newspaper	iton	עִיתוֹן (ז)
nightclub	mo'adon 'laila	מוֹעֲדוֹן לַיְלָה (ז)
oil (petroleum)	neft	נֶפְט (ז)
courier services	ʃirut ʃliχim	שֵׁירוּת שְׁלִיחִים (ז)
pharmaceutics	rokχut	רוֹקְחוּת (נ)
printing (industry)	beit dfus	בֵּית דְפוּס (ז)
publishing house	hotsa'a la'or	הוֹצָאָה לָאוֹר (נ)
radio (~ station)	'radyo	רַדְיוֹ (ז)
real estate	nadlan	נַדְל"ן (ז)
restaurant	mis'ada	מִסְעָדָה (נ)
security company	χevrat ʃmira	חֶבְרַת שְׁמִירָה (נ)
sports	sport	סְפּוֹרְט (ז)
stock exchange	'bursa	בּוּרְסָה (נ)
store	χanut	חֲנוּת (נ)
supermarket	super'market	סוּפֶּרְמַרְקֶט (ז)
swimming pool (public ~)	breχat sχiya	בְּרֵיכַת שְׂחִייָה (נ)
tailor shop	mitpara	מִתְפָּרָה (נ)
television	tele'vizya	טֶלֶוִוִיזְיָה (נ)
theater	te'atron	תֵיאַטְרוֹן (ז)
trade (commerce)	misχar	מִסְחָר (ז)
transportation	hovalot	הוֹבָלוֹת (נ"ר)
travel	tayarut	תַיָירוּת (נ)
veterinarian	veterinar	וֶטֶרִינָר (ז)
warehouse	maχsan	מַחְסָן (ז)
waste collection	isuf 'zevel	אִיסוּף זֶבֶל (ז)

Job. Business. Part 2

118. Show. Exhibition

exhibition, show	ta'aruxa	תַּעֲרוּכָה (נ)
trade show	ta'aruxa misχarit	תַּעֲרוּכָה מִסְחָרִית (נ)
participation	hiʃtatfut	הִשְׁתַּתְּפוּת (נ)
to participate (vi)	lehiʃtatef	לְהִשְׁתַּתֵּף
participant (exhibitor)	miʃtatef	מִשְׁתַּתֵּף (ז)
director	menahel	מְנַהֵל (ז)
organizers' office	misrad hame'argenim	מִשְׂרַד הַמְאַרְגְּנִים (ז)
organizer	me'argen	מְאַרְגֵן (ז)
to organize (vt)	le'argen	לְאַרְגֵן
participation form	'tofes hiʃtatfut	טוֹפֶס הִשְׁתַּתְּפוּת (ז)
to fill out (vt)	lemale	לְמַלֵּא
details	pratim	פְּרָטִים (ז"ר)
information	meida	מֵידָע (ז)
price (cost, rate)	meχir	מְחִיר (ז)
including	kolel	כּוֹלֵל
to include (vt)	liχlol	לִכְלוֹל
to pay (vi, vt)	leʃalem	לְשַׁלֵּם
registration fee	dmei riʃum	דְּמֵי רִישׁוּם (ז"ר)
entrance	knisa	כְּנִיסָה (נ)
pavilion, hall	bitan	בִּיתָן (ז)
to register (vt)	lirʃom	לִרְשׁוֹם
badge (identity tag)	tag	תָּג (ז)
booth, stand	duχan	דּוּכָן (ז)
to reserve, to book	liʃmor	לִשְׁמוֹר
display case	madaf tetsuga	מַדָף תְּצוּגָה (ז)
spotlight	menorat spot	מְנוֹרַת סְפּוֹט (נ)
design	itsuv	עִיצוּב (ז)
to place (put, set)	la'aroχ	לַעֲרוֹךְ
to be placed	lehimatse	לְהִימָצֵא
distributor	mefits	מֵפִיץ (ז)
supplier	sapak	סַפָּק (ז)
to supply (vt)	lesapek	לְסַפֵּק
country	medina	מְדִינָה (נ)
foreign (adj)	meχul	מְחוּ"ל

product	mutsar	מוֹצָר (ז)
association	amuta	עֲמוּתָה (נ)
conference hall	ulam knasim	אוּלָם כְּנָסִים (ז)
congress	kongres	קוֹנגרֶס (ז)
contest (competition)	taχarut	תַחֲרוּת (נ)

visitor (attendee)	mevaker	מְבַקֵר (ז)
to visit (attend)	levaker	לְבַקֵר
customer	la'koaχ	לָקוֹחַ (ז)

119. Mass Media

newspaper	iton	עִיתוֹן (ז)
magazine	ʒurnal	ז'וּרנָל (ז)
press (printed media)	itonut	עִיתוֹנוּת (נ)
radio	'radyo	רַדִיוֹ (ז)
radio station	taχanat 'radyo	תַחֲנַת רַדִיוֹ (נ)
television	tele'vizya	טֶלֶוִוידִיָה (נ)

presenter, host	manχe	מַנחֶה (ז)
newscaster	karyan	קַריָין (ז)
commentator	parʃan	פַרשָן (ז)

journalist	itonai	עִיתוֹנַאי (ז)
correspondent (reporter)	katav	כַּתָב (ז)
press photographer	tsalam itonut	צַלָם עִיתוֹנוּת (ז)
reporter	katav	כַּתָב (ז)

| editor | oreχ | עוֹרֵך (ז) |
| editor-in-chief | oreχ raʃi | עוֹרֵך רָאשִי (ז) |

to subscribe (to …)	lehasdir manui	לְהַסדִיר מָנוּי
subscription	minui	מָנוּי (ז)
subscriber	manui	מָנוּי (ז)
to read (vi, vt)	likro	לִקרוֹא
reader	kore	קוֹרֵא (ז)

circulation (of newspaper)	tfutsa	תפוּצָה (נ)
monthly (adj)	χodʃi	חוֹדשִי
weekly (adj)	ʃvu'i	שבוּעִי
issue (edition)	gilayon	גִילָיוֹן (ז)
new (~ issue)	tari	טָרִי

headline	ko'teret	כּוֹתֶרֶת (נ)
short article	katava ktsara	כַּתָבָה קצָרָה (נ)
column (regular article)	tur	טוּר (ז)
article	ma'amar	מַאֲמָר (ז)
page	amud	עַמוּד (ז)
reportage, report	katava	כַּתָבָה (נ)
event (happening)	ei'ru'a	אֵירוּעַ (ז)

sensation (news)	sen'satsya	סֶנסַציָה (נ)
scandal	ʃa'aruriya	שַׁעֲרוּרִיָה (נ)
scandalous (adj)	meviʃ	מֵבִישׁ
great (~ scandal)	gadol	גָדוֹל
show (e.g., cooking ~)	toxnit	תוֹכנִית (נ)
interview	ra'ayon	רַאֲיוֹן (ז)
live broadcast	ʃidur xai	שִׁידוּר חַי (ז)
channel	aruts	עָרוּץ (ז)

120. Agriculture

agriculture	xakla'ut	חַקלָאוּת (נ)
peasant (masc.)	ikar	אִיכָּר (ז)
peasant (fem.)	xakla'ut	חַקלָאִית (נ)
farmer	xavai	חַוַואי (ז)
tractor (farm ~)	'traktor	טרַקטוֹר (ז)
combine, harvester	kombain	קוֹמבַּיין (ז)
plow	maxreʃa	מַחרֵשָׁה (נ)
to plow (vi, vt)	laxaroʃ	לַחֲרוֹשׁ
plowland	sade xaruʃ	שָׂדֶה חָרוּשׁ (ז)
furrow (in field)	'telem	תֶלֶם (ז)
to sow (vi, vt)	liz'ro'a	לִזרוֹעַ
seeder	mazre'a	מַזרֵעָה (ז)
sowing (process)	zri'a	זרִיעָה (נ)
scythe	xermeʃ	חֶרמֵשׁ (ז)
to mow, to scythe	liktsor	לִקצוֹר
spade (tool)	et	אֵת (ז)
to till (vt)	leta'teax	לְתַחֵחַ
hoe	ma'ader	מַעֲדֵר (ז)
to hoe, to weed	lenakeʃ	לְנַכֵּשׁ
weed (plant)	'esev ʃote	עֵשֶׂב שׁוֹטֶה (ז)
watering can	maʃpex	מַשׁפֵּך (ז)
to water (plants)	lehaʃkot	לְהַשׁקוֹת
watering (act)	haʃkaya	הַשׁקָיָה (נ)
pitchfork	kilʃon	קִלשׁוֹן (ז)
rake	magrefa	מַגרֵפָה (נ)
fertilizer	'deʃen	דֶשֶׁן (ז)
to fertilize (vt)	ledaʃen	לְדַשֵׁן
manure (fertilizer)	'zevel	זֶבֶל (ז)
field	sade	שָׂדֶה (ז)

meadow	aχu	אָחוּ (ז)
vegetable garden	gan yarak	גַן יָרָק (ז)
orchard (e.g., apple ~)	bustan	בּוּסתָן (ז)
to graze (vt)	lir'ot	לִרעוֹת
herder (herdsman)	ro'e tson	רוֹעֶה צֹאן (ז)
pasture	mir'e	מִרעֶה (ז)
cattle breeding	gidul bakar	גִידוּל בָּקָר (ז)
sheep farming	gidul kvasim	גִידוּל כּבָשִׂים (ז)
plantation	mata	מַטָע (ז)
row (garden bed ~s)	aruga	עֲרוּגָה (נ)
hothouse	χamama	חֲמָמָה (נ)
drought (lack of rain)	ba'tsoret	בַּצוֹרֶת (נ)
dry (~ summer)	yaveʃ	יָבֵש
grain	tvu'a	תבוּאָה (נ)
cereal crops	gidulei dagan	גִידוּלֵי דָגָן (ז"ר)
to harvest, to gather	liktof	לִקטוֹף
miller (person)	toχen	טוֹחֵן (ז)
mill (e.g., gristmill)	taχanat 'kemaχ	טַחֲנַת קֶמַח (נ)
to grind (grain)	litχon	לִטחוֹן
flour	'kemaχ	קֶמַח (ז)
straw	kaʃ	קַש (ז)

121. Building. Building process

construction site	atar bniya	אֲתַר בּנִייָה (ז)
to build (vt)	livnot	לִבנוֹת
construction worker	banai	בַּנַאי (ז)
project	proyekt	פּרוֹייֵקט (ז)
architect	adriχal	אַדרִיכָל (ז)
worker	po'el	פּוֹעֵל (ז)
foundation (of a building)	yesodot	יְסוֹדוֹת (ז"ר)
roof	gag	גַג (ז)
foundation pile	amud yesod	עַמוּד יְסוֹד (ז)
wall	kir	קִיר (ז)
reinforcing bars	mot χizuk	מוֹט חִיזוּק (ז)
scaffolding	pigumim	פִּיגוּמִים (ז"ר)
concrete	beton	בֶּטוֹן (ז)
granite	granit	גרָנִיט (ז)
stone	'even	אֶבֶן (נ)
brick	levena	לְבֵנָה (נ)

sand	χol	חוֹל (ז)
cement	'melet	מֶלֶט (ז)
plaster (for walls)	'tiaχ	טִיחַ (ז)
to plaster (vt)	leta'yeaχ	לְטַיֵּחַ
paint	'tseva	צֶבַע (ז)
to paint (~ a wall)	liʦ'bo'a	לִצְבּוֹעַ
barrel	χavit	חָבִית (נ)

crane	aguran	עֲגוּרָן (ז)
to lift, to hoist (vt)	lehanif	לְהָנִיף
to lower (vt)	lehorid	לְהוֹרִיד

bulldozer	daχpor	דַּחְפּוֹר (ז)
excavator	maχper	מַחְפֵּר (ז)
scoop, bucket	ʃa'ov	שָׁאוֹב (ז)
to dig (excavate)	laχpor	לַחְפּוֹר
hard hat	kasda	קַסְדָּה (נ)

122. Science. Research. Scientists

science	mada	מַדָּע (ז)
scientific (adj)	mada'i	מַדָּעִי
scientist	mad'an	מַדְעָן (ז)
theory	te''orya	תֵּיאוֹרְיָה (נ)

axiom	aks'yoma	אַקְסִיוֹמָה (נ)
analysis	ni'tuaχ	נִיתוּחַ (ז)
to analyze (vt)	lena'teaχ	לְנַתֵּחַ
argument (strong ~)	nimuk	נִימוּק (ז)
substance (matter)	'χomer	חוֹמֶר (ז)

hypothesis	hipo'teza	הִיפּוֹתֵזָה (נ)
dilemma	di'lema	דִּילֶמָה (נ)
dissertation	diser'taʦya	דִּיסֶרְטַצְיָה (נ)
dogma	'dogma	דּוֹגְמָה (נ)

doctrine	dok'trina	דּוֹקְטְרִינָה (נ)
research	meχkar	מֶחְקָר (ז)
to research (vt)	laχkor	לַחְקוֹר
tests (laboratory ~)	nuisuyim	נִיסוּיִים (ז"ר)
laboratory	ma'abada	מַעֲבָּדָה (נ)

method	ʃita	שִׁיטָה (נ)
molecule	mo'lekula	מוֹלֶקוּלָה (נ)
monitoring	nitur	נִיטוּר (ז)
discovery (act, event)	gilui	גִּילוּי (ז)

postulate	aks'yoma	אַקְסִיוֹמָה (נ)
principle	ikaron	עִיקָרוֹן (ז)
forecast	taχazit	תַּחֲזִית (נ)

to forecast (vt)	laχazot	לַחֲזוֹת
synthesis	sin'teza	סִינתֵזָה (נ)
trend (tendency)	megama	מְגַמָה (נ)
theorem	miʃpat	מִשׁפָּט (ז)
teachings	tora	תוֹרָה (נ)
fact	uvda	עוּבדָה (נ)
expedition	miʃ'laχat	מִשׁלַחַת (נ)
experiment	nisui	נִיסוּי (ז)
academician	akademai	אֲקָדמַאי (ז)
bachelor (e.g., ~ of Arts)	'to'ar riʃon	תוֹאַר רִאשׁוֹן (ז)
doctor (PhD)	'doktor	דוֹקטוֹר (ז)
Associate Professor	martse baχir	מַרצֶה בָּכִיר (ז)
Master (e.g., ~ of Arts)	musmaχ	מוּסמָך (ז)
professor	pro'fesor	פּרוֹפֶסוֹר (ז)

Professions and occupations

123. Job search. Dismissal

job	avoda	עֲבוֹדָה (נ)
staff (work force)	'segel	סֶגֶל (ז)
personnel	'segel	סֶגֶל (ז)
career	kar'yera	קַרְיֶירָה (נ)
prospects (chances)	efʃaruyot	אֶפְשָׁרֻיוֹת (נ״ר)
skills (mastery)	meyumanut	מְיֻמָּנוּת (נ)
selection (screening)	sinun	סִינוּן (ז)
employment agency	soχnut 'koaχ adam	סוֹכְנוּת כּוֹחַ אָדָם (נ)
résumé	korot χayim	קוֹרוֹת חַיִּים (נ״ר)
job interview	ra'ayon avoda	רַאָיוֹן עֲבוֹדָה (ז)
vacancy, opening	misra pnuya	מִשְׂרָה פְּנוּיָה (נ)
salary, pay	mas'koret	מַשְׂכּוֹרֶת (נ)
fixed salary	mas'koret kvu'a	מַשְׂכּוֹרֶת קְבוּעָה (נ)
pay, compensation	taʃlum	תַּשְׁלוּם (ז)
position (job)	tafkid	תַּפְקִיד (ז)
duty (of employee)	χova	חוֹבָה (נ)
range of duties	tχum aχrayut	תְּחוּם אַחְרָיוּת (ז)
busy (I'm ~)	asuk	עָסוּק
to fire (dismiss)	lefater	לְפַטֵּר
dismissal	pitur	פִּיטוּר (ז)
unemployment	avtala	אַבְטָלָה (נ)
unemployed (n)	muvtal	מוּבְטָל (ז)
retirement	'pensya	פֶּנְסְיָה (נ)
to retire (from job)	latset legimla'ot	לָצֵאת לְגִימְלָאוֹת

124. Business people

director	menahel	מְנַהֵל (ז)
manager (director)	menahel	מְנַהֵל (ז)
boss	bos	בּוֹס (ז)
superior	memune	מְמוּנֶּה (ז)
superiors	memunim	מְמוּנִּים (ז״ר)
president	nasi	נָשִׂיא (ז)

chairman	yoʃev roʃ	יוֹשֵׁב רֹאשׁ (ז)
deputy (substitute)	sgan	סְגָן (ז)
assistant	ozer	עוֹזֵר (ז)
secretary	mazkir	מַזְכִּיר (ז)
personal assistant	mazkir iʃi	מַזְכִּיר אִישִׁי (ז)
businessman	iʃ asakim	אִישׁ עֲסָקִים (ז)
entrepreneur	yazam	יָזָם (ז)
founder	meyased	מְיַיסֵד (ז)
to found (vt)	leyased	לְיַיסֵד
incorporator	meχonen	מְכוֹנֵן (ז)
partner	ʃutaf	שׁוּתָף (ז)
stockholder	'ba'al menayot	בַּעַל מְנָיוֹת (ז)
millionaire	milyoner	מִילְיוֹנֶר (ז)
billionaire	milyarder	מִילְיַארְדֶר (ז)
owner, proprietor	be'alim	בְּעָלִים (ז)
landowner	'ba'al adamot	בַּעַל אֲדָמוֹת (ז)
client	la'koaχ	לָקוֹחַ (ז)
regular client	la'koaχ ka'vu'a	לָקוֹחַ קָבוּעַ (ז)
buyer (customer)	kone	קוֹנֶה (ז)
visitor	mevaker	מְבַקֵר (ז)
professional (n)	miktso'an	מִקְצוֹעָן (ז)
expert	mumχe	מוּמְחֶה (ז)
specialist	mumχe	מוּמְחֶה (ז)
banker	bankai	בַּנְקַאי (ז)
broker	soχen	סוֹכֵן (ז)
cashier, teller	kupai	קוּפַּאי (ז)
accountant	menahel χeʃbonot	מְנַהֵל חֶשְׁבּוֹנוֹת (ז)
security guard	ʃomer	שׁוֹמֵר (ז)
investor	maʃki'a	מַשְׁקִיעַ (ז)
debtor	'ba'al χov	בַּעַל חוֹב (ז)
creditor	malve	מַלְוֶה (ז)
borrower	love	לוֹוֶה (ז)
importer	yevu'an	יְבוּאָן (ז)
exporter	yetsu'an	יְצוּאָן (ז)
manufacturer	yatsran	יַצְרָן (ז)
distributor	mefits	מֵפִיץ (ז)
middleman	metaveχ	מְתַוֵוךְ (ז)
consultant	yo'ets	יוֹעֵץ (ז)
sales representative	natsig meχirot	נָצִיג מְכִירוֹת (ז)
agent	soχen	סוֹכֵן (ז)
insurance agent	soχen bi'tuaχ	סוֹכֵן בִּיטוּחַ (ז)

125. Service professions

cook	tabaχ	טַבָּח (ז)
chef (kitchen chef)	ʃef	שֶׁף (ז)
baker	ofe	אוֹפֶה (ז)
bartender	'barmen	בַּרמֶן (ז)
waiter	meltsar	מֶלצָר (ז)
waitress	meltsarit	מֶלצָרִית (נ)
lawyer, attorney	oreχ din	עוֹרֵך דִין (ז)
lawyer (legal expert)	oreχ din	עוֹרֵך דִין (ז)
notary	notaryon	נוֹטַריוֹן (ז)
electrician	χaʃmalai	חַשמַלַאי (ז)
plumber	ʃravrav	שְׁרַבּרָב (ז)
carpenter	nagar	נַגָר (ז)
masseur	ma'ase	מְעַסֶה (ז)
masseuse	masa'ʒistit	מַסָז'יסטִית (נ)
doctor	rofe	רוֹפֵא (ז)
taxi driver	nahag monit	נֶהָג מוֹנִית (ז)
driver	nahag	נֶהָג (ז)
delivery man	ʃa'liaχ	שָׁלִיחַ (ז)
chambermaid	χadranit	חַדרָנִית (נ)
security guard	ʃomer	שׁוֹמֵר (ז)
flight attendant (fem.)	da'yelet	דַייֶלֶת (נ)
schoolteacher	more	מוֹרֶה (ז)
librarian	safran	סַפרָן (ז)
translator	metargem	מְתַרגֵם (ז)
interpreter	meturgeman	מְתוּרגְמָן (ז)
guide	madriχ tiyulim	מַדרִיך טִיוּלִים (ז)
hairdresser	sapar	סַפָּר (ז)
mailman	davar	דַווָר (ז)
salesman (store staff)	moχer	מוֹכֵר (ז)
gardener	ganan	גַנָן (ז)
domestic servant	meʃaret	מְשָׁרֵת (ז)
maid (female servant)	meʃa'retet	מְשָׁרֶתֶת (נ)
cleaner (cleaning lady)	menaka	מְנַקָה (נ)

126. Military professions and ranks

private	turai	טוּרָאי (ז)
sergeant	samal	סַמָל (ז)

lieutenant	'segen	סֶגֶן (ז)
captain	'seren	סֶרֶן (ז)
major	rav 'seren	רַב־סֶרֶן (ז)
colonel	aluf miʃne	אַלּוּף מִשְׁנֶה (ז)
general	aluf	אַלּוּף (ז)
marshal	'marʃal	מַרְשָׁל (ז)
admiral	admiral	אַדְמִירָל (ז)
military (n)	iʃ tsava	אִישׁ צָבָא (ז)
soldier	χayal	חַיָּל (ז)
officer	katsin	קָצִין (ז)
commander	mefaked	מְפַקֵּד (ז)
border guard	ʃomer gvul	שׁוֹמֵר גְּבוּל (ז)
radio operator	alχutai	אַלְחוּטַאי (ז)
scout (searcher)	iʃ modi'in kravi	אִישׁ מוֹדִיעִין קְרָבִי (ז)
pioneer (sapper)	χablan	חַבְּלָן (ז)
marksman	tsalaf	צַלָּף (ז)
navigator	navat	נַוָּט (ז)

127. Officials. Priests

king	'meleχ	מֶלֶךְ (ז)
queen	malka	מַלְכָּה (נ)
prince	nasiχ	נָסִיךְ (ז)
princess	nesiχa	נְסִיכָה (נ)
czar	tsar	צָאר (ז)
czarina	tsa'rina	צָארִינָה (נ)
president	nasi	נָשִׂיא (ז)
Secretary (minister)	sar	שַׂר (ז)
prime minister	roʃ memʃala	רֹאשׁ מֶמְשָׁלָה (ז)
senator	se'nator	סֶנָאטוֹר (ז)
diplomat	diplomat	דִיפְּלוֹמָט (ז)
consul	'konsul	קוֹנְסוּל (ז)
ambassador	ʃagrir	שַׁגְרִיר (ז)
counsilor (diplomatic officer)	yo'ets	יוֹעֵץ (ז)
official, functionary (civil servant)	pakid	פָּקִיד (ז)
prefect	prefekt	פְּרֶפֶקְט (ז)
mayor	roʃ ha'ir	רֹאשׁ הָעִיר (ז)
judge	ʃofet	שׁוֹפֵט (ז)
prosecutor (e.g., district attorney)	to've'a	תּוֹבֵעַ (ז)

missionary	misyoner	מִיסיוֹנֶר (ז)
monk	nazir	נָזִיר (ז)
abbot	roʃ minzar ka'toli	רֹאש מִנזָר קָתוֹלִי (ז)
rabbi	rav	רַב (ז)
vizier	vazir	וָזִיר (ז)
shah	ʃaχ	שָׁאח (ז)
sheikh	ʃeiχ	שֵׁיח (ז)

128. Agricultural professions

beekeeper	kavran	כַּוורָן (ז)
herder, shepherd	ro'e tson	רוֹעֵה צֹאן (ז)
agronomist	agronom	אַגרוֹנוֹם (ז)
cattle breeder	megadel bakar	מְגַדֵל בָּקָר (ז)
veterinarian	veterinar	וֶטֶרִינָר (ז)
farmer	χavai	חַוואַי (ז)
winemaker	yeinan	יֵינָן (ז)
zoologist	zo'olog	זוֹאוֹלוֹג (ז)
cowboy	'ka'uboi	קָאוּבּוֹי (ז)

129. Art professions

actor	saχkan	שַׂחקָן (ז)
actress	saχkanit	שַׂחקָנִית (נ)
singer (masc.)	zamar	זַמָר (ז)
singer (fem.)	za'meret	זַמֶרֶת (נ)
dancer (masc.)	rakdan	רַקדָן (ז)
dancer (fem.)	rakdanit	רַקדָנִית (נ)
performer (masc.)	saχkan	שַׂחקָן (ז)
performer (fem.)	saχkanit	שַׂחקָנִית (נ)
musician	muzikai	מוּזִיקַאי (ז)
pianist	psantran	פּסַנתְרָן (ז)
guitar player	nagan gi'tara	נַגָן גִיטָרָה (ז)
conductor (orchestra ~)	mena'tseaχ	מְנַצֵחַ (ז)
composer	malχin	מַלחִין (ז)
impresario	amargan	אָמַרגָן (ז)
film director	bamai	בַּמַאי (ז)
producer	mefik	מֵפִיק (ז)
scriptwriter	tasritai	תַסרִיטַאי (ז)
critic	mevaker	מְבַקֵר (ז)

writer	sofer	סוֹפֵר (ז)
poet	meʃorer	מְשׁוֹרֵר (ז)
sculptor	pasal	פַּסָל (ז)
artist (painter)	tsayar	צַיָיר (ז)

juggler	lahatutan	לַהֲטוּטָן (ז)
clown	leitsan	לֵיצָן (ז)
acrobat	akrobat	אַקרוֹבָּט (ז)
magician	kosem	קוֹסֵם (ז)

130. Various professions

doctor	rofe	רוֹפֵא (ז)
nurse	aχot	אָחוֹת (נ)
psychiatrist	psiχi''ater	פְּסִיכִיאָטֵר (ז)
dentist	rofe ʃi'nayim	רוֹפֵא שִׁינַיִים (ז)
surgeon	kirurg	כִּירוּרג (ז)

astronaut	astro'na'ut	אַסטרוֹנָאוּט (ז)
astronomer	astronom	אַסטרוֹנוֹם (ז)
pilot	tayas	טַייָס (ז)

driver (of taxi, etc.)	nahag	נַהָג (ז)
engineer (train driver)	nahag ra'kevet	נַהָג רַכֶּבֶת (ז)
mechanic	meχonai	מְכוֹנַאי (ז)

miner	kore	כּוֹרֶה (ז)
worker	po'el	פּוֹעֵל (ז)
locksmith	misgad	מַסגֵד (ז)
joiner (carpenter)	nagar	נַגָר (ז)
turner (lathe machine operator)	χarat	חָרָט (ז)
construction worker	banai	בַּנָאי (ז)
welder	rataχ	רַתָּך (ז)

professor (title)	pro'fesor	פּרוֹפֶסוֹר (ז)
architect	adriχal	אַדרִיכָל (ז)
historian	historyon	הִיסטוֹריוֹן (ז)
scientist	mad'an	מַדעָן (ז)
physicist	fizikai	פִיזִיקַאי (ז)
chemist (scientist)	χimai	כִימַאי (ז)

archeologist	arχe'olog	אַרכֵיאוֹלוֹג (ז)
geologist	ge'olog	גֵיאוֹלוֹג (ז)
researcher (scientist)	χoker	חוֹקֵר (ז)

babysitter	ʃmartaf	שמַרטָף (ז)
teacher, educator	more, meχaneχ	מוֹרֶה, מְחַנֵך (ז)
editor	oreχ	עוֹרֵך (ז)
editor-in-chief	oreχ raʃi	עוֹרֵך רָאשִׁי (ז)

correspondent	katav	כַּתָּב (ז)
typist (fem.)	kaldanit	קַלְדָנִית (נ)
designer	me'atsev	מְעַצֵב (ז)
computer expert	mumxe maxʃevim	מֻמְחֶה מַחְשְׁבִים (ז)
programmer	metaxnet	מְתַכְנֵת (ז)
engineer (designer)	mehandes	מְהַנְדֵס (ז)
sailor	yamai	יַמַאי (ז)
seaman	malax	מַלָח (ז)
rescuer	matsil	מַצִיל (ז)
fireman	kabai	כַּבַּאי (ז)
police officer	ʃoter	שׁוֹטֵר (ז)
watchman	ʃomer	שׁוֹמֵר (ז)
detective	balaʃ	בַּלָשׁ (ז)
customs officer	pakid 'mexes	פְּקִיד מֶכֶס (ז)
bodyguard	ʃomer roʃ	שׁוֹמֵר רֹאשׁ (ז)
prison guard	soher	סוֹהֵר (ז)
inspector	mefa'keax	מְפַקֵחַ (ז)
sportsman	sportai	סְפּוֹרְטַאי (ז)
trainer, coach	me'amen	מְאַמֵן (ז)
butcher	katsav	קַצָב (ז)
cobbler (shoe repairer)	sandlar	סַנְדְלָר (ז)
merchant	soxer	סוֹחֵר (ז)
loader (person)	sabal	סַבָּל (ז)
fashion designer	me'atsev ofna	מְעַצֵב אוֹפְנָה (ז)
model (fem.)	dugmanit	דוּגְמָנִית (נ)

131. Occupations. Social status

schoolboy	talmid	תַּלְמִיד (ז)
student (college ~)	student	סְטוּדֶנְט (ז)
philosopher	filosof	פִּילוֹסוֹף (ז)
economist	kalkelan	כַּלְכְּלָן (ז)
inventor	mamtsi	מַמְצִיא (ז)
unemployed (n)	muvtal	מוּבְטָל (ז)
retiree	pensyoner	פֶּנְסְיוֹנֵר (ז)
spy, secret agent	meragel	מְרַגֵל (ז)
prisoner	asir	אָסִיר (ז)
striker	ʃovet	שׁוֹבֵת (ז)
bureaucrat	birokrat	בִּירוֹקְרָט (ז)
traveler (globetrotter)	metayel	מְטַיֵל (ז)
gay, homosexual (n)	'lesbit, 'homo	לֶסְבִּית (נ), הוֹמוֹ (ז)

hacker	'haker	הָאקֶר (ז)
hippie	'hipi	הִיפִּי (ז)
bandit	ʃoded	שׁוֹדֵד (ז)
hit man, killer	ro'tseaχ saχir	רוֹצֵחַ שָׂכִיר (ז)
drug addict	narkoman	נַרקוֹמָן (ז)
drug dealer	soχer samim	סוֹחֵר סַמִּים (ז)
prostitute (fem.)	zona	זוֹנָה (נ)
pimp	sarsur	סַרסוּר (ז)
sorcerer	meχaʃef	מְכַשֵּׁף (ז)
sorceress (evil ~)	maχʃefa	מַכשֵׁפָה (נ)
pirate	ʃoded yam	שׁוֹדֵד יָם (ז)
slave	ʃifχa, 'eved	שִׁפחָה (נ), עֶבֶד (ז)
samurai	samurai	סָמוּרַאי (ז)
savage (primitive)	'pere adam	פֶּרֶא אָדָם (ז)

Sports

132. Kinds of sports. Sportspersons

sportsman	sportai	ספּוֹרְטַאי (ז)
kind of sports	anaf sport	עָנָף ספּוֹרְט (ז)
basketball	kadursal	כַּדוּרְסַל (ז)
basketball player	kadursalan	כַּדוּרְסַלָן (ז)
baseball	'beisbol	בֵּייסְבּוֹל (ז)
baseball player	saχkan 'beisbol	שַׂחֲקָן בֵּייסְבּוֹל (ז)
soccer	kadu'regel	כַּדוּרֶגֶל (ז)
soccer player	kaduraglan	כַּדוּרַגְלָן (ז)
goalkeeper	ʃo'er	שׁוֹעֵר (ז)
hockey	'hoki	הוֹקִי (ז)
hockey player	saχkan 'hoki	שַׂחֲקָן הוֹקִי (ז)
volleyball	kadur'af	כַּדוּרְעָף (ז)
volleyball player	saχkan kadur'af	שַׂחֲקָן כַּדוּרְעָף (ז)
boxing	igruf	אִיגְרוּף (ז)
boxer	mit'agref	מִתְאַגְרֵף (ז)
wrestling	he'avkut	הֵיאָבְקוּת (נ)
wrestler	mit'abek	מִתְאַבֵּק (ז)
karate	karate	קָרָטֶה (ז)
karate fighter	karatist	קָרָטִיסְט (ז)
judo	'dʒudo	ג'וּדוֹ (ז)
judo athlete	dʒudai	ג'וּדָאי (ז)
tennis	'tenis	טֶנִיס (ז)
tennis player	tenisai	טֶנִיסַאי (ז)
swimming	sχiya	שְׂחִייָה (נ)
swimmer	saχyan	שַׂחְייָן (ז)
fencing	'sayif	סַיִף (ז)
fencer	sayaf	סַייָף (ז)
chess	'ʃaχmat	שַׁחְמָט (ז)
chess player	ʃaχmetai	שַׁחְמְטַאי (ז)

alpinism	tipus harim	טִיפּוּס הָרִים (ז)
alpinist	metapes harim	מְטַפֵּס הָרִים (ז)
running	ritsa	רִיצָה (נ)
runner	atsan	אָצָן (ז)
athletics	at'letika kala	אַתְלֶטִיקָה קַלָה (נ)
athlete	atlet	אַתְלֵט (ז)
horseback riding	reχiva al sus	רְכִיבָה עַל סוּס (נ)
horse rider	paraʃ	פָּרָש (ז)
figure skating	haχlaka omanutit	הַחְלָקָה אוֹמָנוּתִית (נ)
figure skater (masc.)	maχlik amanuti	מַחְלִיק אָמָנוּתִי (ז)
figure skater (fem.)	maχlika amanutit	מַחְלִיקָה אָמָנוּתִית (נ)
powerlifting	haramat miʃkolot	הֲרָמַת מִשְׁקוֹלוֹת (נ)
powerlifter	miʃkolan	מִשְׁקוֹלָן (ז)
car racing	merots meχoniyot	מֵירוֹץ מְכוֹנִיוֹת (ז)
racing driver	nahag merotsim	נֶהָג מֵרוֹצִים (ז)
cycling	reχiva al ofa'nayim	רְכִיבָה עַל אוֹפַנַיִים (נ)
cyclist	roχev ofa'nayim	רוֹכֵב אוֹפַנַיִים (ז)
broad jump	kfitsa la'roχav	קְפִיצָה לָרוֹחַק (נ)
pole vault	kfitsa bemot	קְפִיצָה בְּמוֹט (נ)
jumper	kofets	קוֹפֵץ (ז)

133. Kinds of sports. Miscellaneous

football	'futbol	פּוּטְבּוֹל (ז)
badminton	notsit	נוֹצִית (ז)
biathlon	bi'atlon	בִּיאַתְלוֹן (ז)
billiards	bilyard	בִּילְיַארְד (ז)
bobsled	miz'χelet	מִזְחֶלֶת (נ)
bodybuilding	pi'tuaχ guf	פִּיתוּחַ גוּף (ז)
water polo	polo 'mayim	פּוֹלוֹ מַיִם (ז)
handball	kadur yad	כַּדוּר-יָד (ז)
golf	golf	גוֹלְף (ז)
rowing, crew	χatira	חֲתִירָה (נ)
scuba diving	tslila	צְלִילָה (נ)
cross-country skiing	ski bemiʃor	סְקִי בְּמִישׁוֹר (ז)
table tennis (ping-pong)	'tenis ʃulχan	טֶנִיס שׁוּלְחָן (ז)
sailing	'ʃayit	שַׁיִט (ז)
rally racing	'rali	רָאלִי (ז)
rugby	'rogbi	רוֹגְבִּי (ז)

| snowboarding | gliʃat 'ʃeleg | גְּלִישַׁת שֶׁלֶג (נ) |
| archery | kaʃatut | קַשָּׁתוּת (נ) |

134. Gym

| barbell | miʃ'kolet | מִשְׁקוֹלֶת (נ) |
| dumbbells | miʃkolot | מִשְׁקוֹלוֹת (נ״ר) |

training machine	maxʃir 'koʃer	מַכְשִׁיר כּוֹשֶׁר (ז)
exercise bicycle	ofanei 'koʃer	אוֹפַנֵּי כּוֹשֶׁר (ז״ר)
treadmill	halixon	הֲלִיכוֹן (ז)

horizontal bar	'metax	מֶתַח (ז)
parallel bars	makbilim	מַקְבִּילִים (ז״ר)
vault (vaulting horse)	sus	סוּס (ז)
mat (exercise ~)	mizron	מִזְרוֹן (ז)

jump rope	dalgit	דַּלְגִּית (נ)
aerobics	ei'robika	אֵירוֹבִּיקָה (נ)
yoga	'yoga	יוֹגָה (נ)

135. Hockey

hockey	'hoki	הוֹקִי (ז)
hockey player	saxkan 'hoki	שַׂחְקָן הוֹקִי (ז)
to play hockey	lesaxek 'hoki	לְשַׂחֵק הוֹקִי
ice	'kerax	קֶרַח (ז)

puck	diskit	דִּיסְקִית (נ)
hockey stick	makel 'hoki	מַקֵּל הוֹקִי (ז)
ice skates	maxli'kayim	מַחְלִיקַיִם (ז״ר)

board (ice hockey rink ~)	'dofen	דּוֹפֶן (ז)
shot	kli'a	קְלִיעָה (נ)
goaltender	ʃo'er	שׁוֹעֵר (ז)
goal (score)	'ʃa'ar	שַׁעַר (ז)
to score a goal	lehav'ki'a 'ʃa'ar	לְהַבְקִיעַ שַׁעַר

period	ʃliʃ	שְׁלִישׁ (ז)
second period	ʃliʃ ʃeni	שְׁלִישׁ שֵׁנִי (ז)
substitutes bench	safsal maxlifim	סַפְסַל מַחְלִיפִים (ז)

136. Soccer

| soccer | kadu'regel | כַּדּוּרֶגֶל (ז) |
| soccer player | kaduraglan | כַּדּוּרַגְלָן (ז) |

to play soccer	lesaχek kadu'regel	לְשַׂחֵק כַּדוּרֶגֶל
major league	'liga elyona	לִיגָה עֶלְיוֹנָה (נ)
soccer club	mo'adon kadu'regel	מוֹעֲדוֹן כַּדוּרֶגֶל (ז)
coach	me'amen	מְאַמֵּן (ז)
owner, proprietor	be'alim	בְּעָלִים (ז)
team	kvutsa, niv'χeret	קְבוּצָה, נִבחֶרֶת (נ)
team captain	'kepten	קַפּטֶן (ז)
player	saχkan	שַׂחְקָן (ז)
substitute	saχkan maχlif	שַׂחְקָן מַחֲלִיף (ז)
forward	χaluts	חָלוּץ (ז)
center forward	χaluts merkazi	חָלוּץ מֶרְכָּזִי (ז)
scorer	mavki	מַבְקִיעַ (ז)
defender, back	balam, megen	בַּלָם, מֵגֵן (ז)
midfielder, halfback	mekaʃer	מְקַשֵּׁר (ז)
match	misχak	מִשְׂחָק (ז)
to meet (vi, vt)	lehipageʃ	לְהִיפָּגֵשׁ
final	gmar	גְמָר (ז)
semi-final	χatsi gmar	חֲצִי גְמָר (ז)
championship	alifut	אֲלִיפוּת (נ)
period, half	maχatsit	מַחֲצִית (נ)
first period	maχatsit riʃona	מַחֲצִית רִאשׁוֹנָה (נ)
half-time	hafsaka	הַפְסָקָה (נ)
goal	'ʃa'ar	שַׁעַר (ז)
goalkeeper	ʃo'er	שׁוֹעֵר (ז)
goalpost	amud ha'ʃa'ar	עַמוּד הַשַּׁעַר (ז)
crossbar	maʃkof	מַשְׁקוֹף (ז)
net	'reʃet	רֶשֶׁת (נ)
to concede a goal	lispog 'ʃa'ar	לִסְפּוֹג שַׁעַר
ball	kadur	כַּדוּר (ז)
pass	mesira	מְסִירָה (נ)
kick	be'ita	בְּעִיטָה (נ)
to kick (~ the ball)	liv'ot	לִבְעוֹט
free kick (direct ~)	be'itat onʃin	בְּעִיטַת עוֹנְשִׁין (נ)
corner kick	be'itat 'keren	בְּעִיטַת קֶרֶן (נ)
attack	hatkafa	הַתְקָפָה (נ)
counterattack	hatkafat 'neged	הַתְקָפַת נֶגֶד (נ)
combination	ʃiluv	שִׁילוּב (ז)
referee	ʃofet	שׁוֹפֵט (ז)
to blow the whistle	liʃrok	לִשְׁרוֹק
whistle (sound)	ʃrika	שְׁרִיקָה (נ)
foul, misconduct	avira	עֲבִירָה (נ)
to commit a foul	leva'tse'a avira	לְבַצֵּע עֲבִירָה
to send off	leharχik	לְהַרְחִיק
yellow card	kartis tsahov	כַּרטִיס צָהוֹב (ז)

red card	kartis adom	כַּרְטִיס אָדוֹם (ז)
disqualification	psila, ʃlila	פְּסִילָה, שְׁלִילָה (נ)
to disqualify (vt)	lefsol	לִפְסוֹל
penalty kick	'pendel	פֶּנְדֶל (ז)
wall	χoma	חוֹמָה (נ)
to score (vi, vt)	lehav'ki'a	לְהַבְקִיעַ
goal (score)	'ʃa'ar	שַׁעַר (ז)
to score a goal	lehav'ki'a 'ʃa'ar	לְהַבְקִיעַ שַׁעַר
substitution	haχlata	הַחְלָטָה (נ)
to replace (a player)	lehaχlif	לְהַחְלִיף
rules	klalim	כְּלָלִים (ז"ר)
tactics	'taktika	טַקְטִיקָה (נ)
stadium	itstadyon	אִצְטַדְיוֹן (ז)
stand (bleachers)	bama	בָּמָה (נ)
fan, supporter	ohed	אוֹהֵד (ז)
to shout (vi)	lits'ok	לִצְעוֹק
scoreboard	'luaχ totsa'ot	לוּחַ תוֹצָאוֹת (ז)
score	totsa'a	תוֹצָאָה (נ)
defeat	tvusa	תְּבוּסָה (נ)
to lose (not win)	lehafsid	לְהַפְסִיד
tie	'teku	תֵּיקוּ (ז)
to tie (vi)	lesayem be'teku	לְסַיֵם בְּתֵיקוּ
victory	nitsaχon	נִיצָחוֹן (ז)
to win (vi, vt)	lena'tseaχ	לְנַצֵחַ
champion	aluf	אַלוּף (ז)
best (adj)	hatov beyoter	הַטוֹב בְּיוֹתֵר
to congratulate (vt)	levareχ	לְבָרֵךְ
commentator	parʃan	פַּרְשָׁן (ז)
to commentate (vt)	lefarʃen	לְפַרְשֵׁן
broadcast	ʃidur	שִׁידוּר (ז)

137. Alpine skiing

skis	migla'ʃayim	מִגְלָשַׁיִים (ז"ר)
to ski (vi)	la'asot ski	לַעֲשׂוֹת סְקִי
mountain-ski resort	atar ski	אָתַר סְקִי (ז)
ski lift	ma'alit ski	מַעֲלִית סְקִי (נ)
ski poles	maklot ski	מַקְלוֹת סְקִי (ז"ר)
slope	midron	מִדְרוֹן (ז)
slalom	merots akalaton	מֵירוֹץ עֲקַלָתוֹן (ז)

138. Tennis. Golf

golf	golf	גּוֹלְף (ז)
golf club	mo'adon golf	מוֹעֲדוֹן גּוֹלְף (ז)
golfer	saxkan golf	שַׂחְקָן גּוֹלְף (ז)
hole	guma	גּוּמָה (נ)
club	makel golf	מַקֵּל גּוֹלְף (ז)
golf trolley	eglat golf	עֶגְלַת גּוֹלְף (נ)
tennis	'tenis	טֶנִיס (ז)
tennis court	migraʃ 'tenis	מִגְרַשׁ טֶנִיס (ז)
serve	xavatat hagaʃa	חֲבָטַת הַגָּשָׁה (נ)
to serve (vt)	lehagiʃ	לְהַגִּישׁ
racket	maxbet 'tenis	מַחְבֵּט טֶנִיס (ז)
net	'reʃet	רֶשֶׁת (נ)
ball	kadur	כַּדּוּר (ז)

139. Chess

chess	'ʃaxmat	שַׁחְמָט (ז)
chessmen	klei 'ʃaxmat	כְּלֵי שַׁחְמָט (ז"ר)
chess player	ʃaxmetai	שַׁחְמְטַאי (ז)
chessboard	'luax 'ʃaxmat	לוּחַ שַׁחְמָט (ז)
chessman	kli	כְּלִי (ז)
White (white pieces)	levanim	לְבָנִים (ז)
Black (black pieces)	ʃxorim	שְׁחוֹרִים (ז)
pawn	xayal	חַיָּל (ז)
bishop	rats	רָץ (ז)
knight	paraʃ	פָּרָשׁ (ז)
rook	'tsriax	צְרִיחַ (ז)
queen	malka	מַלְכָּה (נ)
king	'melex	מֶלֶךְ (ז)
move	'tsa'ad	צַעַד (ז)
to move (vi, vt)	la'nu'a	לָנוּעַ
to sacrifice (vt)	lehakriv	לְהַקְרִיב
castling	hatsraxa	הַצְרָחָה (נ)
check	ʃax	שָׁח (ז)
checkmate	mat	מָט (ז)
chess tournament	taxarut 'ʃaxmat	תַּחֲרוּת שַׁחְמָט (נ)
Grand Master	rav oman	רַב־אוֹמָן (ז)
combination	ʃiluv	שִׁילּוּב (ז)
game (in chess)	misxak	מִשְׂחָק (ז)
checkers	'damka	דַּמְקָה (נ)

140. Boxing

boxing	igruf	אִיגְרוּף (ז)
fight (bout)	krav	קְרָב (ז)
boxing match	du krav	דּוּ־קְרָב (ז)
round (in boxing)	sivuv	סִיבוּב (ז)
ring	zira	זִירָה (נ)
gong	gong	גּוֹנג (ז)
punch	mahaluma	מַהֲלוּמָה (נ)
knockdown	nefila lekrafim	נְפִילָה לִקְרָשִׁים (נ)
knockout	'nok'a'ut	נוֹקְאָאוּט (ז)
to knock out	lifloax le'nok'a'ut	לִשְׁלוֹחַ לְנוֹקְאָאוּט
boxing glove	kfafat igruf	כְּפָפַת אִיגְרוּף (נ)
referee	fofet	שׁוֹפֵט (ז)
lightweight	mifkal notsa	מִשְׁקָל נוֹצָה (ז)
middleweight	mifkal beinoni	מִשְׁקָל בֵּינוֹנִי (ז)
heavyweight	mifkal kaved	מִשְׁקָל כָּבֵד (ז)

141. Sports. Miscellaneous

Olympic Games	hamisxakim ha'o'limpiyim	הַמִּשְׂחָקִים הָאוֹלִימְפִּיִּים (ז"ר)
winner	mena'tseax	מְנַצֵּחַ (ז)
to be winning	lena'tseax	לְנַצֵּחַ
to win (vi)	lena'tseax	לְנַצֵּחַ
leader	manhig	מַנְהִיג (ז)
to lead (vi)	lehovil	לְהוֹבִיל
first place	makom rifon	מָקוֹם רִאשׁוֹן (ז)
second place	makom feni	מָקוֹם שֵׁנִי (ז)
third place	makom flifi	מָקוֹם שְׁלִישִׁי (ז)
medal	me'dalya	מֶדַלְיָה (נ)
trophy	pras	פְּרָס (ז)
prize cup (trophy)	ga'vi'a nitsaxon	גָּבִיעַ נִיצָּחוֹן (ז)
prize (in game)	pras	פְּרָס (ז)
main prize	pras rifon	פְּרָס רִאשׁוֹן (ז)
record	si	שִׂיא (ז)
to set a record	lik'bo'a si	לִקְבּוֹעַ שִׂיא
final	gmar	גְּמָר (ז)
final (adj)	fel hagmar	שֶׁל הַגְּמָר
champion	aluf	אַלּוּף (ז)
championship	alifut	אַלִּיפוּת (נ)

stadium	itstadyon	אָצְטָדִיוֹן (ז)
stand (bleachers)	bama	בָּמָה (נ)
fan, supporter	ohed	אוֹהֵד (ז)
opponent, rival	yariv	יָרִיב (ז)

| start (start line) | kav zinuk | קַו זִינוּק (ז) |
| finish line | kav hagmar | קַו הַגְמָר (ז) |

| defeat | tvusa | תבוּסָה (נ) |
| to lose (not win) | lehafsid | לְהַפְסִיד |

referee	ʃofet	שׁוֹפֵט (ז)
jury (judges)	χaver ʃoftim	חֶבֶר שׁוֹפְטִים (ז)
score	totsa'a	תוֹצָאָה (נ)
tie	'teku	תֵּיקוּ (ז)
to tie (vi)	lesayem be'teku	לְסַיֵּם בְּתֵיקוּ
point	nekuda	נְקוּדָה (נ)
result (final score)	totsa'a	תוֹצָאָה (נ)

period	sivuv	סִיבוּב (ז)
half-time	hafsaka	הַפְסָקָה (נ)
doping	sam	סַם (ז)
to penalize (vt)	leha'aniʃ	לְהַעֲנִישׁ
to disqualify (vt)	lefsol	לְפְסוֹל

apparatus	maχʃir	מַכְשִׁיר (ז)
javelin	kidon	כִּידוֹן (ז)
shot (metal ball)	kadur barzel	כַּדּוּר בַּרְזֶל (ז)
ball (snooker, etc.)	kadur	כַּדּוּר (ז)

aim (target)	matara	מַטָּרָה (נ)
target	matara	מַטָּרָה (נ)
to shoot (vi)	lirot	לִירוֹת
accurate (~ shot)	meduyak	מְדוּיָק

trainer, coach	me'amen	מְאַמֵּן (ז)
to train (sb)	le'amen	לְאַמֵּן
to train (vi)	lehit'amen	לְהִתְאַמֵּן
training	imun	אִימוּן (ז)

gym	'χeder 'koʃer	חֶדֶר כּוֹשֶׁר (ז)
exercise (physical)	imun	אִימוּן (ז)
warm-up (athlete ~)	χimum	חִימוּם (ז)

Education

142. School

school	beit 'sefer	בֵּית סֵפֶר (ז)
principal (headmaster)	menahel beit 'sefer	מְנַהֵל בֵּית סֵפֶר (ז)
pupil (boy)	talmid	תַּלְמִיד (ז)
pupil (girl)	talmida	תַּלְמִידָה (נ)
schoolboy	talmid	תַּלְמִיד (ז)
schoolgirl	talmida	תַּלְמִידָה (נ)
to teach (sb)	lelamed	לְלַמֵד
to learn (language, etc.)	lilmod	לִלְמוֹד
to learn by heart	lilmod be'al pe	לִלְמוֹד בְּעַל פֶּה
to learn (~ to count, etc.)	lilmod	לִלְמוֹד
to be in school	lilmod	לִלְמוֹד
to go to school	la'leχet le'beit 'sefer	לָלֶכֶת לְבֵית סֵפֶר
alphabet	alefbeit	אָלֶפְבֵּית (ז)
subject (at school)	mik'tso'a	מִקְצוֹעַ (ז)
classroom	kita	כִּיתָה (נ)
lesson	ʃi'ur	שִׁיעוּר (ז)
recess	hafsaka	הַפְסָקָה (נ)
school bell	pa'amon	פַּעֲמוֹן (ז)
school desk	ʃulχan limudim	שׁוּלחַן לִימוּדִים (ז)
chalkboard	'luaχ	לוּחַ (ז)
grade	tsiyun	צִיוּן (ז)
good grade	tsiyun tov	צִיוּן טוֹב (ז)
bad grade	tsiyun ga'ru'a	צִיוּן גָרוּעַ (ז)
to give a grade	latet tsiyun	לָתֵת צִיוּן
mistake, error	ta'ut	טָעוּת (נ)
to make mistakes	la'asot ta'uyot	לַעֲשׂוֹת טָעוּיוֹת
to correct (an error)	letaken	לְתַקֵן
cheat sheet	ʃlif	שְׁלִיף (ז)
homework	ʃi'urei 'bayit	שִׁיעוּרֵי בַּיִת (ז"ר)
exercise (in education)	targil	תַרגִיל (ז)
to be present	lihyot no'χeaχ	לִהיוֹת נוֹכֵחַ
to be absent	lehe'ader	לְהֵיעָדֵר
to miss school	lehaχsir	לְהַחסִיר

to punish (vt)	leha'aniʃ	לְהַעֲנִיש
punishment	'oneʃ	עוֹנֶש (ז)
conduct (behavior)	hitnahagut	הִתנַהֲגוּת (נ)

report card	yoman beit 'sefer	יוֹמָן בֵּית סֵפֶר (ז)
pencil	iparon	עִיפָּרוֹן (ז)
eraser	'maxak	מַחַק (ז)
chalk	gir	גִיר (ז)
pencil case	kalmar	קַלמָר (ז)

schoolbag	yalkut	יַלקוּט (ז)
pen	et	עֵט (ז)
school notebook	max'beret	מַחבֶּרֶת (נ)
textbook	'sefer limud	סֵפֶר לִימוּד (ז)
compasses	mexuga	מְחוּגָה (נ)

to make technical drawings	lesartet	לְשַׂרטֵט
technical drawing	sirtut	שִׂרטוּט (ז)

poem	ʃir	שִיר (ז)
by heart (adv)	be'al pe	בְּעַל פֶּה
to learn by heart	lilmod be'al pe	לִלמוֹד בְּעַל פֶּה

school vacation	xufʃa	חוּפשָה (נ)
to be on vacation	lihyot bexufʃa	לִהיוֹת בְּחוּפשָה
to spend one's vacation	leha'avir 'xofeʃ	לְהַעֲבִיר חוֹפֶש

test (written math ~)	mivxan	מִבחָן (ז)
essay (composition)	xibur	חִיבּוּר (ז)
dictation	haxtava	הַכתָבָה (נ)
exam (examination)	bxina	בּחִינָה (נ)
to take an exam	lehibaxen	לְהִיבָּחֵן
experiment (e.g., chemistry ~)	nisui	נִיסוּי (ז)

143. College. University

academy	aka'demya	אֲקָדֶמיָה (נ)
university	uni'versita	אוּנִיבֶּרסִיטָה (נ)
faculty (e.g., ~ of Medicine)	fa'kulta	פָקוּלטָה (נ)

student (masc.)	student	סטוּדֶנט (ז)
student (fem.)	stu'dentit	סטוּדֶנטִית (נ)
lecturer (teacher)	martse	מַרצֶה (ז)

lecture hall, room	ulam hartsa'ot	אוּלַם הַרצָאוֹת (ז)
graduate	boger	בּוֹגֵר (ז)
diploma	di'ploma	דִיפלוֹמָה (נ)

dissertation	diser'tatsya	דִיסֶרְטַצְיָה (נ)
study (report)	meχkar	מֶחְקָר (ז)
laboratory	ma'abada	מַעֲבָּדָה (נ)
lecture	hartsa'a	הַרְצָאָה (נ)
coursemate	χaver lelimudim	חָבֵר לְלִימוּדִים (ז)
scholarship	milga	מִלְגָה (נ)
academic degree	'to'ar aka'demi	תּוֹאַר אָקָדֶמִי (ז)

144. Sciences. Disciplines

mathematics	mate'matika	מָתֶמָטִיקָה (נ)
algebra	'algebra	אַלְגֶּבְרָה (נ)
geometry	ge'o'metriya	גֵּיאוֹמֶטְרִיָה (נ)
astronomy	astro'nomya	אַסְטְרוֹנוֹמְיָה (נ)
biology	bio'logya	בִּיוֹלוֹגְיָה (נ)
geography	ge'o'grafya	גֵּיאוֹגְרַפְיָה (נ)
geology	ge'o'logya	גֵּיאוֹלוֹגְיָה (נ)
history	his'torya	הִיסְטוֹרִיָה (נ)
medicine	refu'a	רְפוּאָה (נ)
pedagogy	χinuχ	חִינוּךְ (ז)
law	miʃpatim	מִשְׁפָּטִים (ז״ר)
physics	'fizika	פִּיזִיקָה (נ)
chemistry	'χimya	כִימְיָה (נ)
philosophy	filo'sofya	פִּילוֹסוֹפְיָה (נ)
psychology	psiχo'logya	פְּסִיכוֹלוֹגְיָה (נ)

145. Writing system. Orthography

grammar	dikduk	דִקְדוּק (ז)
vocabulary	otsar milim	אוֹצַר מִילִים (ז)
phonetics	torat ha'hege	תּוֹרַת הַהֶגֶה (נ)
noun	ʃem 'etsem	שֵׁם עֶצֶם (ז)
adjective	ʃem 'to'ar	שֵׁם תּוֹאַר (ז)
verb	po'el	פּוֹעַל (ז)
adverb	'to'ar 'po'al	תּוֹאַר פּוֹעַל (ז)
pronoun	ʃem guf	שֵׁם גוּף (ז)
interjection	milat kri'a	מִילַת קְרִיאָה (נ)
preposition	milat 'yaχas	מִילַת יַחַס (נ)
root	'ʃoreʃ	שׁוֹרֶשׁ (ז)
ending	si'yomet	סִיוֹמֶת (נ)
prefix	tχilit	תְחִילִית (נ)

syllable	havara	הֲבָרָה (נ)
suffix	si'yomet	סִיוֹמֶת (נ)
stress mark	'ta'am	טַעַם (ז)
apostrophe	'gereʃ	גֶרֶשׁ (ז)
period, dot	nekuda	נְקוּדָה (נ)
comma	psik	פְּסִיק (ז)
semicolon	nekuda ufsik	נְקוּדָה וּפְסִיק (נ)
colon	nekudo'tayim	נְקוּדוֹתַיִים (נ״ר)
ellipsis	ʃaloʃ nekudot	שָׁלוֹשׁ נְקוּדוֹת (נ״ר)
question mark	siman ʃe'ela	סִימָן שְׁאֵלָה (ז)
exclamation point	siman kri'a	סִימָן קְרִיאָה (ז)
quotation marks	merχa'ot	מֵרְכָאוֹת (נ״ר)
in quotation marks	bemerχa'ot	בְּמֵרְכָאוֹת
parenthesis	sog'rayim	סוֹגְרַיִים (ז״ר)
in parenthesis	besog'rayim	בְּסוֹגְרַיִים
hyphen	makaf	מַקָף (ז)
dash	kav mafrid	קַו מַפְרִיד (ז)
space (between words)	'revaχ	רֶוַוח (ז)
letter	ot	אוֹת (נ)
capital letter	ot gdola	אוֹת גְדוֹלָה (נ)
vowel (n)	tnu'a	תְנוּעָה (נ)
consonant (n)	itsur	עִיצוּר (ז)
sentence	miʃpat	מִשְׁפָּט (ז)
subject	nose	נוֹשֵׂא (ז)
predicate	nasu	נָשׂוּא (ז)
line	ʃura	שׁוּרָה (נ)
on a new line	beʃura χadaʃa	בְּשׁוּרָה חֲדָשָׁה
paragraph	piska	פְּסְקָה (נ)
word	mila	מִילָה (נ)
group of words	tsiruf milim	צֵירוּף מִילִים (ז)
expression	bitui	בִּיטוּי (ז)
synonym	mila nir'defet	מִילָה נִרְדֶפֶת (נ)
antonym	'hefeχ	הֶפֶּךְ (ז)
rule	klal	כְּלָל (ז)
exception	yotse min haklal	יוֹצֵא מְן הַכְּלָל (ז)
correct (adj)	naχon	נָכוֹן
conjugation	hataya	הַטָיָיה (נ)
declension	hataya	הַטָיָיה (נ)
nominal case	yaχasa	יַחֲסָה (נ)
question	ʃe'ela	שְׁאֵלָה (נ)

| to underline (vt) | lehadgiʃ | לְהַדְגִּיש |
| dotted line | kav nakud | קַו נָקוד (ז) |

146. Foreign languages

language	safa	שָׂפָה (נ)
foreign (adj)	zar	זָר
foreign language	safa zara	שָׂפָה זָרָה (נ)
to study (vt)	lilmod	לִלְמֹוד
to learn (language, etc.)	lilmod	לִלְמֹוד

to read (vi, vt)	likro	לִקְרֹוא
to speak (vi, vt)	ledaber	לְדַבֵּר
to understand (vt)	lehavin	לְהָבִין
to write (vt)	liχtov	לכתֹוב

fast (adv)	maher	מַהֵר
slowly (adv)	le'at	לְאַט
fluently (adv)	χofʃi	חֹופְשִׁי

rules	klalim	כְּלָלִים (ז״ר)
grammar	dikduk	דִּקְדּוּק (ז)
vocabulary	otsar milim	אֹוצַר מִילִים (ז)
phonetics	torat ha'hege	תֹּורַת הַהֶגֶה (נ)

textbook	'sefer limud	סֵפֶר לִימוד (ז)
dictionary	milon	מִילֹון (ז)
teach-yourself book	'sefer lelimud atsmi	סֵפֶר לְלִימוד עַצְמִי (ז)
phrasebook	siχon	שִׂיחֹון (ז)

cassette, tape	ka'letet	קַלֶטֶת (נ)
videotape	ka'letet 'vide'o	קַלֶטֶת וִידֵיאֹו (נ)
CD, compact disc	taklitor	תַּקְלִיטֹור (ז)
DVD	di vi di	דִּי. וִי. דִּי. (ז)

alphabet	alefbeit	אָלֶפְבֵּית (ז)
to spell (vt)	le'ayet	לְאַיֵּת
pronunciation	hagiya	הֲגִייָה (נ)

accent	mivta	מִבְטָא (ז)
with an accent	im mivta	עִם מִבְטָא
without an accent	bli mivta	בְּלִי מִבְטָא

| word | mila | מִילָה (נ) |
| meaning | maʃma'ut | מַשְׁמָעוּת (נ) |

course (e.g., a French ~)	kurs	קוּרְס (ז)
to sign up	leheraʃem lekurs	לְהֵירָשֵׁם לְקוּרְס
teacher	more	מֹורֶה (ז)
translation (process)	tirgum	תַּרְגוּם (ז)

translation (text, etc.)	tirgum	תִּרְגּוּם (ז)
translator	metargem	מְתַרְגֵּם (ז)
interpreter	meturgeman	מְתוּרְגְּמָן (ז)
polyglot	poliglot	פּוֹלִיגְלוֹט (ז)
memory	zikaron	זִיכָּרוֹן (ז)

147. Fairy tale characters

Santa Claus	'santa 'kla'us	סַנְטָה קְלָאוּס (ז)
Cinderella	sinde'rela	סִינְדֶּרֶלָה
mermaid	bat yam, betulat hayam	בַּת יָם, בְּתוּלַת הַיָּם (נ)
Neptune	neptun	נֶפְטוּן (ז)
magician, wizard	kosem	קוֹסֵם (ז)
fairy	'feya	פֵייָה (נ)
magic (adj)	kasum	קָסוּם
magic wand	ʃarvit 'kesem	שַׁרְבִיט קֶסֶם (ז)
fairy tale	agada	אַגָּדָה (נ)
miracle	nes	נֵס (ז)
dwarf	gamad	גַּמָּד (ז)
to turn into ...	lahafoχ le...	לַהֲפוֹךְ לְ...
ghost	'ruaχ refa''im	רוּחַ רְפָאִים (נ)
phantom	'ruaχ refa''im	רוּחַ רְפָאִים (נ)
monster	mif'letset	מִפְלֶצֶת (נ)
dragon	drakon	דְּרָקוֹן (ז)
giant	anak	עֲנָק (ז)

148. Zodiac Signs

Aries	tale	טָלֶה (ז)
Taurus	ʃor	שׁוֹר (ז)
Gemini	te'omim	תְּאוֹמִים (ז"ר)
Cancer	sartan	סַרְטָן (ז)
Leo	arye	אַרְיֵה (ז)
Virgo	betula	בְּתוּלָה (נ)
Libra	moz'nayim	מאֹזְנַיִים (ז"ר)
Scorpio	akrav	עַקְרָב (ז)
Sagittarius	kaʃat	קַשָּׁת (ז)
Capricorn	gdi	גְּדִי (ז)
Aquarius	dli	דְּלִי (ז)
Pisces	dagim	דָּגִים (ז"ר)
character	'ofi	אוֹפִי (ז)
character traits	tχunot 'ofi	תְּכוּנוֹת אוֹפִי (נ"ר)

behavior	hitnahagut	הִתְנַהֲגוּת (נ)
to tell fortunes	lenabe et ha'atid	לְנַבֵּא אֶת הֶעָתִיד
fortune-teller	ma'gedet atidot	מַגֶּדֶת עֲתִידוֹת (נ)
horoscope	horoskop	הוֹרוֹסקוֹפ (ז)

Arts

149. Theater

theater	te'atron	תֵּיאַטְרוֹן (ז)
opera	'opera	אוֹפֵּרָה (נ)
operetta	ope'reta	אוֹפֵּרֶטָּה (נ)
ballet	balet	בָּלֶט (ז)
theater poster	kraza	כְּרָזָה (נ)
troupe	lahaka	לַהֲקָה (נ)
(theatrical company)		
tour	masa hofa'ot	מַסַע הוֹפָעוֹת (ז)
to be on tour	latset lemasa hofa'ot	לָצֵאת לְמַסַע הוֹפָעוֹת
to rehearse (vi, vt)	la'arox xazara	לַעֲרוֹך חֲזָרָה
rehearsal	xazara	חֲזָרָה (נ)
repertoire	repertu'ar	רֶפֶּרְטוּאָר (ז)
performance	hofa'a	הוֹפָעָה (נ)
theatrical show	hatsaga	הַצָּגָה (נ)
play	maxaze	מַחֲזֶה (ז)
ticket	kartis	כַּרְטִיס (ז)
box office (ticket booth)	kupa	קוּפָּה (נ)
lobby, foyer	'lobi	לוֹבִּי (ז)
coat check (cloakroom)	meltaxa	מֶלְתָּחָה (נ)
coat check tag	mispar meltaxa	מִסְפַּר מֶלְתָּחָה (ז)
binoculars	mif'kefet	מִשְׁקֶפֶת (נ)
usher	sadran	סַדְרָן (ז)
orchestra seats	parter	פַּרְטֵר (ז)
balcony	mir'peset	מִרְפֶּסֶת (נ)
dress circle	ya'tsi'a	יָצִיע (ז)
box	ta	תָּא (ז)
row	ʃura	שׁוּרָה (נ)
seat	moʃav	מוֹשָׁב (ז)
audience	'kahal	קָהָל (ז)
spectator	tsofe	צוֹפֶה (ז)
to clap (vi, vt)	limxo ka'payim	לִמְחוֹא כַּפַּיִם
applause	mexi'ot ka'payim	מְחִיאוֹת כַּפַּיִם (נ״ר)
ovation	tʃu'ot	תְּשׁוּאוֹת (נ״ר)
stage	bama	בָּמָה (נ)
curtain	masax	מָסָך (ז)
scenery	taf'ura	תַּפְאוּרָה (נ)

backstage	klayim	קְלָעִים
scene (e.g., the last ~)	'stsena	סְצֶנָה (נ)
act	ma'araχa	מַעֲרָכָה (נ)
intermission	hafsaka	הַפְסָקָה (נ)

150. Cinema

| actor | saχkan | שַׂחְקָן (ז) |
| actress | saχkanit | שַׂחְקָנִית (נ) |

movies (industry)	kol'no'a	קוֹלְנוֹעַ (ז)
movie	'seret	סֶרֶט (ז)
episode	epi'zoda	אֶפִּיזוֹדָה (נ)

detective movie	'seret balaʃi	סֶרֶט בַּלָשִׁי (ז)
action movie	ma'arvon	מַעֲרְבּוֹן (ז)
adventure movie	'seret harpatka'ot	סֶרֶט הַרְפַּתְקָאוֹת (ז)
science fiction movie	'seret mada bidyoni	סֶרֶט מַדָע בִּדְיוֹנִי (ז)
horror movie	'seret eima	סֶרֶט אֵימָה (ז)

comedy movie	ko'medya	קוֹמֶדְיָה (נ)
melodrama	melo'drama	מֶלוֹדְרָמָה (נ)
drama	'drama	דְרָמָה (נ)

fictional movie	'seret alilati	סֶרֶט עֲלִילָתִי (ז)
documentary	'seret ti'udi	סֶרֶט תִיעוּדִי (ז)
cartoon	'seret ani'matsya	סֶרֶט אֲנִימַצְיָה (ז)
silent movies	sratim ilmim	סְרָטִים אִילְמִים (ז"ר)

role (part)	tafkid	תַפְקִיד (ז)
leading role	tafkid raʃi	תַפְקִיד רָאשִׁי (ז)
to play (vi, vt)	lesaχek	לְשַׂחֵק

movie star	koχav kol'no'a	כּוֹכַב קוֹלְנוֹעַ (ז)
well-known (adj)	mefursam	מְפוּרְסָם
famous (adj)	mefursam	מְפוּרְסָם
popular (adj)	popu'lari	פּוֹפּוּלָרִי

script (screenplay)	tasrit	תַסְרִיט (ז)
scriptwriter	tasritai	תַסְרִיטַאי (ז)
movie director	bamai	בַּמַאי (ז)
producer	mefik	מֵפִיק (ז)
assistant	ozer	עוֹזֵר (ז)
cameraman	tsalam	צַלָם (ז)
stuntman	pa'alulan	פַּעֲלוּלָן (ז)
double (stuntman)	saχkan maχlif	שַׂחְקָן מַחֲלִיף (ז)

to shoot a movie	letsalem 'seret	לְצַלֵם סֶרֶט
audition, screen test	mivdak	מִבְדָק (ז)
shooting	hasrata	הַסְרָטָה (נ)

movie crew	'tsevet ha'seret	צֶוֶת הַסֶּרֶט (ז)
movie set	atar hatsilum	אֲתַר הַצִּילוּם (ז)
camera	matslema	מַצְלֵמָה (נ)
movie theater	beit kol'no'a	בֵּית קוֹלְנוֹעַ (ז)
screen (e.g., big ~)	masax	מָסָךְ (ז)
to show a movie	lehar'ot 'seret	לְהַרְאוֹת סֶרֶט
soundtrack	paskol	פַּסְקוֹל (ז)
special effects	e'fektim meyuxadim	אֶפֶּקְטִים מְיוּחָדִים (ז"ר)
subtitles	ktuviyot	כְּתוּבִיּוֹת (נ"ר)
credits	ktuviyot	כְּתוּבִיּוֹת (נ"ר)
translation	tirgum	תִּרְגּוּם (ז)

151. Painting

art	amanut	אָמָנוּת (נ)
fine arts	omanuyot yafot	אוֹמָנוּיוֹת יָפוֹת (נ"ר)
art gallery	ga'lerya le'amanut	גָּלֶרְיָה לְאָמָנוּת (נ)
art exhibition	ta'aruxat amanut	תַּעֲרוּכַת אָמָנוּת (נ)
painting (art)	tsiyur	צִיּוּר (ז)
graphic art	'grafika	גְרָפִיקָה (נ)
abstract art	amanut muf'fetet	אָמָנוּת מוּפְשֶׁטֶת (נ)
impressionism	impresyonizm	אִימְפְּרֶסְיוֹנִיזְם (ז)
picture (painting)	tmuna	תְּמוּנָה (נ)
drawing	tsiyur	צִיּוּר (ז)
poster	'poster	פּוֹסְטֶר (ז)
illustration (picture)	iyur	אִיּוּר (ז)
miniature	minya'tura	מִינְיָאטוּרָה (נ)
copy (of painting, etc.)	he'etek	הֶעְתֵּק (ז)
reproduction	ʃi'atuk	שִׁיעָתוּק (ז)
mosaic	psefas	פְּסֵיפָס (ז)
stained glass window	vitraʒ	וִיטְרָאז' (ז)
fresco	fresko	פְרֶסְקוֹ (ז)
engraving	taxrit	תַּחְרִיט (ז)
bust (sculpture)	pro'toma	פְּרוֹטוֹמָה (נ)
sculpture	'pesel	פֶּסֶל (ז)
statue	'pesel	פֶּסֶל (ז)
plaster of Paris	'geves	גֶּבֶס (ז)
plaster (as adj)	mi'geves	מְגֻבָּס
portrait	dyukan	דְיוֹקָן (ז)
self-portrait	dyukan atsmi	דְיוֹקָן עַצְמִי (ז)
landscape painting	tsiyur nof	צִיּוּר נוֹף (ז)
still life	'teva domem	טֶבַע דּוֹמֵם (ז)

caricature	karika'tura	קָרִיקָטוּרָה (נ)
sketch	tarʃim	תַּרְשִׁים (ז)
paint	'tseva	צֶבַע (ז)
watercolor paint	'tseva 'mayim	צֶבַע מַיִם (ז)
oil (paint)	'ʃemen	שֶׁמֶן (ז)
pencil	iparon	עִיפָּרוֹן (ז)
India ink	tuʃ	טוּשׁ (ז)
charcoal	peχam	פֶּחָם (ז)
to draw (vi, vt)	letsayer	לְצַיֵּיר
to paint (vi, vt)	letsayer	לְצַיֵּיר
to pose (vi)	ledagmen	לְדַגְמֵן
artist's model (masc.)	dugman eirom	דּוּגְמָן עֵירוֹם (ז)
artist's model (fem.)	dugmanit erom	דּוּגְמָנִית עֵירוֹם (נ)
artist (painter)	tsayar	צַיָּיר (ז)
work of art	yetsirat amanut	יְצִירַת אָמָנוּת (נ)
masterpiece	yetsirat mofet	יְצִירַת מוֹפֵת (נ)
studio (artist's workroom)	'studyo	סְטוּדִיוֹ (ז)
canvas (cloth)	bad piʃtan	בַּד פִּשְׁתָּן (ז)
easel	kan tsiyur	כֵּן צִיּוּר (ז)
palette	'plata	פָלֶטָה (נ)
frame (picture ~, etc.)	mis'geret	מִסְגֶּרֶת (נ)
restoration	ʃixzur	שִׁחְזוּר (ז)
to restore (vt)	leʃaχzer	לְשַׁחְזֵר

152. Literature & Poetry

literature	sifrut	סִפְרוּת (נ)
author (writer)	sofer	סוֹפֵר (ז)
pseudonym	ʃem badui	שֵׁם בָּדוּי (ז)
book	'sefer	סֵפֶר (ז)
volume	'kereχ	כֶּרֶךְ (ז)
table of contents	'toχen inyanim	תּוֹכֶן עְנְיָנִים (ז)
page	amud	עָמוּד (ז)
main character	hagibor haraʃi	הַגִּיבּוֹר הָרָאשִׁי (ז)
autograph	χatima	חֲתִימָה (נ)
short story	sipur katsar	סִיפּוּר קָצָר (ז)
story (novella)	sipur	סִיפּוּר (ז)
novel	roman	רוֹמָן (ז)
work (writing)	χibur	חִיבּוּר (ז)
fable	maʃal	מָשָׁל (ז)
detective novel	roman balaʃi	רוֹמָן בַּלָשִׁי (ז)
poem (verse)	ʃir	שִׁיר (ז)

poetry	ʃira	שִׁירָה (נ)
poem (epic, ballad)	po''ema	פּוֹאֵמָה (נ)
poet	meʃorer	מְשׁוֹרֵר (ז)
fiction	sifrut yafa	סִפְרוּת יָפָה (נ)
science fiction	mada bidyoni	מַדָּע בִּדְיוֹנִי (ז)
adventures	harpatka'ot	הַרְפַּתְקָאוֹת (נ"ר)
educational literature	sifrut limudit	סִפְרוּת לִימּוּדִית (נ)
children's literature	sifrut yeladim	סִפְרוּת יְלָדִים (נ)

153. Circus

circus	kirkas	קִרְקָס (ז)
traveling circus	kirkas nayad	קִרְקָס נַיָּיד (ז)
program	toxnit	תּוֹכְנִית (נ)
performance	hofa'a	הוֹפָעָה (נ)
act (circus ~)	hofa'a	הוֹפָעָה (נ)
circus ring	zira	זִירָה (נ)
pantomime (act)	panto'mima	פַּנְטוֹמִימָה (נ)
clown	leiʦan	לֵיצָן (ז)
acrobat	akrobat	אַקְרוֹבָּט (ז)
acrobatics	akro'batika	אַקְרוֹבָּטִיקָה (נ)
gymnast	mit'amel	מִתְעַמֵּל (ז)
gymnastics	hit'amlut	הִתְעַמְּלוּת (נ)
somersault	'salta	סַלְטָה (נ)
athlete (strongman)	atlet	אַתְלֵט (ז)
tamer (e.g., lion ~)	me'alef	מְאַלֵּף (ז)
rider (circus horse ~)	roxev	רוֹכֵב (ז)
assistant	ozer	עוֹזֵר (ז)
stunt	pa'alul	פַּעֲלוּל (ז)
magic trick	'kesem	קֶסֶם (ז)
conjurer, magician	kosem	קוֹסֵם (ז)
juggler	lahatutan	לַהֲטוּטָן (ז)
to juggle (vi, vt)	lelahtet	לְלַהְטֵט
animal trainer	me'alef hayot	מְאַלֵּף חַיּוֹת (ז)
animal training	iluf xayot	אִילּוּף חַיּוֹת (ז)
to train (animals)	le'alef	לְאַלֵּף

154. Music. Pop music

| music | 'muzika | מוּזִיקָה (נ) |
| musician | muzikai | מוּזִיקַאי (ז) |

musical instrument	kli negina	כְּלִי נְגִינָה (ז)
to play ...	lenagen be...	לְנַגֵן בְּ...
guitar	gi'tara	גִיטָרָה (נ)
violin	kinor	כִּינוֹר (ז)
cello	'tʃelo	צֶ'לוֹ (ז)
double bass	kontrabas	קוֹנטרַבָּס (ז)
harp	'nevel	נֶבֶל (ז)
piano	psanter	פְּסַנתֵר (ז)
grand piano	psanter kanaf	פְּסַנתֵר כָּנָף (ז)
organ	ugav	עוּגָב (ז)
wind instruments	klei neʃifa	כְּלֵי נְשִיפָה (ז"ר)
oboe	abuv	אַבּוּב (ז)
saxophone	saksofon	סַקסוֹפוֹן (ז)
clarinet	klarinet	קלָרִינֶט (ז)
flute	χalil	חָלִיל (ז)
trumpet	χatsotsra	חֲצוֹצְרָה (נ)
accordion	akordyon	אָקוֹרדיוֹן (ז)
drum	tof	תוֹף (ז)
duo	'du'o	דוּאוֹ (ז)
trio	ʃliʃiya	שְלִישִיָיה (נ)
quartet	revi'iya	רְבִיעִיָיה (נ)
choir	makhela	מַקהֵלָה (נ)
orchestra	tiz'moret	תִזמוֹרֶת (נ)
pop music	'muzikat pop	מוּזִיקַת פּוֹפ (נ)
rock music	'muzikat rok	מוּזִיקַת רוֹק (נ)
rock group	lehakat rok	לַהֲקַת רוֹק (נ)
jazz	dʒez	גָ'ז (ז)
idol	koχav	כּוֹכָב (ז)
admirer, fan	ohed	אוֹהֵד (ז)
concert	kontsert	קוֹנצֶרט (ז)
symphony	si'fonya	סִימפוֹניָה (נ)
composition	yetsira	יְצִירָה (נ)
to compose (write)	leχaber	לְחַבֵּר
singing (n)	ʃira	שִירָה (נ)
song	ʃir	שִיר (ז)
tune (melody)	mangina	מַנגִינָה (נ)
rhythm	'ketsev	קֶצֶב (ז)
blues	bluz	בּלוּז (ז)
sheet music	tavim	תָוִים (ז"ר)
baton	ʃarvit ni'tsuaχ	שַרבִיט נִיצוּחַ (ז)
bow	'keʃet	קֶשֶת (נ)
string	meitar	מֵיתָר (ז)
case (e.g., guitar ~)	nartik	נַרתִיק (ז)

Rest. Entertainment. Travel

155. Trip. Travel

tourism, travel	tayarut	תַּיָּירוּת (נ)
tourist	tayar	תַּיָּיר (ז)
trip, voyage	tiyul	טִיּוּל (ז)
adventure	harpatka	הַרְפַּתְקָה (נ)
trip, journey	nesi'a	נְסִיעָה (נ)
vacation	χuffa	חוּפְשָׁה (נ)
to be on vacation	lihyot beχuffa	לִהְיוֹת בְּחוּפְשָׁה
rest	menuχa	מְנוּחָה (נ)
train	ra'kevet	רַכֶּבֶת (נ)
by train	bera'kevet	בְּרַכֶּבֶת
airplane	matos	מָטוֹס (ז)
by airplane	bematos	בְּמָטוֹס
by car	bemeχonit	בִּמְכוֹנִית
by ship	be'oniya	בְּאוֹנִיָּיה
luggage	mit'an	מִטְעָן (ז)
suitcase	mizvada	מִזְוָודָה (נ)
luggage cart	eglat mit'an	עֶגְלַת מִטְעָן (נ)
passport	darkon	דַּרְכּוֹן (ז)
visa	'viza, affra	וִיזָה, אַשְׁרָה (נ)
ticket	kartis	כַּרְטִיס (ז)
air ticket	kartis tisa	כַּרְטִיס טִיסָה (ז)
guidebook	madriχ	מַדְרִיךְ (ז)
map (tourist ~)	mapa	מַפָּה (נ)
area (rural ~)	ezor	אֵזוֹר (ז)
place, site	makom	מָקוֹם (ז)
exotica (n)	ek'zotika	אֶקְזוֹטִיקָה (נ)
exotic (adj)	ek'zoti	אֶקְזוֹטִי
amazing (adj)	nifla	נִפְלָא
group	kvuffa	קְבוּצָה (נ)
excursion, sightseeing tour	tiyul	טִיּוּל (ז)
guide (person)	madriχ tiyulim	מַדְרִיךְ טִיּוּלִים (ז)

156. Hotel

hotel	malon	מָלוֹן (ז)
motel	motel	מוֹטֶל (ז)
three-star (~ hotel)	ʃloʃa koxavim	שְׁלוֹשָׁה כּוֹכָבִים
five-star	xamiʃa koxavim	חֲמִישָׁה כּוֹכָבִים
to stay (in a hotel, etc.)	lehit'axsen	לְהִתְאַכְסֵן
room	'xeder	חֶדֶר (ז)
single room	'xeder yaxid	חֶדֶר יָחִיד (ז)
double room	'xeder zugi	חֶדֶר זוּגִי (ז)
to book a room	lehazmin 'xeder	לְהַזְמִין חֶדֶר
half board	xatsi pensiyon	חֲצִי פֶּנְסִיוֹן (ז)
full board	pensyon male	פֶּנְסִיוֹן מָלֵא (ז)
with bath	im am'batya	עִם אַמְבַּטְיָה
with shower	im mik'laxat	עִם מִקְלַחַת
satellite television	tele'vizya bekvalim	טֶלֶוִיזְיָה בְּכְבָלִים (נ)
air-conditioner	mazgan	מַזְגָן (ז)
towel	ma'gevet	מַגֶבֶת (נ)
key	maf'teax	מַפְתֵחַ (ז)
administrator	amarkal	אֲמַרְכָּל (ז)
chambermaid	xadranit	חַדְרָנִית (נ)
porter, bellboy	sabal	סַבָּל (ז)
doorman	pakid kabala	פְּקִיד קַבָּלָה (ז)
restaurant	mis'ada	מִסְעָדָה (נ)
pub, bar	bar	בָּר (ז)
breakfast	aruxat 'boker	אֲרוּחַת בּוֹקֶר (נ)
dinner	aruxat 'erev	אֲרוּחַת עֶרֶב (נ)
buffet	miznon	מִזְנוֹן (ז)
lobby	'lobi	לוֹבִּי (ז)
elevator	ma'alit	מַעֲלִית (נ)
DO NOT DISTURB	lo lehafri'a	לֹא לְהַפְרִיעַ
NO SMOKING	asur le'aʃen!	אָסוּר לְעַשֵׁן!

157. Books. Reading

book	'sefer	סֵפֶר (ז)
author	sofer	סוֹפֵר (ז)
writer	sofer	סוֹפֵר (ז)
to write (~ a book)	lixtov	לִכְתּוֹב
reader	kore	קוֹרֵא (ז)
to read (vi, vt)	likro	לִקְרוֹא

reading (activity)	kri'a	קְרִיאָה (נ)
silently (to oneself)	belev, be'ʃeket	בְּלֵב, בְּשֶׁקֶט
aloud (adv)	bekol ram	בְּקוֹל רָם
to publish (vt)	lehotsi la'or	לְהוֹצִיא לָאוֹר
publishing (process)	hotsa'a la'or	הוֹצָאָה לָאוֹר (נ)
publisher	motsi le'or	מוֹצִיא לְאוֹר (ז)
publishing house	hotsa'a la'or	הוֹצָאָה לָאוֹר (נ)
to come out (be released)	latset le'or	לָצֵאת לְאוֹר
release (of a book)	hafatsa	הֲפָצָה (נ)
print run	tfutsa	תפוּצָה (נ)
bookstore	χanut sfarim	חֲנוּת סְפָרִים (נ)
library	sifriya	סְפְרִיָה (נ)
story (novella)	sipur	סִיפּוּר (ז)
short story	sipur katsar	סִיפּוּר קָצָר (ז)
novel	roman	רוֹמָן (ז)
detective novel	roman balaʃi	רוֹמָן בַּלָשִׁי (ז)
memoirs	ziχronot	זִיכרוֹנוֹת (ז"ר)
legend	agada	אַגָדָה (נ)
myth	'mitos	מִיתוֹס (ז)
poetry, poems	ʃirim	שִׁירִים (ז"ר)
autobiography	otobio'grafya	אוֹטוֹבִּיוֹגרַפיָה (נ)
selected works	mivχar ktavim	מִבחָר כְּתָבִים (ז)
science fiction	mada bidyoni	מַדָע בְּדִיוֹנִי (ז)
title	kotar	כּוֹתָר (ז)
introduction	mavo	מָבוֹא (ז)
title page	amud ha'ʃa'ar	עָמוּד הַשַׁעַר (ז)
chapter	'perek	פֶּרֶק (ז)
extract	'keta	קֶטַע (ז)
episode	epi'zoda	אֶפִּיזוֹדָה (נ)
plot (storyline)	alila	עֲלִילָה (נ)
contents	'toχen	תוֹכֶן (ז)
table of contents	'toχen inyanim	תוֹכֶן עְנָיָינִים (ז)
main character	hagibor haraʃi	הַגִיבּוֹר הָרָאשִׁי (ז)
volume	'kereχ	כֶּרֶך (ז)
cover	kriχa	כְּרִיכָה (נ)
binding	kriχa	כְּרִיכָה (נ)
bookmark	simaniya	סִימָנִיָה (נ)
page	amud	עָמוּד (ז)
to page through	ledafdef	לְדַפדֵף
margins	ʃu'layim	שׁוּלַיִים (ז"ר)
annotation	he'ara	הֶעָרָה (נ)
(marginal note, etc.)		

footnote	he'arat ʃu'layim	הֶעָרַת שׁוּלַיִים (נ)
text	tekst	טֶקְסְט (ז)
type, font	gufan	גּוּפָן (ז)
misprint, typo	ta'ut dfus	טָעוּת דְּפוּס (נ)
translation	tirgum	תִּרְגּוּם (ז)
to translate (vt)	letargem	לְתַרְגֵּם
original (n)	makor	מָקוֹר (ז)
famous (adj)	mefursam	מְפוּרְסָם
unknown (not famous)	lo ya'du'a	לֹא יָדוּעַ
interesting (adj)	me'anyen	מְעַנְיֵין
bestseller	rav 'meχer	רַב־מֶכֶר (ז)
dictionary	milon	מִילּוֹן (ז)
textbook	'sefer limud	סֵפֶר לִימוּד (ז)
encyclopedia	entsiklo'pedya	אֶנְצִיקְלוֹפֶּדְיָה (נ)

158. Hunting. Fishing

hunting	'tsayid	צַיִד (ז)
to hunt (vi, vt)	latsud	לָצוּד
hunter	tsayad	צַיָּיד (ז)
to shoot (vi)	lirot	לִירוֹת
rifle	rove	רוֹבֶה (ז)
bullet (shell)	kadur	כַּדּוּר (ז)
shot (lead balls)	kaduriyot	כַּדּוּרִיּוֹת (נ״ר)
steel trap	mal'kodet	מַלְכּוֹדֶת (נ)
snare (for birds, etc.)	mal'kodet	מַלְכּוֹדֶת (נ)
to fall into the steel trap	lehilaχed bemal'kodet	לְהִילָּכֵד בְּמַלְכּוֹדֶת
to lay a steel trap	leha'niaχ mal'kodet	לְהָנִיחַ מַלְכּוֹדֶת
poacher	tsayad lelo reʃut	צַיָּיד לְלֹא רְשׁוּת (ז)
game (in hunting)	χayot bar	חַיּוֹת בַּר (נ״ר)
hound dog	'kelev 'tsayid	כֶּלֶב צַיִד (ז)
safari	sa'fari	סָפָארִי (ז)
mounted animal	puχlats	פּוּחְלָץ (ז)
fisherman, angler	dayag	דַּיָּיג (ז)
fishing (angling)	'dayig	דַּיִג (ז)
to fish (vi)	ladug	לָדוּג
fishing rod	χaka	חַכָּה (נ)
fishing line	χut haχaka	חוּט הַחַכָּה (ז)
hook	'keres	קֶרֶס (ז)
float, bobber	matsof	מָצוֹף (ז)
bait	pitayon	פִּיתָיוֹן (ז)
to cast a line	lizrok et haχaka	לִזְרוֹק אֶת הַחַכָּה

to bite (ab. fish)	liv'lo'a pitayon	לִבְלוֹעַ פִּתָיוֹן
catch (of fish)	ʃlal 'dayig	שְׁלַל דַּיִג (ז)
ice-hole	mivka 'keraχ	מִבְקַע קֶרַח (ז)

fishing net	'refet dayagim	רֶשֶׁת דַּיָּגִים (נ)
boat	sira	סִירָה (נ)
to net (to fish with a net)	ladug be'refet	לָדוּג בְּרֶשֶׁת
to cast[throw] the net	lizrok 'refet	לִזְרוֹק רֶשֶׁת
to haul the net in	ligror 'refet	לִגְרוֹר רֶשֶׁת
to fall into the net	lehilaχed be'refet	לְהִילָכֵד בְּרֶשֶׁת

whaler (person)	tsayad livyatanim	צַיָּיד לִוְויָתָנִים (ז)
whaleboat	sfinat tseid livyetanim	סְפִינַת צֵיד לִוְויָתָנִית (נ)
harpoon	tsiltsal	צִלְצָל (ז)

159. Games. Billiards

billiards	bilyard	בִּילְיַארְד (ז)
billiard room, hall	'χeder bilyard	חֶדֶר בִּילְיַארְד (ז)
ball (snooker, etc.)	kadur bilyard	כַּדּוּר בִּילְיַארְד (ז)

to pocket a ball	lehaχnis kadur lekis	לְהַכְנִיס כַּדּוּר לְכִּיס
cue	makel bilyard	מַקֵּל בִּילְיַארְד (ז)
pocket	kis	כִּיס (ז)

160. Games. Playing cards

diamonds	yahalom	יַהֲלוֹם (ז)
spades	ale	עָלֶה (ז)
hearts	lev	לֵב (ז)
clubs	tiltan	תִּלְתָּן (ז)

ace	as	אָס (ז)
king	'meleχ	מֶלֶךְ (ז)
queen	malka	מַלְכָּה (נ)
jack, knave	nasiχ	נָסִיךְ (ז)

| playing card | klaf | קְלָף (ז) |
| cards | klafim | קְלָפִים (ז"ר) |

| trump | klaf nitsaχon | קְלָף נִיצָחוֹן (ז) |
| deck of cards | χafisat klafim | חֲפִיסַת קְלָפִים (נ) |

point	nekuda	נְקוּדָה (נ)
to deal (vi, vt)	leχalek klafim	לְחַלֵּק קְלָפִים
to shuffle (cards)	litrof	לִטְרוֹף
lead, turn (n)	tor	תּוֹר (ז)
cardsharp	noχel klafim	נוֹכֵל קְלָפִים (ז)

161. Casino. Roulette

casino	ka'zino	קָזִינוֹ (ז)
roulette (game)	ru'leta	רוּלֶטָה (נ)
bet	menat misχak	מְנָת מִשְׂחָק (נ)
to place bets	leha'niaχ menat misχak	לְהָנִיחַ מְנָת מִשְׂחָק
red	adom	אָדוֹם
black	ʃaχor	שָׁחוֹר
to bet on red	lehamer al adom	לְהַמֵּר עַל אָדוֹם
to bet on black	lehamer al ʃaχor	לְהַמֵּר עַל שָׁחוֹר
croupier (dealer)	'diler	דִּילֶר (ז)
to spin the wheel	lesovev et hagalgal	לְסוֹבֵב אֶת הַגַּלְגַּל
rules (of game)	klalei hamisχak	כְּלָלֵי הַמִּשְׂחָק (ז״ר)
chip	asimon	אֲסִימוֹן (ז)
to win (vi, vt)	lizkot	לִזְכּוֹת
win (winnings)	zχiya	זְכִיָּה (נ)
to lose (~ 100 dollars)	lehafsid	לְהַפְסִיד
loss (losses)	hefsed	הֶפְסֵד (ז)
player	saχkan	שַׂחְקָן (ז)
blackjack (card game)	esrim ve'eχad	עֶשְׂרִים וְאֶחָד (ז)
craps (dice game)	misχak kubiyot	מִשְׂחַק קוּבִּיּוֹת (ז)
dice (a pair of ~)	kubiyot	קוּבִּיּוֹת (נ״ר)
slot machine	meχonat misχak	מְכוֹנַת מִשְׂחָק (נ)

162. Rest. Games. Miscellaneous

to stroll (vi, vt)	letayel ba'regel	לְטַיֵּיל בָּרֶגֶל
stroll (leisurely walk)	tiyul ragli	טִיּוּל רַגְלִי (ז)
car ride	nesi'a bameχonit	נְסִיעָה בָּמְכוֹנִית (נ)
adventure	harpatka	הַרְפַּתְקָה (נ)
picnic	'piknik	פִּיקְנִיק (ז)
game (chess, etc.)	misχak	מִשְׂחָק (ז)
player	saχkan	שַׂחְקָן (ז)
game (one ~ of chess)	misχak	מִשְׂחָק (ז)
collector (e.g., philatelist)	asfan	אַסְפָן (ז)
to collect (stamps, etc.)	le'esof	לֶאֱסוֹף
collection	'osef	אוֹסֶף (ז)
crossword puzzle	taʃbets	תַשְׁבֵּץ (ז)
racetrack (horse racing venue)	hipodrom	הִיפּוֹדְרוֹם (ז)
disco (discotheque)	diskotek	דִיסְקוֹטֶק (ז)

sauna	'sa'una	סָאוּנָה (נ)
lottery	'loto	לוֹטוֹ (ז)
camping trip	tiyul maxana'ut	טִיּוּל מַחֲנָאוּת (ז)
camp	maxane	מַחֲנֶה (ז)
tent (for camping)	'ohel	אֹהֶל (ז)
compass	matspen	מַצְפֵּן (ז)
camper	maxnai	מַחֲנָאִי (ז)
to watch (movie, etc.)	lir'ot	לִרְאוֹת
viewer	tsofe	צוֹפֶה (ז)
TV show (TV program)	toxnit tele'vizya	תּוֹכְנִית טֶלֶוִיזְיָה (נ)

163. Photography

camera (photo)	matslema	מַצְלֵמָה (נ)
photo, picture	tmuna	תְּמוּנָה (נ)
photographer	tsalam	צַלָּם (ז)
photo studio	'studyo letsilum	סְטוּדִיוֹ לְצִילּוּם (ז)
photo album	albom tmunot	אַלְבּוֹם תְּמוּנוֹת (ז)
camera lens	adaʃa	עֲדָשָׁה (נ)
telephoto lens	a'deʃet teleskop	עֲדֶשֶׁת טֶלֶסְקוֹפ (נ)
filter	masnen	מַסְנֵן (ז)
lens	adaʃa	עֲדָשָׁה (נ)
optics (high-quality ~)	'optika	אוֹפְּטִיקָה (נ)
diaphragm (aperture)	tsamtsam	צַמְצָם (ז)
exposure time (shutter speed)	zman hahe'ara	זְמַן הַהֶאָרָה (ז)
viewfinder	einit	עֵינִית (נ)
digital camera	matslema digi'talit	מַצְלֵמָה דִּיגִיטָלִית (נ)
tripod	xatsuva	חֲצוּבָה (נ)
flash	mavzek	מַבְזֵק (ז)
to photograph (vt)	letsalem	לְצַלֵּם
to take pictures	letsalem	לְצַלֵּם
to have one's picture taken	lehitstalem	לְהִצְטַלֵּם
focus	moked	מוֹקֵד (ז)
to focus	lemaked	לְמַקֵּד
sharp, in focus (adj)	xad, memukad	חַד, מְמוּקָד
sharpness	xadut	חַדּוּת (נ)
contrast	nigud	נִיגוּד (ז)
contrast (as adj)	menugad	מְנוּגָד
picture (photo)	tmuna	תְּמוּנָה (נ)
negative (n)	taʃlil	תַּשְׁלִיל (ז)

film (a roll of ~)	'seret	סֶרֶט (ז)
frame (still)	freim	פְרֵיים (ז)
to print (photos)	lehadpis	לְהַדְפִּיס

164. Beach. Swimming

beach	χof yam	חוֹף יָם (ז)
sand	χol	חוֹל (ז)
deserted (beach)	ʃomem	שׁוֹמֵם
suntan	ʃizuf	שִׁיזוּף (ז)
to get a tan	lehiʃtazef	לְהִשְׁתַּזֵּף
tan (adj)	ʃazuf	שָׁזוּף
sunscreen	krem hagana	קְרֶם הֲגָנָה (ז)
bikini	bi'kini	בִּיקִינִי (ז)
bathing suit	'beged yam	בֶּגֶד יָם (ז)
swim trunks	'beged yam	בֶּגֶד יָם (ז)
swimming pool	breχa	בְּרֵיכָה (נ)
to swim (vi)	lisχot	לִשְׂחוֹת
shower	mik'laχat	מִקְלַחַת (נ)
to change (one's clothes)	lehaχlif bgadim	לְהַחְלִיף בְּגָדִים
towel	ma'gevet	מַגֶּבֶת (נ)
boat	sira	סִירָה (נ)
motorboat	sirat ma'no'a	סִירַת מָנוֹעַ (נ)
water ski	ski 'mayim	סְקִי מַיִם (ז)
paddle boat	sirat pe'dalim	סִירַת פֶּדָלִים (נ)
surfing	gliʃat galim	גְלִישַׁת גַלִים
surfer	goleʃ	גוֹלֵשׁ (ז)
scuba set	'skuba	סְקוּבָּה (נ)
flippers (swim fins)	snapirim	סְנַפִּירִים (ז"ר)
mask (diving ~)	maseχa	מַסֵּכָה (נ)
diver	tsolelan	צוֹלְלָן (ז)
to dive (vi)	litslol	לִצְלוֹל
underwater (adv)	mi'taχat lifnei ha'mayim	מִתַּחַת לִפְנֵי הַמַיִם
beach umbrella	ʃimʃiya	שִׁמְשִׁיָה (נ)
sunbed (lounger)	kise 'noaχ	כִּיסֵא נוֹחַ (ז)
sunglasses	miʃkefei 'ʃemeʃ	מִשְׁקְפֵי שֶׁמֶשׁ (ז"ר)
air mattress	mizron mitna'peaχ	מִזְרוֹן מִתְנַפֵּחַ (ז)
to play (amuse oneself)	lesaχek	לְשַׂחֵק
to go for a swim	lehitraχets	לְהִתְרַחֵץ
beach ball	kadur yam	כַּדוּר יָם (ז)
to inflate (vt)	lena'peaχ	לְנַפֵּחַ

inflatable, air (adj)	menupaχ	מְנוּפָּח
wave	gal	גַל (ז)
buoy (line of ~s)	matsof	מָצוֹף (ז)
to drown (ab. person)	lit'bo'a	לִטְבּוֹעַ
to save, to rescue	lehatsil	לְהַצִיל
life vest	χagorat hatsala	חֲגוֹרַת הַצָלָה (נ)
to observe, to watch	litspot, lehaʃkif	לִצְפּוֹת, לְהַשְקִיף
lifeguard	matsil	מַצִיל (ז)

TECHNICAL EQUIPMENT. TRANSPORTATION

Technical equipment

165. Computer

computer	maxʃev	מַחשֵׁב (ז)
notebook, laptop	maxʃev nayad	מַחשֵׁב נַייָד (ז)
to turn on	lehadlik	לְהַדלִיק
to turn off	lexabot	לְכַבּוֹת
keyboard	mik'ledet	מִקלֶדֶת (נ)
key	makaʃ	מַקָּש (ז)
mouse	axbar	עַכבָּר (ז)
mouse pad	ʃa'tiax le'axbar	שָׁטִיחַ לְעַכבָּר (ז)
button	kaftor	כַּפתוֹר (ז)
cursor	saman	סַמָּן (ז)
monitor	masax	מָסָך (ז)
screen	tsag	צָג (ז)
hard disk	disk ka'ʃiax	דִיסק קָשִׁיחַ (ז)
hard disk capacity	'nefax disk ka'ʃiax	נֶפַח דִיסק קָשִׁיחַ (ז)
memory	zikaron	זִיכָּרוֹן (ז)
random access memory	zikaron giʃa akra'it	זִיכָּרוֹן גִישָׁה אַקרָאִית (ז)
file	'kovets	קוֹבֶץ (ז)
folder	tikiya	תִיקִייָה (נ)
to open (vt)	lif'toax	לִפתוֹחַ
to close (vt)	lisgor	לִסגוֹר
to save (vt)	liʃmor	לִשמוֹר
to delete (vt)	limxok	לִמחוֹק
to copy (vt)	leha'atik	לְהַעֲתִיק
to sort (vt)	lemayen	לְמַייֵן
to transfer (copy)	leha'avir	לְהַעֲבִיר
program	toxna	תוֹכנָה (נ)
software	toxna	תוֹכנָה (נ)
programmer	metaxnet	מְתַכנֵת (ז)
to program (vt)	letaxnet	לְתַכנֵת
hacker	'haker	הָאקֶר (ז)
password	sisma	סִיסמָה (נ)

virus	'virus	וִירוּס (ז)
to find, to detect	limtso, le'ater	לִמצוֹא, לְאַתֵר
byte	bait	בַּייט (ז)
megabyte	megabait	מֶגַבַּייט (ז)
data	netunim	נְתוּנִים (ז״ר)
database	bsis netunim	בְּסִיס נְתוּנִים (ז)
cable (USB, etc.)	'kevel	כֶּבֶל (ז)
to disconnect (vt)	lenatek	לְנַתֵק
to connect (sth to sth)	lexaber	לְחַבֵּר

166. Internet. E-mail

Internet	'internet	אִינטֶרנֶט (ז)
browser	dafdefan	דַפדְפָן (ז)
search engine	ma'no'a xipus	מָנוֹעַ חִיפּוּשׂ (ז)
provider	sapak	סַפָּק (ז)
webmaster	menahel ha'atar	מְנַהֵל הָאֲתָר (ז)
website	atar	אֲתָר (ז)
webpage	daf 'internet	דַף אִינטֶרנֶט (ז)
address (e-mail ~)	'ktovet	כּתוֹבֶת (נ)
address book	'sefer ktovot	סֵפֶר כתוֹבוֹת (ז)
mailbox	teivat 'do'ar	תֵיבַת דוֹאַר (נ)
mail	'do'ar, 'do'al	דוֹאַר (ז), דוֹא״ל (ז)
full (adj)	gaduʃ	גָדוּשׁ
message	hoda'a	הוֹדָעָה (נ)
incoming messages	hoda'ot nixnasot	הוֹדָעוֹת נְכנָסוֹת (נ״ר)
outgoing messages	hoda'ot yots'ot	הוֹדָעוֹת יוֹצאוֹת (נ״ר)
sender	ʃo'leax	שׁוֹלֵחַ (ז)
to send (vt)	liʃ'loax	לִשׁלוֹחַ
sending (of mail)	ʃlixa	שׁלִיחָה (ז)
receiver	nim'an	נִמעָן (ז)
to receive (vt)	lekabel	לְקַבֵּל
correspondence	hitkatvut	הִתכַּתבוּת (נ)
to correspond (vi)	lehitkatev	לְהִתכַּתֵב
file	'kovets	קוֹבֶץ (ז)
to download (vt)	lehorid	לְהוֹרִיד
to create (vt)	litsor	לִיצוֹר
to delete (vt)	limxok	לִמחוֹק
deleted (adj)	maxuk	מָחוּק
connection (ADSL, etc.)	xibur	חִיבּוּר (ז)

speed	mehirut	מְהִירוּת (נ)
modem	'modem	מוֹדֶם (ז)
access	giʃa	גִּישָׁה (נ)
port (e.g., input ~)	port	פּוֹרְט (ז)
connection (make a ~)	χibur	חִיבּוּר (ז)
to connect to … (vi)	lehitχaber	לְהִתְחַבֵּר
to select (vt)	livχor	לִבְחוֹר
to search (for …)	leχapes	לְחַפֵּשׂ

167. Electricity

electricity	χaʃmal	חַשְׁמַל (ז)
electric, electrical (adj)	χaʃmali	חַשְׁמַלִי
electric power plant	taχanat 'koaχ	תַּחֲנַת כּוֹחַ (נ)
energy	e'nergya	אֶנֶרְגִיָה (נ)
electric power	e'nergya χaʃmalit	אֶנֶרְגִיָה חַשְׁמַלִית (נ)
light bulb	nura	נוּרָה (נ)
flashlight	panas	פָּנָס (ז)
street light	panas reχov	פָּנָס רְחוֹב (ז)
light	or	אוֹר (ז)
to turn on	lehadlik	לְהַדְלִיק
to turn off	leχabot	לְכַבּוֹת
to turn off the light	leχabot	לְכַבּוֹת
to burn out (vi)	lehisaref	לְהִישָׂרֵף
short circuit	'ketser	קֶצֶר (ז)
broken wire	χut ka'ru'a	חוּט קָרוּעַ (ז)
contact (electrical ~)	maga	מַגָּע (ז)
light switch	'meteg	מֶתֶג (ז)
wall socket	'ʃeka	שֶׁקַע (ז)
plug	'teka	תֶּקַע (ז)
extension cord	'kabel ma'ariχ	כֶּבֶל מַאֲרִיך (ז)
fuse	natiχ	נָתִיך (ז)
cable, wire	χut	חוּט (ז)
wiring	χivut	חִיווּט (ז)
ampere	amper	אַמְפֶּר (ז)
amperage	'zerem χaʃmali	זֶרֶם חַשְׁמַלִי (ז)
volt	volt	ווֹלְט (ז)
voltage	'metaχ	מֶתַח (ז)
electrical device	maχʃir χaʃmali	מַכְשִׁיר חַשְׁמַלִי (ז)
indicator	maχvan	מַחְווָן (ז)
electrician	χaʃmalai	חַשְׁמַלַאי (ז)

to solder (vt)	lehalχim	לְהַלְחִים
soldering iron	malχem	מַלְחֵם (ז)
electric current	'zerem	זֶרֶם (ז)

168. Tools

tool, instrument	kli	כְּלִי (ז)
tools	klei avoda	כְּלֵי עֲבוֹדָה (ז״ר)
equipment (factory ~)	tsiyud	צִיוּד (ז)

hammer	patiʃ	פַּטִּישׁ (ז)
screwdriver	mavreg	מַבְרֵג (ז)
ax	garzen	גַּרְזֶן (ז)

saw	masor	מַסּוֹר (ז)
to saw (vt)	lenaser	לְנַסֵּר
plane (tool)	maktso'a	מַקְצוּעָה (נ)
to plane (vt)	lehak'tsi'a	לְהַקְצִיעַ
soldering iron	malχem	מַלְחֵם (ז)
to solder (vt)	lehalχim	לְהַלְחִים

file (tool)	ptsira	פְּצִירָה (נ)
carpenter pincers	tsvatot	צְבָתוֹת (נ״ר)
lineman's pliers	mel'kaχat	מֶלְקָחַת (נ)
chisel	izmel	אִזְמֵל (ז)

drill bit	mak'deaχ	מַקְדֵּחַ (ז)
electric drill	makdeχa	מַקְדֵּחָה (נ)
to drill (vi, vt)	lik'doaχ	לִקְדּוֹחַ

knife	sakin	סַכִּין (ז, נ)
pocket knife	olar	אוֹלָר (ז)
blade	'lahav	לַהַב (ז)

sharp (blade, etc.)	χad	חַד
dull, blunt (adj)	kehe	קֵהֶה
to get blunt (dull)	lehitkahot	לְהִתְקַהוֹת
to sharpen (vt)	lehaʃχiz	לְהַשְׁחִיז

bolt	'boreg	בּוֹרֶג (ז)
nut	om	אֹם (ז)
thread (of a screw)	tavrig	תַּבְרִיג (ז)
wood screw	'boreg	בּוֹרֶג (ז)

| nail | masmer | מַסְמֵר (ז) |
| nailhead | roʃ hamasmer | רֹאשׁ הַמַּסְמֵר (ז) |

ruler (for measuring)	sargel	סַרְגֵּל (ז)
tape measure	'seret meida	סֶרֶט מֵידָה (ז)
spirit level	'peles	פֶּלֶס (ז)

magnifying glass	zχuχit mag'delet	זְכוּכִית מַגְדֶּלֶת (נ)
measuring instrument	maχʃir medida	מַכְשִׁיר מְדִידָה (ז)
to measure (vt)	limdod	לִמְדּוֹד
scale	'skala	סְקָאלָה (נ)
(of thermometer, etc.)		
readings	medida	מְדִידָה (נ)
compressor	madχes	מַדְחֵס (ז)
microscope	mikroskop	מִיקְרוֹסְקוֹפּ (ז)
pump (e.g., water ~)	maʃeva	מַשְׁאֵבָה (נ)
robot	robot	רוֹבּוֹט (ז)
laser	'leizer	לֵייזֶר (ז)
wrench	maf'teaχ bragim	מַפְתֵּחַ בְּרָגִים (ז)
adhesive tape	neyar 'devek	נְיָיר דֶּבֶק (ז)
glue	'devek	דֶּבֶק (ז)
sandpaper	neyar zχuχit	נְיָיר זְכוּכִית (ז)
spring	kfits	קְפִיץ (ז)
magnet	magnet	מַגְנֵט (ז)
gloves	kfafot	כְּפָפוֹת (נ״ר)
rope	'χevel	חֶבֶל (ז)
cord	sroχ	שְׂרוֹךְ (ז)
wire (e.g., telephone ~)	χut	חוּט (ז)
cable	'kevel	כֶּבֶל (ז)
sledgehammer	kurnas	קוּרְנָס (ז)
prybar	lom	לוֹם (ז)
ladder	sulam	סוּלָם (ז)
stepladder	sulam	סוּלָם (ז)
to screw (tighten)	lehavrig	לְהַבְרִיג
to unscrew (lid, filter, etc.)	lif'toaχ, lehavrig	לִפְתּוֹחַ, לְהַבְרִיג
to tighten	lehadek	לְהַדֵּק
(e.g., with a clamp)		
to glue, to stick	lehadbik	לְהַדְבִּיק
to cut (vt)	laχtoχ	לַחְתּוֹךְ
malfunction (fault)	takala	תַּקָלָה (נ)
repair (mending)	tikun	תִּיקוּן (ז)
to repair, to fix (vt)	letaken	לְתַקֵּן
to adjust (machine, etc.)	leχavnen	לְכַוְונֵן
to check (to examine)	livdok	לִבְדּוֹק
checking	bdika	בְּדִיקָה (נ)
readings	kri'a	קְרִיאָה (נ)
reliable, solid (machine)	amin	אָמִין
complex (adj)	murkav	מוּרְכָּב
to rust (get rusted)	lehaχlid	לְהַחְלִיד

rusty, rusted (adj)	χalud	חָלוּד
rust	χaluda	חֲלוּדָה (נ)

Transportation

169. Airplane

airplane	matos	מָטוֹס (ז)
air ticket	kartis tisa	כַּרְטִיס טִיסָה (ז)
airline	xevrat te'ufa	חֶבְרַת תְּעוּפָה (נ)
airport	nemal te'ufa	נְמַל תְּעוּפָה (ז)
supersonic (adj)	al koli	עַל קוֹלִי
captain	kabarnit	קַבַּרְנִיט (ז)
crew	'tsevet	צֶווֶת (ז)
pilot	tayas	טַייָס (ז)
flight attendant (fem.)	da'yelet	דַייֶלֶת (נ)
navigator	navat	נַווָט (ז)
wings	kna'fayim	כְּנָפַיים (נ"ר)
tail	zanav	זָנָב (ז)
cockpit	'kokpit	קוֹקפִּיט (ז)
engine	ma'no'a	מָנוֹעַ (ז)
undercarriage (landing gear)	kan nesi'a	כַּן נְסִיעָה (ז)
turbine	tur'bina	טוּרבִּינָה (נ)
propeller	madxef	מַדחֵף (ז)
black box	kufsa ʃxora	קוּפסָה שְׁחוֹרָה (נ)
yoke (control column)	'hege	הֶגֶה (ז)
fuel	'delek	דֶלֶק (ז)
safety card	hora'ot betixut	הוֹרָאוֹת בְּטִיחוּת (נ"ר)
oxygen mask	masexat xamtsan	מַסֵיכַת חַמצָן (נ)
uniform	madim	מַדִים (ז"ר)
life vest	xagorat hatsala	חֲגוֹרַת הַצָלָה (נ)
parachute	mitsnax	מִצנָח (ז)
takeoff	hamra'a	הַמרָאָה (נ)
to take off (vi)	lehamri	לְהַמרִיא
runway	maslul hamra'a	מַסלוּל הַמרָאָה (ז)
visibility	re'ut	רְאוּת (נ)
flight (act of flying)	tisa	טִיסָה (נ)
altitude	'gova	גוֹבַה (ז)
air pocket	kis avir	כִּיס אֲווִיר (ז)
seat	moʃav	מוֹשָׁב (ז)
headphones	ozniyot	אוֹזנִיוֹת (נ"ר)

folding tray (tray table)	magaʃ mitkapel	מַגָּשׁ מִתְקַפֵּל (ז)
airplane window	tsohar	צֹהַר (ז)
aisle	ma'avar	מַעֲבָר (ז)

170. Train

train	ra'kevet	רַכֶּבֶת (נ)
commuter train	ra'kevet parvarim	רַכֶּבֶת פַּרְבָרִים (נ)
express train	ra'kevet mehira	רַכֶּבֶת מְהִירָה (נ)
diesel locomotive	katar 'dizel	קַטָּר דִּיזֶל (ז)
steam locomotive	katar	קַטָּר (ז)
passenger car	karon	קָרוֹן (ז)
dining car	kron mis'ada	קְרוֹן מִסְעָדָה (ז)
rails	mesilot	מְסִילוֹת (נ״ר)
railroad	mesilat barzel	מְסִילַת בַּרְזֶל (נ)
railway tie	'eden	אֶדֶן (ז)
platform (railway ~)	ratsif	רָצִיף (ז)
track (~ 1, 2, etc.)	mesila	מְסִילָה (נ)
semaphore	ramzor	רַמְזוֹר (ז)
station	taxana	תַּחֲנָה (נ)
engineer (train driver)	nahag ra'kevet	נֶהָג רַכֶּבֶת (ז)
porter (of luggage)	sabal	סַבָּל (ז)
car attendant	sadran ra'kevet	סַדְרָן רַכֶּבֶת (ז)
passenger	no'se'a	נוֹסֵעַ (ז)
conductor (ticket inspector)	bodek	בּוֹדֵק (ז)
corridor (in train)	prozdor	פְּרוֹזְדּוֹר (ז)
emergency brake	ma'atsar xirum	מַעֲצָר חֵירוּם (ז)
compartment	ta	תָּא (ז)
berth	dargaʃ	דַּרְגָּשׁ (ז)
upper berth	dargaʃ elyon	דַּרְגָּשׁ עֶלְיוֹן (ז)
lower berth	dargaʃ taxton	דַּרְגָּשׁ תַּחְתּוֹן (ז)
bed linen, bedding	matsa'im	מַצָּעִים (ז״ר)
ticket	kartis	כַּרְטִיס (ז)
schedule	'luax zmanim	לוּחַ זְמַנִּים (ז)
information display	'ʃelet meida	שֶׁלֶט מֵידָע (ז)
to leave, to depart	latset	לָצֵאת
departure (of train)	yetsi'a	יְצִיאָה (נ)
to arrive (ab. train)	leha'gi'a	לְהַגִּיעַ
arrival	haga'a	הַגָּעָה (נ)
to arrive by train	leha'gi'a bera'kevet	לְהַגִּיעַ בְּרַכֶּבֶת
to get on the train	la'alot lera'kevet	לַעֲלוֹת לְרַכֶּבֶת

to get off the train	la'redet mehara'kevet	לָרֶדֶת מֵהָרַכֶּבֶת
train wreck	hitraskut	הִתְרַסְּקוּת (נ)
to derail (vi)	la'redet mipasei ra'kevet	לָרֶדֶת מִפַּסֵּי רַכֶּבֶת
steam locomotive	katar	קַטָר (ז)
stoker, fireman	masik	מַסִּיק (ז)
firebox	kivʃan	כִּבְשָׁן (ז)
coal	peχam	פֶּחָם (ז)

171. Ship

ship	sfina	סְפִינָה (נ)
vessel	sfina	סְפִינָה (נ)
steamship	oniyat kitor	אוֹנִיַת קִיטוֹר (נ)
riverboat	sfinat nahar	סְפִינַת נָהָר (נ)
cruise ship	oniyat ta'anugot	אוֹנִיַת תַּעֲנוּגוֹת (נ)
cruiser	sa'yeret	סַיֶּרֶת (נ)
yacht	'yaχta	יַכְטָה (נ)
tugboat	go'reret	גוֹרֶרֶת (נ)
barge	arba	אַרְבָּה (נ)
ferry	ma'a'boret	מַעֲבּוֹרֶת (נ)
sailing ship	sfinat mifras	סְפִינַת מִפְרָשׁ (נ)
brigantine	briganit	בְּרִיגָנִית (נ)
ice breaker	ʃo'veret 'keraχ	שׁוֹבֶרֶת קֶרַח (נ)
submarine	tso'lelet	צוֹלֶלֶת (נ)
boat (flat-bottomed ~)	sira	סִירָה (נ)
dinghy	sira	סִירָה (נ)
lifeboat	sirat hatsala	סִירַת הַצָּלָה (נ)
motorboat	sirat ma'no'a	סִירַת מָנוֹעַ (נ)
captain	rav χovel	רַב־חוֹבֵל (ז)
seaman	malaχ	מַלָּח (ז)
sailor	yamai	יַמַּאי (ז)
crew	'tsevet	צֶוֶת (ז)
boatswain	rav malaχim	רַב־מַלָּחִים (ז)
ship's boy	'na'ar sipun	נַעַר סִיפּוּן (ז)
cook	tabaχ	טַבָּח (ז)
ship's doctor	rofe ha'oniya	רוֹפֵא הָאוֹנִיָה (ז)
deck	sipun	סִיפּוּן (ז)
mast	'toren	תּוֹרֶן (ז)
sail	mifras	מִפְרָשׂ (ז)
hold	'beten oniya	בֶּטֶן אוֹנִיָה (נ)
bow (prow)	χartom	חַרְטוֹם (ז)

stern	yarketei hasfina	יַרכְּתֵי הַסְּפִינָה (ז״ר)
oar	maʃot	מָשׁוֹט (ז)
screw propeller	madχef	מַדחֵף (ז)
cabin	ta	תָא (ז)
wardroom	mo'adon ktsinim	מוֹעֲדוֹן קְצִינִים (ז)
engine room	χadar meχonot	חֲדַר מְכוֹנוֹת (ז)
bridge	'geʃer hapikud	גֶּשֶׁר הַפִּיקוּד (ז)
radio room	ta alχutan	תָא אַלחוּטָן (ז)
wave (radio)	'teder	תֶדֶר (ז)
logbook	yoman ha'oniya	יוֹמַן הָאוֹנִיָּה (ז)
spyglass	miʃ'kefet	מִשׁקֶפֶת (נ)
bell	pa'amon	פַּעֲמוֹן (ז)
flag	'degel	דֶּגֶל (ז)
hawser (mooring ~)	avot ha'oniya	עֲבוֹת הָאוֹנִיָּה (נ)
knot (bowline, etc.)	'keʃer	קֶשֶׁר (ז)
deckrails	ma'ake hasipun	מַעֲקֵה הַסִּיפּוּן (ז)
gangway	'keveʃ	כֶּבֶשׁ (ז)
anchor	'ogen	עוֹגֶן (ז)
to weigh anchor	leharim 'ogen	לְהָרִים עוֹגֶן
to drop anchor	la'agon	לַעֲגוֹן
anchor chain	ʃar'ʃeret ha'ogen	שַׁרשֶׁרֶת הָעוֹגֶן (נ)
port (harbor)	namal	נָמֵל (ז)
quay, wharf	'mezaχ	מֶזַח (ז)
to berth (moor)	la'agon	לַעֲגוֹן
to cast off	lehaflig	לְהַפלִיג
trip, voyage	masa, tiyul	מַסָּע (ז), טִיוּל (ז)
cruise (sea trip)	'ʃayit	שַׁיִט (ז)
course (route)	kivun	כִּיוּון (ז)
route (itinerary)	nativ	נָתִיב (ז)
fairway	nativ 'ʃayit	נָתִיב שַׁיִט (ז)
(safe water channel)		
shallows	sirton	שִׂרטוֹן (ז)
to run aground	la'alot al hasirton	לַעֲלוֹת עַל הַשִּׂרטוֹן
storm	sufa	סוּפָה (נ)
signal	ot	אוֹת (ז)
to sink (vi)	lit'bo'a	לִטבּוֹעַ
Man overboard!	adam ba'mayim!	אָדָם בַּמַּיִם!
SOS (distress signal)	kri'at hatsala	קְרִיאַת הַצָּלָה (נ)
ring buoy	galgal hatsala	גַּלגַּל הַצָּלָה (ז)

172. Airport

airport	nemal te'ufa	נְמַל תְּעוּפָה (ז)
airplane	matos	מָטוֹס (ז)
airline	xevrat te'ufa	חֶבְרַת תְּעוּפָה (נ)
air traffic controller	bakar tisa	בַּקָּר טִיסָה (ז)
departure	hamra'a	הַמְרָאָה (נ)
arrival	nexita	נְחִיתָה (נ)
to arrive (by plane)	leha'gi'a betisa	לְהַגִּיעַ בְּטִיסָה
departure time	zman hamra'a	זְמַן הַמְרָאָה (ז)
arrival time	zman nexita	זְמַן נְחִיתָה (ז)
to be delayed	lehit'akev	לְהִתְעַכֵּב
flight delay	ikuv hatisa	עִיכּוּב הַטִּיסָה (ז)
information board	'luax meida	לוּחַ מֵידָע (ז)
information	meida	מֵידָע (ז)
to announce (vt)	leho'dia	לְהוֹדִיעַ
flight (e.g., next ~)	tisa	טִיסָה (נ)
customs	'mexes	מֶכֶס (ז)
customs officer	pakid 'mexes	פָּקִיד מֶכֶס (ז)
customs declaration	hatsharat mexes	הַצְהָרַת מֶכֶס (נ)
to fill out (vt)	lemale	לְמַלֵּא
to fill out the declaration	lemale 'tofes hatshara	לְמַלֵּא טוֹפֶס הַצְהָרָה
passport control	bdikat darkonim	בְּדִיקַת דַּרְכּוֹנִים (נ)
luggage	kvuda	כְּבוּדָה (נ)
hand luggage	kvudat yad	כְּבוּדַת יָד (נ)
luggage cart	eglat kvuda	עֶגְלַת כְּבוּדָה (נ)
landing	nexita	נְחִיתָה (נ)
landing strip	maslul nexita	מַסְלוּל נְחִיתָה (ז)
to land (vi)	linxot	לִנְחוֹת
airstairs	'kevef	כֶּבֶשׁ (ז)
check-in	tfek in	צֶ'ק אִין (ז)
check-in counter	dalpak tfek in	דַּלְפָּק צֶ'ק אִין (ז)
to check-in (vi)	leva'tse'a tfek in	לְבַצֵּעַ צֶ'ק אִין
boarding pass	kartis aliya lematos	כַּרְטִיס עֲלִיָּה לְמָטוֹס (ז)
departure gate	'fa'ar yetsi'a	שַׁעַר יְצִיאָה (ז)
transit	ma'avar	מַעֲבָר (ז)
to wait (vt)	lehamtin	לְהַמְתִּין
departure lounge	traklin tisa	טְרַקְלִין טִיסָה (ז)
to see off	lelavot	לְלַוּוֹת
to say goodbye	lomar lehitra'ot	לוֹמַר לְהִתְרָאוֹת

173. Bicycle. Motorcycle

bicycle	ofa'nayim	אוֹפַנַּיִם (ז״ר)
scooter	kat'no'a	קַטְנוֹעַ (ז)
motorcycle, bike	of'no'a	אוֹפְנוֹעַ (ז)
to go by bicycle	lirkov al ofa'nayim	לִרְכּוֹב עַל אוֹפַנַּיִם
handlebars	kidon	כִּידוֹן (ז)
pedal	davʃa	דַּוְושָׁה (נ)
brakes	blamim	בְּלָמִים (ז״ר)
bicycle seat (saddle)	ukaf	אוּכָּף (ז)
pump	maʃeva	מַשְׁאֵבָה (נ)
luggage rack	sabal	סַבָּל (ז)
front lamp	panas kidmi	פָּנָס קִדְמִי (ז)
helmet	kasda	קַסְדָּה (נ)
wheel	galgal	גַּלְגַּל (ז)
fender	kanaf	כָּנָף (נ)
rim	xiʃuk	חִישׁוּק (ז)
spoke	xiʃur	חִישׁוּר (ז)

Cars

174. Types of cars

automobile, car	meχonit	מְכוֹנִית (נ)
sports car	meχonit sport	מְכוֹנִית ספּוֹרט (נ)
limousine	limu'zina	לִימוּזִינָה (נ)
off-road vehicle	'reχev 'ʃetaχ	רֶכֶב שֶׁטַח (ז)
convertible (n)	meχonit gag niftaχ	מְכוֹנִית גַג נִפתַח (נ)
minibus	'minibus	מִינִיבּוּס (ז)
ambulance	'ambulans	אַמבּוּלַנס (ז)
snowplow	maf'leset 'ʃeleg	מַפלֶסֶת שֶׁלֶג (נ)
truck	masa'it	מַשָּׂאִית (נ)
tanker truck	meχalit 'delek	מֵיכָלִית דֶלֶק (נ)
van (small truck)	masa'it kala	מַשָּׂאִית קַלָה (נ)
road tractor (trailer truck)	gorer	גוֹרֵר (ז)
trailer	garur	גָרוּר (ז)
comfortable (adj)	'noaχ	נוֹחַ
used (adj)	meʃumaʃ	מְשׁוּמָשׁ

175. Cars. Bodywork

hood	miχse hama'no'a	מִכסֶה הַמָנוֹעַ (ז)
fender	kanaf	כָּנָף (נ)
roof	gag	גַג (ז)
windshield	ʃimʃa kidmit	שִׁמשָׁה קִדמִית (נ)
rear-view mirror	mar'a aχorit	מַראָה אָחוֹרִית (נ)
windshield washer	mataz	מַתָז (ז)
windshield wipers	magev	מַגֵב (ז)
side window	ʃimʃat tsad	שִׁמשַׁת צַד (נ)
window lift (power window)	χalon χaʃmali	חַלוֹן חַשׁמַלִי (ז)
antenna	an'tena	אַנטֶנָה (נ)
sunroof	χalon gag	חַלוֹן גַג (ז)
bumper	pagoʃ	פָּגוֹשׁ (ז)
trunk	ta mit'an	תָא מִטעָן (ז)
roof luggage rack	gagon	גָגוֹן (ז)
door	'delet	דֶלֶת (נ)

| door handle | yadit | יָדִית (נ) |
| door lock | man'ul | מַנעוּל (ז) |

license plate	luχit riʃui	לוֹחִית רִישוּי (נ)
muffler	am'am	עַמעָם (ז)
gas tank	meiχal 'delek	מֵיכָל דֶלֶק (ז)
tailpipe	maflet	מַפלֵט (ז)

gas, accelerator	gaz	גָז (ז)
pedal	davʃa	דַוושָה (נ)
gas pedal	davʃat gaz	דַוושַת גָז (נ)

brake	'belem	בֶּלֶם (ז)
brake pedal	davʃat hablamim	דַוושַת הַבּלָמִים (נ)
to brake (use the brake)	livlom	לִבלוֹם
parking brake	'belem χaniya	בֶּלֶם חֲנָיָה (ז)

clutch	matsmed	מַצמֵד (ז)
clutch pedal	davʃat hamatsmed	דַוושַת הַמַצמֵד (נ)
clutch disc	luχit hamatsmed	לוֹחִית הַמַצמֵד (נ)
shock absorber	bolem za'a'zu'a	בּוֹלֵם זַעֲזוּעִים (ז)

| wheel | galgal | גַלגַל (ז) |
| spare tire | galgal χilufi | גַלגַל חִילוּפִי (ז) |

| tire | tsmig | צמִיג (ז) |
| hubcap | tsa'laχat galgal | צַלַחַת גַלגַל (נ) |

| driving wheels | galgalim meni'im | גַלגַלִים מֵנִיעִים (ז״ר) |
| front-wheel drive (as adj) | shel hana'a kidmit | שֶל הֲנָעָה קִדמִית |

| rear-wheel drive (as adj) | shel hana'a aχorit | שֶל הֲנָעָה אֲחוֹרִית |
| all-wheel drive (as adj) | shel hana'a male'a | שֶל הֲנָעָה מָלֵאָה |

| gearbox | teivat hiluχim | תֵיבַת הִילוּכִים (נ) |
| automatic (adj) | oto'mati | אוֹטוֹמָטִי |

| mechanical (adj) | me'χani | מֶכָנִי |
| gear shift | yadit hiluχim | יָדִית הִילוּכִים (נ) |

| headlight | panas kidmi | פָּנָס קִדמִי (ז) |
| headlights | panasim | פָּנָסִים (ז״ר) |

low beam	or namuχ	אוֹר נָמוּך (ז)
high beam	or ga'voha	אוֹר גָבוֹהַ (ז)
brake light	or 'belem	אוֹר בֶּלֶם (ז)

parking lights	orot χanaya	אוֹרוֹת חֲנָיָה (ז״ר)
hazard lights	orot χerum	אוֹרוֹת חֵירוּם (ז״ר)
fog lights	orot arafel	אוֹרוֹת עֲרָפֶל (ז״ר)
turn signal	panas itut	פָּנָס אִיתוּת (ז)
back-up light	orot revers	אוֹרוֹת רֶבֶרס (ז״ר)

176. Cars. Passenger compartment

car inside (interior)	ta hanos'im	תָּא הַנּוֹסְעִים (ז)
leather (as adj)	asui me'or	עָשׂוּי מֵעוֹר
velour (as adj)	ktifati	קְטִיפָתִי
upholstery	ripud	רִיפּוּד (ז)
instrument (gage)	maχven	מַכְוֵון (ז)
dashboard	'luaχ maχvenim	לוּחַ מַכְוֵונִים (ז)
speedometer	mad mehirut	מַד מְהִירוּת (ז)
needle (pointer)	'maχat	מַחַט (נ)
odometer	mad merχak	מַד מֶרְחָק (ז)
indicator (sensor)	χaiʃan	חַיְישָׁן (ז)
level	ramat mi'lui	רָמַת מִילוּי (נ)
warning light	nurat azhara	נוּרַת אַזְהָרָה (נ)
steering wheel	'hege	הֶגֶה (ז)
horn	tsofar	צוֹפָר (ז)
button	kaftor	כַּפְתּוֹר (ז)
switch	'meteg	מֶתֶג (ז)
seat	moʃav	מוֹשָׁב (ז)
backrest	miʃ'enet	מִשְׁעֶנֶת (נ)
headrest	miʃ'enet roʃ	מִשְׁעֶנֶת רֹאשׁ (נ)
seat belt	χagorat betiχut	חֲגוֹרַת בְּטִיחוּת (נ)
to fasten the belt	lehadek χagora	לְהַדֵּק חֲגוֹרָה
adjustment (of seats)	kivnun	כִּיוּונוּן (ז)
airbag	karit avir	כָּרִית אֲוֵויר (נ)
air-conditioner	mazgan	מַזְגָּן (ז)
radio	'radyo	רַדְיוֹ (ז)
CD player	'diskmen	דִיסְקְמֶן (ז)
to turn on	lehadlik	לְהַדְלִיק
antenna	an'tena	אַנְטֶנָה (נ)
glove box	ta kfafot	תָּא כְּפָפוֹת (ז)
ashtray	ma'afera	מַאֲפֵרָה (נ)

177. Cars. Engine

engine, motor	ma'no'a	מָנוֹעַ (ז)
diesel (as adj)	shel 'dizel	שֶׁל דִיזֶל
gasoline (as adj)	'delek	דֶלֶק
engine volume	'nefaχ ma'no'a	נֶפַח מָנוֹעַ (ז)
power	otsma	עוֹצְמָה (נ)
horsepower	'koaχ sus	כּוֹחַ סוּס (ז)
piston	buχna	בּוּכְנָה (נ)

| cylinder | tsi'linder | צִילִינְדֶר (ז) |
| valve | ʃastom | שַׁסְתּוֹם (ז) |

injector	mazrek	מַזְרֵק (ז)
generator (alternator)	meχolel	מְחוֹלֵל (ז)
carburetor	me'ayed	מְאַיֵּד (ז)
motor oil	'ʃemen mano'im	שֶׁמֶן מָנוֹעִים (ז)

radiator	matsnen	מַצְנֵן (ז)
coolant	nozel kirur	נוֹזֶל קִירוּר (ז)
cooling fan	me'avrer	מְאַוְרֵר (ז)

battery (accumulator)	matsber	מַצְבֵּר (ז)
starter	mat'ne'a	מַתְנֵעַ (ז)
ignition	hatsata	הַצָּתָה (נ)
spark plug	matset	מַצֵת (ז)

terminal (of battery)	'hedek	הֶדֵק (ז)
positive terminal	'hedek χiyuvi	הֶדֵק חִיּוּבִי (ז)
negative terminal	'hedek ʃlili	הֶדֵק שְׁלִילִי (ז)
fuse	natiχ	נָתִיךְ (ז)

air filter	masnen avir	מַסְנֵן אֲוִויר (ז)
oil filter	masnen 'ʃemen	מַסְנֵן שֶׁמֶן (ז)
fuel filter	masnen 'delek	מַסְנֵן דֶּלֶק (ז)

178. Cars. Crash. Repair

car crash	te'una	תְּאוּנָה (נ)
traffic accident	te'unat draχim	תְּאוּנַת דְּרָכִים (נ)
to crash (into the wall, etc.)	lehitnageʃ	לְהִתְנַגֵּשׁ

to get smashed up	lehima'eχ	לְהִימָעֵךְ
damage	'nezek	נֶזֶק (ז)
intact (unscathed)	ʃalem	שָׁלֵם

breakdown	takala	תַּקָּלָה (נ)
to break down (vi)	lehitkalkel	לְהִתְקַלְקֵל
towrope	'χevel grar	חֶבֶל גְּרָר (ז)

puncture	'teker	תֶּקֶר (ז)
to be flat	lehitpantʃer	לְהִתְפַנְצֶ'ר
to pump up	lena'peaχ	לְנַפֵּחַ
pressure	'laχats	לַחַץ (ז)
to check (to examine)	livdok	לִבְדּוֹק

repair	ʃiputs	שִׁיפּוּץ (ז)
auto repair shop	musaχ	מוּסָךְ (ז)
spare part	'χelek χiluf	חֵלֶק חִילוּף (ז)
part	'χelek	חֵלֶק (ז)

bolt (with nut)	'boreg	בּוֹרֶג (ז)
screw (fastener)	'boreg	בּוֹרֶג (ז)
nut	om	אוֹם (ז)
washer	diskit	דִּיסְקִית (נ)
bearing	mesav	מֵסַב (ז)

tube	tsinorit	צִינוֹרִית (נ)
gasket (head ~)	'etem	אֶטֶם (ז)
cable, wire	χut	חוּט (ז)

jack	dʒek	גֶ'ק (ז)
wrench	maf'teaχ bragim	מַפְתֵּחַ בְּרָגִים (ז)
hammer	patiʃ	פַּטִּישׁ (ז)
pump	maʃeva	מַשְׁאֵבָה (נ)
screwdriver	mavreg	מַבְרֵג (ז)

| fire extinguisher | mataf | מַטָּף (ז) |
| warning triangle | meʃulaʃ χirum | מְשׁוּלָשׁ חִירוּם (ז) |

to stall (vi)	ledomem	לְדוֹמֵם
stall (n)	hadmama	הַדְמָמָה (נ)
to be broken	lihyot ʃavur	לִהְיוֹת שָׁבוּר

to overheat (vi)	lehitχamem yoter midai	לְהִתְחַמֵּם יוֹתֵר מִדַי
to be clogged up	lehisatem	לְהֵיסָתֵם
to freeze up (pipes, etc.)	likpo	לִקְפּוֹא
to burst (vi, ab. tube)	lehitpa'ke'a	לְהִתְפַּקֵּעַ

pressure	'laχats	לַחַץ (ז)
level	ramat mi'lui	רָמַת מִילוּי (נ)
slack (~ belt)	rafe	רָפֶה

dent	dfika	דְּפִיקָה (נ)
knocking noise (engine)	'ra'aʃ	רַעַשׁ (ז)
crack	'sedek	סֶדֶק (ז)
scratch	srita	שְׂרִיטָה (נ)

179. Cars. Road

road	'dereχ	דֶּרֶךְ (נ)
highway	kviʃ mahir	כְּבִישׁ מָהִיר (ז)
freeway	kviʃ mahir	כְּבִישׁ מָהִיר (ז)
direction (way)	kivun	כִּיווּן (ז)
distance	merχak	מֶרְחָק (ז)

bridge	'geʃer	גֶּשֶׁר (ז)
parking lot	χanaya	חֲנָיָה (נ)
square	kikar	כִּיכָּר (נ)
interchange	meχlaf	מֶחְלָף (ז)
tunnel	minhara	מִנְהָרָה (נ)

gas station	taxanat 'delek	תַּחֲנַת דֶּלֶק (נ)
parking lot	migraʃ xanaya	מִגְרָשׁ חֲנָיָה (ז)
gas pump (fuel dispenser)	maʃevat 'delek	מַשְׁאֵבַת דֶּלֶק (נ)
auto repair shop	musax	מוּסָךְ (ז)
to get gas (to fill up)	letadlek	לְתַדְלֵק
fuel	'delek	דֶּלֶק (ז)
jerrycan	'dʒerikan	גֶ'רִיקָן (ז)
asphalt	asfalt	אַסְפַלְט (ז)
road markings	simun	סִימוּן (ז)
curb	sfat midraxa	שְׂפַת מִדְרָכָה (נ)
guardrail	ma'ake betixut	מַעֲקֶה בְּטִיחוּת (ז)
ditch	te'ala	תְּעָלָה (נ)
roadside (shoulder)	ʃulei ha'derex	שׁוּלֵי הַדֶּרֶךְ (ז"ר)
lamppost	amud te'ura	עַמּוּד תְּאוּרָה (ז)
to drive (a car)	linhog	לִנְהוֹג
to turn (e.g., ~ left)	lifnot	לִפְנוֹת
to make a U-turn	leva'tse'a pniyat parsa	לְבַצֵּעַ פְּנִיַּת פַּרְסָה
reverse (~ gear)	hilux axori	הִילוּךְ אֲחוֹרִי (ז)
to honk (vi)	liʦpor	לִצְפּוֹר
honk (sound)	ʦfira	צְפִירָה (נ)
to get stuck (in the mud, etc.)	lehitaka	לְהִיתָּקַע
to spin the wheels	lesovev et hagalgal al rek	לְסוֹבֵב אֶת הַגַּלְגַּלִּים עַל רֵיק
to cut, to turn off (vt)	ledomem	לְדוֹמֵם
speed	mehirut	מְהִירוּת (נ)
to exceed the speed limit	linhog bemehirut muf'rezet	לִנְהוֹג בִּמְהִירוּת מוּפְרֶזֶת
to give a ticket	liknos	לִקְנוֹס
traffic lights	ramzor	רַמְזוֹר (ז)
driver's license	riʃyon nehiga	רִשְׁיוֹן נְהִיגָה (ז)
grade crossing	ma'avar pasei ra'kevet	מַעֲבַר פַּסֵּי רַכֶּבֶת (ז)
intersection	'ʦomet	צֹמֶת (ז)
crosswalk	ma'avar xaʦaya	מַעֲבַר חֲצָיָה (ז)
bend, curve	pniya	פְּנִיָּה (נ)
pedestrian zone	midrexov	מִדְרְחוֹב (ז)

180. Traffic signs

rules of the road	xukei hatnu'a	חוּקֵי הַתְּנוּעָה (ז"ר)
road sign (traffic sign)	tamrur	תַּמְרוּר (ז)
passing (overtaking)	akifa	עֲקִיפָה (נ)
curve	pniya	פְּנִיָּה (נ)
U-turn	sivuv parsa	סִיבוּב פַּרְסָה (ז)
traffic circle	ma'agal tnu'a	מַעֲגַל תְּנוּעָה (ז)
No entry	ein knisa	אֵין כְּנִיסָה
No vehicles allowed	ein knisat rexavim	אֵין כְּנִיסַת רְכָבִים

No passing	akifa asura	עֲקִיפָה אֲסוּרָה
No parking	χanaya asura	חֲנָיָה אֲסוּרָה
No stopping	atsira asura	עֲצִירָה אֲסוּרָה
dangerous bend	sivuv χad	סִיבוּב חַד (ז)
steep descent	yerida tlula	יְרִידָה תְּלוּלָה (נ)
one-way traffic	tnu'a χad sitrit	תְּנוּעָה חַד־סְטְרִית (נ)
crosswalk	ma'avar χatsaya	מַעֲבָר חֲצָיָה (ז)
slippery road	kviʃ χalaklak	כְּבִיש חֲלַקְלַק (ז)
YIELD	zχut kdima	זְכוּת קְדִימָה

PEOPLE. LIFE EVENTS

Life events

181. Holidays. Event

celebration, holiday	χagiga	חֲגִיגָה (נ)
national day	χag le'umi	חַג לְאוּמִי (ז)
public holiday	yom χag	יוֹם חַג (ז)
to commemorate (vt)	laχgog	לַחְגוֹג
event (happening)	hitraχaʃut	הִתרַחֲשׁוּת (נ)
event (organized activity)	ei'ru'a	אֵירוּעַ (ז)
banquet (party)	se'uda χagigit	סְעוּדָה חֲגִיגִית (נ)
reception (formal party)	ei'ruaχ	אֵירוּחַ (ז)
feast	miʃte	מִשׁתֶה (ז)
anniversary	yom haʃana	יוֹם הַשָׁנָה (ז)
jubilee	χag hayovel	חַג הַיוֹבֵל (ז)
to celebrate (vt)	laχgog	לַחְגוֹג
New Year	ʃana χadaʃa	שָׁנָה חֲדָשָׁה (נ)
Happy New Year!	ʃana tova!	שָׁנָה טוֹבָה!
Santa Claus	'santa 'kla'us	סַנטָה קלָאוּס
Christmas	χag hamolad	חַג הַמוֹלָד (ז)
Merry Christmas!	χag hamolad sa'meaχ!	חַג הַמוֹלָד שָׂמֵחַ!
Christmas tree	ets χag hamolad	עֵץ חַג הַמוֹלָד (ז)
fireworks (fireworks show)	zikukim	זִיקוּקִים (ז"ר)
wedding	χatuna	חֲתוּנָה (נ)
groom	χatan	חָתָן (ז)
bride	kala	כַּלָה (נ)
to invite (vt)	lehazmin	לְהַזמִין
invitation card	hazmana	הַזמָנָה (נ)
guest	o'reaχ	אוֹרֵחַ (ז)
to visit	levaker	לְבַקֵר
(~ your parents, etc.)		
to meet the guests	lekabel orχim	לְקַבֵּל אוֹרחִים
gift, present	matana	מַתָנָה (נ)
to give (sth as present)	latet matana	לָתֵת מַתָנָה
to receive gifts	lekabel matanot	לְקַבֵּל מַתָנוֹת

bouquet (of flowers)	zer	זֵר (ז)
congratulations	braxa	בְּרָכָה (נ)
to congratulate (vt)	levarex	לְבָרֵךְ
greeting card	kartis braxa	כַּרְטִיס בְּרָכָה (ז)
to send a postcard	liʃloax gluya	לִשְׁלוֹחַ גלוֹיָה
to get a postcard	lekabel gluya	לְקַבֵּל גלוֹיָה
toast	leharim kosit	לְהָרִים כּוֹסִית
to offer (a drink, etc.)	lexabed	לְכַבֵּד
champagne	ʃam'panya	שַׁמפַּניָה (נ)
to enjoy oneself	lehanot	לֵיהָנוֹת
merriment (gaiety)	alitsut	עֲלִיצוּת (נ)
joy (emotion)	simxa	שִׂמחָה (נ)
dance	rikud	רִיקוּד (ז)
to dance (vi, vt)	lirkod	לִרקוֹד
waltz	vals	וַלס (ז)
tango	'tango	טַנגוֹ (ז)

182. Funerals. Burial

cemetery	beit kvarot	בֵּית קבָרוֹת (ז)
grave, tomb	'kever	קֶבֶר (ז)
cross	tslav	צְלָב (ז)
gravestone	matseva	מַצֵבָה (נ)
fence	gader	גָדֵר (נ)
chapel	beit tfila	בֵּית תפִילָה (ז)
death	'mavet	מָוֶות (ז)
to die (vi)	lamut	לָמוּת
the deceased	niftar	נִפטָר (ז)
mourning	'evel	אֵבֶל (ז)
to bury (vt)	likbor	לִקבּוֹר
funeral home	beit levayot	בֵּית לְוָיוֹת (ז)
funeral	levaya	לְוָיָה (נ)
wreath	zer	זֵר (ז)
casket, coffin	aron metim	אֲרוֹן מֵתִים (ז)
hearse	kron hamet	קְרוֹן הַמֵת (ז)
shroud	taxrixim	תַכרִיכִים (ז״ר)
funeral procession	tahaluxat 'evel	תַהֲלוּכַת אֵבֶל (נ)
funerary urn	kad 'efer	כַּד אֵפֶר (ז)
crematory	misrafa	מִשׂרָפָה (נ)
obituary	moda'at 'evel	מוֹדָעַת אֵבֶל (נ)
to cry (weep)	livkot	לִבכּוֹת
to sob (vi)	lehitya'peax	לְהִתיַיפֵּחַ

183. War. Soldiers

platoon	maχlaka	מַחְלָקָה (נ)
company	pluga	פְּלוּגָה (נ)
regiment	χativa	חֲטִיבָה (נ)
army	tsava	צָבָא (ז)
division	ugda	אוּגְדָה (נ)
section, squad	kita	כִּיתָה (נ)
host (army)	'χayil	חַיִל (ז)
soldier	χayal	חַיָּיל (ז)
officer	katsin	קָצִין (ז)
private	turai	טוּרָאי (ז)
sergeant	samal	סַמָּל (ז)
lieutenant	'segen	סֶגֶן (ז)
captain	'seren	סֶרֶן (ז)
major	rav 'seren	רַב־סֶרֶן (ז)
colonel	aluf miʃne	אַלּוּף מִשְׁנֶה (ז)
general	aluf	אַלּוּף (ז)
sailor	yamai	יַמַּאי (ז)
captain	rav χovel	רַב־חוֹבֵל (ז)
boatswain	rav malaχim	רַב־מַלָּחִים (ז)
artilleryman	totχan	תּוֹתְחָן (ז)
paratrooper	tsanχan	צַנְחָן (ז)
pilot	tayas	טַיָּס (ז)
navigator	navat	נַוָּט (ז)
mechanic	meχonai	מְכוֹנַאי (ז)
pioneer (sapper)	χablan	חַבְּלָן (ז)
parachutist	tsanχan	צַנְחָן (ז)
reconnaissance scout	iʃ modi'in kravi	אִישׁ מוֹדִיעִין קְרָבִי (ז)
sniper	tsalaf	צַלָּף (ז)
patrol (group)	siyur	סִיוּר (ז)
to patrol (vt)	lefatrel	לְפַטְרֵל
sentry, guard	zakif	זָקִיף (ז)
warrior	loχem	לוֹחֵם (ז)
patriot	patriyot	פַּטְרִיוֹט (ז)
hero	gibor	גִּיבּוֹר (ז)
heroine	gibora	גִּיבּוֹרָה (נ)
traitor	boged	בּוֹגֵד (ז)
to betray (vt)	livgod	לִבְגּוֹד
deserter	arik	עָרִיק (ז)
to desert (vi)	la'arok	לַעֲרוֹק
mercenary	sχir 'χerev	שְׂכִיר חֶרֶב (ז)

| recruit | tiron | טִירוֹן (ז) |
| volunteer | mitnadev | מִתְנַדֵּב (ז) |

dead (n)	harug	הָרוּג (ז)
wounded (n)	pa'tsu'a	פָּצוּעַ (ז)
prisoner of war	ʃavui	שָׁבוּי (ז)

184. War. Military actions. Part 1

war	milχama	מִלְחָמָה (נ)
to be at war	lehilaχem	לְהִילָחֵם
civil war	mil'χemet ezraχim	מִלְחֶמֶת אֶזְרָחִים (נ)

treacherously (adv)	bogdani	בּוֹגְדָנִי
declaration of war	haχrazat milχama	הַכְרָזַת מִלְחָמָה (נ)
to declare (~ war)	lehaχriz	לְהַכְרִיז
aggression	tokfanut	תּוֹקְפָנוּת (נ)
to attack (invade)	litkof	לִתְקוֹף

to invade (vt)	liχboʃ	לִכְבּוֹשׁ
invader	koveʃ	כּוֹבֵשׁ (ז)
conqueror	koveʃ	כּוֹבֵשׁ (ז)

defense	hagana	הֲגָנָה (נ)
to defend (a country, etc.)	lehagen al	לְהָגֵן עַל
to defend (against ...)	lehitgonen	לְהִתְגּוֹנֵן

enemy	oyev	אוֹיֵב (ז)
foe, adversary	yariv	יָרִיב (ז)
enemy (as adj)	ʃel oyev	שֶׁל אוֹיֵב

| strategy | astra'tegya | אַסְטְרָטֶגְיָה (נ) |
| tactics | 'taktika | טַקְטִיקָה (נ) |

order	pkuda	פְּקוּדָה (נ)
command (order)	pkuda	פְּקוּדָה (נ)
to order (vt)	lifkod	לִפְקוֹד
mission	mesima	מְשִׂימָה (נ)
secret (adj)	sodi	סוֹדִי

| battle | ma'araχa | מַעֲרָכָה (נ) |
| combat | krav | קְרָב (ז) |

attack	hatkafa	הַתְקָפָה (נ)
charge (assault)	hista'arut	הִסְתָּעֲרוּת (נ)
to storm (vt)	lehista'er	לְהִסְתָּעֵר
siege (to be under ~)	matsor	מָצוֹר (ז)

| offensive (n) | mitkafa | מִתְקָפָה (נ) |
| to go on the offensive | latset lemitkafa | לָצֵאת לְמִתְקָפָה |

retreat	nesiga	נְסִיגָה (נ)
to retreat (vi)	la'seget	לָסֶגֶת
encirclement	kitur	כִּיתוּר (ז)
to encircle (vt)	leχater	לְכַתֵּר
bombing (by aircraft)	haftsatsa	הַפְצָצָה (נ)
to drop a bomb	lehatil ptsatsa	לְהָטִיל פְצָצָה
to bomb (vt)	lehaftsits	לְהַפְצִיץ
explosion	pitsuts	פִּיצוּץ (ז)
shot	yeriya	יְרִייָה (נ)
to fire (~ a shot)	lirot	לִירוֹת
firing (burst of ~)	'yeri	יְרִי (ז)
to aim (to point a weapon)	leχaven 'nefek	לְכַוֵון נֶשֶק
to point (a gun)	leχaven	לְכַוֵון
to hit (the target)	lik'lo‘a	לִקְלוֹעַ
to sink (~ a ship)	lehat'bi‘a	לְהַטְבִּיעַ
hole (in a ship)	pirtsa	פִּרְצָה (נ)
to founder, to sink (vi)	lit'bo‘a	לִטְבּוֹעַ
front (war ~)	χazit	חָזִית (נ)
evacuation	pinui	פִּינוּי (ז)
to evacuate (vt)	lefanot	לְפַנוֹת
trench	te‘ala	תְעָלָה (נ)
barbwire	'tayil dokrani	תַיִל דוֹקְרָנִי (ז)
barrier (anti tank ~)	maχsom	מַחְסוֹם (ז)
watchtower	migdal ʃmira	מִגְדַל שמִירָה (ז)
military hospital	beit χolim tsva‘i	בֵּית חוֹלִים צבָאִי (ז)
to wound (vt)	lif'tso‘a	לִפְצוֹעַ
wound	'petsa	פֶּצַע (ז)
wounded (n)	pa'tsu‘a	פָּצוּעַ (ז)
to be wounded	lehipatsa	לְהִיפָּצַע
serious (wound)	kaʃe	קָשֶה

185. War. Military actions. Part 2

captivity	'ʃevi	שֶבִי (ז)
to take captive	la'kaχat be'ʃevi	לָקַחַת בְּשֶבִי
to be held captive	lihyot be'ʃevi	לִהיוֹת בְּשֶבִי
to be taken captive	lipol be'ʃevi	לִיפּוֹל בַּשֶבִי
concentration camp	maχane rikuz	מַחֲנֶה רִיכּוּז (ז)
prisoner of war	ʃavui	שָבוּי (ז)
to escape (vi)	liv'roaχ	לִברוֹחַ
to betray (vt)	livgod	לִבגוֹד

| betrayer | boged | בּוֹגֵד (ז) |
| betrayal | bgida | בְּגִידָה (נ) |

| to execute (by firing squad) | lehotsi la'horeg | לְהוֹצִיא לַהוֹרֵג |
| execution (by firing squad) | hotsa'a le'horeg | הוֹצָאָה לְהוֹרֵג (נ) |

equipment (military gear)	tsiyud	צִיוּד (ז)
shoulder board	ko'tefet	כּוֹתֶפֶת (נ)
gas mask	maseχat 'abaχ	מַסֵּכַת אַבָּ"ך (נ)

field radio	maχʃir 'keʃer	מַכְשִׁיר קֶשֶׁר (ז)
cipher, code	'tsofen	צוֹפֶן (ז)
secrecy	χaʃa'iut	חַשָׁאִיוּת (נ)
password	sisma	סִיסְמָה (נ)

land mine	mokeʃ	מוֹקֵשׁ (ז)
to mine (road, etc.)	lemakeʃ	לְמַקֵּשׁ
minefield	sde mokʃim	שְׂדֵה מוֹקְשִׁים (ז)

air-raid warning	az'aka	אַזְעָקָה (נ)
alarm (alert signal)	az'aka	אַזְעָקָה (נ)
signal	ot	אוֹת (ז)
signal flare	zikuk az'aka	זִיקוּק אַזְעָקָה (ז)

headquarters	mifkada	מִפְקָדָה (נ)
reconnaissance	isuf modi'in	אִיסוּף מוֹדִיעִין (ז)
situation	matsav	מַצָּב (ז)
report	doχ	דוֹ"ח (ז)
ambush	ma'arav	מַאֲרָב (ז)
reinforcement (of army)	tig'boret	תִּגְבּוֹרֶת (נ)

target	matara	מַטָּרָה (נ)
proving ground	sde imunim	שְׂדֵה אִימוּנִים (ז)
military exercise	timronim	תִּמְרוֹנִים (ז"ר)

panic	behala	בֶּהָלָה (נ)
devastation	'heres	הֶרֶס (ז)
destruction, ruins	harisot	הֲרִיסוֹת (נ"ר)
to destroy (vt)	laharos	לַהֲרוֹס

to survive (vi, vt)	lisrod	לִשְׂרוֹד
to disarm (vt)	lifrok mi'neʃek	לִפְרוֹק מִנֶּשֶׁק
to handle (~ a gun)	lehiʃtameʃ be...	לְהִשְׁתַּמֵּשׁ בְּ...

| Attention! | amod dom! | עֲמוֹד דּוֹם! |
| At ease! | amod 'noaχ! | עֲמוֹד נוֹחַ! |

act of courage	ma'ase gvura	מַעֲשֵׂה גְבוּרָה (ז)
oath (vow)	ʃvu'a	שְׁבוּעָה (נ)
to swear (an oath)	lehiʃava	לְהִישָּׁבַע
decoration (medal, etc.)	itur	עִיטוּר (ז)

to award (give medal to)	leha'anik	לְהַעֲנִיק
medal	me'dalya	מֶדַלְיָה (נ)
order (e.g., ~ of Merit)	ot hitstainut	אוֹת הִצְטַיְּינוּת (ז)

victory	nitsaxon	נִיצָחוֹן (ז)
defeat	tvusa	תְּבוּסָה (נ)
armistice	hafsakat eʃ	הַפְסָקַת אֵשׁ (נ)

standard (battle flag)	'degel	דֶּגֶל (ז)
glory (honor, fame)	tehila	תְּהִילָה (נ)
parade	mits'ad	מִצְעָד (ז)
to march (on parade)	lits'od	לִצְעוֹד

186. Weapons

weapons	'neʃek	נֶשֶׁק (ז)
firearms	'neʃek xam	נֶשֶׁק חַם (ז)
cold weapons (knives, etc.)	'neʃek kar	נֶשֶׁק קַר (ז)

chemical weapons	'neʃek 'ximi	נֶשֶׁק כִימִי (ז)
nuclear (adj)	gar'ini	גַּרְעִינִי
nuclear weapons	'neʃek gar'ini	נֶשֶׁק גַּרְעִינִי (ז)

| bomb | ptsatsa | פְּצָצָה (נ) |
| atomic bomb | ptsatsa a'tomit | פְּצָצָה אָטוֹמִית (נ) |

pistol (gun)	ekdax	אֶקְדָּח (ז)
rifle	rove	רוֹבֶה (ז)
submachine gun	tat mak'le'a	תַּת-מַקְלֵעַ (ז)
machine gun	mak'le'a	מַקְלֵעַ (ז)

muzzle	kane	קָנֶה (ז)
barrel	kane	קָנֶה (ז)
caliber	ka'liber	קָלִיבֶּר (ז)

trigger	'hedek	הֶדֶק (ז)
sight (aiming device)	ka'venet	כַּוֶּנֶת (נ)
magazine	maxsanit	מַחְסָנִית (נ)
butt (shoulder stock)	kat	קַת (נ)

| hand grenade | rimon | רִימוֹן (ז) |
| explosive | 'xomer 'nefets | חוֹמֶר נֶפֶץ (ז) |

bullet	ka'li'a	קָלִיעַ (ז)
cartridge	kadur	כַּדוּר (ז)
charge	te'ina	טְעִינָה (נ)
ammunition	tax'moʃet	תַּחְמוֹשֶׁת (נ)
bomber (aircraft)	maftsits	מַפְצִיץ (ז)
fighter	metos krav	מְטוֹס קְרָב (ז)

helicopter	masok	מָסוֹק (ז)
anti-aircraft gun	totaχ 'neged metosim	תּוֹתָח נֶגֶד מְטוֹסִים (ז)
tank	tank	טַנק (ז)
tank gun	totaχ	תּוֹתָח (ז)

artillery	arti'lerya	אַרטִילֶריָה (נ)
gun (cannon, howitzer)	totaχ	תּוֹתָח (ז)
to lay (a gun)	leχaven	לְכַוֵון

shell (projectile)	pagaz	פָּגָז (ז)
mortar bomb	ptsatsat margema	פְּצָצַת מַרגֵמָה (נ)
mortar	margema	מַרגֵמָה (נ)
splinter (shell fragment)	resis	רְסִיס (ז)

submarine	tso'lelet	צוֹלֶלֶת (נ)
torpedo	tor'pedo	טוֹרפֶּדוֹ (ז)
missile	til	טִיל (ז)

to load (gun)	lit'on	לִטעוֹן
to shoot (vi)	lirot	לִירוֹת
to point at (the cannon)	leχaven	לְכַוֵון
bayonet	kidon	כִּידוֹן (ז)

rapier	'χerev	חֶרֶב (נ)
saber (e.g., cavalry ~)	'χerev parashim	חֶרֶב פָּרָשִים (ז)
spear (weapon)	χanit	חֲנִית (נ)
bow	'keshet	קֶשֶת (נ)
arrow	χets	חֵץ (ז)
musket	musket	מוּסקֶט (ז)
crossbow	'keshet metsu'levet	קֶשֶת מְצוּלֶבֶת (נ)

187. Ancient people

primitive (prehistoric)	kadmon	קַדמוֹן
prehistoric (adj)	prehis'tori	פּרֶהִיסטוֹרִי
ancient (~ civilization)	atik	עַתִיק

Stone Age	idan ha''even	עִידָן הָאֶבֶן (ז)
Bronze Age	idan ha'arad	עִידָן הָאָרָד (ז)
Ice Age	idan ha'keraχ	עִידָן הַקֶרַח (ז)

tribe	'shevet	שֶבֶט (ז)
cannibal	oχel adam	אוֹכֵל אָדָם (ז)
hunter	tsayad	צַייָד (ז)
to hunt (vi, vt)	latsud	לָצוּד
mammoth	ma'muta	מָמוּטָה (נ)

cave	me'ara	מְעָרָה (נ)
fire	esh	אֵש (נ)
campfire	medura	מְדוּרָה (נ)

cave painting	pet'roglif	פֶּטרוֹגלִיף (ז)
tool (e.g., stone ax)	kli	כּלִי (ז)
spear	xanit	חֲנִית (נ)
stone ax	garzen ha'even	גַרזֶן הָאֶבֶן (ז)
to be at war	lehilaxem	לְהִילָחֵם
to domesticate (vt)	levayet	לְבַיֵית
idol	'pesel	פֶּסֶל (ז)
to worship (vt)	la'avod et	לַעֲבוֹד אֶת
superstition	emuna tfela	אֱמוּנָה תפֵלָה (נ)
rite	'tekes	טֶקֶס (ז)
evolution	evo'lutsya	אֶבוֹלוּציָה (נ)
development	hitpatxut	הִתפַּתחוּת (נ)
disappearance (extinction)	he'almut	הֵיעָלמוּת (נ)
to adapt oneself	lehistagel	לְהִסתַגֵל
archeology	arxe'o'logya	אַרכֵיאוֹלוֹגיָה (נ)
archeologist	arxe'olog	אַרכֵיאוֹלוֹג (ז)
archeological (adj)	arxe'o'logi	אַרכֵיאוֹלוֹגִי
excavation site	atar xafirot	אֲתַר חֲפִירוֹת (ז)
excavations	xafirot	חֲפִירוֹת (נ"ר)
find (object)	mimtsa	מִמצָא (ז)
fragment	resis	רְסִיס (ז)

188. Middle Ages

people (ethnic group)	am	עַם (ז)
peoples	amim	עַמִים (ז"ר)
tribe	'fevet	שֵבֶט (ז)
tribes	fvatim	שבָטִים (ז"ר)
barbarians	bar'barim	בַּרבָּרִים (ז"ר)
Gauls	'galim	גָאלִים (ז"ר)
Goths	'gotim	גוֹתִים (ז"ר)
Slavs	'slavim	סלָאבִים (ז"ר)
Vikings	'vikingim	וִיקִינגִים (ז"ר)
Romans	roma'im	רוֹמָאִים (ז"ר)
Roman (adj)	'romi	רוֹמִי
Byzantines	bi'zantim	בִּיזַנטִים (ז"ר)
Byzantium	bizantion, bizants	בִּיזַנטִיוֹן, בִּיזַנץ (נ)
Byzantine (adj)	bi'zanti	בִּיזַנטִי
emperor	keisar	קֵיסָר (ז)
leader, chief (tribal ~)	manhig	מַנהִיג (ז)
powerful (~ king)	rav 'koax	רַב-כּוֹחַ
king	'melex	מֶלֶך (ז)

ruler (sovereign)	ʃalit	שַׁלִיט (ז)
knight	abir	אַבִּיר (ז)
feudal lord	fe'odal	פֵיאוֹדָל (ז)
feudal (adj)	fe'o'dali	פֵיאוֹדָלִי
vassal	vasal	וַסָל (ז)
duke	dukas	דוּכָּס (ז)
earl	rozen	רוֹזֵן (ז)
baron	baron	בָּרוֹן (ז)
bishop	'biʃof	בִּישׁוֹף (ז)
armor	ʃiryon	שִׁרְיוֹן (ז)
shield	magen	מָגֵן (ז)
sword	'xerev	חֶרֶב (נ)
visor	magen panim	מָגֵן פָּנִים (ז)
chainmail	ʃiryon kaskasim	שִׁרְיוֹן קַשְׂקַשִׂים (ז)
Crusade	masa tslav	מַסָע צְלָב (ז)
crusader	tsalban	צַלְבָּן (ז)
territory	'ʃetax	שֶׁטַח (ז)
to attack (invade)	litkof	לִתְקוֹף
to conquer (vt)	lixboʃ	לִכְבּוֹשׁ
to occupy (invade)	lehiʃtalet	לְהִשְׁתַּלֵט
siege (to be under ~)	matsor	מָצוֹר (ז)
besieged (adj)	natsur	נָצוּר
to besiege (vt)	latsur	לָצוּר
inquisition	inkvi'zitsya	אִינְקְוִוִיזִיצְיָה (נ)
inquisitor	inkvi'zitor	אִינְקְוִוִיזִיטוֹר (ז)
torture	inui	עִינוּי (ז)
cruel (adj)	axzari	אַכְזָרִי
heretic	kofer	כּוֹפֵר (ז)
heresy	kfira	כְּפִירָה (נ)
seafaring	haflaga bayam	הַפְלָגָה בַיָם (נ)
pirate	ʃoded yam	שׁוֹדֵד יָם (ז)
piracy	pi'ratiyut	פִּירָטִיוּת (נ)
boarding (attack)	la'alot al	לַעֲלוֹת עַל
loot, booty	ʃalal	שָׁלָל (ז)
treasures	otsarot	אוֹצָרוֹת (ז"ר)
discovery	taglit	תַּגְלִית (נ)
to discover (new land, etc.)	legalot	לְגַלוֹת
expedition	miʃlaxat	מִשְׁלַחַת (נ)
musketeer	musketer	מוּסְקֶטֶר (ז)
cardinal	xaʃman	חַשְׁמָן (ז)
heraldry	he'raldika	הֶרַלְדִיקָה (נ)
heraldic (adj)	he'raldi	הֶרַלְדִי

189. Leader. Chief. Authorities

king	'meleχ	מֶלֶךְ (ז)
queen	malka	מַלְכָּה (נ)
royal (adj)	malχuti	מַלְכוּתִי
kingdom	mamlaχa	מַמְלָכָה (נ)
prince	nasiχ	נָסִיךְ (ז)
princess	nesiχa	נְסִיכָה (נ)
president	nasi	נָשִׂיא (ז)
vice-president	sgan nasi	סְגַן נָשִׂיא (ז)
senator	se'nator	סֶנָאטוֹר (ז)
monarch	'meleχ	מֶלֶךְ (ז)
ruler (sovereign)	ʃalit	שַׁלִּיט (ז)
dictator	rodan	רוֹדָן (ז)
tyrant	aruts	עָרוּץ (ז)
magnate	eil hon	אֵיל הוֹן (ז)
director	menahel	מְנַהֵל (ז)
chief	menahel, roʃ	מְנַהֵל (ז), רֹאשׁ (ז)
manager (director)	menahel	מְנַהֵל (ז)
boss	bos	בּוֹס (ז)
owner	'ba'al	בַּעַל (ז)
leader	manhig	מַנְהִיג (ז)
head (~ of delegation)	roʃ	רֹאשׁ (ז)
authorities	ʃiltonot	שִׁלְטוֹנוֹת (ז"ר)
superiors	memunim	מְמוּנִים (ז"ר)
governor	moʃel	מוֹשֵׁל (ז)
consul	'konsul	קוֹנְסוּל (ז)
diplomat	diplomat	דִּיפְּלוֹמָט (ז)
mayor	roʃ ha'ir	רֹאשׁ הָעִיר (ז)
sheriff	ʃerif	שֶׁרִיף (ז)
emperor	keisar	קֵיסָר (ז)
tsar, czar	tsar	צָאר (ז)
pharaoh	par'o	פַּרְעֹה (ז)
khan	χan	חָאן (ז)

190. Road. Way. Directions

road	'dereχ	דֶּרֶךְ (נ)
way (direction)	kivun	כִּיוּוּן (ז)
freeway	kviʃ mahir	כְּבִישׁ מָהִיר (ז)
highway	kviʃ mahir	כְּבִישׁ מָהִיר (ז)

interstate	kviʃ le'umi	כְּבִישׁ לְאוּמִי (ז)
main road	kviʃ raʃi	כְּבִישׁ רָאשִׁי (ז)
dirt road	'derex afar	דֶּרֶךְ עָפָר (נ)

| pathway | ʃvil | שְׁבִיל (ז) |
| footpath (troddenpath) | ʃvil | שְׁבִיל (ז) |

Where?	'eifo?	אֵיפֹה?
Where (to)?	le'an?	לְאָן?
From where?	me''eifo?	מֵאֵיפֹה?

| direction (way) | kivun | כִּיווּן (ז) |
| to point (~ the way) | lenatev | לְנַתֵּב |

to the left	'smola	שְׂמֹאלָה
to the right	ya'mina	יָמִינָה
straight ahead (adv)	yaʃar	יָשָׁר
back (e.g., to turn ~)	a'xora	אֲחוֹרָה
bend, curve	ikul	עִיקּוּל (ז)
to turn (e.g., ~ left)	lifnot	לִפְנוֹת
to make a U-turn	leva'tse'a pniyat parsa	לְבַצֵּעַ פְּנִיַּת פַּרְסָה

| to be visible (mountains, castle, etc.) | lihyot nir'a | לִהְיוֹת נִרְאָה |
| to appear (come into view) | leho'fi'a | לְהוֹפִיעַ |

stop, halt (e.g., during a trip)	taxana	תַּחֲנָה (נ)
to rest, to pause (vi)	la'nuax	לָנוּחַ
rest (pause)	menuxa	מְנוּחָה (נ)

to lose one's way	lit'ot	לִתְעוֹת
to lead to … (ab. road)	lehovil le…	לְהוֹבִיל לְ…
to come out (e.g., on the highway)	latset le…	לָצֵאת לְ…
stretch (of road)	'keta	קֶטַע (ז)

asphalt	asfalt	אַסְפַלְט (ז)
curb	sfat midraxa	שְׂפַת מִדְרָכָה (נ)
ditch	te'ala	תְּעָלָה (נ)
manhole	bor	בּוֹר (ז)
roadside (shoulder)	ʃulei ha'derex	שׁוּלֵי הַדֶּרֶךְ (ז"ר)
pit, pothole	bor	בּוֹר (ז)

| to go (on foot) | la'lexet | לָלֶכֶת |
| to pass (overtake) | la'akof | לַעֲקֹוף |

step (footstep)	'tsa'ad	צַעַד (ז)
on foot (adv)	ba'regel	בָּרֶגֶל
to block (road)	laxsom	לַחְסֹום
boom gate	maxsom	מַחְסוֹם (ז)
dead end	mavoi satum	מָבוֹי סָתוּם (ז)

191. Breaking the law. Criminals. Part 1

bandit	ʃoded	שׁוֹדֵד (ז)
crime	'peʃa	פֶּשַׁע (ז)
criminal (person)	po'ʃe'a	פּוֹשֵׁעַ (ז)
thief	ganav	גַּנָּב (ז)
to steal (vi, vt)	lignov	לִגְנוֹב
stealing (larceny)	gneva	גְּנֵיבָה (נ)
theft	gneva	גְּנֵיבָה (נ)
to kidnap (vt)	laχatof	לַחֲטוֹף
kidnapping	χatifa	חֲטִיפָה (נ)
kidnapper	χotef	חוֹטֵף (ז)
ransom	'kofer	כּוֹפֶר (ז)
to demand ransom	lidroʃ 'kofer	לִדְרוֹשׁ כּוֹפֶר
to rob (vt)	liʃdod	לִשְׁדוֹד
robbery	ʃod	שׁוֹד (ז)
robber	ʃoded	שׁוֹדֵד (ז)
to extort (vt)	lisχot	לִסְחוֹט
extortionist	saχtan	סַחְטָן (ז)
extortion	saχtanut	סַחְטָנוּת (נ)
to murder, to kill	lir'tsoaχ	לִרְצוֹחַ
murder	'retsaχ	רֶצַח (ז)
murderer	ro'tseaχ	רוֹצֵחַ (ז)
gunshot	yeriya	יְרִיָּה (נ)
to fire (~ a shot)	lirot	לִירוֹת
to shoot to death	lirot la'mavet	לִירוֹת לַמָּוֶת
to shoot (vi)	lirot	לִירוֹת
shooting	'yeri	יְרִי (ז)
incident (fight, etc.)	takrit	תַּקְרִית (נ)
fight, brawl	ktata	קְטָטָה (נ)
Help!	ha'tsilu!	הַצִּילוּ!
victim	nifga	נִפְגָּע (ז)
to damage (vt)	lekalkel	לְקַלְקֵל
damage	'nezek	נֶזֶק (ז)
dead body, corpse	gufa	גּוּפָה (נ)
grave (~ crime)	χamur	חָמוּר
to attack (vt)	litkof	לִתְקוֹף
to beat (to hit)	lehakot	לְהַכּוֹת
to beat up	lehakot	לְהַכּוֹת
to take (rob of sth)	la'kaχat be'koaχ	לָקַחַת בְּכוֹחַ
to stab to death	lidkor le'mavet	לִדְקוֹר לְמָוֶת

to maim (vt)	lehatil mum	לְהָטִיל מוּם
to wound (vt)	lif'tso'a	לִפְצוֹעַ
blackmail	saxtanut	סַחטָנוּת (נ)
to blackmail (vt)	lisxot	לִסחוֹט
blackmailer	saxtan	סַחטָן (ז)
protection racket	dmei xasut	דמֵי חָסוּת (ז"ר)
racketeer	gove xasut	גוֹבֶה חָסוּת (ז)
gangster	'gangster	גַנגסטֶר (ז)
mafia, Mob	'mafya	מָאפִיָה (נ)
pickpocket	kayas	כַּיָיס (ז)
burglar	porets	פּוֹרֵץ (ז)
smuggling	havraxa	הַברָחָה (נ)
smuggler	mav'riax	מַברִיחַ (ז)
forgery	ziyuf	זִיוּף (ז)
to forge (counterfeit)	lezayef	לְזַיֵיף
fake (forged)	mezuyaf	מְזוּיָף

192. Breaking the law. Criminals. Part 2

rape	'ones	אוֹנֶס (ז)
to rape (vt)	le'enos	לֶאֱנוֹס
rapist	anas	אַנָס (ז)
maniac	'manyak	מַניָאק (ז)
prostitute (fem.)	zona	זוֹנָה (נ)
prostitution	znut	זנוּת (נ)
pimp	sarsur	סַרסוּר (ז)
drug addict	narkoman	נַרקוֹמָן (ז)
drug dealer	soxer samim	סוֹחֵר סָמִים (ז)
to blow up (bomb)	lefotsets	לְפוֹצֵץ
explosion	pitsuts	פִּיצוּץ (ז)
to set fire	lehatsit	לְהַצִית
arsonist	matsit	מַצִית (ז)
terrorism	terorizm	טֶרוֹרִיזם (ז)
terrorist	mexabel	מְחַבֵּל (ז)
hostage	ben aruba	בֶּן עָרוּבָּה (ז)
to swindle (deceive)	lehonot	לְהוֹנוֹת
swindle, deception	hona'a	הוֹנָאָה (נ)
swindler	ramai	רַמַאי (ז)
to bribe (vt)	lefaxed	לְשַׁחֵד
bribery	'foxad	שׁוֹחַד (ז)

bribe	ʃoχad	שׁוֹחַד (ז)
poison	'ra'al	רַעַל (ז)
to poison (vt)	lehar'il	לְהַרְעִיל
to poison oneself	lehar'il et atsmo	לְהַרְעִיל אֶת עַצמוֹ
suicide (act)	hit'abdut	הִתאַבְּדוּת (נ)
suicide (person)	mit'abed	מִתאַבֵּד (ז)
to threaten (vt)	le'ayem	לְאַיֵם
threat	iyum	אִיוּם (ז)
to make an attempt	lehitnakeʃ	לְהִתנַקֵש
attempt (attack)	nisayon hitnakʃut	נִיסָיוֹן הִתנַקְשׁוּת (ז)
to steal (a car)	lignov	לִגנוֹב
to hijack (a plane)	laχatof matos	לַחֲטוֹף מָטוֹס
revenge	nekama	נְקָמָה (נ)
to avenge (get revenge)	linkom	לִנקוֹם
to torture (vt)	la'anot	לְעַנוֹת
torture	inui	עִינוּי (ז)
to torment (vt)	leyaser	לְייַסֵר
pirate	ʃoded yam	שׁוֹדֵד יָם (ז)
hooligan	χuligan	חוּלִיגָאן (ז)
armed (adj)	mezuyan	מְזוּיָן
violence	alimut	אַלִימוּת (נ)
illegal (unlawful)	'bilti le'gali	בִּלתִי לְגָלִי
spying (espionage)	rigul	רִיגוּל (ז)
to spy (vi)	leragel	לְרַגֵל

193. Police. Law. Part 1

justice	'tsedek	צֶדֶק (ז)
court (see you in ~)	beit miʃpat	בֵּית מִשׁפָּט (ז)
judge	ʃofet	שׁוֹפֵט (ז)
jurors	muʃba'im	מוּשׁבָּעִים (ז"ר)
jury trial	χaver muʃba'im	חָבֶר מוּשׁבָּעִים (ז)
to judge (vt)	liʃpot	לִשׁפּוֹט
lawyer, attorney	oreχ din	עוֹרֵך דִין (ז)
defendant	omed lemiʃpat	עוֹמֵד לְמִשׁפָּט (ז)
dock	safsal ne'eʃamim	סַפסָל נֶאֱשָׁמִים (ז)
charge	ha'aʃama	הַאֲשָׁמָה (נ)
accused	ne'eʃam	נֶאֱשָׁם (ז)
sentence	gzar din	גְזַר דִין (ז)
to sentence (vt)	lifsok	לִפסוֹק

guilty (culprit)	aʃem	אָשֵׁם (ז)
to punish (vt)	leha'aniʃ	לְהַעֲנִישׁ
punishment	'oneʃ	עוֹנֶשׁ (ז)
fine (penalty)	knas	קְנָס (ז)
life imprisonment	ma'asar olam	מַאֲסַר עוֹלָם (ז)
death penalty	'oneʃ 'mavet	עוֹנֶשׁ מָוֶת (ז)
electric chair	kise χaʃmali	כִּיסֵּא חַשְׁמַלִי (ז)
gallows	gardom	גַרְדוֹם (ז)
to execute (vt)	lehotsi la'horeg	לְהוֹצִיא לַהוֹרֵג
execution	hatsa'a le'horeg	הוֹצָאָה לְהוֹרֵג (נ)
prison, jail	beit 'sohar	בֵּית סוֹהַר (ז)
cell	ta	תָא (ז)
escort	miʃmar livui	מִשְׁמָר לִיוּוי (ז)
prison guard	soher	סוֹהֵר (ז)
prisoner	asir	אָסִיר (ז)
handcuffs	azikim	אֲזִיקִים (ז"ר)
to handcuff (vt)	liχbol be'azikim	לִכְבּוֹל בַּאֲזִיקִים
prison break	briχa	בְּרִיחָה (נ)
to break out (vi)	liv'roaχ	לִבְרוֹח
to disappear (vi)	lehe'alem	לְהֵיעָלֵם
to release (from prison)	leʃaχrer	לְשַׁחְרֵר
amnesty	χanina	חֲנִינָה (נ)
police	miʃtara	מִשְׁטָרָה (נ)
police officer	ʃoter	שׁוֹטֵר (ז)
police station	taχanat miʃtara	תַחֲנַת מִשְׁטָרָה (נ)
billy club	ala	אַלָה (נ)
bullhorn	megafon	מֶגָפוֹן (ז)
patrol car	na'yedet	נַייֶדֶת (נ)
siren	tsofar	צוֹפָר (ז)
to turn on the siren	lehaf'il tsofar	לְהַפְעִיל צוֹפָר
siren call	tsfira	צְפִירָה (נ)
crime scene	zirat 'peʃa	זִירַת פֶּשַׁע (נ)
witness	ed	עֵד (ז)
freedom	'χofeʃ	חוֹפֶשׁ (ז)
accomplice	ʃutaf	שׁוּתָף (ז)
to flee (vi)	lehiχave	לְהֵיחָבֵא
trace (to leave a ~)	akev	עָקֵב (ז)

194. Police. Law. Part 2

search (investigation)	χipus	חִיפּוּשׂ (ז)
to look for ...	leχapes	לְחַפֵּשׂ

suspicion	χaʃad	חָשָׁד (ז)
suspicious (e.g., ~ vehicle)	χaʃud	חָשׁוד
to stop (cause to halt)	la'atsor	לַעֲצוֹר
to detain (keep in custody)	la'atsor	לַעֲצוֹר
case (lawsuit)	tik	תִּיק (ז)
investigation	χakira	חֲקִירָה (נ)
detective	balaʃ	בַּלָשׁ (ז)
investigator	χoker	חוֹקֵר (ז)
hypothesis	haʃara	הַשׁעָרָה (נ)
motive	me'ni'a	מֵנִיע (ז)
interrogation	χakira	חֲקִירָה (נ)
to interrogate (vt)	laχkor	לַחקוֹר
to question (~ neighbors, etc.)	letaʃ'el	לְתַשׁאֵל
check (identity ~)	bdika	בּדִיקָה (נ)
round-up	matsod	מָצוֹד (ז)
search (~ warrant)	χipus	חִיפּוּשׂ (ז)
chase (pursuit)	mirdaf	מִרדָף (ז)
to pursue, to chase	lirdof aχarei	לִרדוֹף אַחֲרֵי
to track (a criminal)	la'akov aχarei	לַעֲקוֹב אַחֲרֵי
arrest	ma'asar	מַאֲסָר (ז)
to arrest (sb)	le'esor	לֶאֱסוֹר
to catch (thief, etc.)	lilkod	לִלכּוֹד
capture	leχida	לְכִידָה (נ)
document	mismaχ	מִסמָך (ז)
proof (evidence)	hoχaχa	הוֹכָחָה (נ)
to prove (vt)	leho'χiaχ	לְהוֹכִיח
footprint	akev	עָקֵב (ז)
fingerprints	tvi'ot etsba'ot	טבִיעוֹת אֶצבָּעוֹת (נ״ר)
piece of evidence	re'aya	רְאָיָה (נ)
alibi	'alibi	אָלִיבִּי (ז)
innocent (not guilty)	χaf mi'peʃa	חַף מִפֶּשַׁע
injustice	i 'tsedek	אִי צֶדֶק (ז)
unjust, unfair (adj)	lo tsodek	לֹא צוֹדֵק
criminal (adj)	plili	פּלִילִי
to confiscate (vt)	lehaχrim	לְהַחרִים
drug (illegal substance)	sam	סַם (ז)
weapon, gun	'neʃek	נֶשֶׁק (ז)
to disarm (vt)	lifrok mi'neʃek	לְפָרוֹק מִנֶשֶׁק
to order (command)	lifkod	לִפקוֹד
to disappear (vi)	lehe'alem	לְהֵיעָלֵם
law	χok	חוֹק (ז)
legal, lawful (adj)	χuki	חוּקִי
illegal, illicit (adj)	'bilti χuki	בִּלתִי חוּקִי

responsibility (blame)	aχrayut	אַחְרָיוּת (נ)
responsible (adj)	aχrai	אַחְרַאי

NATURE

The Earth. Part 1

195. Outer space

space	χalal	חָלָל (ז)
space (as adj)	ʃel χalal	שֶׁל חָלָל
outer space	χalal χitson	חָלָל חִיצוֹן (ז)
world	olam	עוֹלָם (ז)
universe	yekum	יְקוּם (ז)
galaxy	ga'laksya	גָּלַקְסְיָה (נ)
star	koχav	כּוֹכָב (ז)
constellation	tsvir koχavim	צְבִיר כּוֹכָבִים (ז)
planet	koχav 'leχet	כּוֹכָב לֶכֶת (ז)
satellite	lavyan	לַוְיָן (ז)
meteorite	mete'orit	מֶטֵאוֹרִיט (ז)
comet	koχav ʃavit	כּוֹכָב שָׁבִיט (ז)
asteroid	aste'ro'id	אַסְטֵרוֹאִיד (ז)
orbit	maslul	מַסְלוּל (ז)
to revolve (~ around the Earth)	lesovev	לְסוֹבֵב
atmosphere	atmos'fera	אַטְמוֹסְפֵרָה (נ)
the Sun	'ʃemeʃ	שֶׁמֶשׁ (נ)
solar system	ma'a'reχet ha'ʃemeʃ	מַעֲרֶכֶת הַשֶּׁמֶשׁ (נ)
solar eclipse	likui χama	לִיקּוּי חַמָה (ז)
the Earth	kadur ha''arets	כַּדוּר הָאָרֶץ (ז)
the Moon	ya'reaχ	יָרֵחַ (ז)
Mars	ma'adim	מַאֲדִים (ז)
Venus	'noga	נוֹגַה (ז)
Jupiter	'tsedek	צֶדֶק (ז)
Saturn	ʃabtai	שַׁבְּתַאי (ז)
Mercury	koχav χama	כּוֹכָב חַמָה (ז)
Uranus	u'ranus	אוּרָנוּס (ז)
Neptune	neptun	נֶפְּטוּן (ז)
Pluto	'pluto	פְּלוּטוֹ (ז)
Milky Way	ʃvil haχalav	שְׁבִיל הֶחָלָב (ז)
Great Bear (Ursa Major)	duba gdola	דוּבָּה גְדוֹלָה (נ)

North Star	koχav hatsafon	כּוֹכַב הַצָּפוֹן (ז)
Martian	toʃav ma'adim	תּוֹשַׁב מַאֲדִים (ז)
extraterrestrial (n)	χutsan	חוּצָן (ז)
alien	χaizar	חייזָר (ז)
flying saucer	tsa'laχat me'o'fefet	צַלַחַת מְעוֹפֶפֶת (נ)
spaceship	χalalit	חָלָלִית (נ)
space station	taχanat χalal	תַּחֲנַת חָלָל (נ)
blast-off	hamra'a	הַמרָאָה (נ)
engine	ma'no'a	מָנוֹעַ (ז)
nozzle	neχir	נְחִיר (ז)
fuel	'delek	דֶלֶק (ז)
cockpit, flight deck	'kokpit	קוֹקפִּיט (ז)
antenna	an'tena	אַנטֶנָה (נ)
porthole	eʃnav	אֶשׁנָב (ז)
solar panel	'luaχ so'lari	לוּחַ סוֹלָרִי (ז)
spacesuit	χalifat χalal	חֲלִיפַת חָלָל (נ)
weightlessness	'χoser miʃkal	חוֹסֶר מִשׁקָל (ז)
oxygen	χamtsan	חַמצָן (ז)
docking (in space)	agina	עֲגִינָה (נ)
to dock (vi, vt)	la'agon	לַעֲגוֹן
observatory	mitspe koχavim	מִצפֵּה כּוֹכָבִים (ז)
telescope	teleskop	טֶלֶסקוֹפ (ז)
to observe (vt)	litspot, lehaʃkif	לִצפּוֹת, לְהַשׁקִיף
to explore (vt)	laχkor	לַחקוֹר

196. The Earth

the Earth	kadur ha''arets	כַּדוּר הָאָרֶץ (ז)
the globe (the Earth)	kadur ha''arets	כַּדוּר הָאָרֶץ (ז)
planet	koχav 'leχet	כּוֹכַב לֶכֶת (ז)
atmosphere	atmos'fera	אַטמוֹספֶרָה (נ)
geography	ge'o'grafya	גֵּיאוֹגרַפיָה (נ)
nature	'teva	טֶבַע (ז)
globe (table ~)	'globus	גלוֹבּוּס (ז)
map	mapa	מַפָּה (נ)
atlas	'atlas	אַטלָס (ז)
Europe	ei'ropa	אֵירוֹפָּה (נ)
Asia	'asya	אַסיָה (נ)
Africa	'afrika	אַפרִיקָה (נ)
Australia	ost'ralya	אוֹסטרַליָה (נ)
America	a'merika	אָמֶרִיקָה (נ)

North America	a'merika hatsfonit	אָמֶרִיקָה הַצְפוֹנִית (נ)
South America	a'merika hadromit	אָמֶרִיקָה הַדְרוֹמִית (נ)
Antarctica	ya'beʃet an'tarktika	יַבֶּשֶׁת אַנְטַארְקְטִיקָה (נ)
the Arctic	'arktika	אַרְקְטִיקָה (נ)

197. Cardinal directions

north	tsafon	צָפוֹן (ז)
to the north	tsa'fona	צָפוֹנָה
in the north	batsafon	בַּצָפוֹן
northern (adj)	tsfoni	צְפוֹנִי
south	darom	דָרוֹם (ז)
to the south	da'roma	דָרוֹמָה
in the south	badarom	בַּדָרוֹם
southern (adj)	dromi	דְרוֹמִי
west	ma'arav	מַעֲרָב (ז)
to the west	ma'a'rava	מַעֲרָבָה
in the west	bama'arav	בַּמַעֲרָב
western (adj)	ma'aravi	מַעֲרָבִי
east	mizraχ	מִזְרָח (ז)
to the east	miz'raχa	מִזְרָחָה
in the east	bamizraχ	בַּמִזְרָח
eastern (adj)	mizraχi	מִזְרָחִי

198. Sea. Ocean

sea	yam	יָם (ז)
ocean	ok'yanos	אוֹקְיָאנוֹס (ז)
gulf (bay)	mifrats	מִפְרָץ (ז)
straits	meitsar	מֵיצָר (ז)
land (solid ground)	yabaʃa	יַבָּשָׁה (נ)
continent (mainland)	ya'beʃet	יַבֶּשֶׁת (נ)
island	i	אִי (ז)
peninsula	χatsi i	חֲצִי אִי (ז)
archipelago	arχipelag	אַרְכִיפֶּלָג (ז)
bay, cove	mifrats	מִפְרָץ (ז)
harbor	namal	נָמָל (ז)
lagoon	la'guna	לָגוּנָה (נ)
cape	kef	כֵּף (ז)
atoll	atol	אָטוֹל (ז)
reef	ʃunit	שׁוּנִית (נ)

coral	almog	אַלְמוֹג (ז)
coral reef	ʃunit almogim	שׁוּנִית אַלְמוֹגִים (נ)
deep (adj)	amok	עָמוֹק
depth (deep water)	'omek	עוֹמֶק (ז)
abyss	tehom	תְּהוֹם (נ)
trench (e.g., Mariana ~)	maxteʃ	מַכְתֵּשׁ (ז)
current (Ocean ~)	'zerem	זֶרֶם (ז)
to surround (bathe)	lehakif	לְהַקִּיף
shore	xof	חוֹף (ז)
coast	xof yam	חוֹף יָם (ז)
flow (flood tide)	ge'ut	גֵּאוּת (נ)
ebb (ebb tide)	'ʃefel	שֵׁפֶל (ז)
shoal	sirton	שִׂרְטוֹן (ז)
bottom (~ of the sea)	karka'it	קַרְקָעִית (נ)
wave	gal	גַּל (ז)
crest (~ of a wave)	pisgat hagal	פִּסְגַּת הַגַּל (נ)
spume (sea foam)	'ketsef	קֶצֶף (ז)
storm (sea storm)	sufa	סוּפָה (נ)
hurricane	hurikan	הוֹרִיקָן (ז)
tsunami	tsu'nami	צוּנָאמִי (ז)
calm (dead ~)	'roga	רוֹגַע (ז)
quiet, calm (adj)	ʃalev	שָׁלֵו
pole	'kotev	קוֹטֶב (ז)
polar (adj)	kotbi	קוֹטְבִּי
latitude	kav 'roxav	קַו רוֹחַב (ז)
longitude	kav 'orex	קַו אוֹרֶךְ (ז)
parallel	kav 'roxav	קַו רוֹחַב (ז)
equator	kav hamaʃve	קַו הַמַּשְׁוֶה (ז)
sky	ʃa'mayim	שָׁמַיִם (ז"ר)
horizon	'ofek	אוֹפֶק (ז)
air	avir	אֲוִיר (ז)
lighthouse	migdalor	מִגְדַּלּוֹר (ז)
to dive (vi)	litslol	לִצְלֹל
to sink (ab. boat)	lit'bo'a	לִטְבֹּעַ
treasures	otsarot	אוֹצָרוֹת (ז"ר)

199. Seas' and Oceans' names

| Atlantic Ocean | ha'ok'yanus ha'at'lanti | הָאוֹקְיָנוֹס הָאַטְלַנְטִי (ז) |
| Indian Ocean | ha'ok'yanus ha'hodi | הָאוֹקְיָנוֹס הַהוֹדִי (ז) |

Pacific Ocean	ha'ok'yanus haʃaket	הָאוֹקְיָינוֹס הַשָׁקֵט (ז)
Arctic Ocean	ok'yanos ha'keraχ hatsfoni	אוֹקְיָינוֹס הַקֶּרַח הַצְּפוֹנִי (ז)
Black Sea	hayam haʃaχor	הַיָּם הַשָׁחוֹר (ז)
Red Sea	yam suf	יַם סוּף (ז)
Yellow Sea	hayam hatsahov	הַיָּם הַצָּהֹב (ז)
White Sea	hayam halavan	הַיָּם הַלָּבָן (ז)
Caspian Sea	hayam ha'kaspi	הַיָּם הַכַּסְפִּי (ז)
Dead Sea	yam ha'melaχ	יַם הַמֶּלַח (ז)
Mediterranean Sea	hayam hatiχon	הַיָּם הַתִּיכוֹן (ז)
Aegean Sea	hayam ha'e'ge'i	הַיָּם הָאֵגֵאִי (ז)
Adriatic Sea	hayam ha'adri'yati	הַיָּם הָאַדְרִיָאתִי (ז)
Arabian Sea	hayam ha'aravi	הַיַּם הָעֲרָבִי (ז)
Sea of Japan	hayam haya'pani	הַיָּם הַיַפָּנִי (ז)
Bering Sea	yam 'bering	יַם בֶּרִינג (ז)
South China Sea	yam sin hadromi	יַם סִין הַדְּרוֹמִי (ז)
Coral Sea	yam ha'almogim	יַם הָאַלְמוֹגִים (ז)
Tasman Sea	yam tasman	יַם טַסְמַן (ז)
Caribbean Sea	hayam haka'ribi	הַיָּם הַקָרִיבִּי (ז)
Barents Sea	yam 'barents	ים בֶּרֶנץ (ז)
Kara Sea	yam 'kara	יַם קָאׁרָה (ז)
North Sea	hayam hatsfoni	הַיָּם הַצְּפוֹנִי (ז)
Baltic Sea	hayam ha'balti	הַיָּם הַבַּלְטִי (ז)
Norwegian Sea	hayam hanor'vegi	הַיָּם הַנּוֹרְבֶגִי (ז)

200. Mountains

mountain	har	הַר (ז)
mountain range	'reχes harim	רֶכֶס הָרִים (ז)
mountain ridge	'reχes har	רֶכֶס הַר (ז)
summit, top	pisga	פִּסְגָּה (נ)
peak	pisga	פִּסְגָּה (נ)
foot (~ of the mountain)	margelot	מַרְגְּלוֹת (נ"ר)
slope (mountainside)	midron	מִדְרוֹן (ז)
volcano	har 'ga'aʃ	הַר גַעַש (ז)
active volcano	har 'ga'aʃ pa'il	הַר גַעַש פָּעִיל (ז)
dormant volcano	har 'ga'aʃ radum	הַר גַעַש רָדוּם (ז)
eruption	hitpartsut	הִתְפָּרְצוּת (נ)
crater	lo'a	לֹעַ (ז)
magma	megama	מֶגְמָה (נ)
lava	'lava	לָאבָה (נ)

molten (~ lava)	lohet	לוֹהֵט
canyon	kanyon	קַנְיוֹן (ז)
gorge	gai	גַּיְא (ז)
crevice	'beka	בֶּקַע (ז)
abyss (chasm)	tehom	תְּהוֹם (נ)
pass, col	ma'avar harim	מַעֲבָר הָרִים (ז)
plateau	rama	רָמָה (נ)
cliff	tsuk	צוּק (ז)
hill	giv'a	גִּבְעָה (נ)
glacier	karxon	קַרְחוֹן (ז)
waterfall	mapal 'mayim	מַפַּל מַיִם (ז)
geyser	'geizer	גֵּייזֶר (ז)
lake	agam	אֲגַם (ז)
plain	miʃor	מִישׁוֹר (ז)
landscape	nof	נוֹף (ז)
echo	hed	הֵד (ז)
alpinist	metapes harim	מְטַפֵּס הָרִים (ז)
rock climber	metapes sla'im	מְטַפֵּס סְלָעִים (ז)
to conquer (in climbing)	lixboʃ	לִכְבּוֹשׁ
climb (an easy ~)	tipus	טִיפּוּס (ז)

201. Mountains names

The Alps	harei ha''alpim	הָרֵי הָאַלְפִּים (ז"ר)
Mont Blanc	mon blan	מוֹן בְּלָאן (ז)
The Pyrenees	pire'ne'im	פִּירֶנָאִים (ז"ר)
The Carpathians	kar'patim	קַרְפָּטִים (ז"ר)
The Ural Mountains	harei ural	הָרֵי אוּרָל (ז"ר)
The Caucasus Mountains	harei hakavkaz	הָרֵי הַקַוְקָז (ז"ר)
Mount Elbrus	elbrus	אֶלְבְּרוּס (ז)
The Altai Mountains	harei altai	הָרֵי אַלְטַאי (ז"ר)
The Tian Shan	tyan ʃan	טְיָאן שָׁאן (ז)
The Pamir Mountains	harei pamir	הָרֵי פָּאמִיר (ז"ר)
The Himalayas	harei hehima'laya	הָרֵי הֶהִימָלָאיָה (ז"ר)
Mount Everest	everest	אֶוֶורֶסְט (ז)
The Andes	harei ha''andim	הָרֵי הָאַנְדִים (ז"ר)
Mount Kilimanjaro	kiliman'dʒaro	קִילִימַנְגַ'רוֹ (ז)

202. Rivers

river	nahar	נָהָר (ז)
spring (natural source)	ma'ayan	מַעְיָין (ז)

riverbed (river channel)	afik	אָפִיק (ז)
basin (river valley)	agan nahar	אַגַּן נָהָר (ז)
to flow into ...	lehiʃapeχ	לְהִישָׁפֵךְ
tributary	yuval	יוּבַל (ז)
bank (of river)	χof	חוֹף (ז)
current (stream)	'zerem	זֶרֶם (ז)
downstream (adv)	bemorad hanahar	בְּמוֹרַד הַנָּהָר
upstream (adv)	bema'ale hanahar	בְּמַעֲלֵה הַזֶּרֶם
inundation	hatsafa	הַצָּפָה (נ)
flooding	ʃitafon	שִׁיטָפוֹן (ז)
to overflow (vi)	la'alot al gdotav	לַעֲלוֹת עַל גדוֹתָיו
to flood (vt)	lehatsif	לְהָצִיף
shallow (shoal)	sirton	שִׂרטוֹן (ז)
rapids	'eʃed	אֶשֶׁד (ז)
dam	'seχer	סֶכֶר (ז)
canal	te'ala	תְּעָלָה (נ)
reservoir (artificial lake)	ma'agar 'mayim	מַאֲגַר מַיִם (ז)
sluice, lock	ta 'ʃayit	תָּא שַׁיִט (ז)
water body (pond, etc.)	ma'agar 'mayim	מַאֲגַר מַיִם (ז)
swamp (marshland)	bitsa	בִּיצָה (נ)
bog, marsh	bitsa	בִּיצָה (נ)
whirlpool	me'ar'bolet	מְעַרבּוֹלֶת (נ)
stream (brook)	'naχal	נַחַל (ז)
drinking (ab. water)	ʃel ʃtiya	שֶׁל שתִייָה
fresh (~ water)	metukim	מְתוּקִים
ice	'keraχ	קֶרַח (ז)
to freeze over	likpo	לִקפּוֹא
(ab. river, etc.)		

203. Rivers' names

Seine	hasen	הַסֶן (ז)
Loire	lu'ar	לוּאָר (ז)
Thames	'temza	תָמזָה (ז)
Rhine	hrain	הרַיין (ז)
Danube	da'nuba	דָנוּבָּה (ז)
Volga	'volga	וֹולגָה (ז)
Don	nahar don	נָהָר דוֹן (ז)
Lena	'lena	לֶנָה (ז)
Yellow River	hvang ho	הוַונג הוֹ (ז)

Yangtze	yangtse	יָאנגצֶה (ז)
Mekong	mekong	מֶקוֹנג (ז)
Ganges	'ganges	גַנגֶס (ז)

Nile River	'nilus	נִילוּס (ז)
Congo River	'kongo	קוֹנגוֹ (ז)
Okavango River	ok'vango	אוֹקבַנגוֹ (ז)
Zambezi River	zam'bezi	זַמבֶּזִי (ז)
Limpopo River	limpopo	לִימפּוֹפּוֹ (ז)
Mississippi River	misi'sipi	מִיסִיסִיפִּי (ז)

204. Forest

| forest, wood | 'ya'ar | יַעַר (ז) |
| forest (as adj) | ʃel 'ya'ar | שֶׁל יַעַר |

thick forest	avi ha'ya'ar	עֲבִי הַיַעַר (ז)
grove	χurʃa	חוּרשָׁה (נ)
forest clearing	ka'raχat 'ya'ar	קָרַחַת יַעַר (נ)

| thicket | svaχ | סבַךְ (ז) |
| scrubland | 'siaχ | שִׂיחַ (ז) |

| footpath (troddenpath) | ʃvil | שבִיל (ז) |
| gully | 'emek tsar | עֵמֶק צַר (ז) |

tree	ets	עֵץ (ז)
leaf	ale	עָלֶה (ז)
leaves (foliage)	alva	עַלוָוה (נ)

fall of leaves	ʃa'leχet	שַׁלֶכֶת (נ)
to fall (ab. leaves)	linʃor	לִנשׁוֹר
top (of the tree)	tsa'meret	צַמֶרֶת (נ)

branch	anaf	עָנָף (ז)
bough	anaf ave	עָנָף עָבֶה (ז)
bud (on shrub, tree)	nitsan	נִיצָן (ז)
needle (of pine tree)	'maχat	מַחַט (נ)
pine cone	itstrubal	אָצטרוּבָּל (ז)

hollow (in a tree)	χor ba'ets	חוֹר בָּעֵץ (ז)
nest	ken	קֵן (ז)
burrow (animal hole)	meχila	מְחִילָה (נ)

trunk	'geza	גֶזַע (ז)
root	'ʃoreʃ	שׁוֹרֶשׁ (ז)
bark	klipa	קלִיפָּה (נ)
moss	taχav	טַחַב (ז)
to uproot (remove trees or tree stumps)	la'akor	לַעֲקוֹר

to chop down	liχrot	לִכְרוֹת
to deforest (vt)	levare	לְבָרֵא
tree stump	'gedem	גֶּדֶם (ז)

campfire	medura	מְדוּרָה (נ)
forest fire	srefa	שְׂרֵיפָה (נ)
to extinguish (vt)	leχabot	לְכַבּוֹת

forest ranger	ʃomer 'ya'ar	שׁוֹמֵר יַעַר (ז)
protection	ʃmira	שְׁמִירָה (נ)
to protect (~ nature)	liʃmor	לִשְׁמוֹר
poacher	tsayad lelo reʃut	צַיָּיד לְלֹא רְשׁוּת (ז)
steel trap	mal'kodet	מַלְכּוֹדֶת (נ)

| to gather, to pick (vt) | lelaket | לְלַקֵּט |
| to lose one's way | lit'ot | לִתְעוֹת |

205. Natural resources

natural resources	otsarot 'teva	אוֹצְרוֹת טֶבַע (ז"ר)
minerals	mine'ralim	מִינֵרָלִים (ז"ר)
deposits	mirbats	מִרְבָּץ (ז)
field (e.g., oilfield)	mirbats	מִרְבָּץ (ז)

to mine (extract)	liχrot	לִכְרוֹת
mining (extraction)	kriya	כְּרִיָּיה (נ)
ore	afra	עַפְרָה (נ)
mine (e.g., for coal)	miχre	מִכְרֶה (ז)
shaft (mine ~)	pir	פִּיר (ז)
miner	kore	כּוֹרֶה (ז)

| gas (natural ~) | gaz | גָּז (ז) |
| gas pipeline | tsinor gaz | צִינוֹר גָּז (ז) |

oil (petroleum)	neft	נֵפְט (ז)
oil pipeline	tsinor neft	צִינוֹר נֵפְט (ז)
oil well	be'er neft	בְּאֵר נֵפְט (נ)
derrick (tower)	migdal ki'duaχ	מִגְדָּל קִידּוּחַ (ז)
tanker	meχalit	מֵיכָלִית (נ)

sand	χol	חוֹל (ז)
limestone	'even gir	אֶבֶן גִּיר (נ)
gravel	χatsats	חָצָץ (ז)
peat	kavul	כָּבוּל (ז)
clay	tit	טִיט (ז)
coal	peχam	פֶּחָם (ז)

iron (ore)	barzel	בַּרְזֶל (ז)
gold	zahav	זָהָב (ז)
silver	'kesef	כֶּסֶף (ז)

nickel	'nikel	נִיקֶל (ז)
copper	ne'χoʃet	נְחוֹשֶׁת (נ)
zinc	avats	אָבָץ (ז)
manganese	mangan	מַנְגָּן (ז)
mercury	kaspit	כַּסְפִּית (נ)
lead	o'feret	עוֹפֶרֶת (נ)
mineral	mineral	מִינְרָל (ז)
crystal	gaviʃ	גָּבִישׁ (ז)
marble	'ʃayiʃ	שַׁיִשׁ (ז)
uranium	u'ranyum	אוּרָנְיוּם (ז)

The Earth. Part 2

206. Weather

weather	'mezeg avir	מֶזֶג אֲוֹוִיר (ז)
weather forecast	taχazit 'mezeg ha'avir	תַּחֲזִית מֶזֶג הָאֲוֹוִיר (נ)
temperature	tempera'tura	טֶמְפֶּרָטוּרָה (נ)
thermometer	madχom	מַדְחוֹם (ז)
barometer	ba'rometer	בָּרוֹמֶטֶר (ז)
humid (adj)	laχ	לַח
humidity	laχut	לַחוּת (נ)
heat (extreme ~)	χom	חוֹם (ז)
hot (torrid)	χam	חַם
it's hot	χam	חַם
it's warm	χamim	חָמִים
warm (moderately hot)	χamim	חָמִים
it's cold	kar	קַר
cold (adj)	kar	קַר
sun	'ʃemeʃ	שֶׁמֶשׁ (נ)
to shine (vi)	lizhor	לִזְהוֹר
sunny (day)	ʃimʃi	שִׁמְשִׁי
to come up (vi)	liz'roaχ	לִזְרוֹחַ
to set (vi)	liʃko'a	לִשְׁקוֹעַ
cloud	anan	עָנָן (ז)
cloudy (adj)	me'unan	מְעוֹנָן
rain cloud	av	עָב (ז)
somber (gloomy)	sagriri	סַגְרִירִי
rain	'geʃem	גֶּשֶׁם (ז)
it's raining	yored 'geʃem	יוֹרֵד גֶּשֶׁם
rainy (~ day, weather)	gaʃum	גָשׁוּם
to drizzle (vi)	letaftef	לְטַפְטֵף
pouring rain	matar	מָטָר (ז)
downpour	mabul	מַבּוּל (ז)
heavy (e.g., ~ rain)	χazak	חָזָק
puddle	ʃlulit	שְׁלוּלִית (נ)
to get wet (in rain)	lehitratev	לְהִתְרַטֵּב
fog (mist)	arapel	עֲרָפֶל (ז)
foggy	me'urpal	מְעוֹרְפָל

| snow | 'ʃeleg | שֶׁלֶג (ז) |
| it's snowing | yored 'ʃeleg | יוֹרֵד שֶׁלֶג |

207. Severe weather. Natural disasters

thunderstorm	sufat re'amim	סוּפַת רְעָמִים (נ)
lightning (~ strike)	barak	בָּרָק (ז)
to flash (vi)	livhok	לִבהוֹק
thunder	'ra'am	רַעַם (ז)
to thunder (vi)	lir'om	לִרעוֹם
it's thundering	lir'om	לִרעוֹם
hail	barad	בָּרָד (ז)
it's hailing	yored barad	יוֹרֵד בָּרָד
to flood (vt)	lehatsif	לְהָצִיף
flood, inundation	ʃitafon	שִׁיטָפוֹן (ז)
earthquake	re'idat adama	רְעִידַת אֲדָמָה (נ)
tremor, quake	re'ida	רְעִידָה (נ)
epicenter	moked	מוֹקֵד (ז)
eruption	hitpartsut	הִתפָּרצוּת (נ)
lava	'lava	לָאבָה (נ)
twister	hurikan	הוֹרִיקָן (ז)
tornado	tor'nado	טוֹרנָדוֹ (ז)
typhoon	taifun	טַייפוּן (ז)
hurricane	hurikan	הוֹרִיקָן (ז)
storm	sufa	סוּפָה (נ)
tsunami	tsu'nami	צוּנָאמִי (ז)
cyclone	tsiklon	צִיקלוֹן (ז)
bad weather	sagrir	סַגרִיר (ז)
fire (accident)	srefa	שׂרֵיפָה (נ)
disaster	ason	אָסוֹן (ז)
meteorite	mete'orit	מֶטֶאוֹרִיט (ז)
avalanche	ma'polet ʃlagim	מַפּוֹלֶת שלָגִים (נ)
snowslide	ma'polet ʃlagim	מַפּוֹלֶת שלָגִים (נ)
blizzard	sufat ʃlagim	סוּפַת שלָגִים (נ)
snowstorm	sufat ʃlagim	סוּפַת שלָגִים (נ)

208. Noises. Sounds

| silence (quiet) | 'ʃeket | שֶׁקֶט (ז) |
| sound | tslil | צלִיל (ז) |

noise	'ra'aʃ	רַעַשׁ (ז)
to make noise	lir'oʃ	לִרְעוֹשׁ
noisy (adj)	ro'eʃ	רוֹעֵשׁ
loudly (to speak, etc.)	bekol	בְּקוֹל
loud (voice, etc.)	ram	רָם
constant (e.g., ~ noise)	ka'vu'a	קָבוּעַ
cry, shout (n)	tse'aka	צְעָקָה (נ)
to cry, to shout (vi)	lits'ok	לִצְעוֹק
whisper	leχiʃa	לְחִישָׁה (נ)
to whisper (vi, vt)	lilχoʃ	לִלְחוֹשׁ
barking (dog's ~)	neviχa	נְבִיחָה (נ)
to bark (vi)	lin'boaχ	לִנְבּוֹחַ
groan (of pain, etc.)	anaka	אֲנָקָה (נ)
to groan (vi)	lehe'anek	לְהֵיאָנֵק
cough	ʃi'ul	שִׁיעוּל (ז)
to cough (vi)	lehiʃta'el	לְהִשְׁתַּעֵל
whistle	ʃrika	שְׁרִיקָה (נ)
to whistle (vi)	liʃrok	לִשְׁרוֹק
knock (at the door)	hakaʃa	הַקָּשָׁה (נ)
to knock (at the door)	lidfok	לִדְפוֹק
to crack (vi)	lehitba'ke'a	לְהִתְבַּקֵעַ
crack (cracking sound)	naftsuts	נַפְצוּץ (ז)
siren	tsofar	צוֹפָר (ז)
whistle (factory ~, etc.)	tsfira	צְפִירָה (נ)
to whistle (ab. train)	litspor	לִצְפּוֹר
honk (car horn sound)	tsfira	צְפִירָה (נ)
to honk (vi)	litspor	לִצְפּוֹר

209. Winter

winter (n)	'χoref	חוֹרֶף (ז)
winter (as adj)	χorpi	חוֹרְפִּי
in winter	ba'χoref	בַּחוֹרֶף
snow	'ʃeleg	שֶׁלֶג (ז)
it's snowing	yored 'ʃeleg	יוֹרֵד שֶׁלֶג
snowfall	yeridat 'ʃeleg	יְרִידַת שֶׁלֶג (נ)
snowdrift	aremat 'ʃeleg	עֲרֵימַת שֶׁלֶג (נ)
snowflake	ptit 'ʃeleg	פְּתִית שֶׁלֶג (ז)
snowball	kadur 'ʃeleg	כַּדּוּר שֶׁלֶג (ז)
snowman	iʃ 'ʃeleg	אִישׁ שֶׁלֶג (ז)
icicle	netif 'keraχ	נְטִיף קֶרַח (ז)

December	de'tsember	דֶּצֶמְבֶּר (ז)
January	'yanu'ar	יָנוּאָר (ז)
February	'febru'ar	פֶבְּרוּאָר (ז)
frost (severe ~, freezing cold)	kfor	כְּפוֹר (ז)
frosty (weather, air)	kfori	כְּפוֹרִי
below zero (adv)	mi'taχat la''efes	מִתַּחַת לָאֶפֶס
first frost	kara	קָרָה (נ)
hoarfrost	kfor	כְּפוֹר (ז)
cold (cold weather)	kor	קוֹר (ז)
it's cold	kar	קַר
fur coat	me'il parva	מְעִיל פַּרְוָה (ז)
mittens	kfafot	כְּפָפוֹת (נ״ר)
to get sick	laχalot	לַחֲלוֹת
cold (illness)	hitstanenut	הִצְטַנְּנוּת (נ)
to catch a cold	lehitstanen	לְהִצְטַנֵּן
ice	'keraχ	קֶרַח (ז)
black ice	ʃiχvat 'keraχ	שִׁכְבַת קֶרַח (נ)
to freeze over (ab. river, etc.)	likpo	לִקְפּוֹא
ice floe	karχon	קַרְחוֹן (ז)
skis	ski	סְקִי (ז)
skier	goleʃ	גּוֹלֵשׁ (ז)
to ski (vi)	la'asot ski	לַעֲשׂוֹת סְקִי
to skate (vi)	lehaχlik	לְהַחֲלִיק

Fauna

210. Mammals. Predators

predator	χayat 'teref	חַיַּת טֶרֶף (נ)
tiger	'tigris	טִיגְרִיס (ז)
lion	arye	אַרְיֵה (ז)
wolf	ze'ev	זְאֵב (ז)
fox	ʃu'al	שׁוּעָל (ז)
jaguar	yagu'ar	יָגוּאָר (ז)
leopard	namer	נָמֵר (ז)
cheetah	bardelas	בַּרְדְּלָס (ז)
black panther	panter	פַּנְתֵּר (ז)
puma	'puma	פּוּמָה (נ)
snow leopard	namer 'ʃeleg	נָמֵר שֶׁלֶג (ז)
lynx	ʃunar	שׁוּנָר (ז)
coyote	ze'ev ha'aravot	זְאֵב הָעֲרָבוֹת (ז)
jackal	tan	תַּן (ז)
hyena	tsa'vo'a	צָבוֹעַ (ז)

211. Wild animals

animal	'ba'al χayim	בַּעַל חַיִּים (ז)
beast (animal)	χaya	חַיָּה (נ)
squirrel	sna'i	סְנָאִי (ז)
hedgehog	kipod	קִיפּוֹד (ז)
hare	arnav	אַרְנָב (ז)
rabbit	ʃafan	שָׁפָן (ז)
badger	girit	גִּירִית (נ)
raccoon	dvivon	דְּבִיבוֹן (ז)
hamster	oger	אוֹגֵר (ז)
marmot	mar'mita	מַרְמִיטָה (נ)
mole	χafar'peret	חֲפַרְפֶּרֶת (נ)
mouse	aχbar	עַכְבָּר (ז)
rat	χulda	חוּלְדָּה (נ)
bat	atalef	עֲטַלֵּף (ז)
ermine	hermin	הֶרְמִין (ז)
sable	tsobel	צוֹבֶּל (ז)

marten	dalak	דָלָק (ז)
weasel	χamus	חָמוֹס (ז)
mink	χorfan	חוֹרפָן (ז)
beaver	bone	בּוֹנֶה (ז)
otter	lutra	לוֹטרָה (נ)
horse	sus	סוּס (ז)
moose	ayal hakore	אַייָל הַקוֹרֵא (ז)
deer	ayal	אַייָל (ז)
camel	gamal	גָמָל (ז)
bison	bizon	בִּיזוֹן (ז)
aurochs	bizon ei'ropi	בִּיזוֹן אֵירוֹפִי (ז)
buffalo	te'o	תְאוֹ (ז)
zebra	'zebra	זֶבּרָה (נ)
antelope	anti'lopa	אַנטִילוֹפָּה (ז)
roe deer	ayal hakarmel	אַייָל הַכַּרמֶל (ז)
fallow deer	yaχmur	יַחמוּר (ז)
chamois	ya'el	יָעֵל (ז)
wild boar	χazir bar	חֲזִיר בָּר (ז)
whale	livyatan	לִווייָתָן (ז)
seal	'kelev yam	כֶּלֶב יָם (ז)
walrus	sus yam	סוּס יָם (ז)
fur seal	dov yam	דוֹב יָם (ז)
dolphin	dolfin	דוֹלפִין (ז)
bear	dov	דוֹב (ז)
polar bear	dov 'kotev	דוֹב קוֹטֶב (ז)
panda	'panda	פַּנדָה (נ)
monkey	kof	קוֹף (ז)
chimpanzee	ʃimpanze	שִימפַּנזֶה (נ)
orangutan	orang utan	אוֹרַנג-אוּטָן (ז)
gorilla	go'rila	גוֹרִילָה (נ)
macaque	makak	מָקָק (ז)
gibbon	gibon	גִיבּוֹן (ז)
elephant	pil	פִּיל (ז)
rhinoceros	karnaf	קַרנַף (ז)
giraffe	dʒi'rafa	ג'יִרָפָּה (נ)
hippopotamus	hipopotam	הִיפּוֹפּוֹטָם (ז)
kangaroo	'kenguru	קֶנגוּרוּ (ז)
koala (bear)	ko''ala	קוֹאָלָה (ז)
mongoose	nemiya	נְמִייָה (נ)
chinchilla	tʃin'tʃila	צ'יִנצ'יִילָה (נ)
skunk	bo'eʃ	בּוֹאֵש (ז)
porcupine	darban	דַרבָּן (ז)

212. Domestic animals

cat	χatula	חֲתוּלָה (נ)
tomcat	χatul	חָתוּל (ז)
dog	'kelev	כֶּלֶב (ז)
horse	sus	סוּס (ז)
stallion (male horse)	sus harba'a	סוּס הַרְבָּעָה (ז)
mare	susa	סוּסָה (נ)
cow	para	פָּרָה (נ)
bull	ʃor	שׁוֹר (ז)
ox	ʃor	שׁוֹר (ז)
sheep (ewe)	kivsa	כִּבְשָׂה (נ)
ram	'ayil	אַיִל (ז)
goat	ez	עֵז (נ)
billy goat, he-goat	'tayiʃ	תַּיִשׁ (ז)
donkey	χamor	חֲמוֹר (ז)
mule	'pered	פֶּרֶד (ז)
pig, hog	χazir	חֲזִיר (ז)
piglet	χazarzir	חֲזַרְזִיר (ז)
rabbit	arnav	אַרְנָב (ז)
hen (chicken)	tarne'golet	תַּרְנְגֹלֶת (נ)
rooster	tarnegol	תַּרְנְגוֹל (ז)
duck	barvaz	בַּרְוָז (ז)
drake	barvaz	בַּרְוָז (ז)
goose	avaz	אַוָּז (ז)
tom turkey, gobbler	tarnegol 'hodu	תַּרְנְגוֹל הוֹדוּ (ז)
turkey (hen)	tarne'golet 'hodu	תַּרְנְגֹלֶת הוֹדוּ (נ)
domestic animals	χayot 'bayit	חַיּוֹת בַּיִת (נ״ר)
tame (e.g., ~ hamster)	mevuyat	מְבוּיָת
to tame (vt)	levayet	לְבַיֵּת
to breed (vt)	lehar'bi'a	לְהַרְבִּיעַ
farm	χava	חַוָּה (נ)
poultry	ofot 'bayit	עוֹפוֹת בַּיִת (נ״ר)
cattle	bakar	בָּקָר (ז)
herd (cattle)	'eder	עֵדֶר (ז)
stable	urva	אֻרְוָה (נ)
pigpen	dir χazirim	דִּיר חֲזִירִים (ז)
cowshed	'refet	רֶפֶת (נ)
rabbit hutch	arnaviya	אַרְנָבִיָּה (נ)
hen house	lul	לוּל (ז)

213. Dogs. Dog breeds

dog	'kelev	כֶּלֶב (ז)
sheepdog	'kelev ro'e	כֶּלֶב רוֹעֶה (ז)
German shepherd	ro'e germani	רוֹעֶה גֶּרמָנִי (ז)
poodle	'pudel	פּוּדֶל (ז)
dachshund	'taxaʃ	תַּחַש (ז)
bulldog	buldog	בּוּלדוֹג (ז)
boxer	'bokser	בּוֹקסֶר (ז)
mastiff	mastif	מָסטִיף (ז)
Rottweiler	rot'vailer	רוֹטוַוילֶר (ז)
Doberman	'doberman	דוֹבֶּרמָן (ז)
basset	'baset 'ha'und	בָּאסֶט־הָאוּנד (ז)
bobtail	bobteil	בּוֹבּטֵייל (ז)
Dalmatian	dal'mati	דַלמָטִי (ז)
cocker spaniel	'koker 'spani'el	קוֹקֶר סֹפָּנִיאֶל (ז)
Newfoundland	nyu'fa'undlend	נִיוּפָאוּנדלֶנד (ז)
Saint Bernard	sen bernard	סֶן בֶּרנָרד (ז)
husky	'haski	הָאסקִי (ז)
Chow Chow	'tʃa'u 'tʃa'u	צַ'אוּ צַ'אוּ (ז)
spitz	ʃpits	שפִּיץ (ז)
pug	pag	פָּאג (ז)

214. Sounds made by animals

barking (n)	nevixa	נְבִיחָה (נ)
to bark (vi)	lin'boax	לִנבּוֹחַ
to meow (vi)	leyalel	לְיַיֵל
to purr (vi)	legarger	לְגַרגֵּר
to moo (vi)	lig'ot	לִגעוֹת
to bellow (bull)	lig'ot	לִגעוֹת
to growl (vi)	linhom	לִנהוֹם
howl (n)	yelala	יְלָלָה (נ)
to howl (vi)	leyalel	לְיַיֵל
to whine (vi)	leyabev	לְיַיבֵּב
to bleat (sheep)	lif'ot	לִפעוֹת
to oink, to grunt (pig)	lexarxer	לְחַרחֵר
to squeal (vi)	lits'voax	לִצווֹחַ
to croak (vi)	lekarker	לְקַרקֵר
to buzz (insect)	lezamzem	לְזַמזֵם
to chirp (crickets, grasshopper)	letsartser	לְצַרצֵר

215. Young animals

cub	gur	גּוּר (ז)
kitten	χataltul	חֲתַלְתּוּל (ז)
baby mouse	aχbaron	עַכְבָּרוֹן (ז)
puppy	klavlav	כְּלַבְלַב (ז)
leveret	arnavon	אַרְנָבוֹן (ז)
baby rabbit	ʃfanfan	שְׁפַנְפַּן (ז)
wolf cub	gur ze'evim	גּוּר זְאֵבִים (ז)
fox cub	ʃu'alon	שׁוּעָלוֹן (ז)
bear cub	dubon	דֻּבּוֹן (ז)
lion cub	gur arye	גּוּר אַרְיֵה (ז)
tiger cub	gur namerim	גּוּר נְמֵרִים (ז)
elephant calf	pilon	פִּילוֹן (ז)
piglet	χazarzir	חֲזַרְזִיר (ז)
calf (young cow, bull)	'egel	עֵגֶל (ז)
kid (young goat)	gdi	גְּדִי (ז)
lamb	tale	טָלֶה (ז)
fawn (young deer)	'ofer	עוֹפֶר (ז)
young camel	'beχer	בֶּכֶר (ז)
snakelet (baby snake)	gur naχaʃim	גּוּר נְחָשִׁים (ז)
froglet (baby frog)	tsfarde'on	צְפַרְדְּעוֹן (ז)
baby bird	gozal	גּוֹזָל (ז)
chick (of chicken)	ef'roaχ	אֶפְרוֹחַ (ז)
duckling	barvazon	בַּרְוָזוֹן (ז)

216. Birds

bird	tsipor	צִיפּוֹר (נ)
pigeon	yona	יוֹנָה (נ)
sparrow	dror	דְּרוֹר (ז)
tit (great tit)	yargazi	יַרְגָּזִי (ז)
magpie	orev neχalim	עוֹרֵב נְחָלִים (ז)
raven	orev ʃaχor	עוֹרֵב שָׁחוֹר (ז)
crow	orev afor	עוֹרֵב אָפוֹר (ז)
jackdaw	ka'ak	קָאָק (ז)
rook	orev hamizra	עוֹרֵב הַמִּזְרָע (ז)
duck	barvaz	בַּרְוָז (ז)
goose	avaz	אַוָּז (ז)
pheasant	pasyon	פַּסְיוֹן (ז)
eagle	'ayit	עַיִט (ז)
hawk	nets	נֵץ (ז)

falcon	baz	בַּז (ז)
vulture	ozniya	עוֹזְנִיָּה (נ)
condor (Andean ~)	kondor	קוֹנְדוֹר (ז)
swan	barbur	בַּרְבּוּר (ז)
crane	agur	עָגוּר (ז)
stork	xasida	חֲסִידָה (נ)
parrot	'tuki	תֻּכִּי (ז)
hummingbird	ko'libri	קוֹלִיבְרִי (ז)
peacock	tavas	טַוָּס (ז)
ostrich	bat ya'ana	בַּת יַעֲנָה (נ)
heron	anafa	אֲנָפָה (נ)
flamingo	fla'mingo	פְלָמִינְגוֹ (ז)
pelican	saknai	שַׂקְנַאי (ז)
nightingale	zamir	זָמִיר (ז)
swallow	snunit	סְנוּנִית (נ)
thrush	kixli	קִיכְלִי (ז)
song thrush	kixli mezamer	קִיכְלִי מְזַמֵּר (ז)
blackbird	kixli ʃaxor	קִיכְלִי שָׁחוֹר (ז)
swift	sis	סִיס (ז)
lark	efroni	עֶפְרוֹנִי (ז)
quail	slav	שְׂלָיו (ז)
woodpecker	'neker	נֶקֶר (ז)
cuckoo	kukiya	קוּקִיָּה (נ)
owl	yanʃuf	יַנְשׁוּף (ז)
eagle owl	'oax	אוֹחַ (ז)
wood grouse	sexvi 'ya'ar	שְׂכְווֵי יַעַר (ז)
black grouse	sexvi	שְׂכְווִי (ז)
partridge	xogla	חָגְלָה (נ)
starling	zarzir	זַרְזִיר (ז)
canary	ka'narit	קָנָרִית (נ)
hazel grouse	sexvi haya'arot	שְׂכְווִי הַיְּעָרוֹת (ז)
chaffinch	paroʃ	פָּרוּשׁ (ז)
bullfinch	admonit	אַדְמוֹנִית (נ)
seagull	'ʃaxaf	שַׁחַף (ז)
albatross	albatros	אַלְבַּטְרוֹס (ז)
penguin	pingvin	פִּינְגְּוִין (ז)

217. Birds. Singing and sounds

| to sing (vi) | laʃir | לָשִׁיר |
| to call (animal, bird) | lits'ok | לִצְעוֹק |

to crow (rooster)	lekarker	לְקַרְקֵר
cock-a-doodle-doo	kuku'riku	קוּקוּרִיקוּ

to cluck (hen)	lekarker	לְקַרְקֵר
to caw (vi)	lits'roax	לִצְרוֹחַ
to quack (duck)	lega'a'ge'a	לְגַעֲגֵעַ
to cheep (vi)	letsayets	לְצַיֵּץ
to chirp, to twitter	letsaftsef, letsayets	לְצַפְצֵף, לְצַיֵּץ

218. Fish. Marine animals

bream	avroma	אַבְרוֹמָה (נ)
carp	karpiyon	קַרְפְּיוֹן (ז)
perch	'okunus	אוֹקוּנוּס (ז)
catfish	sfamnun	שְׂפַמְנוּן (ז)
pike	ze'ev 'mayim	זְאֵב מַיִם (ז)

salmon	'salmon	סַלְמוֹן (ז)
sturgeon	xidkan	חִדְקָן (ז)

herring	ma'liax	מָלִיחַ (ז)
Atlantic salmon	iltit	אִילְתִּית (נ)
mackerel	makarel	מָקָרֵל (ז)
flatfish	dag mofe ra'benu	דַּג מֹשֶׁה רַבֵּנוּ (ז)

zander, pike perch	amnun	אַמְנוּן (ז)
cod	ʃibut	שִׁיבּוּט (ז)
tuna	'tuna	טוּנָה (נ)
trout	forel	פּוֹרֵל (ז)
eel	tslofax	צְלוֹפָח (ז)
electric ray	trisanit	תְּרִיסָנִית (נ)
moray eel	mo'rena	מוֹרֵנָה (נ)
piranha	pi'ranya	פִּירָנְיָה (נ)

shark	kariʃ	כָּרִישׁ (ז)
dolphin	dolfin	דוֹלְפִין (ז)
whale	livyatan	לִוְיָתָן (ז)

crab	sartan	סַרְטָן (ז)
jellyfish	me'duza	מֶדוּזָה (נ)
octopus	tamnun	תַּמְנוּן (ז)

starfish	koxav yam	כּוֹכַב יָם (ז)
sea urchin	kipod yam	קִיפּוֹד יָם (ז)
seahorse	suson yam	סוּסוֹן יָם (ז)

oyster	tsidpa	צִדְפָּה (נ)
shrimp	xasilon	חֲסִילוֹן (ז)
lobster	'lobster	לוֹבּסְטֶר (ז)
spiny lobster	'lobster kotsani	לוֹבּסְטֶר קוֹצָנִי (ז)

219. Amphibians. Reptiles

snake	naχaʃ	נָחָשׁ (ז)
venomous (snake)	arsi	אַרְסִי
viper	'tsefa	צֶפַע (ז)
cobra	'peten	פֶּתֶן (ז)
python	piton	פִּיתוֹן (ז)
boa	χanak	חֲנָק (ז)
grass snake	naχaʃ 'mayim	נָחָשׁ מַיִם (ז)
rattle snake	ʃfifon	שְׁפִיפוֹן (ז)
anaconda	ana'konda	אֲנָקוֹנְדָה (נ)
lizard	leta'a	לְטָאָה (נ)
iguana	igu''ana	אִיגוּאָנָה (נ)
monitor lizard	'koaχ	כּוֹחַ (ז)
salamander	sala'mandra	סָלָמַנְדְרָה (נ)
chameleon	zikit	זִיקִית (נ)
scorpion	akrav	עַקְרָב (ז)
turtle	tsav	צָב (ז)
frog	tsfar'de'a	צְפַרְדֵּעַ (נ)
toad	karpada	קַרְפָּדָה (נ)
crocodile	tanin	תַנִּין (ז)

220. Insects

insect, bug	χarak	חָרָק (ז)
butterfly	parpar	פַּרְפַּר (ז)
ant	nemala	נְמָלָה (נ)
fly	zvuv	זְבוּב (ז)
mosquito	yatuʃ	יַתּוּשׁ (ז)
beetle	χipuʃit	חִיפּוּשִׁית (נ)
wasp	tsir'a	צִרְעָה (נ)
bee	dvora	דְּבוֹרָה (נ)
bumblebee	dabur	דַּבּוּר (ז)
gadfly (botfly)	zvuv hasus	זְבוּב הַסּוּס (ז)
spider	akaviʃ	עַכָּבִישׁ (ז)
spiderweb	kurei akaviʃ	קוּרֵי עַכָּבִישׁ (ז"ר)
dragonfly	ʃapirit	שְׁפִּירִית (נ)
grasshopper	χagav	חָגָב (ז)
moth (night butterfly)	aʃ	עָשׁ (ז)
cockroach	makak	מַקָּק (ז)
tick	kartsiya	קַרְצִיָּה (נ)

| flea | par'oʃ | פַּרְעוֹשׁ (ז) |
| midge | yavχuʃ | יַבְחוּשׁ (ז) |

locust	arbe	אַרְבֶּה (ז)
snail	χilazon	חִילָזוֹן (ז)
cricket	ʦarʦar	צְרָצַר (ז)

lightning bug	gaχlilit	גַחְלִילִית (נ)
ladybug	parat moʃe ra'benu	פָּרַת מֹשֶׁה רַבֵּנוּ (נ)
cockchafer	χipuʃit aviv	חִיפּוּשִׁית אָבִיב (נ)

leech	aluka	עֲלוּקָה (נ)
caterpillar	zaχal	זַחַל (ז)
earthworm	to'la'at	תּוֹלַעַת (נ)
larva	'deren	דֶרֶן (ז)

221. Animals. Body parts

beak	makor	מַקוֹר (ז)
wings	kna'fayim	כְּנָפַיִם (ז"ר)
foot (of bird)	'regel	רֶגֶל (נ)
feathers (plumage)	pluma	פְּלוּמָה (נ)

| feather | noʦa | נוֹצָה (נ) |
| crest | ʦiʦa | צִיצָה (נ) |

gills	zimim	זִימִים (ז"ר)
spawn	beiʦei dagim	בֵּיצֵי דָגִים (נ"ר)
larva	'deren	דֶרֶן (ז)

| fin | snapir | סְנַפִּיר (ז) |
| scales (of fish, reptile) | kaskasim | קַשְׂקַשִׂים (ז"ר) |

fang (canine)	niv	נִיב (ז)
paw (e.g., cat's ~)	'regel	רֶגֶל (נ)
muzzle (snout)	parʦuf	פַּרְצוּף (ז)
mouth (of cat, dog)	lo'a	לוֹעַ (ז)

| tail | zanav | זָנָב (ז) |
| whiskers | safam | שָׂפָם (ז) |

| hoof | parsa | פַּרְסָה (נ) |
| horn | 'keren | קֶרֶן (נ) |

carapace	ʃiryon	שִׁרְיוֹן (ז)
shell (of mollusk)	konχiya	קוֹנְכִיָה (נ)
eggshell	klipa	קְלִיפָּה (נ)

| animal's hair (pelage) | parva | פַּרְוָה (נ) |
| pelt (hide) | or | עוֹר (ז) |

222. Actions of animals

to fly (vi)	la'uf	לָעוּף
to fly in circles	laxug	לָחוּג
to fly away	la'uf	לָעוּף
to flap (~ the wings)	lenafnef	לְנַפְנֵף
to peck (vi)	lenaker	לְנַקֵּר
to sit on eggs	lidgor	לִדְגּוֹר
to hatch out (vi)	liv'ko'a	לִבְקוֹעַ
to build a nest	lekanen	לְקַנֵּן
to slither, to crawl	lizxol	לִזְחוֹל
to sting, to bite (insect)	la'akots	לַעֲקוֹץ
to bite (ab. animal)	linʃox	לִנְשׁוֹךְ
to sniff (vt)	lerax'reax	לְכַחֲרֵם
to bark (vi)	lin'boax	לִנְבּוֹחַ
to hiss (snake)	lirʃof	לִרְשׁוֹף
to scare (vt)	lehafxid	לְהַפְחִיד
to attack (vt)	litkof	לִתְקוֹף
to gnaw (bone, etc.)	lexarsem	לְכַרְסֵם
to scratch (with claws)	lisrot	לִשְׂרוֹט
to hide (vi)	lehistater	לְהִסְתַּתֵּר
to play (kittens, etc.)	lesaxek	לְשַׂחֵק
to hunt (vi, vt)	latsud	לָצוּד
to hibernate (vi)	laxrof	לַחֲרוֹף
to go extinct	lehikaxed	לְהִיכָחֵד

223. Animals. Habitats

habitat	beit gidul	בֵּית גִּידוּל (ז)
migration	hagira	הַגִּירָה (נ)
mountain	har	הַר (ז)
reef	ʃunit	שׁוּנִית (נ)
cliff	'sela	סֶלַע (ז)
forest	'ya'ar	יַעַר (ז)
jungle	'dʒungel	גִ׳ונְגֶל (ז)
savanna	sa'vana	סָוַונָה (נ)
tundra	'tundra	טוּנְדְּרָה (נ)
steppe	arava	עֲרָבָה (נ)
desert	midbar	מִדְבָּר (ז)
oasis	neve midbar	נְוֵוה מִדְבָּר (ז)
sea	yam	יָם (ז)

lake	agam	אֲגַם (ז)
ocean	ok'yanos	אוֹקְיָאנוֹס (ז)
swamp (marshland)	bitsa	בִּיצָה (נ)
freshwater (adj)	ʃel 'mayim metukim	שֶׁל מַיִם מְתוּקִים
pond	breχa	בְּרֵיכָה (נ)
river	nahar	נָהָר (ז)
den (bear's ~)	me'ura	מְאוּרָה (נ)
nest	ken	קַן (ז)
hollow (in a tree)	χor ba'ets	חוֹר בָּעֵץ (ז)
burrow (animal hole)	meχila	מְחִילָה (נ)
anthill	kan nemalim	קַן נְמָלִים (ז)

224. Animal care

zoo	gan hayot	גַּן חַיּוֹת (ז)
nature preserve	ʃmurat 'teva	שְׁמוּרַת טֶבַע (נ)
breeder (cattery, kennel, etc.)	beit gidul	בֵּית גִּידּוּל (ז)
open-air cage	kluv	כְּלוּב (ז)
cage	kluv	כְּלוּב (ז)
doghouse (kennel)	meluna	מְלוּנָה (נ)
dovecot	ʃovaχ	שׁוֹבָךְ (ז)
aquarium (fish tank)	ak'varyum	אָקְוַורְיוּם (ז)
dolphinarium	dolfi'naryum	דוֹלְפִינָרְיוּם (ז)
to breed (animals)	legadel	לְגַדֵּל
brood, litter	tse'etsa'im	צֶאֱצָאִים (ז"ר)
to tame (vt)	levayet	לְבַיֵּית
to train (animals)	le'alef	לְאַלֵּף
feed (fodder, etc.)	mazon, mispo	מָזוֹן (ז), מִסְפּוֹא (ז)
to feed (vt)	leha'aχil	לְהַאֲכִיל
pet store	χanut χayot	חֲנוּת חַיּוֹת (נ)
muzzle (for dog)	maχsom	מַחְסוֹם (ז)
collar (e.g., dog ~)	kolar	קוֹלָר (ז)
name (of animal)	kinui	כִּינּוּי (ז)
pedigree (of dog)	ʃal'ʃelet yuχsin	שַׁלְשֶׁלֶת יוּחְסִין (נ)

225. Animals. Miscellaneous

pack (wolves)	lahaka	לַהֲקָה (נ)
flock (birds)	lahaka	לַהֲקָה (נ)
shoal, school (fish)	lahaka	לַהֲקָה (נ)
herd (horses)	'eder	עֵדֶר (ז)

male (n)	zaχar	זָכָר (ז)
female (n)	nekeva	נְקֵבָה (נ)
hungry (adj)	ra'ev	רָעֵב
wild (adj)	pra'i	פְּרָאִי
dangerous (adj)	mesukan	מְסוּכָּן

226. Horses

horse	sus	סוּס (ז)
breed (race)	'geza	גֶּזַע (ז)
foal	syaχ	סְיָח (ז)
mare	susa	סוּסָה (נ)
mustang	mustang	מוּסטַנג (ז)
pony	'poni	פּוֹנִי (ז)
draft horse	sus avoda	סוּס עֲבוֹדָה (ז)
mane	ra'ama	רַעֲמָה (נ)
tail	zanav	זָנָב (ז)
hoof	parsa	פַּרסָה (נ)
horseshoe	parsa	פַּרסָה (נ)
to shoe (vt)	lefarzel	לְפַרזֵל
blacksmith	'nefaχ	נַפָּח (ז)
saddle	ukaf	אוּכָּף (ז)
stirrup	arkuba	אַרכּוּבָּה (נ)
bridle	'resen	רֶסֶן (ז)
reins	moʃχot	מוֹשְׁכוֹת (נ"ר)
whip (for riding)	ʃot	שׁוֹט (ז)
rider	roχev	רוֹכֵב (ז)
to saddle up (vt)	le'akef	לְאַכֵּף
to mount a horse	la'alot al sus	לַעֲלוֹת עַל סוּס
gallop	dehira	דְּהִירָה (נ)
to gallop (vi)	lidhor	לִדהוֹר
trot (n)	tfifa	טְפִיפָה (נ)
at a trot (adv)	bidhira	בִּדהִירָה
to go at a trot	litpof	לִטפּוֹף
racehorse	sus merots	סוּס מֵירוֹץ (ז)
horse racing	merots susim	מֵירוֹץ סוּסִים (ז)
stable	urva	אוּרוָוה (נ)
to feed (vt)	leha'aχil	לְהַאֲכִיל
hay	χatsil	חָצִיל (ז)
to water (animals)	lehaʃkot	לְהַשׁקוֹת

to wash (horse)	lirχots	לִרְחוֹץ
horse-drawn cart	agala	עֲגָלָה (נ)
to graze (vi)	lir'ot	לִרְעוֹת
to neigh (vi)	litshol	לִצְהוֹל
to kick (about horse)	liv'ot	לִבְעוֹט

Flora

227. Trees

tree	ets	עֵץ (ז)
deciduous (adj)	naʃir	נָשִׁיר
coniferous (adj)	maxtani	מַחְטָנִי
evergreen (adj)	yarok ad	יָרוֹק עַד
apple tree	ta'puax	תַּפּוּחַ (ז)
pear tree	agas	אַגָּס (ז)
sweet cherry tree	gudgedan	גּוּדְגְּדָן (ז)
sour cherry tree	duvdevan	דּוּבְדְּבָן (ז)
plum tree	ʃezif	שְׁזִיף (ז)
birch	ʃadar	שָׁדָר (ז)
oak	alon	אַלּוֹן (ז)
linden tree	'tilya	טִילְיָה (נ)
aspen	aspa	אַסְפָּה (נ)
maple	'eder	אֶדֶר (ז)
spruce	a'ʃuax	אַשׁוּחַ (ז)
pine	'oren	אוֹרֶן (ז)
larch	arzit	אַרְזִית (נ)
fir tree	a'ʃuax	אַשׁוּחַ (ז)
cedar	'erez	אֶרֶז (ז)
poplar	tsaftsefa	צַפְצָפָה (נ)
rowan	ben xuzrar	בֶּן־חוּזְרָר (ז)
willow	arava	עֲרָבָה (נ)
alder	alnus	אַלְנוּס (ז)
beech	aʃur	אַשׁוּר (ז)
elm	bu'kitsa	בּוּקִיצָה (נ)
ash (tree)	mela	מֵילָה (נ)
chestnut	armon	עַרְמוֹן (ז)
magnolia	mag'nolya	מַגְנוֹלִיָה (נ)
palm tree	'dekel	דֶּקֶל (ז)
cypress	broʃ	בְּרוֹשׁ (ז)
mangrove	mangrov	מַנְגְּרוֹב (ז)
baobab	ba'obab	בָּאוֹבָּב (ז)
eucalyptus	eika'liptus	אִיקָלִיפְּטוּס (ז)
sequoia	sek'voya	סְקְווֹיָה (נ)

228. Shrubs

bush	'siaχ	שִׂיחַ (ז)
shrub	'siaχ	שִׂיחַ (ז)
grapevine	'gefen	גֶּפֶן (ז)
vineyard	'kerem	כֶּרֶם (ז)
raspberry bush	'petel	פֶּטֶל (ז)
blackcurrant bush	'siaχ dumdemaniyot ʃχorot	שִׂיחַ דּוּמְדְּמָנִיּוֹת שְׁחוֹרוֹת (ז)
redcurrant bush	'siaχ dumdemaniyot adumot	שִׂיחַ דּוּמְדְּמָנִיּוֹת אֲדֻמּוֹת (ז)
gooseberry bush	χazarzar	חֲזַרְזָר (ז)
acacia	ʃita	שִׁיטָה (נ)
barberry	berberis	בֶּרְבֶּרִיס (ז)
jasmine	yasmin	יַסְמִין (ז)
juniper	ar'ar	עַרְעָר (ז)
rosebush	'siaχ vradim	שִׂיחַ וְרָדִים (ז)
dog rose	'vered bar	וֶרֶד בָּר (ז)

229. Mushrooms

mushroom	pitriya	פִּטְרִיָּה (נ)
edible mushroom	pitriya ra'uya lema'aχal	פִּטְרִיָּה רְאוּיָה לְמַאֲכָל
poisonous mushroom	pitriya ra'ila	פִּטְרִיָּה רְעִילָה (נ)
cap (of mushroom)	kipat pitriya	כִּיפַּת פִּטְרִיָּה (נ)
stipe (of mushroom)	'regel	רֶגֶל (נ)
cep (Boletus edulis)	por'tʃini	פּוֹרְצִ׳ינִי (ז)
orange-cap boletus	pitriyat 'kova aduma	פִּטְרִיַּת כּוֹבַע אֲדֻמָּה (נ)
birch bolete	pitriyat 'ya'ar	פִּטְרִיַּת יַעַר (נ)
chanterelle	gvi'onit ne'e'χelet	גְּבִיעוֹנִית נֶאֱכֶלֶת (נ)
russula	χarifit	חֲרִיפִית (נ)
morel	gamtsuts	גַּמְצוּץ (ז)
fly agaric	zvuvanit	זְבוּבָנִית (נ)
death cap	pitriya ra'ila	פִּטְרִיָּה רְעִילָה (נ)

230. Fruits. Berries

fruit	pri	פְּרִי (ז)
fruits	perot	פֵּירוֹת (ז״ר)
apple	ta'puaχ	תַּפּוּחַ (ז)
pear	agas	אַגָּס (ז)
plum	ʃezif	שְׁזִיף (ז)

strawberry (garden ~)	tut sade	תּוּת שָׂדֶה (ז)
sour cherry	duvdevan	דּוּבְדְּבָן (ז)
sweet cherry	gudgedan	גּוּדְגְּדָן (ז)
grape	anavim	עֲנָבִים (ז"ר)
raspberry	'petel	פֶּטֶל (ז)
blackcurrant	dumdemanit ʃxora	דּוּמְדְּמָנִית שְׁחוֹרָה (נ)
redcurrant	dumdemanit aduma	דּוּמְדְּמָנִית אֲדוּמָה (נ)
gooseberry	xazarzar	חֲזַרְזַר (ז)
cranberry	xamutsit	חֲמוּצִית (נ)
orange	tapuz	תַּפּוּז (ז)
mandarin	klemen'tina	קְלֵמֶנְטִינָה (נ)
pineapple	'ananas	אֲנָנָס (ז)
banana	ba'nana	בָּנָנָה (נ)
date	tamar	תָּמָר (ז)
lemon	limon	לִימוֹן (ז)
apricot	'miʃmeʃ	מִשְׁמֵשׁ (ז)
peach	afarsek	אֲפַרְסֵק (ז)
kiwi	'kivi	קִיוִוי (ז)
grapefruit	eʃkolit	אֶשְׁכּוֹלִית (נ)
berry	garger	גַּרְגֵּר (ז)
berries	gargerim	גַּרְגְּרִים (ז"ר)
cowberry	uxmanit aduma	אוּכְמָנִית אֲדוּמָה (נ)
wild strawberry	tut 'ya'ar	תּוּת יַעַר (ז)
bilberry	uxmanit	אוּכְמָנִית (נ)

231. Flowers. Plants

flower	'perax	פֶּרַח (ז)
bouquet (of flowers)	zer	זֵר (ז)
rose (flower)	'vered	וֶרֶד (ז)
tulip	tsiv'oni	צִבְעוֹנִי (ז)
carnation	tsi'poren	צִיפּוֹרֶן (ז)
gladiolus	glad'yola	גְּלַדִיוֹלָה (נ)
cornflower	dganit	דְּגָנִית (נ)
harebell	pa'amonit	פַּעֲמוֹנִית (נ)
dandelion	ʃinan	שִׁינָן (ז)
camomile	kamomil	קָמוֹמִיל (ז)
aloe	alvai	אַלְוַוי (ז)
cactus	'kaktus	קַקְטוּס (ז)
rubber plant, ficus	'fikus	פִיקוּס (ז)
lily	ʃoʃana	שׁוֹשַׁנָּה (נ)
geranium	ge'ranyum	גֵּרַנְיוּם (ז)

hyacinth	yakinton	יָקִינטוֹן (ז)
mimosa	mi'moza	מִימוֹזָה (נ)
narcissus	narkis	נַרקִיס (ז)
nasturtium	'kova hanazir	כּוֹבַע הַנָזִיר (ז)
orchid	saxlav	סַחלָב (ז)
peony	admonit	אַדמוֹנִית (נ)
violet	sigalit	סִיגָלִית (נ)

pansy	amnon vetamar	אַמנוֹן וְתָמָר (ז)
forget-me-not	zix'rini	זִכרִינִי (ז)
daisy	marganit	מַרגָנִית (נ)

poppy	'pereg	פֶּרֶג (ז)
hemp	ka'nabis	קָנָאבִּיס (ז)
mint	'menta	מֶנתָה (נ)

lily of the valley	zivanit	זִיוָנִית (נ)
snowdrop	ga'lantus	גָלַנטוּס (ז)
nettle	sirpad	סִרפָּד (ז)
sorrel	xum'a	חוּמעָה (נ)
water lily	nufar	נוּפָר (ז)
fern	ʃarax	שְׂרָך (ז)
lichen	xazazit	חֲזָזִית (נ)

greenhouse (tropical ~)	xamama	חֲמָמָה (נ)
lawn	midʃa'a	מִדשָׁאָה (נ)
flowerbed	arugat praxim	עֲרוּגַת פּרָחִים (נ)

plant	'tsemax	צֶמַח (ז)
grass	'deʃe	דֶשֶׁא (ז)
blade of grass	giv'ol 'esev	גִבעוֹל עֵשֶׂב (ז)

leaf	ale	עָלֶה (ז)
petal	ale ko'teret	עָלֶה כּוֹתֶרֶת (ז)
stem	giv'ol	גִבעוֹל (ז)
tuber	'pka'at	פְּקַעַת (נ)

| young plant (shoot) | 'nevet | נֶבֶט (ז) |
| thorn | kots | קוֹץ (ז) |

to blossom (vi)	lif'roax	לִפרוֹחַ
to fade, to wither	linbol	לִנבּוֹל
smell (odor)	'reax	רֵיחַ (ז)
to cut (flowers)	ligzom	לִגזוֹם
to pick (a flower)	liktof	לִקטוֹף

232. Cereals, grains

| grain | tvu'a | תבוּאָה (נ) |
| cereal crops | dganim | דגָנִים (ז״ר) |

ear (of barley, etc.)	ʃi'bolet	שִׁיבּוֹלֶת (נ)
wheat	χita	חִיטָה (נ)
rye	ʃifon	שִׁיפוֹן (ז)
oats	ʃi'bolet ʃu'al	שִׁיבּוֹלֶת שׁוּעָל (נ)
millet	'doχan	דּוֹחַן (ז)
barley	se'ora	שְׂעוֹרָה (נ)
corn	'tiras	תִּירָס (ז)
rice	'orez	אוֹרֶז (ז)
buckwheat	ku'semet	כּוּסֶמֶת (נ)
pea plant	afuna	אֲפוּנָה (נ)
kidney bean	ʃu'it	שְׁעוּעִית (נ)
soy	'soya	סוֹיָה (נ)
lentil	adaʃim	עֲדָשִׁים (נ"ר)
beans (pulse crops)	pol	פּוֹל (ז)

233. Vegetables. Greens

vegetables	yerakot	יְרָקוֹת (ז"ר)
greens	'yerek	יֶרֶק (ז)
tomato	agvaniya	עַגְבָנִיָה (נ)
cucumber	melafefon	מְלָפְפוֹן (ז)
carrot	'gezer	גֶּזֶר (ז)
potato	ta'puaχ adama	תַּפּוּחַ אֲדָמָה (ז)
onion	batsal	בָּצָל (ז)
garlic	ʃum	שׁוּם (ז)
cabbage	kruv	כְּרוּב (ז)
cauliflower	kruvit	כְּרוּבִית (נ)
Brussels sprouts	kruv nitsanim	כְּרוּב נִצָנִים (ז)
broccoli	'brokoli	בְּרוֹקוֹלִי (ז)
beetroot	'selek	סֶלֶק (ז)
eggplant	χatsil	חָצִיל (ז)
zucchini	kiʃu	קִישׁוּא (ז)
pumpkin	'dla'at	דְלַעַת (נ)
turnip	'lefet	לֶפֶת (נ)
parsley	petro'zilya	פֶּטְרוֹזִילְיָה (נ)
dill	ʃamir	שָׁמִיר (ז)
lettuce	'χasa	חַסָה (נ)
celery	'seleri	סֶלֶרִי (ז)
asparagus	aspa'ragos	אַסְפָּרָגוֹס (ז)
spinach	'tered	תֶּרֶד (ז)
pea	afuna	אֲפוּנָה (נ)
beans	pol	פּוֹל (ז)
corn (maize)	'tiras	תִּירָס (ז)

kidney bean	ʃu'it	שְׁעוּעִית (נ)
pepper	'pilpel	פִּלְפֵּל (ז)
radish	tsnonit	צְנוֹנִית (נ)
artichoke	artiʃok	אַרְטִישׁוֹק (ז)

REGIONAL GEOGRAPHY

Countries. Nationalities

234. Western Europe

Europe	ei'ropa	אֵירוֹפָּה (נ)
European Union	ha'iχud ha'eiro'pe'i	הָאִיחוּד הָאֵירוֹפִּי (ז)
European (n)	eiro'pe'i	אֵירוֹפָּאִי (ז)
European (adj)	eiro'pe'i	אֵירוֹפָּאִי
Austria	'ostriya	אוֹסְטְרִיָה (נ)
Austrian (masc.)	'ostri	אוֹסְטְרִי (ז)
Austrian (fem.)	'ostrit	אוֹסְטְרִית (נ)
Austrian (adj)	'ostri	אוֹסְטְרִי
Great Britain	bri'tanya hagdola	בְּרִיטַנְיָה הַגְדוֹלָה (נ)
England	'angliya	אַנְגְלִיָה (נ)
British (masc.)	'briti	בְּרִיטִי (ז)
British (fem.)	'btitit	בְּרִיטִית (נ)
English, British (adj)	angli	אַנְגְלִי
Belgium	'belgya	בֶּלְגִיָה (נ)
Belgian (masc.)	'belgi	בֶּלְגִי (ז)
Belgian (fem.)	'belgit	בֶּלְגִית (נ)
Belgian (adj)	'belgi	בֶּלְגִי
Germany	ger'manya	גֶרְמַנְיָה (נ)
German (masc.)	germani	גֶרְמָנִי (ז)
German (fem.)	germaniya	גֶרְמַנְיָה (נ)
German (adj)	germani	גֶרְמָנִי
Netherlands	'holand	הוֹלַנד (נ)
Holland	'holand	הוֹלַנד (נ)
Dutch (masc.)	ho'landi	הוֹלַנְדִי (ז)
Dutch (fem.)	ho'landit	הוֹלַנְדִית (נ)
Dutch (adj)	ho'landi	הוֹלַנְדִי
Greece	yavan	יָוָן (נ)
Greek (masc.)	yevani	יְוָנִי (ז)
Greek (fem.)	yevaniya	יְוָנִיָה (נ)
Greek (adj)	yevani	יְוָנִי
Denmark	'denemark	דֶנֶמַרק (נ)
Dane (masc.)	'deni	דֶנִי (ז)

| Dane (fem.) | 'denit | דֶּנִית (נ) |
| Danish (adj) | 'deni | דֶּנִי |

Ireland	'irland	אִירְלַנְד (נ)
Irish (masc.)	'iri	אִירִי (ז)
Irish (fem.)	ir'landit	אִירְלַנְדִּית (נ)
Irish (adj)	'iri	אִירִי

Iceland	'island	אִיסְלַנְד (נ)
Icelander (masc.)	is'landi	אִיסְלַנְדִּי (ז)
Icelander (fem.)	is'landit	אִיסְלַנְדִּית (נ)
Icelandic (adj)	is'landi	אִיסְלַנְדִּי

Spain	sfarad	סְפָרַד (נ)
Spaniard (masc.)	sfaradi	סְפָרַדִּי (ז)
Spaniard (fem.)	sfaradiya	סְפָרַדְיָה (נ)
Spanish (adj)	sfaradi	סְפָרַדִּי

Italy	i'talya	אִיטַלְיָה (נ)
Italian (masc.)	italki	אִיטַלְקִי (ז)
Italian (fem.)	italkiya	אִיטַלְקִיָה (נ)
Italian (adj)	italki	אִיטַלְקִי

Cyprus	kafrisin	קַפְרִיסִין (נ)
Cypriot (masc.)	kafri'sa'i	קַפְרִיסָאִי (ז)
Cypriot (fem.)	kafri'sa'it	קַפְרִיסָאִית (נ)
Cypriot (adj)	kafri'sa'i	קַפְרִיסָאִי

Malta	'malta	מַלְטָה (נ)
Maltese (masc.)	'malti	מַלְטִי (ז)
Maltese (fem.)	'maltit	מַלְטִית (נ)
Maltese (adj)	'malti	מַלְטִי

Norway	nor'vegya	נוֹרְבֶּגְיָה (נ)
Norwegian (masc.)	nor'vegi	נוֹרְבֶּגִי (ז)
Norwegian (fem.)	nor'vegit	נוֹרְבֶּגִית (נ)
Norwegian (adj)	nor'vegi	נוֹרְבֶּגִי

Portugal	portugal	פּוֹרְטוּגָל (נ)
Portuguese (masc.)	portu'gali	פּוֹרְטוּגָלִי (ז)
Portuguese (fem.)	portu'galit	פּוֹרְטוּגָלִית (נ)
Portuguese (adj)	portu'gezi	פּוֹרְטוּגֶזִי

Finland	'finland	פִינְלַנְד (נ)
Finn (masc.)	'fini	פִינִי (ז)
Finn (fem.)	'finit	פִינִית (נ)
Finnish (adj)	'fini	פִינִי

France	tsarfat	צָרְפַת (נ)
French (masc.)	tsarfati	צָרְפָתִי (ז)
French (fem.)	tsarfatiya	צָרְפָתְיָה (נ)
French (adj)	tsarfati	צָרְפָתִי

Sweden	'ʃvedya	שְׁבֶדְיָה (נ)
Swede (masc.)	'ʃvedi	שְׁבֶדִי (ז)
Swede (fem.)	'ʃvedit	שְׁבֶדִית (נ)
Swedish (adj)	'ʃvedi	שְׁבֶדִי

Switzerland	'ʃvaits	שְׁוַיץ (נ)
Swiss (masc.)	ʃvei'tsari	שְׁוַיצָרִי (ז)
Swiss (fem.)	ʃvei'tsarit	שְׁוַיצָרִית (נ)
Swiss (adj)	ʃve'tsari	שְׁוַיצָרִי

Scotland	'skotland	סְקוֹטְלַנד (נ)
Scottish (masc.)	'skoti	סְקוֹטִי (ז)
Scottish (fem.)	'skotit	סְקוֹטִית (נ)
Scottish (adj)	'skoti	סְקוֹטִי

Vatican	vatikan	וָתִיקָן (ז)
Liechtenstein	liχtenʃtain	לִיכְטֶנְשְׁטַיין (נ)
Luxembourg	luksemburg	לוּקְסֶמְבּוּרג (נ)
Monaco	mo'nako	מוֹנָקוֹ (נ)

235. Central and Eastern Europe

Albania	al'banya	אַלְבַּנְיָה (נ)
Albanian (masc.)	al'bani	אַלְבָּנִי (ז)
Albanian (fem.)	al'banit	אַלְבָּנִית (נ)
Albanian (adj)	al'bani	אַלְבָּנִי

Bulgaria	bul'garya	בּוּלְגַרְיָה (נ)
Bulgarian (masc.)	bul'gari	בּוּלְגָרִי (ז)
Bulgarian (fem.)	bulgariya	בּוּלְגָרְיָה (נ)
Bulgarian (adj)	bul'gari	בּוּלְגָרִי

Hungary	hun'garya	הוּנְגַרְיָה (נ)
Hungarian (masc.)	hungari	הוּנְגָרִי (ז)
Hungarian (fem.)	hungariya	הוּנְגַרְיָה (נ)
Hungarian (adj)	hun'gari	הוּנְגָרִי

Latvia	'latviya	לַטְבְיָה (נ)
Latvian (masc.)	'latvi	לַטְבִי (ז)
Latvian (fem.)	'latvit	לַטְבִית (נ)
Latvian (adj)	'latvi	לַטְבִי

Lithuania	'lita	לִישָׁא (נ)
Lithuanian (masc.)	lita'i	לִישָׁאִי (ז)
Lithuanian (fem.)	lita'it	לִישָׁאִית (נ)
Lithuanian (adj)	lita'i	לִישָׁאִי

Poland	polin	פּוֹלִין (נ)
Pole (masc.)	polani	פּוֹלָנִי (ז)
Pole (fem.)	polaniya	פּוֹלָנְיָה (נ)

Polish (adj)	polani	פּוֹלָנִי
Romania	ro'manya	רוֹמַנְיָה (נ)
Romanian (masc.)	romani	רוֹמָנִי (ז)
Romanian (fem.)	romaniya	רוֹמָנִיָה (נ)
Romanian (adj)	ro'mani	רוֹמָנִי

Serbia	'serbya	סֶרְבְּיָה (נ)
Serbian (masc.)	'serbi	סֶרְבִּי (ז)
Serbian (fem.)	'serbit	סֶרְבִּית (נ)
Serbian (adj)	'serbi	סֶרְבִּי

Slovakia	slo'vakya	סלוֹבָקְיָה (נ)
Slovak (masc.)	slo'vaki	סלוֹבָקִי (ז)
Slovak (fem.)	slo'vakit	סלוֹבָקִית (נ)
Slovak (adj)	slo'vaki	סלוֹבָקִי

Croatia	kro''atya	קרוֹאָטְיָה (נ)
Croatian (masc.)	kro''ati	קרוֹאָטִי (ז)
Croatian (fem.)	kro''atit	קרוֹאָטִית (נ)
Croatian (adj)	kro''ati	קרוֹאָטִי

Czech Republic	'tʃeχya	צֶ׳כְיָה (נ)
Czech (masc.)	'tʃeχi	צֶ׳כִי (ז)
Czech (fem.)	'tʃeχit	צֶ׳כִית (נ)
Czech (adj)	'tʃeχi	צֶ׳כִי

Estonia	es'tonya	אֶסטוֹנְיָה (נ)
Estonian (masc.)	es'toni	אֶסטוֹנִי (ז)
Estonian (fem.)	es'tonit	אֶסטוֹנִית (נ)
Estonian (adj)	es'toni	אֶסטוֹנִי

Bosnia and Herzegovina	'bosniya	בּוֹסנִיָה (נ)
Macedonia (Republic of ~)	make'donya	מָקֶדוֹנְיָה (נ)
Slovenia	slo'venya	סלוֹבֶנְיָה (נ)
Montenegro	monte'negro	מוֹנטֶנֶגרוֹ (נ)

236. Former USSR countries

Azerbaijan	azerbaidʒan	אָזֶרְבַּייג׳ָן (נ)
Azerbaijani (masc.)	azerbai'dʒani	אָזֶרְבַּייג׳ָנִי (ז)
Azerbaijani (fem.)	azerbai'dʒanit	אָזֶרְבַּייג׳ָנִית (נ)
Azerbaijani, Azeri (adj)	azerbai'dʒani	אָזֶרְבַּייג׳ָנִי

Armenia	ar'menya	אַרמֶנְיָה (נ)
Armenian (masc.)	ar'meni	אַרמֶנִי (ז)
Armenian (fem.)	ar'menit	אַרמֶנִית (נ)
Armenian (adj)	ar'meni	אַרמֶנִי

| Belarus | 'belarus | בֶּלָרוּס (נ) |
| Belarusian (masc.) | bela'rusi | בֶּלָרוּסִי (ז) |

| Belarusian (fem.) | bela'rusit | בֶּלָרוּסִית (נ) |
| Belarusian (adj) | byelo'rusi | בִּילוֹרוּסִי |

Georgia	'gruzya	גרוזְיָה (נ)
Georgian (masc.)	gru'zini	גרוזִינִי (ז)
Georgian (fem.)	gru'zinit	גרוזִינִית (נ)
Georgian (adj)	gru'zini	גרוזִינִי
Kazakhstan	kazaχstan	קָזַחסטָן (נ)
Kazakh (masc.)	ka'zaχi	קָזָחִי (ז)
Kazakh (fem.)	ka'zaχit	קָזָחִית (נ)
Kazakh (adj)	ka'zaχi	קָזָחִי

Kirghizia	kirgizstan	קִירגִיזסטָן (נ)
Kirghiz (masc.)	kir'gizi	קִירגִיזִי (ז)
Kirghiz (fem.)	kir'gizit	קִירגִיזִית (נ)
Kirghiz (adj)	kir'gizi	קִירגִיזִי

Moldova, Moldavia	mol'davya	מוֹלדַבָיָה (נ)
Moldavian (masc.)	mol'davi	מוֹלדָבִי (ז)
Moldavian (fem.)	mol'davit	מוֹלדָבִית (נ)
Moldavian (adj)	mol'davi	מוֹלדָבִי
Russia	'rusya	רוֹסיָה (נ)
Russian (masc.)	rusi	רוֹסִי (ז)
Russian (fem.)	rusiya	רוֹסִיָּה (נ)
Russian (adj)	rusi	רוֹסִי

Tajikistan	tadʒikistan	טָגִ'יקִיסטָן (נ)
Tajik (masc.)	ta'dʒiki	טָגִ'יקִי (ז)
Tajik (fem.)	ta'dʒikit	טָגִ'יקִית (נ)
Tajik (adj)	ta'dʒiki	טָגִ'יקִי

Turkmenistan	turkmenistan	טוּרקמֶנִיסטָן (נ)
Turkmen (masc.)	turk'meni	טוּרקמֶנִי (ז)
Turkmen (fem.)	turk'menit	טוּרקמֶנִית (נ)
Turkmenian (adj)	turk'meni	טוּרקמֶנִי

Uzbekistan	uzbekistan	אוּזבָּקִיסטָן (נ)
Uzbek (masc.)	uz'beki	אוּזבָּקִי (ז)
Uzbek (fem.)	uz'bekit	אוּזבָּקִית (נ)
Uzbek (adj)	uz'beki	אוּזבָּקִי

Ukraine	uk'rayna	אוּקרָאִינָה (נ)
Ukrainian (masc.)	ukra''ini	אוּקרָאִינִי (ז)
Ukrainian (fem.)	ukra''init	אוּקרָאִינִית (נ)
Ukrainian (adj)	ukra''ini	אוּקרָאִינִי

237. Asia

| Asia | 'asya | אַסיָה (נ) |
| Asian (adj) | as'yati | אַסיָיתִי |

Vietnam	vyetnam	וְיֶיטְנָאם (נ)
Vietnamese (masc.)	vyet'nami	וְיֶיטְנָאמִי (ז)
Vietnamese (fem.)	vyet'namit	וְיֶיטְנָאמִית (נ)
Vietnamese (adj)	vyet'nami	וְיֶיטְנָאמִי
India	'hodu	הוֹדוּ (נ)
Indian (masc.)	'hodi	הוֹדִי (ז)
Indian (fem.)	'hodit	הוֹדִית (נ)
Indian (adj)	'hodi	הוֹדִי
Israel	yisra'el	יִשְׂרָאֵל (נ)
Israeli (masc.)	yisra'eli	יִשְׂרָאֵלִי (ז)
Israeli (fem.)	yisra'elit	יִשְׂרָאֵלִית (נ)
Israeli (adj)	yisra'eli	יִשְׂרָאֵלִי
Jew (n)	yehudi	יְהוּדִי (ז)
Jewess (n)	yehudiya	יְהוּדִיָה (נ)
Jewish (adj)	yehudi	יְהוּדִי
China	sin	סִין (נ)
Chinese (masc.)	'sini	סִינִי (נ)
Chinese (fem.)	'sinit	סִינִית (נ)
Chinese (adj)	'sini	סִינִי
Korean (masc.)	korei"ani	קוֹרֵיאָנִי (ז)
Korean (fem.)	korei"anit	קוֹרֵיאָנִית (נ)
Korean (adj)	korei"ani	קוֹרֵיאָנִי
Lebanon	levanon	לְבָנוֹן (נ)
Lebanese (masc.)	leva'noni	לְבָנוֹנִי (ז)
Lebanese (fem.)	leva'nonit	לְבָנוֹנִית (נ)
Lebanese (adj)	leva'noni	לְבָנוֹנִי
Mongolia	mon'golya	מוֹנגוֹלְיָה (נ)
Mongolian (masc.)	mon'goli	מוֹנגוֹלִי (ז)
Mongolian (fem.)	mon'golit	מוֹנגוֹלִית (נ)
Mongolian (adj)	mon'goli	מוֹנגוֹלִי
Malaysia	ma'lezya	מָלֶזְיָה (נ)
Malaysian (masc.)	ma'la'i	מָלָאִי (ז)
Malaysian (fem.)	ma'la'it	מָלָאִית (נ)
Malaysian (adj)	ma'la'i	מָלָאִי
Pakistan	pakistan	פָּקִיסטָן (נ)
Pakistani (masc.)	pakis'tani	פָּקִיסטָנִי (ז)
Pakistani (fem.)	pakis'tanit	פָּקִיסטָנִית (נ)
Pakistani (adj)	pakis'tani	פָּקִיסטָנִי
Saudi Arabia	arav hasa'udit	עֲרָב הַסָעוּדִית (נ)
Arab (masc.)	aravi	עֲרָבִי (ז)
Arab (fem.)	araviya	עֲרָבִיָה (נ)
Arab, Arabic (adj)	aravi	עֲרָבִי

Thailand	'tailand	תָּאִילֶנד (נ)
Thai (masc.)	tai'landi	תָּאִילֶנדִי (ז)
Thai (fem.)	tai'landit	תָּאִילֶנדִית (נ)
Thai (adj)	tai'landi	תָּאִילֶנדִי

Taiwan	taivan	טַייוָון (נ)
Taiwanese (masc.)	tai'vani	טַייוָונִי (ז)
Taiwanese (fem.)	tai'vanit	טַייוָונִית (נ)
Taiwanese (adj)	tai'vani	טַייוָונִי

Turkey	'turkiya	טוּרקְיָה (נ)
Turk (masc.)	turki	טוּרקִי (ז)
Turk (fem.)	turkiya	טוּרקְיָה (נ)
Turkish (adj)	turki	טוּרקִי

Japan	yapan	יַפָּן (נ)
Japanese (masc.)	ya'pani	יַפָּנִי (ז)
Japanese (fem.)	ya'panit	יַפָּנִית (נ)
Japanese (adj)	ya'pani	יַפָּנִי

Afghanistan	afganistan	אַפְגָנִיסטָן (נ)
Bangladesh	bangladeʃ	בַּנגלָדָש (נ)
Indonesia	indo'nezya	אִינדוֹנֶזיָה (נ)
Jordan	yarden	יַרדֵן (נ)

Iraq	irak	עִירָאק (נ)
Iran	iran	אִירָן (נ)
Cambodia	kam'bodya	קַמבּוֹדִיָה (נ)
Kuwait	kuveit	כּוּוֵית (נ)

Laos	la'os	לָאוֹס (נ)
Myanmar	miyanmar	מְיַאנמַר (נ)
Nepal	nepal	נֶפָּאל (נ)
United Arab Emirates	iχud ha'emi'royot ha'araviyot	אִיחוּד הָאֲמִירוּיוֹת הָעַרָבִיוֹת (ז)

Syria	'surya	סוּריָה (נ)
Palestine	falastin	פָּלַסטִין (נ)
South Korea	ko'rei'a hadromit	קוֹרֵיאָה הַדרוֹמִית (נ)
North Korea	ko'rei'a haʦfonit	קוֹרֵיאָה הַצפוֹנִית (נ)

238. North America

United States of America	arʦot habrit	אַרצוֹת הַבּרִית (נ״ר)
American (masc.)	ameri'ka'i	אֲמֶרִיקָאִי (ז)
American (fem.)	ameri'ka'it	אֲמֶרִיקָאִית (נ)
American (adj)	ameri'ka'i	אֲמֶרִיקָאִי

| Canada | 'kanada | קַנָדָה (נ) |
| Canadian (masc.) | ka'nadi | קַנָדִי (ז) |

| Canadian (fem.) | ka'nadit | קָנָדִית (נ) |
| Canadian (adj) | ka'nadi | קָנָדִי |

Mexico	'meksiko	מֶקְסִיקוֹ (נ)
Mexican (masc.)	meksi'kani	מֶקְסִיקָנִי (ז)
Mexican (fem.)	meksi'kanit	מֶקְסִיקָנִית (נ)
Mexican (adj)	meksi'kani	מֶקְסִיקָנִי

239. Central and South America

Argentina	argen'tina	אַרְגֶּנְטִינָה (נ)
Argentinian (masc.)	argentinai	אַרְגֶּנְטִינָאִי (ז)
Argentinian (fem.)	argenti'na'it	אַרְגֶּנְטִינָאִית (נ)
Argentinian (adj)	argenti'na'it	אַרְגֶּנְטִינָאִי

Brazil	brazil	בְּרָזִיל (נ)
Brazilian (masc.)	brazil'a'i	בְּרָזִילָאִי (ז)
Brazilian (fem.)	brazi'la'it	בְּרָזִילָאִית (נ)
Brazilian (adj)	brazi'la'i	בְּרָזִילָאִי

Colombia	ko'lombya	קוֹלוֹמְבִּיָה (נ)
Colombian (masc.)	kolom'byani	קוֹלוֹמְבִּיָאנִי (ז)
Colombian (fem.)	kolomb'yanit	קוֹלוֹמְבִּיָאנִית (נ)
Colombian (adj)	kolom'byani	קוֹלוֹמְבִּיָאנִי

Cuba	'kuba	קוּבָּה (נ)
Cuban (masc.)	ku'bani	קוּבָּנִי (ז)
Cuban (fem.)	ku'banit	קוּבָּנִית (נ)
Cuban (adj)	ku'bani	קוּבָּנִי

Chile	'tʃile	צִ'ילֶה (נ)
Chilean (masc.)	tʃili''ani	צִ'ילִיאָנִי (ז)
Chilean (fem.)	tʃili''anit	צִ'ילִיאָנִית (נ)
Chilean (adj)	tʃili''ani	צִ'ילִיאָנִי

Bolivia	bo'livya	בּוֹלִיבִיָה (נ)
Venezuela	venetsu''ela	וֶנֶצוּאֶלָה (נ)
Paraguay	paragvai	פָּרָגוּוַאי (נ)
Peru	peru	פֶּרוּ (נ)

Suriname	surinam	סוּרִינָאם (נ)
Uruguay	urugvai	אוּרוּגוּוַאי (נ)
Ecuador	ekvador	אֶקוָודוֹר (נ)

The Bahamas	iyey ba'hama	אִיֵי בָּהָאמָה (ז"ר)
Haiti	ha''iti	הָאִיטִי (נ)
Dominican Republic	hare'publika hadomeni'kanit	הָרֶפּוּבְּלִיקָה הַדוֹמִינִיקָנִית (נ)
Panama	pa'nama	פָּנָמָה (נ)
Jamaica	dʒa'maika	גַ'מַייקָה (נ)

240. Africa

Egypt	mits'rayim	מִצְרַיִם (נ)
Egyptian (masc.)	mitsri	מִצְרִי (ז)
Egyptian (fem.)	mitsriya	מִצְרִייָה (נ)
Egyptian (adj)	mitsri	מִצְרִי
Morocco	ma'roko	מָרוֹקוֹ (נ)
Moroccan (masc.)	maro'ka'i	מָרוֹקָאִי (ז)
Moroccan (fem.)	maro'ka'it	מָרוֹקָאִית (נ)
Moroccan (adj)	maro'ka'i	מָרוֹקָאִי
Tunisia	tu'nisya	טוּנִיסְיָה (נ)
Tunisian (masc.)	tuni'sa'i	טוּנִיסָאִי (ז)
Tunisian (fem.)	tuni'sa'it	טוּנִיסָאִית (נ)
Tunisian (adj)	tuni'sa'i	טוּנִיסָאִי
Ghana	'gana	גָאנָה (נ)
Zanzibar	zanzibar	זַנְזִיבָּר (נ)
Kenya	'kenya	קֶנְיָה (נ)
Libya	luv	לוּב (נ)
Madagascar	madagaskar	מָדָגַסְקָר (ז)
Namibia	na'mibya	נָמִיבִּיָה (נ)
Senegal	senegal	סֶנֶגָל (נ)
Tanzania	tan'zanya	טַנְזַנְיָה (נ)
South Africa	drom 'afrika	דרוֹם אַפְרִיקָה (נ)
African (masc.)	afri'ka'i	אַפְרִיקָאִי (ז)
African (fem.)	afri'ka'it	אַפְרִיקָאִית (נ)
African (adj)	afri'ka'i	אַפְרִיקָאִי

241. Australia. Oceania

Australia	ost'ralya	אוֹסְטְרַלְיָה (נ)
Australian (masc.)	ost'rali	אוֹסְטְרָלִי (ז)
Australian (fem.)	ost'ralit	אוֹסְטְרָלִית (נ)
Australian (adj)	ost'rali	אוֹסְטְרָלִי
New Zealand	nyu 'ziland	נִיוֹ זִילַנד (נ)
New Zealander (masc.)	nyu zi'landi	נִיוֹ זִילַנדִי (ז)
New Zealander (fem.)	nyu zi'landit	נִיוֹ זִילַנדִית (נ)
New Zealand (as adj)	nyu zi'landi	נִיוֹ זִילַנדִי
Tasmania	tas'manya	טַסְמַנְיָה (נ)
French Polynesia	poli'nezya hatsarfatit	פּוֹלִינֶזִיָה הַצָרְפָתִית (נ)

242. Cities

Amsterdam	'amsterdam	אָמְסְטֶרְדָם (נ)
Ankara	ankara	אַנְקָרָה (נ)
Athens	a'tuna	אָתוּנָה (נ)
Baghdad	bagdad	בַּגְדָד (נ)
Bangkok	bangkok	בַּנְגְקוֹק (נ)
Barcelona	bartse'lona	בַּרְצֶלוֹנָה (נ)
Beijing	beiʤing	בֵּייגִ'ינג (נ)
Beirut	beirut	בֵּירוּת (נ)
Berlin	berlin	בֶּרְלִין (נ)
Mumbai (Bombay)	bombei	בּוֹמְבֵּיִ (נ)
Bonn	bon	בּוֹן (נ)
Bordeaux	bordo	בּוֹרְדוֹ (נ)
Bratislava	bratis'lava	בְּרָטִיסְלָאבָה (נ)
Brussels	brisel	בְּרִיסֶל (נ)
Bucharest	'bukareʃt	בּוּקָרֶשְט (נ)
Budapest	'budapeʃt	בּוּדַפֶּשְט (נ)
Cairo	kahir	קָהִיר (נ)
Kolkata (Calcutta)	kol'kata	קוֹלְקָטָה (נ)
Chicago	ʃi'kago	שִׁיקָאגוֹ (נ)
Copenhagen	kopen'hagen	קוֹפֶּנְהָגֶן (נ)
Dar-es-Salaam	dar e salam	דָאר אֶ-סָלָאם (נ)
Delhi	'delhi	דֶלְהִי (נ)
Dubai	dubai	דוּבַּאי (נ)
Dublin	'dablin	דַבְּלִין (נ)
Düsseldorf	'diseldorf	דִיסֶלְדוֹרְף (נ)
Florence	fi'rentse	פִירֶנְצֶה (נ)
Frankfurt	'frankfurt	פְרַנְקְפוּרְט (נ)
Geneva	ʤe'neva	גְ'נֶבָה (נ)
The Hague	hag	הָאג (נ)
Hamburg	'hamburg	הַמְבּוּרְג (נ)
Hanoi	hanoi	הָאנוֹי (נ)
Havana	ha'vana	הָוָואנָה (נ)
Helsinki	'helsinki	הֶלְסִינְקִי (נ)
Hiroshima	hiro'ʃima	הִירוֹשִׁימָה (נ)
Hong Kong	hong kong	הוֹנג קוֹנג (נ)
Istanbul	istanbul	אִיסְטַנְבּוּל (נ)
Jerusalem	yeruʃa'layim	יְרוּשָׁלַיִם (נ)
Kyiv	'kiyev	קִייֶב (נ)
Kuala Lumpur	ku''ala lumpur	קוּאָלָה לוּמְפּוּר (נ)
Lisbon	lisbon	לִיסְבּוֹן (נ)
London	'london	לוֹנְדוֹן (נ)
Los Angeles	los 'anʤeles	לוֹס אַנגְ'לֶס (נ)

Lyons	li'on	לִיאוֹן (נ)
Madrid	madrid	מַדְרִיד (נ)
Marseille	marsei	מַרְסֵי (נ)
Mexico City	'meksiko 'siti	מֶקְסִיקוֹ סִיטִי (נ)
Miami	ma'yami	מַיָאמִי (נ)
Montreal	montri'ol	מוֹנְטְרִיאוֹל (נ)
Moscow	'moskva	מוֹסְקְבָה (נ)
Munich	'minχen	מִינְכֶן (נ)

Nairobi	nai'robi	נַיירוֹבִּי (נ)
Naples	'napoli	נָפּוֹלִי (נ)
New York	nyu york	נִיו יוֹרק (נ)
Nice	nis	נִיס (נ)
Oslo	'oslo	אוֹסְלוֹ (נ)
Ottawa	'otava	אוֹטָוָוה (נ)

Paris	pariz	פָּרִיז (נ)
Prague	prag	פְּרָאג (נ)
Rio de Janeiro	'riyo de ʒa'nero	רִיוֹ דֶה זָ'נֶרוֹ (נ)
Rome	'roma	רוֹמָא (נ)

Saint Petersburg	sant 'petersburg	סָנט פֶּטֶרסבּוּרג (נ)
Seoul	se'ul	סָאוּל (נ)
Shanghai	ʃanχai	שַׁנְחַאי (נ)
Singapore	singapur	סִינגַפּוּר (נ)
Stockholm	'stokholm	סטוֹקהוֹלם (נ)
Sydney	'sidni	סִידְנִי (נ)

Taipei	taipe	טַייפֶּה (נ)
Tokyo	'tokyo	טוֹקִיוֹ (נ)
Toronto	to'ronto	טוֹרוֹנְטוֹ (נ)

Venice	ve'netsya	וֶנֶצְיָה (נ)
Vienna	'vina	וִינָה (נ)
Warsaw	'varʃa	וַרשָׁה (נ)
Washington	'voʃington	ווֹשִׁינגטוֹן (נ)

243. Politics. Government. Part 1

politics	po'litika	פּוֹלִיטִיקָה (נ)
political (adj)	po'liti	פּוֹלִיטִי
politician	politikai	פּוֹלִיטִיקַאי (ז)

state (country)	medina	מְדִינָה (נ)
citizen	ezraχ	אֶזְרָח (ז)
citizenship	ezraχut	אֶזְרָחוּת (נ)

national emblem	'semel le'umi	סֶמֶל לְאוּמִי (ז)
national anthem	himnon le'umi	הִמְנוֹן לְאוּמִי (ז)
government	memʃala	מֶמשָׁלָה (נ)

head of state	roʃ medina	רֹאשׁ מְדִינָה (ז)
parliament	parlament	פַּרְלָמֶנט (ז)
party	miflaga	מִפְלָגָה (נ)
capitalism	kapitalizm	קָפִּיטָלִיזֶם (ז)
capitalist (adj)	kapita'listi	קָפִּיטָלִיסטִי
socialism	sotsyalizm	סוֹצִיאָלִיזֶם (ז)
socialist (adj)	sotsya'listi	סוֹצִיאָלִיסטִי
communism	komunizm	קוֹמוּנִיזֶם (ז)
communist (adj)	komu'nisti	קוֹמוּנִיסטִי
communist (n)	komunist	קוֹמוּנִיסט (ז)
democracy	demo'kratya	דֶמוֹקרַטיָה (נ)
democrat	demokrat	דֶמוֹקרָט (ז)
democratic (adj)	demo'krati	דֶמוֹקרָטִי
Democratic party	miflaga demo'kratit	מִפְלָגָה דֶמוֹקרָטִית (נ)
liberal (n)	libe'rali	לִיבֶּרָלִי (ז)
liberal (adj)	libe'rali	לִיבֶּרָלִי
conservative (n)	ʃamran	שַׁמְרָן (ז)
conservative (adj)	ʃamrani	שַׁמְרָנִי
republic (n)	re'publika	רֶפּוּבּלִיקָה (נ)
republican (n)	republi'kani	רֶפּוּבּלִיקָנִי (ז)
Republican party	miflaga republi'kanit	מִפְלָגָה רֶפּוּבּלִיקָנִית (נ)
elections	bχirot	בְּחִירוֹת (נ"ר)
to elect (vt)	livχor	לִבְחוֹר
elector, voter	mats'bi'a	מַצְבִּיעַ (ז)
election campaign	masa bχirot	מַסָע בְּחִירוֹת (ז)
voting (n)	hatsba'a	הַצְבָּעָה (נ)
to vote (vi)	lehats'bi'a	לְהַצְבִּיעַ
suffrage, right to vote	zχut hatsba'a	זכוּת הַצְבָּעָה (נ)
candidate	mu'amad	מוֹעֲמָד (ז)
to be a candidate	lehatsig mu'amadut	לְהַצִיג מוֹעֲמָדוּת
campaign	masa	מַסָע (ז)
opposition (as adj)	opozitsyoni	אוֹפּוֹזִיציוֹנִי
opposition (n)	opo'zitsya	אוֹפּוֹזִיציָה (נ)
visit	bikur	בִּיקוּר (ז)
official visit	bikur riʃmi	בִּיקוּר רִשְׁמִי (ז)
international (adj)	benle'umi	בֵּינלְאוּמִי
negotiations	masa umatan	מַשָׂא וּמַתָן (ז)
to negotiate (vi)	laset velatet	לָשֵׂאת וְלָתֵת

244. Politics. Government. Part 2

society	χevra	חֶבְרָה (נ)
constitution	χuka	חוּקָה (נ)
power (political control)	ʃilton	שִׁלְטוֹן (ז)
corruption	ʃχitut	שְׁחִיתוּת (נ)
law (justice)	χok	חוֹק (ז)
legal (legitimate)	χuki	חוּקִי
justice (fairness)	'tsedek	צֶדֶק (ז)
just (fair)	tsodek	צוֹדֵק
committee	'va'ad	וַעַד (ז)
bill (draft law)	hatsa'at χok	הַצָעַת חוֹק (נ)
budget	taktsiv	תַקְצִיב (ז)
policy	mediniyut	מְדִינִיוּת (נ)
reform	re'forma	רֶפוֹרְמָה (נ)
radical (adj)	radi'kali	רָדִיקָלִי
power (strength, force)	otsma	עוֹצְמָה (נ)
powerful (adj)	rav 'koaχ	רַב־כּוֹחַ
supporter	tomeχ	תוֹמֵךְ (ז)
influence	haʃpa'a	הַשְׁפָּעָה (נ)
regime (e.g., military ~)	miʃtar	מִשְׁטָר (ז)
conflict	siχsuχ	סִכְסוּךְ (ז)
conspiracy (plot)	'keʃer	קֶשֶׁר (ז)
provocation	provo'katsya, hitgarut	פְּרוֹבוֹקַצְיָה, הִתְגָרוּת (נ)
to overthrow (regime, etc.)	leha'diaχ	לְהָדִיחַ
overthrow (of government)	hadaχa mikes malχut	הַדָחָה מִכֶּס מַלְכוּת (נ)
revolution	mahapeχa	מַהְפֵּכָה (נ)
coup d'état	hafiχa	הֲפִיכָה (נ)
military coup	mahapaχ tsva'i	מַהֲפָךְ צְבָאִי (ז)
crisis	maʃber	מַשְׁבֵּר (ז)
economic recession	mitun kalkali	מִיתוּן כַּלְכָּלִי (ז)
demonstrator (protester)	mafgin	מַפְגִין (ז)
demonstration	hafgana	הַפְגָנָה (נ)
martial law	miʃtar tsva'i	מִשְׁטָר צְבָאִי (ז)
military base	basis tsva'i	בָּסִיס צְבָאִי (ז)
stability	yatsivut	יַצִיבוּת (נ)
stable (adj)	yatsiv	יַצִיב
exploitation	nitsul	נִיצוּל (ז)
to exploit (workers)	lenatsel	לְנַצֵל
racism	giz'anut	גִזְעָנוּת (נ)
racist	giz'ani	גִזְעָנִי (ז)

fascism	faʃizm	פָּשִׁיזם (ז)
fascist	faʃist	פָּשִׁיסט (ז)

245. Countries. Miscellaneous

foreigner	zar	זָר (ז)
foreign (adj)	zar	זָר
abroad (in a foreign country)	beχul	בְּחו"ל
emigrant	mehager	מְהַגֵּר (ז)
emigration	hagira	הֲגִירָה (נ)
to emigrate (vi)	lehager	לְהַגֵּר
the West	ma'arav	מַעֲרָב (ז)
the East	mizraχ	מִזרָח (ז)
the Far East	hamizraχ haraχok	הַמִזרָח הָרָחוֹק (ז)
civilization	tsivili'zatsya	צִיבִילִיזַצִיָה (נ)
humanity (mankind)	enoʃut	אֱנוֹשוּת (נ)
the world (earth)	olam	עוֹלָם (ז)
peace	ʃalom	שָׁלוֹם (ז)
worldwide (adj)	olami	עוֹלָמִי
homeland	mo'ledet	מוֹלֶדֶת (נ)
people (population)	am	עַם (ז)
population	oχlusiya	אוֹכְלוּסִיָה (נ)
people (a lot of ~)	anaʃim	אֲנָשִׁים (ז"ר)
nation (people)	uma	אוּמָה (נ)
generation	dor	דוֹר (ז)
territory (area)	'ʃetaχ	שֶׁטַח (ז)
region	ezor	אֵזוֹר (ז)
state (part of a country)	medina	מְדִינָה (נ)
tradition	ma'soret	מָסוֹרֶת (נ)
custom (tradition)	minhag	מִנהָג (ז)
ecology	eko'logya	אֵקוֹלוֹגִיָה (נ)
Indian (Native American)	ind'yani	אִינדיָאנִי (ז)
Gypsy (masc.)	tso'ani	צוֹעֲנִי (ז)
Gypsy (fem.)	tso'aniya	צוֹעֲנִיָה (נ)
Gypsy (adj)	tso'ani	צוֹעֲנִי
empire	im'perya	אִימפֶּריָה (נ)
colony	ko'lonya	קוֹלוֹנִיָה (נ)
slavery	avdut	עַבדוּת (נ)
invasion	pliʃa	פְּלִישָׁה (נ)
famine	'ra'av	רָעָב (ז)

246. Major religious groups. Confessions

religion	dat	דָת (נ)
religious (adj)	dati	דָתִי
faith, belief	emuna	אֱמוּנָה (נ)
to believe (in God)	leha'amin	לְהַאֲמִין
believer	ma'amin	מַאֲמִין
atheism	ate'izm	אָתֵאִיזם (ז)
atheist	ate'ist	אָתֵאִיסט (ז)
Christianity	natsrut	נַצרוּת (נ)
Christian (n)	notsri	נוֹצרִי (ז)
Christian (adj)	notsri	נוֹצרִי
Catholicism	ka'toliyut	קָתוֹלִיוּת (נ)
Catholic (n)	ka'toli	קָתוֹלִי (ז)
Catholic (adj)	ka'toli	קָתוֹלִי
Protestantism	protes'tantiyut	פּרוֹטֶסטַנטִיוּת (נ)
Protestant Church	knesiya protes'tantit	כּנֵסִייָה פּרוֹטֶסטַנטִית (נ)
Protestant (n)	protestant	פּרוֹטֶסטַנט (ז)
Orthodoxy	natsrut orto'doksit	נַצרוּת אוֹרתוֹדוֹקסִית (נ)
Orthodox Church	knesiya orto'doksit	כּנֵסִייָה אוֹרתוֹדוֹקסִית (נ)
Orthodox (n)	orto'doksi	אוֹרתוֹדוֹקסִי
Presbyterianism	presbiteryanizm	פּרֶסבִּיטֶריָאנִיזם (ז)
Presbyterian Church	knesiya presviteri''anit	כּנֵסִייָה פּרֶסבִּיטֶריָאנִית (נ)
Presbyterian (n)	presbiter'yani	פּרֶסבִּיטֶריָאנִי (ז)
Lutheranism	knesiya lute'ranit	כּנֵסִייָה לוּתֶרָנִית (נ)
Lutheran (n)	lute'rani	לוּתֶרָנִי (ז)
Baptist Church	knesiya bap'tistit	כּנֵסִייָה בַּפּטִיסטִית (נ)
Baptist (n)	baptist	בַּפּטִיסט (ז)
Anglican Church	knesiya angli'kanit	כּנֵסִייָה אַנגלִיקָנִית (נ)
Anglican (n)	angli'kani	אַנגלִיקָנִי (ז)
Mormonism	mor'monim	מוֹרמוֹנִים (ז)
Mormon (n)	mormon	מוֹרמוֹן (ז)
Judaism	yahadut	יַהֲדוּת (נ)
Jew (n)	yehudi, yehudiya	יְהוּדִי (ז), יְהוּדִיָה (נ)
Buddhism	budhizm	בּוּדהִיזם (ז)
Buddhist (n)	budhist	בּוּדהִיסט (ז)
Hinduism	hindu'izm	הִינדוּאִיזם (ז)
Hindu (n)	'hindi	הִינדִי (ז)

Islam	islam	(ז) אִיסלָאם
Muslim (n)	'muslemi	(ז) מוּסלְמִי
Muslim (adj)	'muslemi	מוּסלְמִי

Shiah Islam	islam 'ʃi'i	(ז) אָסלָאם שִיעִי
Shiite (n)	'ʃi'i	(ז) שִיעִי
Sunni Islam	islam 'suni	(ז) אָסלָאם סוּנִי
Sunnite (n)	'suni	(ז) סוּנִי

247. Religions. Priests

| priest | 'komer | (ז) כּוֹמֶר |
| the Pope | apifyor | (ז) אַפִּיפיוֹר |

monk, friar	nazir	(ז) נָזִיר
nun	nazira	(נ) נָזִירָה
pastor	'komer	(ז) כּוֹמֶר

abbot	roʃ minzar	(ז) רֹאש מִנזָר
vicar (parish priest)	'komer hakehila	(ז) כּוֹמֶר הַקְהִילָה
bishop	'biʃof	(ז) בִּישוֹף
cardinal	χaʃman	(ז) חַשמָן

preacher	matif	(ז) מַטִיף
preaching	hatafa, draʃa	(נ) הַטָפָה, דְרָשָה
parishioners	χaver kehila	(ז) חָבֵר קְהִילָה

| believer | ma'amin | (ז) מַאֲמִין |
| atheist | ate'ist | (ז) אָתֵאִיסט |

248. Faith. Christianity. Islam

| Adam | adam | אָדָם |
| Eve | χava | חַוָה |

God	elohim	אֱלוֹהִים
the Lord	adonai	אֲדוֹנָי
the Almighty	kol yaχol	כָּל יָכוֹל

sin	χet	(ז) חֵטא
to sin (vi)	laχato	לַחֲטוֹא
sinner (masc.)	χote	(ז) חוֹטֵא
sinner (fem.)	χo'ta'at	(נ) חוֹטָאת

hell	gehinom	(ז) גֵיהִינוֹם
paradise	gan 'eden	(ז) גַן עֵדֶן
Jesus	'yeʃu	יֵשוּ
Jesus Christ	'yeʃu hanotsri	יֵשוּ הַנוֹצרִי

the Holy Spirit	'ruaχ ha'kodeʃ	רוּחַ הַקּוֹדֶשׁ (ז)
the Savior	mo'ʃi'a	מוֹשִׁיעַ (ז)
the Virgin Mary	'miryam hakdoʃa	מִרְיָם הַקְּדוֹשָׁה
the Devil	satan	שָׂטָן (ז)
devil's (adj)	stani	שְׂטָנִי
Satan	satan	שָׂטָן (ז)
satanic (adj)	stani	שְׂטָנִי
angel	mal'aχ	מַלְאָךְ (ז)
guardian angel	mal'aχ ʃomer	מַלְאָךְ שׁוֹמֵר (ז)
angelic (adj)	mal'aχi	מַלְאָכִי
apostle	ʃa'liaχ	שָׁלִיחַ (ז)
archangel	arχimalaχ	אַרְכִימַלְאָךְ (ז)
the Antichrist	an'tikrist	אַנְטִיכְּרִיסְט (ז)
Church	knesiya	כְּנֵסִיָּה (נ)
Bible	tanaχ	תנַ"ךְ (ז)
biblical (adj)	tanaχi	תנַ"כִי
Old Testament	habrit hayeʃana	הַבְּרִית הַיְשָׁנָה (נ)
New Testament	habrit haχadaʃa	הַבְּרִית הַחֲדָשָׁה (נ)
Gospel	evangelyon	אֶוָונְגֶּלְיוֹן (ז)
Holy Scripture	kitvei ha'kodeʃ	כִּתְבֵי הַקּוֹדֶשׁ (ז"ר)
Heaven	malχut ʃa'mayim, gan 'eden	מַלְכוּת שָׁמַיִים (נ), גַּן עֵדֶן (ז)
Commandment	mitsva	מִצְוָוה (נ)
prophet	navi	נָבִיא (ז)
prophecy	nevu'a	נְבוּאָה (נ)
Allah	'alla	אַלְלָה
Mohammed	mu'χamad	מוּחַמַד
the Koran	kur'an	קוֹרְאָן (ז)
mosque	misgad	מִסְגָּד (ז)
mullah	'mula	מוּלָא (ז)
prayer	tfila	תְּפִילָה (נ)
to pray (vi, vt)	lehitpalel	לְהִתְפַּלֵל
pilgrimage	aliya le'regel	עֲלִיָּה לְרֶגֶל (נ)
pilgrim	tsalyan	צַלְיָין (ז)
Mecca	'meka	מֶכָּה (נ)
church	knesiya	כְּנֵסִיָּה (נ)
temple	mikdaʃ	מִקְדָּשׁ (ז)
cathedral	kated'rala	קָתֶדְרָלָה (נ)
Gothic (adj)	'goti	גוֹתִי
synagogue	beit 'kneset	בֵּית כְּנֶסֶת (ז)
mosque	misgad	מִסְגָּד (ז)
chapel	beit tfila	בֵּית תְּפִילָה (ז)

abbey	minzar	מִנְזָר (ז)
convent	minzar	מִנְזָר (ז)
monastery	minzar	מִנְזָר (ז)
bell (church ~s)	pa'amon	פַּעֲמוֹן (ז)
bell tower	migdal pa'amonim	מִגְדַל פַּעֲמוֹנִים (ז)
to ring (ab. bells)	letsaltsel	לְצַלְצֵל
cross	tslav	צְלָב (ז)
cupola (roof)	kipa	כִּיפָּה (נ)
icon	ikonin	אִיקוֹנִין (ז)
soul	nefama	נְשָׁמָה (נ)
fate (destiny)	goral	גּוֹרָל (ז)
evil (n)	'ro'a	רוֹעַ (ז)
good (n)	tuv	טוּב (ז)
vampire	arpad	עַרְפָּד (ז)
witch (evil ~)	maxfefa	מַכְשֵׁפָה (נ)
demon	fed	שֵׁד (ז)
spirit	'ruax	רוּחַ (נ)
redemption (giving us ~)	kapara	כַּפָּרָה (נ)
to redeem (vt)	lexaper al	לְכַפֵּר עַל
church service, mass	'misa	מִיסָה (נ)
to say mass	la'arox 'misa	לַעֲרוֹךְ מִיסָה
confession	vidui	וִידוּי (ז)
to confess (vi)	lehitvadot	לְהִתְוַדּוֹת
saint (n)	kadof	קָדוֹש (ז)
sacred (holy)	mekudaf	מְקוּדָש
holy water	'mayim kdofim	מַיִם קְדוֹשִׁים (ז"ר)
ritual (n)	'tekes	טֶקֶס (ז)
ritual (adj)	fel 'tekes	שֶׁל טֶקֶס
sacrifice	korban	קוֹרְבָּן (ז)
superstition	emuna tfela	אֱמוּנָה תְפֵלָה (נ)
superstitious (adj)	ma'amin emunot tfelot	מַאֲמִין אֱמוּנוֹת תְפֵלוֹת
afterlife	ha'olam haba	הָעוֹלָם הַבָּא (ז)
eternal life	xayei olam, xayei 'netsax	חַיֵּי עוֹלָם (ז"ר), חַיֵּי נֶצַח (ז"ר)

MISCELLANEOUS

249. Various useful words

background (green ~)	'reka	רֶקַע (ז)
balance (of situation)	izun	אִיזּוּן (ז)
barrier (obstacle)	mixʃol	מִכְשׁוֹל (ז)
base (basis)	basis	בָּסִיס (ז)
beginning	hatxala	הַתְחָלָה (נ)
category	kate'gorya	קָטֵגוֹרִיָה (נ)
cause (reason)	siba	סִיבָּה (נ)
choice	bxina	בְּחִינָה (נ)
coincidence	hat'ama	הַתְאָמָה (נ)
comfortable (~ chair)	'noax	נוֹחַ
comparison	haʃvaʾa	הַשְׁוָואָה (נ)
compensation	pitsui	פִּיצוּי (ז)
degree (extent, amount)	darga	דַרְגָה (נ)
development	hitpatxut	הִתְפַּתְחוּת (נ)
difference	'ʃoni	שׁוֹנִי (ז)
effect (e.g., of drugs)	efekt	אֶפֶקְט (ז)
effort (exertion)	ma'amats	מַאֲמָץ (ז)
element	element	אֶלֶמֶנְט (ז)
end (finish)	sof	סוֹף (ז)
example (illustration)	dugma	דוּגמָה (נ)
fact	uvda	עוּבדָה (נ)
frequent (adj)	tadir	תָדִיר
growth (development)	gidul	גִידוּל (ז)
help	ezra	עֶזְרָה (נ)
ideal	ide'al	אִידֵיאָל (ז)
kind (sort, type)	sug	סוּג (ז)
labyrinth	mavox	מָבוֹךְ (ז)
mistake, error	ta'ut	טָעוּת (נ)
moment	'rega	רֶגַע (ז)
object (thing)	'etsem	עֶצֶם (ז)
obstacle	maxsom	מַחסוֹם (ז)
original (original copy)	makor	מָקוֹר (ז)
part (~ of sth)	'xelek	חֵלֶק (ז)
particle, small part	xelkik	חֶלְקִיק (ז)
pause (break)	hafuga	הֲפוּגָה (נ)

position	emda	עֶמְדָּה (נ)
principle	ikaron	עִיקָרוֹן (ז)
problem	be'aya	בְּעָיָה (נ)
process	tahaliχ	תַּהֲלִיךְ (ז)
progress	kidma	קִדְמָה (נ)
property (quality)	tχuna, sgula	תְּכוּנָה, סְגוּלָה (נ)
reaction	tguva	תְּגוּבָה (נ)
risk	sikun	סִיכּוּן (ז)
secret	sod	סוֹד (ז)
series	sidra	סִדְרָה (נ)
shape (outer form)	tsura	צוּרָה (נ)
situation	matsav	מַצָּב (ז)
solution	pitaron	פִּיתָרוֹן (ז)
standard (adj)	tikni	תִּקְנִי
standard (level of quality)	'teken	תֶּקֶן (ז)
stop (pause)	hafsaka	הַפְסָקָה (נ)
style	signon	סִגְנוֹן (ז)
system	ʃita	שִׁיטָה (נ)
table (chart)	tavla	טַבְלָה (נ)
tempo, rate	'ketsev	קֶצֶב (ז)
term (word, expression)	musag	מוּשָׂג (ז)
thing (object, item)	'χefets	חֵפֶץ (ז)
truth (e.g., moment of ~)	emet	אֱמֶת (נ)
turn (please wait your ~)	tor	תּוֹר (ז)
type (sort, kind)	min	מִין (ז)
urgent (adj)	daχuf	דָּחוּף
urgently (adv)	bidχifut	בִּדְחִיפוּת
utility (usefulness)	to''elet	תּוֹעֶלֶת (נ)
variant (alternative)	girsa	גִּירְסָה (נ)
way (means, method)	'ofen	אוֹפֶן (ז)
zone	ezor	אֵזוֹר (ז)

250. Modifiers. Adjectives. Part 1

additional (adj)	nosaf	נוֹסָף
ancient (~ civilization)	atik	עַתִּיק
artificial (adj)	melaχuti	מְלָאכוּתִי
back, rear (adj)	aχorani	אֲחוֹרָנִי
bad (adj)	ra	רַע
beautiful (~ palace)	mefo'ar	מְפוֹאָר
beautiful (person)	yafe	יָפֶה
big (in size)	gadol	גָּדוֹל

bitter (taste)	marir	מָרִיר
blind (sightless)	iver	עִיוֵּר
calm, quiet (adj)	ʃaket	שָׁקֵט
careless (negligent)	meruʃal	מְרוּשָׁל
caring (~ father)	do'eg	דוֹאֵג
central (adj)	merkazi	מֶרְכָּזִי
cheap (low-priced)	zol	זוֹל
cheerful (adj)	sa'meax	שָׂמֵחַ
children's (adj)	yaldi	יַלְדִי
civil (~ law)	ezraxi	אֶזְרָחִי
clandestine (secret)	maxtarti	מַחְתַּרְתִי
clean (free from dirt)	naki	נָקִי
clear (explanation, etc.)	barur	בָּרוּר
clever (smart)	pi'keax	פִּיקֵחַ
close (near in space)	karov	קָרוֹב
closed (adj)	sagur	סָגוּר
cloudless (sky)	lelo ananim	לְלֹא עֲנָנִים
cold (drink, weather)	kar	קַר
compatible (adj)	to'em	תּוֹאֵם
contented (satisfied)	merutse	מְרוּצָה
continuous (uninterrupted)	mitmaʃex	מִתְמַשֵׁךְ
cool (weather)	karir	קָרִיר
dangerous (adj)	mesukan	מְסוּכָּן
dark (room)	xaʃux	חָשׁוּךְ
dead (not alive)	met	מֵת
dense (fog, smoke)	tsafuf	צָפוּף
destitute (extremely poor)	ani	עָנִי
different (not the same)	ʃone	שׁוֹנֶה
difficult (decision)	kaʃe	קָשֶׁה
difficult (problem, task)	mesubax	מְסוּבָּךְ
dim, faint (light)	amum	עָמוּם
dirty (not clean)	meluxlax	מְלוּכְלָךְ
distant (in space)	raxok	רָחוֹק
dry (clothes, etc.)	yaveʃ	יָבֵשׁ
easy (not difficult)	kal	קַל
empty (glass, room)	rek	רֵיק
even (e.g., ~ surface)	xalak	חָלָק
exact (amount)	meduyak	מְדוּיָק
excellent (adj)	metsuyan	מְצוּיָן
excessive (adj)	meyutar	מְיוּתָר
expensive (adj)	yakar	יָקָר
exterior (adj)	xitsoni	חִיצוֹנִי
far (the ~ East)	raxok	רָחוֹק

fast (quick)	mahir	מָהִיר
fatty (food)	ʃamen	שָׁמֵן
fertile (land, soil)	pore	פּוֹרֶה
flat (~ panel display)	ʃa'tuaχ	שָׁטוּחַ
foreign (adj)	zar	זָר
fragile (china, glass)	ʃavir	שָׁבִיר
free (at no cost)	χinam	חִינָם
free (unrestricted)	χofʃi	חוֹפְשִׁי
fresh (~ water)	metukim	מְתוּקִים
fresh (e.g., ~ bread)	tari	טָרִי
frozen (food)	kafu	קָפוּא
full (completely filled)	male	מָלֵא
gloomy (house, forecast)	koder	קוֹדֵר
good (book, etc.)	tov	טוֹב
good, kind (kindhearted)	tov	טוֹב
grateful (adj)	asir toda	אֲסִיר תּוֹדָה
happy (adj)	me'uʃar	מְאוּשָׁר
hard (not soft)	kaʃe	קָשֶׁה
heavy (in weight)	kaved	כָּבֵד
hostile (adj)	oyen	עוֹיֵן
hot (adj)	χam	חַם
huge (adj)	anaki	עֲנָקִי
humid (adj)	laχ	לַח
hungry (adj)	ra'ev	רָעֵב
ill (sick, unwell)	χole	חוֹלֶה
immobile (adj)	χasar tnu'a	חֲסַר תנוּעָה
important (adj)	χaʃuv	חָשׁוּב
impossible (adj)	'bilti efʃari	בִּלתִי אֶפְשָׁרִי
incomprehensible	'bilti muvan	בִּלתִי מוּבָן
indispensable (adj)	naχuts	נָחוּץ
inexperienced (adj)	χasar nisayon	חֲסַר נִיסָיוֹן
insignificant (adj)	χasar χaʃivut	חֲסַר חֲשִׁיבוּת
interior (adj)	pnimi	פְּנִימִי
joint (~ decision)	meʃutaf	מְשׁוּתָף
last (e.g., ~ week)	ʃe'avar	שֶׁעָבַר
last (final)	aχaron	אַחֲרוֹן
left (e.g., ~ side)	smali	שְׂמָאלִי
legal (legitimate)	χuki	חוּקִי
light (in weight)	kal	קַל
light (pale color)	bahir	בָּהִיר
limited (adj)	mugbal	מוּגבָּל
liquid (fluid)	nozli	נוֹזְלִי
long (e.g., ~ hair)	aroχ	אָרוֹך

| loud (voice, etc.) | ram | רָם |
| low (voice) | ʃaket | שָׁקֵט |

251. Modifiers. Adjectives. Part 2

main (principal)	raʃi	רָאשִׁי
matt, matte	mat	מַט
meticulous (job)	kapdani	קַפְּדָנִי
mysterious (adj)	mistori	מִסְתּוֹרִי
narrow (street, etc.)	tsar	צַר

native (~ country)	ʃel mo'ledet	שֶׁל מוֹלֶדֶת
nearby (adj)	karov	קָרוֹב
nearsighted (adj)	ktsar re'iya	קְצַר רְאִיָּה
needed (necessary)	daruʃ	דָּרוּשׁ
negative (~ response)	ʃlili	שְׁלִילִי

neighboring (adj)	samux	סָמוּךְ
nervous (adj)	atsbani	עַצְבָּנִי
new (adj)	xadaʃ	חָדָשׁ
next (e.g., ~ week)	haba	הַבָּא

nice (kind)	nexmad	נֶחְמָד
nice (voice)	na'im	נָעִים
normal (adj)	nor'mali	נוֹרְמָלִי
not big (adj)	lo gadol	לֹא גָּדוֹל
not difficult (adj)	lo kaʃe	לֹא קָשֶׁה

obligatory (adj)	hexrexi	הֶכְרֵחִי
old (house)	yaʃan	יָשָׁן
open (adj)	pa'tuax	פָּתוּחַ
opposite (adj)	negdi	נֶגְדִּי

ordinary (usual)	ragil	רָגִיל
original (unusual)	mekori	מְקוֹרִי
past (recent)	ʃe'avar	שֶׁעָבַר
permanent (adj)	ka'vu'a	קָבוּעַ
personal (adj)	prati	פְּרָטִי

polite (adj)	menumas	מְנוּמָס
poor (not rich)	ani	עָנִי
possible (adj)	efʃari	אֶפְשָׁרִי
present (current)	noxexi	נוֹכְחִי
previous (adj)	kodem	קוֹדֵם

principal (main)	ikari	עִיקָרִי
private (~ jet)	iʃi	אִישִׁי
probable (adj)	efʃari	אֶפְשָׁרִי
prolonged (e.g., ~ applause)	memuʃax	מְמוּשָׁךְ

public (open to all)	tsiburi	צִיבּוּרִי
punctual (person)	daikan	דַייקָן
quiet (tranquil)	ʃalev	שָׁלֵו
rare (adj)	nadir	נָדִיר
raw (uncooked)	χai	חַי
right (not left)	yemani	יְמָנִי
right, correct (adj)	naχon	נָכוֹן
ripe (fruit)	baʃel	בָּשֵׁל
risky (adj)	mesukan	מְסוּכָּן
sad (~ look)	atsuv	עָצוּב
sad (depressing)	atsuv	עָצוּב
safe (not dangerous)	ba'tuaχ	בָּטוּחַ
salty (food)	ma'luaχ	מָלוּחַ
satisfied (customer)	mesupak	מְסוּפָּק
second hand (adj)	meʃumaʃ	מְשׁוּמָשׁ
shallow (water)	radud	רָדוּד
sharp (blade, etc.)	χad	חַד
short (in length)	katsar	קָצָר
short, short-lived (adj)	katsar	קָצָר
significant (notable)	χaʃuv	חָשׁוּב
similar (adj)	dome	דוֹמֶה
simple (easy)	paʃut	פָּשׁוּט
skinny	raze	רָזֶה
small (in size)	katan	קָטָן
smooth (surface)	χalak	חָלָק
soft (~ toys)	raχ	רַך
solid (~ wall)	mutsak	מוּצָק
sour (flavor, taste)	χamuts	חָמוּץ
spacious (house, etc.)	meruvaχ	מְרוּוָח
special (adj)	meyuχad	מְיוּחָד
straight (line, road)	yaʃar	יָשָׁר
strong (person)	χazak	חָזָק
stupid (foolish)	tipeʃ	טִיפֵּשׁ
suitable (e.g., ~ for drinking)	mat'im	מַתְאִים
sunny (day)	ʃimʃi	שִׁמְשִׁי
superb, perfect (adj)	metsuyan	מְצוּיָן
swarthy (adj)	ʃaχum	שָׁחוּם
sweet (sugary)	matok	מָתוֹק
tan (adj)	ʃazuf	שָׁזוּף
tasty (delicious)	ta'im	טָעִים
tender (affectionate)	raχ	רַך
the highest (adj)	haga'voha beyoter	הַגָּבוֹהַ בְּיוֹתֵר
the most important	haχaʃuv beyoter	הַחָשׁוּב בְּיוֹתֵר

the nearest	hakarov beyoter	הַקָרוֹב בְּיוֹתֵר
the same, equal (adj)	zehe	זֶהֶה
thick (e.g., ~ fog)	samuχ	סָמוּך
thick (wall, slice)	ave	עָבֶה

thin (person)	raze	רָזֶה
tight (~ shoes)	tsar	צַר
tired (exhausted)	ayef	עָיֵף
tiring (adj)	me'ayef	מְעַיֵף

transparent (adj)	ʃakuf	שָקוּף
unclear (adj)	lo barur	לֹא בָּרוּר
unique (exceptional)	meyuχad bemino	מְיוּחָד בְּמִינוֹ
various (adj)	kol minei	כָּל מִינֵי

warm (moderately hot)	χamim	חָמִים
wet (e.g., ~ clothes)	ratuv	רָטוּב
whole (entire, complete)	ʃalem	שָלֵם
wide (e.g., ~ road)	raχav	רָחָב
young (adj)	tsa'ir	צָעִיר

MAIN 500 VERBS

252. Verbs A-C

to accompany (vt)	lelavot	לְלַוּוֹת
to accuse (vt)	leha'aʃim	לְהַאֲשִׁים
to acknowledge (admit)	lehakir be...	לְהַכִּיר בְּ...
to act (take action)	lif'ol	לִפְעוֹל
to add (supplement)	lehosif	לְהוֹסִיף
to address (speak to)	lifnot el	לִפְנוֹת אֶל
to admire (vi)	lehitpa'el	לְהִתְפַּעֵל
to advertise (vt)	lefarsem	לְפַרְסֵם
to advise (vt)	leya'ets	לְיַיעֵץ
to affirm (assert)	lit'on	לִטְעוֹן
to agree (say yes)	lehaskim	לְהַסְכִּים
to aim (to point a weapon)	leχaven	לְכַוֵּון
to allow (sb to do sth)	leharʃot	לְהַרְשׁוֹת
to amputate (vt)	lik'to'a	לִקְטוֹעַ
to answer (vi, vt)	la'anot	לַעֲנוֹת
to apologize (vi)	lehitnatsel	לְהִתְנַצֵּל
to appear (come into view)	leho'fi'a	לְהוֹפִיעַ
to applaud (vi, vt)	limχo ka'payim	לִמְחוֹא כַּפַּיִים
to appoint (assign)	lemanot	לְמַנּוֹת
to approach (come closer)	lehitkarev	לְהִתְקָרֵב
to arrive (ab. train)	leha'gi'a	לְהַגִּיעַ
to ask (~ sb to do sth)	levakeʃ	לְבַקֵּשׁ
to aspire to ...	liʃ'of	לִשְׁאוֹף
to assist (help)	la'azor	לַעֲזוֹר
to attack (mil.)	litkof	לִתְקוֹף
to attain (objectives)	lehasig	לְהַשִּׂיג
to avenge (get revenge)	linkom	לִנְקוֹם
to avoid (danger, task)	lehimana	לְהִימָּנַע
to award (give medal to)	leha'anik	לְהַעֲנִיק
to battle (vi)	lehilaχem	לְהִילָחֵם
to be (vi)	lihyot	לִהְיוֹת
to be a cause of ...	ligrom le...	לִגְרוֹם לְ...
to be afraid	lefaχed	לְפַחֵד
to be angry (with ...)	lehitragez	לְהִתְרַגֵּז

to be at war	lehilaxem	לְהִילָחֵם
to be based (on ...)	lehitbases	לְהִתְבַּסֵס
to be bored	lehiʃta'amem	לְהִשְׁתַּעֲמֵם
to be convinced	lehiʃtax'ne'a	לְהִשְׁתַּכְנֵעַ
to be enough	lehasmik	לְהַסְמִיק
to be envious	lekane	לְקַנֵּא
to be indignant	lehitra'em	לְהִתְרַעֵם
to be interested in ...	lehit'anyen	לְהִתְעַנְיֵין
to be lost in thought	liʃko'a bemaxʃavot	לִשְׁקוֹעַ בְּמַחֲשָׁבוֹת
to be lying (~ on the table)	lihyot munax	לִהְיוֹת מוּנָח
to be needed	lehidareʃ	לְהִידָרֵשׁ
to be perplexed (puzzled)	lit'moha	לִתְמוֹהַ
to be preserved	lehiʃtamer	לְהִשְׁתַּמֵּר
to be required	lehidareʃ	לְהִידָרֵשׁ
to be surprised	lehitpale	לְהִתְפַּלֵּא
to be worried	lid'og	לִדְאוֹג
to beat (to hit)	lehakot	לְהַכּוֹת
to become (e.g., ~ old)	lahafox le...	לַהֲפוֹךְ לְ...
to behave (vi)	lehitnaheg	לְהִתְנַהֵג
to believe (think)	leha'amin	לְהַאֲמִין
to belong to ...	lehiʃtayex	לְהִשְׁתַּיֵּיךְ
to berth (moor)	la'agon	לַעֲגוֹן
to blind (other drivers)	lisanver	לְסַנְוֵּר
to blow (wind)	linʃov	לִנְשׁוֹב
to blush (vi)	lehasmik	לְהַסְמִיק
to boast (vi)	lehitravrev	לְהִתְרַבְרֵב
to borrow (money)	lilvot	לִלְווֹת
to break (branch, toy, etc.)	liʃbor	לִשְׁבּוֹר
to breathe (vi)	linʃom	לִנְשׁוֹם
to bring (sth)	lehavi	לְהָבִיא
to burn (paper, logs)	lisrof	לִשְׂרוֹף
to buy (purchase)	liknot	לִקְנוֹת
to call (~ for help)	likro	לִקְרוֹא
to call (yell for sb)	likro le...	לִקְרוֹא לְ...
to calm down (vt)	lehar'gi'a	לְהַרְגִּיעַ
can (v aux)	yaxol	יָכוֹל
to cancel (call off)	levatel	לְבַטֵּל
to cast off (of a boat or ship)	lehaflig	לְהַפְלִיג
to catch (e.g., ~ a ball)	litfos	לִתְפּוֹס
to change (~ one's opinion)	leʃanot	לְשַׁנּוֹת
to change (exchange)	lehaxlif	לְהַחְלִיף
to charm (vt)	lehaksim	לְהַקְסִים
to choose (select)	livxor	לִבְחוֹר

to chop off (with an ax)	liχrot	לִכְרוֹת
to clean (e.g., kettle from scale)	lenakot	לְנַקּוֹת
to clean (shoes, etc.)	lenakot	לְנַקּוֹת
to clean up (tidy)	lesader	לְסַדֵּר
to close (vt)	lisgor	לִסְגּוֹר
to comb one's hair	lehistarek	לְהִסְתָּרֵק
to come down (the stairs)	la'redet	לָרֶדֶת
to come out (book)	laʦet le'or	לָצֵאת לְאוֹר
to compare (vt)	lehaʃvot	לְהַשְׁווֹת
to compensate (vt)	lefaʦot	לְפַצּוֹת
to compete (vi)	lehitχarot	לְהִתְחָרוֹת
to compile (~ a list)	lena'seaχ, la'aroχ	לְנַסֵּחַ, לַעֲרוֹךְ
to complain (vi, vt)	lehitlonen	לְהִתְלוֹנֵן
to complicate (vt)	lesabeχ	לְסַבֵּךְ
to compose (music, etc.)	lehalχin	לְהַלְחִין
to compromise (reputation)	lehav'iʃ et reχo	לְהַבְאִישׁ אֶת רֵיחוֹ
to concentrate (vi)	lehitrakez	לְהִתְרַכֵּז
to confess (criminal)	lehodot be...	לְהוֹדוֹת בְּ...
to confuse (mix up)	lehitbalbel	לְהִתְבַּלְבֵּל
to congratulate (vt)	levareχ	לְבָרֵךְ
to consult (doctor, expert)	lehitya'eʦ im	לְהִתְיַיעֵץ עִם
to continue (~ to do sth)	lehamʃiχ	לְהַמְשִׁיךְ
to control (vt)	liʃlot	לִשְׁלוֹט
to convince (vt)	leʃaχ'ne'a	לְשַׁכְנֵעַ
to cooperate (vi)	leʃatef pe'ula	לְשַׁתֵּף פְּעוּלָה
to coordinate (vt)	leta'em	לְתָאֵם
to correct (an error)	letaken	לְתַקֵּן
to cost (vt)	la'alot	לַעֲלוֹת
to count (money, etc.)	lispor	לִסְפּוֹר
to count on ...	lismoχ al	לִסְמוֹךְ עַל
to crack (ceiling, wall)	lehisadek	לְהִיסָדֵק
to create (vt)	liʦor	לִיצוֹר
to crush, to squash (~ a bug)	lirmos	לִרְמוֹס
to cry (weep)	livkot	לִבְכּוֹת
to cut off (with a knife)	laχtoχ	לַחְתוֹךְ

253. Verbs D-G

to dare (~ to do sth)	leha'ez	לְהָעֵז
to date from ...	leta'areχ	לְתָאֲרֵךְ

| to deceive (vi, vt) | leramot | לְרַמוֹת |
| to decide (~ to do sth) | lehaxlit | לְהַחְלִיט |

to decorate (tree, street)	lekaʃet	לְקַשֵׁט
to dedicate (book, etc.)	lehakdiʃ	לְהַקְדִּישׁ
to defend (a country, etc.)	lehagen	לְהָגֵן
to defend oneself	lehitgonen	לְהִתְגּוֹנֵן

to demand (request firmly)	lidroʃ	לִדְרוֹשׁ
to denounce (vt)	lehalʃim	לְהַלְשִׁין
to deny (vt)	liʃlol	לִשְׁלוֹל
to depend on ...	lihyot talui be...	להיוֹת תָּלוּי בְּ...

to deprive (vt)	liʃlol	לִשְׁלוֹל
to deserve (vt)	lihyot ra'ui	להיוֹת רָאוּי
to design (machine, etc.)	letaxnen	לְתַכְנֵן
to desire (want, wish)	lirtsot	לִרְצוֹת

to despise (vt)	lezalzel be...	לְזַלְזֵל בְּ...
to destroy (documents, etc.)	lexasel	לְחַסֵל
to differ (from sth)	lehibadel	לְהִיבָּדֵל
to dig (tunnel, etc.)	laxpor	לַחְפּוֹר
to direct (point the way)	lexaven	לְכַוֵּון

to disappear (vi)	lehe'alem	לְהֵיעָלֵם
to discover (new land, etc.)	legalot	לְגַלּוֹת
to discuss (vt)	ladun	לָדוּן
to distribute (leaflets, etc.)	lehafits	לְהָפִיץ

to disturb (vt)	lehatrid	לְהַטְרִיד
to dive (vi)	litslol	לִצְלוֹל
to divide (math)	lexalek	לְחַלֵּק
to do (vt)	la'asot	לַעֲשׂוֹת

to do the laundry	lexabes	לְכַבֵּס
to double (increase)	lehaxpil	לְהַכְפִּיל
to doubt (have doubts)	lefakpek	לְפַקְפֵּק
to draw a conclusion	lehasik	לְהַסִּיק

to dream (daydream)	laxalom	לַחֲלוֹם
to dream (in sleep)	laxalom	לַחֲלוֹם
to drink (vi, vt)	liʃtot	לִשְׁתּוֹת
to drive a car	linhog	לִנְהוֹג

to drive away (scare away)	legareʃ	לְגָרֵשׁ
to drop (let fall)	lehapil	לְהַפִּיל
to drown (ab. person)	lit'bo'a	לִטְבּוֹעַ
to dry (clothes, hair)	leyabeʃ	לְיַבֵּשׁ

| to eat (vi, vt) | le'exol | לֶאֱכוֹל |
| to eavesdrop (vi) | leha'azin be'seter | לְהַאֲזִין בְּסֵתֶר |

to emit (diffuse - odor, etc.)	lehafits	לְהָפִיץ
to enjoy oneself	lehanot	לֵיהָנוֹת
to enter (on the list)	lehosif	לְהוֹסִיף
to enter (room, house, etc.)	lehikanes	לְהִיכָּנֵס
to entertain (amuse)	levader	לְבַדֵּר
to equip (fit out)	letsayed	לְצַיֵּד
to examine (proposal)	livχon	לבחון
to exchange (sth)	lehitχalef	לְהִתְחַלֵּף
to excuse (forgive)	lis'loaχ	לִסְלוֹחַ
to exist (vi)	lehitkayem	לְהִתְקַיֵּים
to expect (anticipate)	letsapot	לְצַפּוֹת
to expect (foresee)	laχazot	לַחֲזוֹת
to expel (from school, etc.)	lesalek	לְסַלֵּק
to explain (vt)	lehasbir	לְהַסְבִּיר
to express (vt)	levate	לְבַטֵּא
to extinguish (a fire)	leχabot	לְכַבּוֹת
to fall in love (with ...)	lehit'ahev	לְהִתְאַהֵב
to feed (provide food)	leha'aχil	לְהַאֲכִיל
to fight (against the enemy)	lehilaχem	לְהִילָחֵם
to fight (vi)	lehitkotet	לְהִתְקוֹטֵט
to fill (glass, bottle)	lemale	לְמַלֵּא
to find (~ lost items)	limtso	לִמְצוֹא
to finish (vt)	lesayem	לְסַיֵּים
to fish (angle)	ladug	לָדוּג
to fit (ab. dress, etc.)	lehat'im	לְהַתְאִים
to flatter (vt)	lehaχnif	לְהַחֲנִיף
to fly (bird, plane)	la'uf	לָעוּף
to follow ... (come after)	la'akov aχarei	לַעֲקוֹב אַחֲרֵי
to forbid (vt)	le'esor	לֶאֱסוֹר
to force (compel)	lehaχ'riaχ	לְהַכְרִיחַ
to forget (vi, vt)	lif'koaχ	לשכּוֹחַ
to forgive (pardon)	lis'loaχ	לִסְלוֹחַ
to form (constitute)	le'atsev	לְעַצֵּב
to get dirty (vi)	lehitlaχleχ	לְהִתְלַכְלֵךְ
to get infected (with ...)	lehibadek	לְהִידָּבֵק
to get irritated	lehitragez	לְהִתְרַגֵּז
to get married	lehitχaten	לְהִתְחַתֵּן
to get rid of ...	lehipater mi...	לְהִיפָּטֵר מְ...
to get tired	lehit'ayef	לְהִתְעַיֵּיף
to get up (arise from bed)	lakum	לָקוּם

to give (vt)	latet	לָתֵת
to give a bath (to bath)	lirχots	לִרחוֹץ
to give a hug, to hug (vt)	leχabek	לְחַבֵּק
to give in (yield to)	levater	לְוַותֵר
to glimpse (vt)	lir'ot	לִראוֹת
to go (by car, etc.)	lin'so'a	לִנסוֹעַ
to go (on foot)	la'leχet	לָלֶכֶת
to go for a swim	lehitraχets	לְהִתרַחֵץ
to go out (for dinner, etc.)	latset	לָצֵאת
to go to bed (go to sleep)	liʃkav liʃon	לִשכַּב לִישוֹן
to greet (vt)	lomar ʃalom	לוֹמַר שָׁלוֹם
to grow (plants)	legadel	לְגַדֵל
to guarantee (vt)	lehav'tiaχ	לְהַבטִיחַ
to guess (the answer)	lenaχeʃ	לְנַחֵש

254. Verbs H-M

to hand out (distribute)	leχalek	לְחַלֵק
to hang (curtains, etc.)	litlot	לִתלוֹת
to have (vt)	lehaχzik	לְהַחזִיק
to have a try	lenasot	לְנַסוֹת
to have breakfast	le'eχol aruχat 'boker	לֶאֱכוֹל אֲרוּחַת בּוֹקֶר
to have dinner	le'eχol aruχat 'erev	לֶאֱכוֹל אֲרוּחַת עֶרֶב
to have lunch	le'eχol aruχat tsaha'rayim	לֶאֱכוֹל אֲרוּחַת צָהֳרַיים
to head (group, etc.)	la'amod beroʃ	לַעֲמוֹד בְּרֹאש
to hear (vt)	liʃ'mo'a	לִשמוֹעַ
to heat (vt)	leχamem	לְחַמֵם
to help (vt)	la'azor	לַעֲזוֹר
to hide (vt)	lehastir	לְהַסתִיר
to hire (e.g., ~ a boat)	liskor	לִשכּוֹר
to hire (staff)	leha'asik	לְהַעֲסִיק
to hope (vi, vt)	lekavot	לְקַווֹת
to hunt (for food, sport)	latsud	לָצוּד
to hurry (vi)	lemaher	לְמַהֵר
to imagine (to picture)	ledamyen	לְדַמיֵין
to imitate (vt)	leχakot	לְחַקוֹת
to implore (vt)	lehitχanen	לְהִתחַנֵן
to import (vt)	leyabe	לְייַבֵּא
to increase (vi)	ligdol	לִגדוֹל
to increase (vt)	lehagdil	לְהַגדִיל
to infect (vt)	lehadbik	לְהַדבִּיק
to influence (vt)	lehaʃpi'a	לְהַשפִּיעַ
to inform (e.g., ~ the police about)	leya'de'a	לְייַדֵעַ

to inform (vt)	leho'dia	לְהוֹדִיעַ
to inherit (vt)	la'reʃet	לָרֶשֶׁת
to inquire (about …)	levarer	לְבָרֵר
to insert (put in)	lehaxnis	לְהַכְנִיס
to insinuate (imply)	lirmoz	לִרְמוֹז
to insist (vi, vt)	lehit'akeʃ	לְהִתְעַקֵּשׁ
to inspire (vt)	lehalhiv	לְהַלְהִיב
to instruct (teach)	lehadrix	לְהַדְרִיךְ
to insult (offend)	leha'aliv	לְהַעֲלִיב
to interest (vt)	le'anyen	לְעַנְיֵן
to intervene (vi)	lehit'arev	לְהִתְעָרֵב
to introduce (sb to sb)	lehatsig	לְהַצִּיג
to invent (machine, etc.)	lehamtsi	לְהַמְצִיא
to invite (vt)	lehazmin	לְהַזְמִין
to iron (clothes)	legahets	לְגַהֵץ
to irritate (annoy)	le'atsben	לְעַצְבֵּן
to isolate (vt)	levoded	לְבוֹדֵד
to join (political party, etc.)	lehitstaref	לְהִצְטָרֵף
to joke (be kidding)	lehitba'deax	לְהִתְבַּדֵּחַ
to keep (old letters, etc.)	liʃmor	לִשְׁמוֹר
to keep silent	liʃtok	לִשְׁתוֹק
to kill (vt)	laharog	לַהֲרוֹג
to knock (at the door)	lidfok	לִדְפוֹק
to know (sb)	lehakir et	לְהַכִּיר אֶת
to know (sth)	la'da'at	לָדַעַת
to laugh (vi)	litsxok	לִצְחוֹק
to launch (start up)	lehaf'il	לְהַפְעִיל
to leave (~ for Mexico)	la'azov	לַעֲזוֹב
to leave (forget sth)	lehaʃir	לְהַשְׁאִיר
to leave (spouse)	la'azov	לַעֲזוֹב
to liberate (city, etc.)	leʃaxrer	לְשַׁחְרֵר
to lie (~ on the floor)	liʃkav	לִשְׁכַּב
to lie (tell untruth)	leʃaker	לְשַׁקֵּר
to light (campfire, etc.)	lehadlik	לְהַדְלִיק
to light up (illuminate)	leha'ir	לְהָאִיר
to like (I like …)	limtso xen be'ei'nayim	לִמְצוֹא חֵן בְּעֵינַיִים
to limit (vt)	lehagbil	לְהַגְבִּיל
to listen (vi)	lehakʃiv	לְהַקְשִׁיב
to live (~ in France)	lagur	לָגוּר
to live (exist)	lixyot	לִחְיוֹת
to load (gun)	lit'on	לִטְעוֹן
to load (vehicle, etc.)	leha'amis	לְהַעֲמִיס
to look (I'm just ~ing)	lehistakel	לְהִסְתַּכֵּל
to look for … (search)	lexapes	לְחַפֵּשׂ

to look like (resemble)	lihyot dome	לִהְיוֹת דּוֹמֶה
to lose (umbrella, etc.)	le'abed	לְאַבֵּד
to love (e.g., ~ dancing)	le'ehov	לֶאֱהוֹב
to love (sb)	le'ehov	לֶאֱהוֹב
to lower (blind, head)	lehorid	לְהוֹרִיד
to make (~ dinner)	levaʃel	לְבַשֵּׁל
to make a mistake	lit'ot	לִטְעוֹת
to make angry	lehargiz	לְהַרְגִּיז
to make easier	lehakel al	לְהָקֵל עַל
to make multiple copies	leʃaxpel	לְשַׁכְפֵּל
to make the acquaintance	lehakir	לְהַכִּיר
to make use (of ...)	lehiʃtameʃ be...	לְהִשְׁתַּמֵּשׁ בְּ...
to manage, to run	lenahel	לְנַהֵל
to mark (make a mark)	lesamen	לְסַמֵּן
to mean (signify)	lomar	לוֹמַר
to memorize (vt)	lizkor	לִזְכּוֹר
to mention (talk about)	lehazkir	לְהַזְכִּיר
to miss (school, etc.)	lehaxsir	לְהַחְסִיר
to mix (combine, blend)	le'arbev	לְעַרְבֵּב
to mock (make fun of)	lil'og	לִלְעוֹג
to move (to shift)	lehaziz	לְהָזִיז
to multiply (math)	lehaxpil	לְהַכְפִּיל
must (v aux)	lihyot xayav	לִהְיוֹת חַיָּב

255. Verbs N-R

to name, to call (vt)	likro	לִקְרוֹא
to negotiate (vi)	laset velatet	לָשֵׂאת וְלָתֵת
to note (write down)	lesamen	לְסַמֵּן
to notice (see)	lasim lev	לָשִׂים לֵב
to obey (vi, vt)	letsayet	לְצַיֵּת
to object (vi, vt)	lehitnaged	לְהִתְנַגֵּד
to observe (see)	litspot, lehaʃkif	לִצְפּוֹת, לְהַשְׁקִיף
to offend (vt)	lif'go'a	לִפְגּוֹעַ
to omit (word, phrase)	lehaʃmit	לְהַשְׁמִיט
to open (vt)	lif'toax	לִפְתּוֹחַ
to order (in restaurant)	lehazmin	לְהַזְמִין
to order (mil.)	lifkod	לִפְקוֹד
to organize (concert, party)	le'argen	לְאַרְגֵּן
to overestimate (vt)	leha'arix 'yeter al hamida	לְהַעֲרִיךְ יֶתֶר עַל הַמִּידָה
to own (possess)	lihyot 'ba'al ʃel	לִהְיוֹת בַּעַל שֶׁל
to participate (vi)	lehiʃtatef	לְהִשְׁתַּתֵּף
to pass through (by car, etc.)	la'avor	לַעֲבוֹר

to pay (vi, vt)	leʃalem	לְשַׁלֵם
to peep, spy on	lehatsits	לְהָצִיץ
to penetrate (vt)	laxdor	לַחדוֹר
to permit (vt)	leharʃot	לְהַרשוֹת
to pick (flowers)	liktof	לִקטוֹף
to place (put, set)	la'arox	לַעֲרוֹך
to plan (~ to do sth)	letaxnen	לְתַכנֵן
to play (actor)	lesaxek	לְשַׂחֵק
to play (children)	lesaxek	לְשַׂחֵק
to point (~ the way)	lenatev	לְנַתֵב
to pour (liquid)	limzog	לִמזוֹג
to pray (vi, vt)	lehitpalel	לְהִתפַּלֵל
to prefer (vt)	leha'adif	לְהַעֲדִיף
to prepare (~ a plan)	lehaxin	לְהָכִין
to present (sb to sb)	lehatsig	לְהַצִיג
to preserve (peace, life)	leʃamer	לְשַׁמֵר
to prevail (vt)	ligbor	לִגבּוֹר
to progress (move forward)	lehitkadem	לְהִתקַדֵם
to promise (vt)	lehav'tiax	לְהַבטִיחַ
to pronounce (vt)	levate	לְבַטֵא
to propose (vt)	leha'tsi'a	לְהַצִיעַ
to protect (e.g., ~ nature)	liʃmor	לִשמוֹר
to protest (vi)	limxot	לִמחוֹת
to prove (vt)	leho'xiax	לְהוֹכִיחַ
to provoke (vt)	lehitgarot	לְהִתגָרוֹת
to pull (~ the rope)	limʃox	לִמשוֹך
to punish (vt)	leha'aniʃ	לְהַעֲנִיש
to push (~ the door)	lidxof	לִדחוֹף
to put away (vt)	lefanot	לְפַנוֹת
to put in order	lesader	לְסַדֵר
to put, to place	lasim	לָשִׂים
to quote (cite)	letsatet	לְצַטֵט
to reach (arrive at)	lehasig	לְהַשִׂיג
to read (vi, vt)	likro	לִקרוֹא
to realize (a dream)	lehagʃim	לְהַגשִים
to recognize (identify sb)	lezahot	לְזַהוֹת
to recommend (vt)	lehamlits	לְהַמלִיץ
to recover (~ from flu)	lehaxlim	לְהַחלִים
to redo (do again)	la'asot mexadaʃ	לַעֲשׂוֹת מֵחָדָש
to reduce (speed, etc.)	lehaktin	לְהַקטִין
to refuse (~ sb)	lesarev	לְסָרֵב
to regret (be sorry)	lehitsta'er	לְהִצטַעֵר

to reinforce (vt)	leχazek	לְחַזֵק
to remember (Do you ~ me?)	lizkor	לִזְכּוֹר
to remember (I can't ~ her name)	lehizaχer	לְהִיזָכֵר
to remind of …	lehazkir	לְהַזְכִּיר
to remove (~ a stain)	lehasir	לְהָסִיר
to remove (~ an obstacle)	lehasir	לְהָסִיר
to rent (sth from sb)	liskor	לִשְׂכּוֹר
to repair (mend)	letaken	לְתַקֵן
to repeat (say again)	laχazor al	לַחֲזוֹר עַל
to report (make a report)	leda'veaχ	לְדַוֵוחַ
to reproach (vt)	linzof	לִנְזוֹף
to reserve, to book	leʃaryen	לְשַׁרְיֵין
to restrain (hold back)	lerasen	לְרַסֵן
to return (come back)	laʃuv	לָשׁוּב
to risk, to take a risk	la'kaχat sikun	לָקַחַת סִיכּוּן
to rub out (erase)	limχok	לִמְחוֹק
to run (move fast)	laruts	לָרוּץ
to rush (hurry sb)	lezarez	לְזָרֵז

256. Verbs S-W

to satisfy (please)	lesapek	לְסַפֵּק
to save (rescue)	lehatsil	לְהַצִיל
to say (~ thank you)	lomar	לוֹמַר
to scold (vt)	linzof	לִנְזוֹף
to scratch (with claws)	lisrot	לִשְׂרוֹט
to select (to pick)	livχor	לִבְחוֹר
to sell (goods)	limkor	לִמְכּוֹר
to send (a letter)	liʃloaχ	לִשְׁלוֹחַ
to send back (vt)	liʃloaχ baχazara	לִשְׁלוֹחַ בַּחֲזָרָה
to sense (~ danger)	laχuʃ	לָחוּשׁ
to sentence (vt)	ligzor din	לִגְזוֹר דִין
to serve (in restaurant)	leʃaret	לְשָׁרֵת
to settle (a conflict)	lesader	לְסַדֵר
to shake (vt)	lena'er	לְנַעֵר
to shave (vi)	lehitga'leaχ	לְהִתְגַלֵחַ
to shine (gleam)	lizhor	לִזְהוֹר
to shiver (with cold)	lir'od	לִרְעוֹד
to shoot (vi)	lirot	לִירוֹת
to shout (vi)	lits'ok	לִצְעוֹק

to show (to display)	lehar'ot	לְהַרְאוֹת
to shudder (vi)	lir'od	לִרְעוֹד
to sigh (vi)	lehe'anax	לְהֵיאָנַח
to sign (document)	laxtom	לַחְתּוֹם
to signify (mean)	lomar	לוֹמַר
to simplify (vt)	lefaʃet	לְפַשֵּׁט
to sin (vi)	laxato	לַחֲטוֹא
to sit (be sitting)	la'ʃevet	לָשֶׁבֶת
to sit down (vi)	lehityaʃev	לְהִתְיַישֵׁב
to smell (emit an odor)	leha'riax	לְהָרִיחַ
to smell (inhale the odor)	leha'riax	לְהָרִיחַ
to smile (vi)	lexayex	לְחַייֵךְ
to snap (vi, ab. rope)	lehikara	לְהִיקָּרַע
to solve (problem)	liftor	לִפְתּוֹר
to sow (seed, crop)	liz'ro'a	לִזְרוֹעַ
to spill (liquid)	liʃpox	לִשְׁפּוֹךְ
to spill out, scatter (flour, etc.)	lehiʃapex	לְהִישָׁפֵּךְ
to spit (vi)	lirok	לִירוֹק
to stand (toothache, cold)	lisbol	לִסְבּוֹל
to start (begin)	lehatxil	לְהַתְחִיל
to steal (money, etc.)	lignov	לִגְנוֹב
to stop (for pause, etc.)	la'atsor	לַעֲצוֹר
to stop (please ~ calling me)	lehafsik	לְהַפְסִיק
to stop talking	lehiʃtatek	לְהִשְׁתַּתֵּק
to stroke (caress)	lelatef	לְלַטֵּף
to study (vt)	lilmod	לִלְמוֹד
to suffer (feel pain)	lisbol	לִסְבּוֹל
to support (cause, idea)	litmox be...	לִתְמוֹךְ בְּ...
to suppose (assume)	leʃa'er	לְשַׁעֵר
to surface (ab. submarine)	latsuf	לָצוּף
to surprise (amaze)	lehaf'ti'a	לְהַפְתִּיעַ
to suspect (vt)	laxʃod	לַחְשׁוֹד
to swim (vi)	lisxot	לִשְׂחוֹת
to take (get hold of)	la'kaxat	לָקַחַת
to take a bath	lehitraxets	לְהִתְרַחֵץ
to take a rest	la'nuax	לָנוּחַ
to take away (e.g., about waiter)	lehotsi	לְהוֹצִיא
to take off (airplane)	lehamri	לְהַמְרִיא
to take off (painting, curtains, etc.)	lehorid	לְהוֹרִיד

to take pictures	letsalem	לְצַלֵם
to talk to …	ledaber	לְדַבֵּר
to teach (give lessons)	lelamed	לְלַמֵד

to tear off, to rip off (vt)	litloʃ	לתלוֹש
to tell (story, joke)	lesaper	לְסַפֵּר
to thank (vt)	lehodot	לְהוֹדוֹת
to think (believe)	lisbor	לסבּוֹר

to think (vi, vt)	laxʃov	לַחשוֹב
to threaten (vt)	le'ayem	לְאַייֵם
to throw (stone, etc.)	lizrok	לזרוֹק
to tie to …	likʃor	לקשוֹר

to tie up (prisoner)	likʃor	לקשוֹר
to tire (make tired)	le'ayef	לְעַייֵף
to touch (one's arm, etc.)	lin'go'a	לנגוֹעַ
to tower (over …)	lehitromem	לְהִתרוֹמֵם

to train (animals)	le'alef	לְאַלֵף
to train (sb)	le'amen	לְאַמֵן
to train (vi)	lehit'amen	לְהִתאַמֵן
to transform (vt)	leʃanot tsura	לְשָנוֹת צוּרָה

to translate (vt)	letargem	לְתַרגֵם
to treat (illness)	letapel be…	לְטַפֵּל בְּ…
to trust (vt)	liv'toax	לבטוֹחַ
to try (attempt)	lenasot	לְנַסוֹת

to turn (e.g., ~ left)	lifnot	לפנוֹת
to turn away (vi)	lehafnot 'oref le…	לְהַפנוֹת עוֹרֶף לְ…
to turn off (the light)	lexabot	לְכַבּוֹת
to turn on (computer, etc.)	lehadlik	לְהַדלִיק
to turn over (stone, etc.)	lahafox	לַהֲפוֹך

to underestimate (vt)	leham'it be''erex	לְהַמעִיט בְּעֵרֶך
to underline (vt)	lehadgiʃ	לְהַדגִיש
to understand (vt)	lehavin	לְהָבִין
to undertake (vt)	linkot	לנקוֹט

to unite (vt)	le'axed	לְאַחֵד
to untie (vt)	lehatir 'keʃer	לְהַתִיר קֶשֶר
to use (phrase, word)	lehiʃtameʃ be…	לְהִשתַמֵש בְּ…
to vaccinate (vt)	lexasen	לְחַסֵן

to vote (vi)	lehats'bi'a	לְהַצבִּיעַ
to wait (vt)	lehamtin	לְהַמתִין
to wake (sb)	leha'ir	לְהָעִיר
to want (wish, desire)	lirtsot	לרצוֹת

| to warn (of the danger) | lehazhir | לְהַזהִיר |
| to wash (clean) | liʃtof | לשטוֹף |

| to water (plants) | lehaʃkot | לְהַשְׁקוֹת |
| to wave (the hand) | lenafnef | לְנַפְנֵף |

to weigh (have weight)	liʃkol	לִשְׁקוֹל
to work (vi)	la'avod	לַעֲבוֹד
to worry (make anxious)	lehad'ig	לְהַדְאִיג
to worry (vi)	lid'og	לִדְאוֹג

to wrap (parcel, etc.)	le'eroz	לֶאֱרוֹז
to wrestle (sport)	lehe'avek	לְהֵיאָבֵק
to write (vt)	lixtov	לִכְתּוֹב
to write down	lirʃom	לִרְשׁוֹם

Made in United States
Orlando, FL
14 December 2023